PLA... CRICKE... 1980

33rd edition

EDITED BY GORDON ROSS

Statistics by Michael Fordham and Barry McCaully

Front cover: Graham Gooch. Photo: Allsport

Swivel head winner.

THE CROSS-ROADS

by Gordon Ross

Cricket, the world over, stands at the crossroads at the present moment, because genuine followers of the game fear a spreading of what has happened so far only in Australia. To place those events in a nutshell: the Australian Board, when in distress, with Packer at their throat, sought help from the rest of the cricketing world, which was freely given at a substantial cost which cricket could ill afford. Then, when the Australian Board found themselves virtually bankrupt, a marriage was effected between themselves and Packer, the dreaded enemy, amid firm statements that the Australian Board are still very much in control of cricket in Australia; Packer will merely promote and televise. Packer meantime had claimed that he had brought a new audience to cricket with his World Series, and he is right of course, particularly at night games, where alcohol is consumed in excess, and at times behaviour has occurred which would disgrace some football terraces. Constant publicity has created genuine hatred between sections of Australian crowds and the England players. The Fight for the Ashes has always been fiercely contested on the field of play but off the field it was a different matter. How sad that Brearley had to comment on a situation he thought so serious as to provoke him to say that someone in the end may be killed.

The English Test and County Cricket Board had refused to go along with some of the Packer-inspired ideas; declining to put the Ashes at stake in the three-match series and waving aside some of his gimmicks. They were absolutely right, despite a surprising outburst by a member of the Australian Board when those decisions were announced. Whether or not the Australian Board decisions were entirely their own, or Packer-influenced, is debatable, especially over the incident of the aluminium bat brought by Lillee to the wicket and objected to by Brearley who considered that it dented the ball. Lillee then caused a 10 minute delay but was only reprimanded for his performance because so said Bob Parish of the Australian Board: 'There was no dissent'. Could it be that Packer was

3

whispering in his ear: 'Don't suspend Dennis – he's the best piece of television we've got.' If this was not the case, and it was the Board's decision unimpeded by outside influence, then the unanimous view was that it represented a lack of the firmness which has characterised the Board's dealings in the past. What the Packer intrusion has done to cricket is to convince the players that they should be paid a great deal more money – and no-one would criticise him for that – but often when a pendulum starts to swing it can end up by swinging too far, and it could place a number of English counties in a parlous state unless strenuous efforts are made to find the money from somewhere. It is this situation which looks like putting an end to the Gillette Cup at the end of this summer after 18 years, because the Test and County Cricket Board say that they need to extract the very largest sum of money possible for this 18-year-old competition, pioneered and sponsored by Gillette, who feel now that the sort of money talked about does not make it a viable proposition within the confines of their available budget. So it seems likely that the name Gillette will disappear from the cricket scene after being almost a household word for so long.

Packer's television, though no doubt to the taste of his advertisers, caused Tony Lewis to write in the *Sunday Telegraph*: 'The TV advertisements which popped up at the end of every over and those which crawled across the bottom of the screen during the overs, destroyed the whole tempo and character of the game. The commentators have no time to talk at the end of an over, so they all chatter during it, over the pictures of play. Is this a fair representation of the cricket that the Australian Board are offering?' Mr Parish's comment: 'It's a commercial company. It's something we have to live with.' Let us fervently hope that it is not something we have to live with in this country, and that the TCCB in their quest for more money, at least don't sell their souls; or more to the point, the soul of cricket.

It is odd, almost as odd as the Mad Hatter, that when money is so much the dictator these days that Surrey, trying to raise money to preserve county and Test cricket at The Oval, should find themselves faced with a £1,600 bill for bowling their overs too slowly last summer. They fell behind the target set by the TCCB of 19 an hour, ending up with an average rate of 18.38, thus almost wiping out the £1,750 Surrey earned for their third place in the Schweppes County Championship (a fine performance this after some lean years). But the summer of 1979 belonged exclusively to Essex and Somerset, two counties who previously had not won a single honour in their long history. They exacted revenge with a vengeance each winning not one, but two competitions: Essex, The Benson and Hedges Cup and The Schweppes County Championship, and Somerset, in one champagne-filled week-end taking The Gillette Cup and The John Player League on successive days. Somerset were treading along the last few yards of the same road as in 1978, towards the Gillette Cup on the Saturday and the John Player League Championship on the Sunday. In 1978 when favourites for both, it was double failure: a bitter pill to swallow. It was this, perhaps, which made them all the more determined in 1979.

Essex opened up such a lead in the County Championship (largely by fine bowling performances by John Lever) that it soon looked a foregone conclusion. It was said that Essex were lucky that they were able to play when foul weather kept other sides in the dressing-rooms. But this is always the lottery that cricket offers and in any event, who was their chief rival, and who is to say that had they played they would have played better than Essex? No, this was a thoroughly deserved triumph for Essex, as was their Benson and Hedges success when Graham Gooch contributed a magnificent century. But how bravely Surrey fought back against a total of 290 to lose by only 35 runs.

The Prudential World Cup once again put on show the almost inexhaustible talents of cricketers from the Caribbean. In the final at Lord's, England were never in with a chance facing a total of 287 to win, although the West Indies innings was largely confined to Vivian Richards (138) and a hurricane that blew across Lord's in the shape of Collis King, whose swiftly struck 86 put the prize beyond England's grasp. Sri Lanka won the ambitious ICC Trophy and in addition, beat India at Old Trafford, which surely must enhance their claims to full Test status. They beat Canada in the ICC Trophy final by 60 runs at Worcester.

Now to the summer of 1980 and a series with West Indies who will certainly start firm favourites against an England team which still has considerable problems, and the Centenary Test against Australia.

India v West Indies, 1978-79

FIRST TEST MATCH

PLAYED AT BOMBAY, 1, 2, 3, 5, 6 DECEMBER

MATCH DRAWN

INDIA

†S. M. Gavaskar b Clarke	205	c Murray b Clarke	73
C. P. S. Chauhan c Greenidge b Holder	52	c Murray b Parry	84
M. Amarnath b Clarke	4	not out	37
G. R. Viswanath c Bacchus b Parry	52		
D. B. Vengsarkar lbw b Phillip	11	not out	10
†S. M. H. Kirmani b Clarke	17		
Kapil Dev c Bacchus b Holder	42		
S. Venkataraghavan c Murray b Clarke	0		
K. D. Ghavri not out	15		
B. S. Bedi c & b Holder	2		
B. S. Chandrasekhar b Holder	1		
Extras (B6, LB4, NB13)	23	(B4, LB7, NB9)	20
Total	**424**	**(2 wkts)**	**224**

WEST INDIES

A. T. Greenidge c Venkat b Ghavri	0
A. B. Williams b Ghavri	0
H. A. Gomes b Chandrasekhar	63
†A. I. Kallicharran lbw b Dev	187
S. F. A. Bacchus b Chandrasekhar	11
‡D. A. Murray lbw b Chandrasekhar	84
D. R. Parry c Kirmani b Chandrasekhar	55
N. Phillip c Vengsarkar b Venkataraghavan	26
V. A. Holder c Vengsarkar c Chandrasekhar	14
R. R. Jumadeen not out	2
S. T. Clarke c Venkataraghavan b Bedi	8
Extras (B22, LB13, NB8)	43
Total	**493**

BOWLING

WEST INDIES	O	M	R	W	O	M	R	W	FALL OF WICKETS			
										I	WI	I
Phillip	22	4	67	1	—	6	2	19	0			
Clarke	42	9	98	4	—	16	2	53	1		*1st*	*1st*	*2nd*
Holder	27	3	94	4	—	7	2	15	0	1st	35	0	153
Parry	28	4	100	1	—	27	7	77	1	2nd	190	23	194
Jumadeen	17	3	39	0	—	21	6	32	0	3rd	217	122	—
Kallicharran	1	0	3	0	—	4.5	2	6	0	4th	334	150	—
Gomes					—	3	2	2	0	5th	344	317	—
INDIA										6th	390	387	—
Dev	19	3	70	1	—					7th	408	430	—
Ghavri	25	3	71	2	—					8th	411	474	—
Venkataraghavan	34	12	77	1	—					9th	414	480	—
Bedi	36	7	102	1	—					10th	424	493	—
Chandrasekhar	43	7	116	5	—								
Chauhan	1	0	2	0	—								
Amarnath	3	0	12	0	—								

Indian's first innings Chauhan retired hurt at 23-0 and resumed his innings at 217-3.

SECOND TEST MATCH

PLAYED AT BANGALORE, 15, 16, 17, 19, 20 DECEMBER

MATCH DRAWN

WEST INDIES

A. B. Williams st Kirmani b Bedi	44	c Gavaskar b Ghavri	20
S. F. A. Bacchus b Bedi	96	c Chauhan b Ghavri	4
H. A. Gomes c & b Chandrasekhar	51	c Chauhan b Ghavri	82
†A. I. Kallicharran c Viswanath b Ghavri	71	b Ghavri	21
‡D. A. Murray c Kirmani b Ghavri	14	b Dev	9
S. Shivnarine b Venkataraghavan	62	b Chauhan b Dev	0
V. A. Holder b Dev	27	not out	0
D. R. Parry not out	41	c Kirmani b Bedi	38
M. D. Marshall lbw b Chandrasekhar	0	b Ghavri	5
N. Phillip run out	26	not out	13
S. T. Clarke c & b Bedi	0		
Extras (LB3, NB2)	5	(B1, LB3, NB4)	8
Total	**437**	**(8 wkts)**	**200**

INDIA

†S. M. Gavaskar c Shivnarine b Clarke	0
A. D. Gaekwad b Parry	87
D. B. Vengsarkar c Murray b Phillip	73
G. R. Viswanath c Kallicharran b Clarke	70
C. P. S. Chauhan c Parry b Marshall	15
‡S. M. H. Kirmani c Kallicharran b Phillip	15
Kapil Dev c Murray b Clarke	12
K. D. Ghavri b Clarke	43
S. Venkataraghavan c Phillip b Clarke	11
B. S. Bedi c Shivnarine b Phillip	18
B. S. Chandrasekhar not out	0
Extras (B1, LB5, NB21)	27
Total	**371**

BOWLING

INDIA	O	M	R	W	O	M	R	W	FALL OF WICKETS		
Dev	20	5	79	1	— 11	1	30	2			
Ghavri	16	1	77	2	— 24	8	51	5		*WI*	*I*	*WI*
Bedi	29	7	98	3	— 19	8	33	1		*1st*	*1st*	*2nd*
Chandrasekhar	33	4	94	2	— 12	2	39	0	1st	97	0	7
Venkataraghavan	41	15	74	1	— 16	5	39	0	2nd	164	170	38
Gaekwad	1	0	10	0	—				3rd	238	200	74
									4th	268	233	98
									5th	284	266	101
WEST INDIES									6th	343	291	179
Clarke	34.2	3	126	5	—				7th	383	304	181
Phillip	25	6	86	3	—				8th	384	318	192
Marshall	18	2	53	1	—				9th	437	370	—
Holder	24	3	55	0	—				10th	437	371	—
Parry	12	6	22	1	—							
Shivnarine	3	2	2	0	—							

The last day's play was abandoned because of riots in Bangalore following the imprisonment of Mrs. Ghandi.

THIRD TEST MATCH

PLAYED AT CALCUTTA, 29, 30, 31 DECEMBER, 2, 3 JANUARY
MATCH DRAWN

INDIA

†S. M. Gavaskar c Bacchus b Phillip	107	not out		182
C. P. S. Chauhan b Clarke	11			
A. D. Gaekwad c Murray b Marshall	7	b Clarke		5
G. R. Viswanath b Phillip	32			
D. B. Vengsarkar c Williams b Parry	42	not out		157
M. V. Narasimha Rao c Gomes b Parry	1			
K. D. Ghavri c Marshall b Phillip	5			
‡S. M. H. Kirmani lbw b Phillip	0			
Kapil Dev b Parry	61			
S. Venkataraghavan lbw b Holder	7			
B. S. Bedi not out	4			
Extras (B3, LB2, NB18)	23	(B1, LB4, NB12)		17
Total	**300**	(1 wkt dec)		**361**

WEST INDIES

A. B. Williams c & b Ghavri	111	b Ghavri		11
S. F. A. Bacchus b Ghavri	26	c & b Ghavri		20
H. A. Gomes b Venkataraghavan	8	b Venkataraghavan		5
†A. I. Kallicharran c Rao b Venkataraghavan	55	c Viswanath b Rao		46
V. A. Holder c Rao b Venkataraghavan	3	b Ghavri		4
‡D. A. Murray c Dev b Venkataraghavan	2	st Kirmani b Venkataraghavan		66
S. Shivnarine c sub b Ghavri	48	not out		36
D. R. Parry b Bedi	4	c Gavaskar b Venkataraghavan		0
N. Phillip lbw b Dev	47	lbw b Ghavri		0
M. D. Marshall c Kirmani b Dev	1	lbw b Bedi		0
S. T. Clarke not out	4	not out		1
Extras (B5, LB9, NB4)	18	(B4, LB2, NB2)		8
Total	**327**	(9 wkts)		**197**

BOWLING

WEST INDIES	O	M	R	W	O	M	R	W
Clarke	27	8	70	1 — 28	4	104	1	
Phillip	22	6	64	4 — 16	0	81	0	
Holder	21	5	48	1 — 20	3	59	0	
Marshall	14	3	44	1 — 13	3	45	0	
Parry	20.3	7	51	3 — 13	3	50	0	
Gomes	1	1	0	0 — 1	0	3	0	
Shivnarine	1	1	0	0 — 1	0	0	0	
INDIA								
Dev	20.4	3	88	2 — 13	6	21	0	
Ghavri	29	5	74	4 — 23	8	46	4	
Bedi	24	4	59	1 — 22	14	32	1	
Venkataraghavan	33	15	55	4 — 30	13	47	3	
Rao	11	0	33	0 — 17.1	6	43	1	

FALL OF WICKETS

	I	WI	I	WI
	1st	1st	2nd	2nd
1st	20	58	17	35
2nd	48	95	—	45
3rd	110	197	—	133
4th	199	210	—	143
5th	209	215	—	145
6th	220	218	—	164
7th	220	230	—	164
8th	225	313	—	183
9th	283	318	—	197
10th	300	327	—	

FOURTH TEST MATCH

PLAYED AT MADRAS, 12, 13, 14, 16 JANUARY
INDIA WON BY 3 WICKETS

WEST INDIES

S. F. A. Bacchus	c Vengsarakar b Dev	0	c Vengsarkar b Ghavri	4
A. T. Greenidge	b Venkataraghavan	13	c Kirmani b Dev	15
H. A. Gomes	c Rao b Dev	14	c Gavaskar b Venkataraghavan	91
†A. I. Kallicharran	b Venkataraghavan	98	c sub b Venkataraghavan	4
H. S. Chang	c Chauhan b Dev	6	hit wkt b Ghavri	2
‡D. A. Murray	hit wkt b Dev	0	c Rao b Dev	15
S. Shivnarine	c sub b Ghavri	5	c Vengsarkar b Ghavri	9
D. R. Parry	run out	12	c sub b Dev	1
N. Phillip	not out	22	not out	7
V. A. Holder	c Dev b Parsana	20	c Rao b Venkataraghavan	0
S. T. Clarke	lbw b Venkataraghavan	12	st Kirmani b Venkataraghavan	0
Extras	(LB9, W1, NB16)	26	(NB3)	3
Total		**228**		**151**

INDIA

†S. M. Gavaskar	c Bacchus b Phillip	4	c Murray b Clarke	1
C. P. S. Chauhan	c Murray b Holder	20	c Bacchus b Phillip	10
D. B. Vengsarkar	c Bacchus b Clarke	0	c Shivnarine b Clarke	0
G. R. Viswanath	c Shivnarine b Clarke	124	c Kallicharran b Holder	31
A. D. Gaekwad	b Phillip	24	c Murray b Holder	21
M. V. Narasimha Rao	c Greenidge b Parry	6	c Murray b Phillip	4
Kapil Dev	c Bacchus b Clarke	0	not out	26
K. D. Ghavri	c Murray b Clarke	1	c Clarke b Phillip	8
‡S. M. H. Kirmani	c Shivnarine b Phillip	33	not out	4
D. Parsana	c sub b Phillip	0		
S. Venkataraghavan	not out	0		
Extras	(B15, LB11, NB17)	43	(B5, LB1, NB14)	20
Total		**255**	**(7 wkts)**	**125**

BOWLING

INDIA	O	M	R	W		O	M	R	W
Kapil Dev	14	0	38	4	—	14	3	46	3
Ghavri	16	5	41	1	—	13	3	52	3
Parsana	12	3	32	1	—	2	0	7	0
Venkataraghavan	20.5	5	60	3	—	16.5	5	43	4
Narasimha Rao	10	1	31	0	—				
WEST INDIES									
Clarke	29.1	3	75	4	—	21.1	3	46	2
Phillip	22	8	48	4	—	15	5	37	5
Holder	11	2	28	1	—	10	3	22	2
Gomes	1	0	2	0	—				
Parry	15	2	43	1	—				
Shivnarine	1	1	16	0	—				

FALL OF WICKETS

	WI	I	WI	I
	1st	1st	2nd	2nd
1st	0	10	9	16
2nd	25	11	34	17
3rd	45	80	87	17
4th	55	150	100	74
5th	61	174	133	82
6th	68	174	141	84
7th	168	180	143	115
8th	168	250	148	—
9th	210	255	151	—
10th	228	255	151	—

FIFTH TEST MATCH

INDIA

†S. M. Gavaskar	c Murray b Clarke	120
C. P. S. Chauhan	c Parry b Phillip	60
D. B. Vengsarkar	c Murray b Clarke	109
G. R. Viswanath	c Murray b Phillip	9
A. D. Gaekwad	c Murray b Gomes	47
Kapil Dev	not out	126
‡S. M. H. Kirmani	run out	30
K. D. Ghavri	c Murray b Phillip	2
D. Parsana	b Clarke	1
S. Venkataraghavan	not out	8
B. S. Chandrasekhar	did not bat	
Extras	(B7, LB13, NB34)	54
Total	(8 wkts dec)	**566**

WEST INDIES

A. B. Williams	b Venkataraghavan	26		
A. T. Greenidge	c Chauhan b Ghavri	0	b Chandrasekhar	32
H. A. Gomes	c Kirmani b Dev	40	b Venkataraghavan	14
†A. I. Kallicharran	c Chandrasekhar b Ghavri	7	not out	45
S. F. A. Bacchus	c Dev b Ghavri	0	c Gavaskar b Chandrasekhar	61
‡D. A. Murray	c Chandrasekhar	20	not out	7
S. Shivnarine	b Dev	0		
D. R. Parry	lbw b Chandrasekhar	15		
N. Phillip	b Dev	26		
V. A. Holder	not out	11		
S. T. Clarke	c & b Venkataraghavan	15		
Extras	(B1, LB5, NB6)	12	(B15, LB5)	20
Total		**172**	(3 wkts)	**179**

BOWLING

WEST INDIES	O	M	R	W		O	M	R	W	FALL OF WICKETS			
											I	*WI*	*WI*
Clarke	36	7	139	3	—						*1st*	*1st*	*2nd*
Phillip	38.2	3	159	3	—					1st	119	0	89
Holder	40	7	109	0	—					2nd	270	48	106
Parry	17	4	43	0	—					3rd	305	56	140
Shivnarine	2	0	8	0	—					4th	353	57	—
Gomes	9	0	54	1	—					5th	432	89	—
INDIA										6th	518	89	—
Dev	15	2	59	3	—	9	4	32	0	7th	536	106	—
Ghavri	16	3	54	3	—	12	2	50	0	8th	542	133	—
Venkataraghavan	10.4	5	14	2	—	14	8	26	1	9th	—	144	—
Chandrasekhar	16	6	33	2	—	15	4	32	2	10th	—	172	—
Parsana					—	6	3	11	0				
Gaekwad					—	1	0	5	0				
Vengsarkar					—	1	0	3	0				

10

SIXTH TEST MATCH

PLAYED AT KANPUR, 2, 3, 4, 6, 7 FEBRUARY
MATCH DRAWN

INDIA

†S. M. Gavaskar c Murray b Marshall	40
C. P. S. Chauhan st Murray b Parry	79
D. B. Vengsarkar lbw b Phillip	15
G. R. Viswanath c Phillip b Parry	179
A. D. Gaekwad b Jumadeen	102
M. Amarnath not out	101
Kapil Dev c Greenidge b Jumadeen	62
‡S. M. H. Kirmani c Phillip b Jumadeen	2
K. D. Ghavri not out	18
S. Venkataraghavan did not bat	
B. S. Chandrasekhar did not bat	
Extras (B9, LB12, NB25)	46
	—
Total (7 wkts dec)	644

WEST INDIES

A. T. Greenidge lbw b Ghavri	20
S. F. A. Bacchus hit wkt b Venkataraghavan	250
H. A. Gomes c Vengsarkar b Chandrasekhar	37
R. R. Jumadeen b Dev	56
†A. I. Kallicharran c Kirmani b Ghavri	4
‡D. A. Murray c sub (Yajurvendra Singh) b Ghavri	44
S. Shivnarine c Vengsarkar b Armarnath	2
D. R. Parry c Vengsarkar b Ghavri	4
N. Phillip not out	10
M. D. Marshall not out	1
V. A. Holder did not bat	
Extras (B9, LB9, NB6)	24
	—
Total (8 wkts)	452

BOWLING

WEST INDIES	O	M	R	W			FALL OF WICKETS		
								I	WI
Phillip	27	4	89	1 —				1st	1st
Marshall	34	3	123	1 —			1st	51	37
Holder	43	6	118	0 —			2nd	77	134
Gomes	1	0	4	0 —			3rd	221	263
Parry	39	8	127	2 —			4th	393	268
Jumadeen	45.4	4	137	3 —			5th	502	429
INDIA							6th	604	431
Dev	20	0	98	1 —			7th	609	440
Ghavri	31	4	118	4 —			8th	—	443
Chandrasekhar	41	10	117	1 —			9th	—	—
Venkataraghavan	46.1	16	60	1 —			10th	—	—
Amarnath	10	1	35	1 —					

11

FIRST TEST MATCH

PLAYED AT CHRISTCHURCH, 2, 3, 4, 6, 7 FEBRUARY

PAKISTAN WON BY 128 RUNS

PAKISTAN

Mudassar Nazar c Edgar b Bracewell	7	retired hurt	4
Talat Ali c Wright b Hadlee	40	c Coney b Hadlee	61
Mohsin Khan lbw b Hadlee	12	lbw b Coney	7
Javed Miandad b Hadlee	81	not out	160
Haroon Rashid c Howarth b Hadlee	40	b Cairns	35
Wasim Raja c Boock b Cairns	12	c Hadlee b Coney	17
†Mushtaq Mohammad lbw b Hadlee	10	c Burgess b Hadlee	12
Sarfraz Nawaz not out	31	b Hadlee	4
‡Wasim Bari c Cairns	9		
Anwar Khan c Lees b Boock	12	not out	3
Sikhander Bakht c Edgar b Boock	0		
Extras (B5, LB8, NB4)	17	(B1, LB19)	20
Total	**271**	**(6 wkts dec)**	**123**

NEW ZEALAND

J. G. Wright c Bari b Sikander	27	b Mushtaq	21
B. A. Edgar c Bari b Sikander	129	c Sarfraz b Sikander	16
G. P. Howarth c Raja b Mushtaq	19	b Mushtaq	0
‡M. G. Burgess c Javed b Sikander	16	c Sarfraz b Raja	6
J. M. Parker c Bari b Sarfraz	2	lbw b Mushtaq	33
J. V. Coney c Javed b Mushtaq	6	c Mohsin b Raja	36
†W. K. Lees c & b Mushtaq	8	c Bari b Raja	19
R. J. Hadlee c Bari b Raja	42	c Sikander b Raja	4
B. L. Cairns b Mushtaq	11	not out	23
S. L. Boock b Raja	1	c Mohsin b Mushtaq	0
B. P. Bracewell not out	0	st Bari b Mushtaq	5
Extras (B8, LB9, NB12)	29	(B4, LB6, NB3)	13
Total	**290**		**176**

BOWLING

NEW ZEALAND	O	M	R	W		O	M	R	W
Hadlee	25	2	62	5	—	26	4	83	3
Bracewell	12	1	50	1	—	7	0	53	0
Cairns	31	5	96	2	—	23	7	46	1
Coney	7	3	10	0	—	12	1	33	2
Boock	14.6	5	22	2	—	19	4	70	0
Howarth	3	1	14	0	—	6	0	18	0
PAKISTAN									
Sarfraz	24	7	67	1	—	8	3	22	0
Sikander	21	4	88	3	—	6	0	14	1
Anwar	4	0	12	0	—				
Mushtaq	25	4	60	4	—	22	5	59	5
Raja	10.4	5	18	2	—	20	3	68	4
Mudassar									

FALL OF WICKETS

	P	NZ	P	NZ
	1st	1st	2nd	2nd
1st	19	53	24	33
2nd	48	96	128	62
3rd	75	147	209	62
4th	135	151	273	77
5th	183	176	298	98
6th	198	200	316	136
7th	242	254	—	142
8th	255	288	—	152
9th	271	289	—	176
10th	271	290	—	176

In Pakistan's 2nd innings, Mudassar retired at 6-0.

SECOND TEST MATCH

PLAYED AT NAPIER, 16, 17, 18, 19, 20, 21 FEBRUARY
MATCH DRAWN

PAKISTAN

Majid Khan c Lees b Cairns	29	not out		119
Talat Ali b Hadlee	4	b Hadlee		13
Zaheer Abbas c Parker b Cairns	2	c & b Boock		40
Javed Miandad run out	26			
Asif Iqbal b Cairns	104			
†Mushtaq Mohammad c Lees b Hadlee	24	c Cairns b Boock		28
Wasim Raja lbw b Hadlee	74			
Imran Khan c Lees b Hadlee	3	not out		27
Sarfraz Nawaz c Edgar b Coney	31			
‡Wasim Bari not out	37			
Sikander Bakht lbw b Troup	19			
Extras (B2, LB3, NB2)	7	(B2, LB1, W4)		7
Total	**360**	(3 wkts dec)		**234**

NEW ZEALAND

B. A. Edgar c Mushtaq b Imran	3
J. G. Wright c Javed b Sikander	88
G. P. Howarth b Sikander	114
J. M. Parker lbw b Sikander	3
†M. G. Burgess c Javed b Imran	40
J. V. Coney lbw b Sikander	69
S. L. Boock b Imran	4
‡W. K. Lees b Imran	8
R. J. Hadlee c Sikander b Imran	11
B. L. Cairns c Zaheer b Mushtaq	13
G. B. Troup not out	3
Extras (B10, LB14, NB22)	46
Total	**402**

BOWLING

NEW ZEALAND	O	M	R	W	O	M	R	W
Hadlee	25	3	101	4	14	1	56	1
Cairns	19	1	85	3	11	2	23	0
Troup	22.5	2	87	1	16	3	25	0
Coney	25	9	38	1	10	2	21	0
Boock	12	3	41	0	30	6	77	2
Howarth	1	0	1	0	5	1	25	0

PAKISTAN	O	M	R	W
Imran	33	6	106	5
Sarfraz	26	5	90	0
Sikander	17	2	67	4
Mushtaq	17.3	0	70	1
Raja	3	1	10	0
Majid	5	1	13	0

FALL OF WICKETS

	P	NZ	P
	1st	1st	2nd
1st	19	24	27
2nd	23	219	110
3rd	42	230	188
4th	128	241	—
5th	180	292	—
6th	221	301	—
7th	228	318	—
8th	283	351	—
9th	313	388	—
10th	360	402	—

13

THIRD TEST MATCH

NEW ZEALAND

J. G. Wright c Bari b Sikander	32	b Sarfraz		10
B. A. Edgar c Bari b Imran	1	b Imran		0
G. P. Howarth c Bari b Sarfraz	5	c Raja b Sikander		38
J. F. Reid c Bari b Imran	0	c Majid b Mushtaq		19
†M. G. Burgess c Sarfraz b Sikander	3	c Asif b Sarfraz		71
J. V. Coney c Bari b Sarfraz	82	c Mushtaq b Imran		49
‡W. K. Lees c Bari b Sarfraz	25	not out		45
B. L. Cairns c Bari b Asif	17	b Sarfraz		4
R. J. Hadlee not out	53	c Talat b Sarfraz		5
G. B. Troup c Mushtaq b Sikander	7			
S. L. Boock c Javed b Imran	0			
Extras (B5, LB3, NB20, W1)	29	(B8, LB13, W1, NB18)		40
Total	**254**	**(8 wkts dec)**		**281**

PAKISTAN

Majid Khan b Cairns	10	not out	0
Talat Ali c Lees b Hadlee	1	not out	8
Zaheer Abbas c Lees b Troup	135		
Javed Miandad lbw b Cairns	30		
Asif Iqbal c Coney b Cairns	35		
†Mushtaq Mohammad lbw b Hadlee	48		
Wasim Raja c Coney b Troup	19		
Imran Khan c Lees b Hadlee	33		
Sarfraz Nawaz c Howarth b Hadlee	5		
‡Wasim Bari not out	25		
Sikander Bakht c Cairns b Hadlee	6		
Extras (B4, LB7, NB1)	12		
Total	**359**	**(0 wkt)**	**8**

BOWLING

PAKISTAN	O	M	R	W		O	M	R	W
Imran	17	2	77	3	—	32	9	72	2
Sarfraz	15	3	56	3	—	28.2	9	61	4
Asif	7	1	24	1	—	2	0	5	0
Sikander	16	4	68	3	—	18	2	64	1
Mushtaq					—	11	2	39	1
NEW ZEALAND									
Hadlee	27	3	104	5	—	1	0	8	0
Troup	22	2	70	2	—				
Cairns	28	5	94	3	—				
Coney	19	4	51	0	—				
Boock	6	0	28	0	—				
Howarth	1	1	0	0	—				

FALL OF WICKETS

	NZ	P	NZ	P
	1st	1st	2nd	2nd
1st	11	5	1	—
2nd	31	22	52	—
3rd	32	118	85	—
4th	50	195	121	—
5th	60	231	205	—
6th	109	273	261	—
7th	166	321	275	—
8th	209	322	281	—
9th	251	345	—	—
10th	254	359	—	—

Australia v Pakistan 1978-79

FIRST TEST MATCH

PLAYED AT MELBOURNE, 10, 11, 12, 14, 15 MARCH
PAKISTAN WON BY 71 RUNS

PAKISTAN

Majid Khan c Wright b Hogg	1	b Border	108
Mohsin Khan c Hilditch b Hogg	14	c & b Hogg	14
Zaheer Abbas b Hogg	11	b Hogg	59
Javed Miandad b Hogg	19	c Wright b Border	16
Asif Iqbal c Wright b Clark	9	lbw b Hogg	44
†Mushtaq Mohammad c Wright b Hurst	36	c Higgs b Sleep	28
Wasim Raja b Hurst	13	c Wright b Hurst	28
Imran Khan c Wright b Hurst	33	c Clark b Hurst	28
Sarfraz Nawaz c Wright b Sleep	35	lbw b Hurst	1
‡Wasim Bari run out	0	not out	8
Sikander Bakht not out	5		
Extras (B2, LB7, W1, NB10)	20	(B4, LB6, NB9)	19
Total	**196**	(9 wkts dec)	**353**

AUSTRALIA

G. M. Wood not out	5	c Wasim Bari b Sarfraz	0
A. M. Hilditch c Javed b Imran	3	b Sarfraz	62
A. R. Border b Imran	20	b Sarfraz	105
†G. N. Yallop b Imran	25	run out	8
K. J. Hughes run out	19	c Mohsin b Sarfraz	84
D. F. Whatmore lbw b Sarfraz	43	b Sarfraz	15
P. R. Sleep c Wasim Bari b Imran	10	b Sarfraz	0
‡K. J. Wright c Imran b Wasim Raja	9	not out	1
W. M. Clark c Mushtaq b Wasim Raja	9	b Sarfraz	0
R. M. Hogg run out	0	lbw b Sarfraz	0
A. G. Hurst c & b Sarfraz	0	c Wasim Bari b Sarfraz	0
Extras (B1, LB5, W2, NB8)	16	(B13, LB13, NB9)	35
Total	**168**		**310**

BOWLING

AUSTRALIA	O	M	R	W	O	M	R	W	FALL OF WICKETS
Hogg	17	4	49	4	19	2	75	3	*P A P A*
Hurst	20	4	55	3	19.5	1	115	3	*1st 1st 2nd 2nd*
Clark	17	4	56	1	21	6	47	0	1st 2 11 30 49
Sleep	7.7	2	16	1	8	0	62	1	2nd 22 53 165 109
Border					14	5	35	2	3rd 28 63 204 128
PAKISTAN									4th 40 97 209 305
Imran	18	8	26	4	9	73	0		5th 83 109 261 305
Sarfraz	21.6	6	39	2	35.4	7	86	9	6th 99 140 299 306
Sikander	10	1	29	0	7	0	29	0	7th 122 152 330 308
Mushtaq	7	0	35	0	11	0	42	0	8th 173 167 332 309
Wasim Raja	5	0	23	2	3	0	11	0	9th 177 167 353 310
Majid					9	1	34	0	10th 196 168 — 310

SECOND TEST MATCH

PLAYED AT PERTH, 24, 25, 26, 28, 29 MARCH
AUSTRALIA WON BY 7 WICKETS

PAKISTAN

Majid Khan	c Hilditch b Hogg	0	c sub (Laughlin) b Hogg	0
Mudassar Nazar	c Wright b Hurst	5	c Hilditch b Hurst	25
Zaheer Abbas	c Wright b Hurst	29	c Wright b Hogg	18
Javed Miandad	not out	129	c Wright b Hurst	19
Haroon Rashid	c Border b Hurst	4	c Yardley b Dymock	47
Asif Iqbal	run out	35	not out	134
†Mushtaq Mohammad	run out	23	lbw b Yardley	1
Imran Khan	c Wright b Dymock	14	c Wright b Hurst	15
Sarfraz Nawaz	c Wright b Hurst	27	c Yardley b Hurst	3
‡Wasim Bari	c Hilditch b Dymock	0	c Whatmore b Hurst	0
Sikander Bakht	b Dymock	0	run out	0
Extras	(LB3, W3, NB5)	11	(B3, LB8, NB12)	23
Total		**277**		**285**

AUSTRALIA

W. M. Darling	lbw b Mudassar	75	run out	79
A. M. J. Hilditch	c Zaheer b Imran	41	handled ball	29
A. R. Border	c Majid b Javed	85	not out	66
†K. J. Hughes	lbw b Sikander	9		
J. K. Moss	c Wasim b Mudassar	22	not out	38
D. F. Whatmore	c Asif b Imran	15		
‡K. J. Wright	c Wasim b Mudassar	16		
B. Yardley	b Sarfraz	19	run out	1
G. Dymock	not out	5		
R. M. Hogg	b Imran	3		
A. G. Hurst	c Wasim b Sarfraz	16		
Extras	(B3, LB4, W1, NB13)	21	(LB13, NB10)	23
Total		**327**	(3 wkts)	**236**

BOWLING

AUSTRALIA	O	M	R	W		O	M	R	W
Hogg	19	2	88	1	—	20	5	45	2
Hurst	23	4	61	4	—	24.7	2	94	5
Dymock	21.6	4	65	3	—	23	5	72	1
Yardley	14	2	52	0	—	14	3	42	1
Border					—	4	0	9	0
PAKISTAN									
Imran	32	5	105	3	—	17	1	81	0
Sarfraz	35.1	7	112	2	—	19	1	85	0
Sikander	11	1	33	1	—				
Mudassar	16	2	48	3	—	10.1	2	35	0
Javed	2	0	8	1	—	2	0	12	0

FALL OF WICKETS

	P	A	P	A
	1st	1st	2nd	2nd
1st	0	96	0	87
2nd	27	143	35	153
3rd	41	161	67	155
4th	49	219	86	—
5th	90	246	152	—
6th	176	273	153	—
7th	224	297	245	—
8th	276	301	263	—
9th	277	304	263	—
10th	277	327	285	—

England v India, 1979

FIRST CORNHILL TEST MATCH

PLAYED AT EDGBASTON, 12, 13, 14, 16 JULY
ENGLAND WON BY AN INNINGS AND 83 RUNS

ENGLAND

†J. M. Brearley c Reddy b Dev	24
G. Boycott lbw b Dev	155
D. W. Randall c Reddy b Dev	15
G. A. Gooch c Reddy b Dev	83
D. I. Gower not out	200
I. T. Botham b Dev	33
G. Miller not out	63
P. H. Edmonds did not bat	
‡R. W. Taylor did not bat	
R. G. D. Willis did not bat	
M. Hendrick did not bat	
Extras (B4, LB27, W11, NB18)	60
Total (5 wkts dec)	633

INDIA

S. M. Gavaskar run out	61	c Gooch b Hendrick	68
C. P. S. Chauhan c Gooch b Botham	4	c Randall b Willis	56
D. B. Vengsarkar c Gooch b Edmonds	32	c Edmonds b Hendrick	7
G. R. Viswanath c Botham b Edmonds	78	c Taylor b Botham	51
A. D. Gaekwad c Botham b Willis	25	c Gooch b Botham	15
M. Amarnath b Willis	31	lbw b Botham	10
Kapil Dev lbw b Botham	1	c Hendrick b Botham	21
K. D. Ghavri c Brearley b Willis	6	c Randall b Hendrick	4
‡B. Reddy b Hendrick	21	lbw b Hendrick	0
†S. Venkataraghavan c Botham b Hendrick	28	lbw b Botham	0
B. S. Chandrasekhar not out	0	not out	0
Extras (B1, LB4, W3, NB12)	20	(B7, LB12, NB2)	21
Total	297		253

BOWLING

INDIA	O	M	R	W	O	M	R	W	FALL OF WICKETS			
										E	I	I
Dev	48	15	146	5	—					1st	1st	2nd
Ghavri	38	5	129	0	—				1st	66	15	124
Amarnath	13.2	2	47	0	—				2nd	90	59	136
Chandrasekhar	29	1	113	0	—				3rd	235	129	136
Venkataraghavan	31	4	107	0	—				4th	426	205	182
Gaekwad	3	0	12	0	—				5th	468	209	227
Chauhan	3	0	19	0	—				6th	—	210	240
ENGLAND									7th	—	229	249
Willis	24	9	69	3	—	14	3	45	1	8th	—	251	250
Botham	26	4	86	2	—	29	8	70	5	9th	—	294	251
Hendrick	24.1	9	36	2	—	20.3	8	45	4	10th	—	297	253
Edmonds	26	11	60	2	—	17	6	37	0				
Boycott	5	1	8	0	—								
Miller	11	3	18	0	—	9	1	27					
Gooch					—	6	2	8					

Man of the Match: D. I. Gower.

SECOND TEST MATCH

INDIA

S. M. Gavaskar c Taylor b Gooch	42	c Brearley b Botham		59
C. P. S. Chauhan c Randall b Botham	2	c Randall b Edmonds		31
D. B. Vengsarkar c Botham b Hendrick	0	c Boycott b Edmonds		103
G. R. Viswanath c Brearley b Hendrick	21	c Gower b Lever		113
A. D. Gaekwad c Taylor b Botham	13	not out		1
Yashpal Sharma c Taylor b Botham	11	not out		5
Kapil Dev c Miller b Botham	4			
K. D. Ghavri not out	3			
‡B. Reddy lbw b Botham	0			
†S. Venkataraghavan run out	0			
B. S. Bedi b Lever	0			
Extras	0	(B2, LB2, W1, NB1)		6
Total	**96**	**(4 wkts)**		**318**

ENGLAND

†J. M. Brearley c Reddy b Dev	12
G. Boycott c Gavaskar b Ghavri	32
G. A. Gooch b Dev	10
D. I. Gower b Ghavri	82
D. W. Randall run out	57
I. T. Botham c Venkataraghavan	36
G. Miller st Reddy b Bedi	62
P. H. Edmonds c Reddy b Dev	20
‡R. W. Taylor c Vengsarkar b Bedi	64
J. K. Lever not out	6
M. Hendrick did not bat	
Extras (B11, LB21, W2, NB4)	38
Total (9 wkts dec)	**419**

BOWLING

ENGLAND	O	M	R	W	O	M	R	W	FALL OF WICKETS			
										I	E	I
Lever	9.5	3	29	1 —	24	7	69	1		1st	1st	2nd
Botham	19	9	35	5 —	35	13	80	1	1st	12	21	79
Hendrick	15	7	15	2 —	25	12	56	0	2nd	23	60	99
Edmonds	2	1	1	0 —	45	18	62	2	3rd	51	71	309
Gooch	10	5	16	1 —	2	0	8	0	4th	75	185	312
Miller				—	17	6	37	0	5th	79	226	—
INDIA									6th	89	253	—
Dev	38	11	93	3 —					7th	96	291	—
Ghavri	31		2	122	2 —				8th	96	394	—
Bedi	35.5	13	87	2 —					9th	96	419	—
Venkataraghavan	22		2	79	1 —				10th	96	—	—

Man of the Match: D. B. Vengsarkar. Adjudicator: John Arlott.

THIRD TEST MATCH

PLAYED AT HEADINGLEY, 16, 17, 18, 20, 21 AUGUST
MATCH DRAWN

ENGLAND

G. Boycott c Viswanath b Dev	31
†J. M. Brearley c Viswanath b Amarnath	15
G. A. Gooch c Vengsarkar b Dev	4
D. I. Gower lbw b Dev	0
D. W. Randall b Ghavri	11
I. T. Botham c Ghavri b Venkataraghavan	137
G. Miller c Reddy b Amarnath	27
P. H. Edmonds run out	18
‡R. W. Taylor c Chauhan b Bedi	1
R. G. D. Willis not out	4
M. Hendrick c sub (Yajurvindra) b Bedi	0
Extras (B4, LB6, W4, NB8)	22
Total	**270**

INDIA

S. M. Gavaskar b Edmonds	78
C. P. S. Chauhan c Botham b Willis	0
M. Amarnath c Taylor b Willis	0
G. R. Viswanath c Brearley b Hendrick	1
Yashpal Sharma c Botham b Miller	40
D. B. Vengsarkar not out	65
Kapil Dev c Gooch b Miller	3
K. D. Ghavri not out	20
†S. Venkataraghavan did not bat	
‡B. Reddy did not bat	
B. S. Bedi did not bat	
Extras (B11, LB4, W1)	16
Total (6 wkts)	**223**

BOWLING

INDIA	O	M	R	W
Dev	27	7	84	3
Ghavri	18	4	60	1
Amarnath	20	7	53	2
Venkataraghavan	7	2	25	1
Bedi	8.5	2	26	2
ENGLAND				
Willis	18	5	42	2
Hendrick	14	6	13	1
Botham	13	3	39	0
Edmonds	28	8	59	1
Miller	32	13	52	2
Gooch	3	1	2	0
Boycott	2	2	0	0

FALL OF WICKETS

	E	I
	1st	1st
1st	53	1
2nd	57	9
3rd	57	12
4th	58	106
5th	89	156
6th	176	160
7th	264	—
8th	264	—
9th	266	—
10th	270	—

Man of the Match: I. T. Botham. Adjudicator: J. C. Laker.

FOURTH TEST MATCH

PLAYED AT THE OVAL, 30, 31 AUGUST, 1, 3, 4 SEPTEMBER

MATCH DRAWN

ENGLAND

G. Boycott lbw b Dev	35	b Ghavri	125
A. R. Butcher c Yajurvindra b Venkataraghavan	14	c Venkataraghavan b Ghavri	20
G. A. Gooch c Viswanath b Ghavri	79	lbw b Dev	31
D. I. Gower lbw b Dev	0	c Reddy b Bedi	7
P. Willey c Yajurvindra b Bedi	52	c Reddy b Ghavri	31
I. T. Botham st Reddy b Venkataraghavan	38	run out	0
†J. M. Brearley b Ghavri	34	b Venkataraghavan	11
‡D. L. Bairstow c Reddy b Dev	9	c Gavaskar b Dev	59
P. H. Edmonds c Dev b Venkataraghavan	16	not out	27
R. G. D. Willis not out	10		
M. Hendrick c Gavaskar b Bedi	0		
Extras (LB9, W4, NB5)	18	(LB14, W2, NB7)	23
Total	**305**	**(8 wkts dec)**	**334**

INDIA

S. M. Gavaskar c Bairstow b Botham	13	c Gower b Botham	221
C. P. S. Chauhan c Botham b Willis	6	c Botham b Willis	80
D. B. Vengsarkar c Botham b Willis	0	c Botham b Edmonds	52
G. R. Viswanath c Brearley b Botham	62	c Brearley b Willey	15
Yashpal Sharma lbw b Willis	27	lbw b Botham	19
Yajurvindra Singh not out	43	lbw b Botham	1
Kapil Dev b Hendrick	16	c Gooch b Willey	0
K. D. Ghavri c Bairstow b Botham	7	not out	3
‡B. Reddy c Bairstow b Botham	12	not out	5
†S. Venkataraghavan c & b Hendrick	2	run out	6
B. S. Bedi c Brearley b Hendrick	1		
Extras (B2, LB3, W5, NB3)	13	(B11, LB15, W1)	27
Total	**202**	**(8 wkts)**	**429**

BOWLING

INDIA	O	M	R	W		O	M	R	W	FALL OF WICKETS				
											E	*I*	*E*	*I*
Dev	32	12	83	3	—	28.5	4	89	2		*1st*	*1st*	*2nd*	*2nd*
Ghavri	26	8	61	2	—	34	11	76	3	1st	45	9	43	213
Bedi	29.5	4	69	2	—	26	4	67	1	2nd	51	9	107	366
Yajurvindra	8	2	15	0	—	2	0	4	0	3rd	51	47	125	367
Venkataraghavan	29	9	59	2	—	26	4	75	1	4th	148	91	192	389
ENGLAND										5th	203	130	194	410
Willis	18	2	53	3	—	28	4	89	1	6th	245	161	215	411
Botham	28	7	65	4	—	29	5	97	3	7th	272	176	291	419
Hendrick	22.3	7	38	3	—	11	8	15	0	8th	275	192	334	423
Willey	4	1	10	0	—	43.5	15	96	2	9th	304	200	—	—
Gooch	2	0	6	0	—	2	0	0	0	10th	305	202	—	—
Edmonds	5	1	17	0	—	38	11	87	1					
Butcher					—	2	0	9	0					

Man of the Match: S. M. Gavaskar. Adjudicator: J. H. Edrich.

TEST MATCH AVERAGES

ENGLAND—BATTING AND FIELDING

	M	I	NO	Runs	HS	Avge	100	50	Ct	St
G. Miller	3	3	1	152	63*	76.00	—	2	1	—
G. Boycott	4	5	0	378	155	75.60	2	—	1	—
D. I. Gower	4	5	1	289	200*	72.25	1	1	2	—
I. T. Botham	4	5	0	244	137	48.80	1	—	10	—
G. A. Gooch	4	5	0	207	83	41.40	—	2	6	—
R. W. Taylor	3	2	0	65	64	32.50	—	1	5	—
D. W. Randall	3	3	0	83	57	27.66	—	1	4	—
P. H. Edmonds	4	4	1	81	27*	27.00	—	—	1	—
J. M. Brearley	4	5	0	96	34	19.20	—	—	7	—
R. G. D. Willis	3	2	2	14	10*	—	—	—	—	—
M. Hendrick	4	2	0	0	0	0.00	—	—	—	—

Played in one Test: D. L. Bairstow 9, 59 (3ct, 0st); A. R. Butcher 14, 20; J. K. Lever 6*; P. Willey 52, 31.

ENGLAND—BOWLING

	Overs	Mdns	Runs	Wkts	Avge	Best	5wI	10wM
M. Hendrick	129.2	51	218	12	18.16	4/45	—	—
I. T. Botham	179	49	472	20	23.60	5/35	2	—
R. G. D. Willis	102	23	298	10	29.80	3/53	—	—
P. H. Edmonds	161	56	323	6	53.83	2/60	—	—

Also bowled: G. Boycott 7-3-8-0; A. R. Butcher 2-0-9-0; G. A. Gooch 25-9-49-1; J. K. Lever 33.5-10-98-2; G. Miller 69-23-134-2; P. Willey 47.5-16-106-2.

INDIA—BATTING AND FIELDING

	M	I	NO	Runs	HS	Avge	100	50	Ct	St
S. M. Gavaskar	4	7	0	542	221	77.42	1	4	3	—
G. R. Viswanath	4	7	0	341	113	48.71	1	3	3	—
D. B. Vengsarkar	4	7	1	249	103	41.50	1	2	2	—
C. P. S. Chauhan	4	7	0	179	80	25.57	—	2	1	—
Yashpal	3	5	1	102	40	25.50	—	—	—	—
A. D. Gaekwad	2	4	1	54	25	18.00	—	—	—	—
K. D. Ghavri	4	6	3	43	20*	14.33	—	—	1	—
M. Amarnath	2	3	0	41	31	13.66	—	—	—	—
B. Reddy	4	5	1	38	21	9.50	—	—	9	2
Kapil Dev	4	6	0	45	21	7.50	—	—	1	—
S. Venkataraghavan	4	5	0	36	28	7.20	—	—	1	—
B. S. Bedi	3	2	0	1	1	0.50	—	—	—	—

Played in one Test: B. S. Chandrasekhar 0*, 0*; Yajurvindra Singh 43*, 1 (2ct).

INDIA—BOWLING

	Overs	Mdns	Runs	Wkts	Avge	Best	5wI	10wM
Kapil Dev	173.5	49	495	16	30.93	5/146	1	—
B. S. Bedi	103.3	23	249	7	35.57	2/26	—	—
K. D. Ghavri	147	30	448	8	56.00	3/76	—	—
S. Venkataraghavan	115	21	345	6	57.50	3/59	—	—

Also bowled: M. Amarnath 33.2-9-100-2; B. S. Chandrasekhar 29-1-113-0; C. P. S. Chauhan 3-0-19-0; A. D. Gaekwad 3-0-12-0; Yajurvindra Singh 10-2-19-0.

FIRST-CLASS TOUR AVERAGES

BATTING AND FIELDING

	M	I	NO	Runs	HS	Avge	100	50	Ct	St
Yashpal	12	21	6	884	111	58.93	3	3	6	1
S. M. Gavaskar	13	20	1	1062	221	55.89	3	5	15	—
G. R. Viswanath	13	17	2	757	113	50.46	3	4	4	—
M. Amarnath	11	16	3	592	123	45.53	1	3	2	—
D. B. Vengsarkar	12	19	1	751	138	41.72	3	4	12	—
Yajurvindra Singh	9	14	6	293	59	36.62	—	1	10	—
A. D. Gaekwad	12	20	2	574	109	31.88	2	1	4	—
C. P. S. Chauhan	13	22	2	561	108	28.05	1	3	4	—
B. P. Patel	7	10	4	137	36*	22.83	—	—	1	—
K. D. Ghavri	12	12	5	143	33*	20.42	—	—	1	—
Kapil Dev	13	15	0	287	102	19.13	1	—	4	—
S. Khanna	6	4	1	41	20	13.66	—	—	6	4
B. Reddy	10	12	2	101	23	10.10	—	—	21	2
S. Venkataraghavan	13	10	0	101	28	10.10	—	—	3	—
B. S. Bedi	11	7	4	28	20	9.33	—	—	5	—
B. S. Chandrasekhar	9	5	3	2	1*	1.00	—	—	—	—

BOWLING

	Overs	Mdns	Runs	Wkts	Avge	Best	5wI	10wM
B. S. Bedi	377.5	113	847	33	25.66	6/28	2	1
Yajurvindra Singh	138	26	437	15	29.13	5/75	1	—
S. Venkataraghavan	391.5	96	1065	34	31.32	5/33	1	—
M. Amarnath	194.5	47	533	14	38.07	4/88	—	—
K. D. Ghavri	345.5	68	1122	27	41.55	5/23	1	—
Kapil Dev	422	96	1327	31	42.80	5/146	1	—
B. S. Chandrasekhar	204.2	32	655	14	46.78	4/30	—	—

Also bowled: C. P. S. Chauhan 38.3-5-132-4; A. D. Gaekwad 13-4-55-1; S. M. Gavaskar 8-1-23-0; Yashpal 31.1-3-123-3.

India v Australia, 1979—80

FIRST TEST MATCH

PLAYED AT MADRAS, 11, 12, 14, 15, 16 SEPTEMBER

MATCH DRAWN

AUSTRALIA

A. M. Hilditch c Venkataraghavan b Dev	4	lbw b Doshi		55
G. M. Wood lbw b Doshi	33	c Chauhan b Dev		2
A. R. Border run out	162	b Venkataraghavan		50
†K. J. Hughes c Venkataraghavan b Doshi	100	lbw b Venkataraghavan		36
G. N. Yallop c Yajurvindra b Doshi	18	run out		2
D. F. Whatmore c Venkataraghavan b Doshi	20	c Chauhan b Doshi		8
‡K. J. Wright b Venkataraghavan	20	b Venkataraghavan		5
G. Dymock lbw b Dev	16	not out		28
R. M. Hogg c Dev b Doshi	3	not out		8
A. G. Hurst c Kirmani b Doshi	0			
J. D. Higgs not out	1			
Extras (B1, LB7, W1, NB4)	13	(B11, LB4, NB3)		18
Total	390	(7 wkts)		212

INDIA

†S. M. Gavaskar c Wood b Hogg	50
C. P. S. Chauhan c Wright b Higgs	26
‡S. M. H. Kirmani c Border b Hogg	57
G. R. Viswanath c Hughes b Higgs	17
D. B. Vengsarkar c Whatmore b Higgs	65
Yashpal Sharma lbw b Higgs	52
Yajurvindra Singh c Wright b Yallop	15
Kapil Dev c Hurst b Higgs	83
K. D. Ghavri not out	23
S. Venkataraghavan lbw b Higgs	4
D. R. Doshi c Hogg b Higgs	3
Extras (B2, LB5, NB23)	30
Total	425

BOWLING

INDIA	O	M	R	W	O	M	R	W
Dev	25.4	3	95	2	— 9	3	30	1
Ghavri	20	4	49	0	— 17.4	8	23	0
Yajurvindra	9	1	29	0	—			
Venkataraghavan	46	16	101	1	— 45	10	77	3
Doshi	43	10	103	6	— 42	15	64	2

AUSTRALIA	O	M	R	W
Hogg	22	1	85	2
Hurst	23	8	51	0
Higgs	41.3	12	143	7
Dymock	24	6	65	0
Border	14	4	30	0
Yallop	6	1	21	1

FALL OF WICKETS

	A	I	A
	1st	1st	2nd
1st	8	80	2
2nd	75	89	103
3rd	297	122	123
4th	318	221	127
5th	339	240	146
6th	352	281	156
7th	369	371	175
8th	375	394	—
9th	376	417	—
10th	390	425	—

SECOND TEST MATCH

AUSTRALIA

A. M. Hilditch c sub (Arunlal) b Yadav	62	lbw b Yadav	3
W. M. Darling b Dev	7		
A. R. Border c Yadav b Doshi	44	b Yadav	19
†K. J. Hughes c Ghavri b Dev	86	not out	13
G. N. Yallop c Viswanath b Yadav	12	not out	6
B. Yardley c & b Ghavri	47		
G. M. Wood c Kirmani b Ghavri	18	c Viswanath b Yadav	30
‡K. J. Wright not out	16		
R. M. Hogg lbw b Venkataraghavan	19		
J. D. Higgs lbw b Yadav	1		
A. G. Hurst b Yadav	0		
Extras (LB6, W5, NB10)	21	(LB5, NB1)	6
Total	333	(3 wkts)	77

INDIA

†S. M. Gavaskar c Hilditch b Yardley	10
C. P. S. Chauhan c Hilditch b Yardley	31
D. B. Vengsarkar lbw b Yardley	112
‡S. M. H. Kirmani st Wright b Higgs	30
G. R. Viswanath not out	161
Yashpal Sharma c Border b Yardley	37
Kapil Dev not out	38
S. Yadav did not bat	
K. D. Ghavri did not bat	
S. Venkataraghavan did not bat	
D. R. Doshi did not bat	
Extras (B12, LB8, W1, NB17)	38
Total (5 wkts dec)	457

BOWLING

INDIA	O	M	R	W	O	M	R	W
Dev	25	4	89	2 —	3	2	10	0
Ghavri	19	5	68	2 —	3	1	9	0
Doshi	28	6	63	1 —	8	4	11	0
Venkataraghavan	20	6	43	1 —	8	2	18	0
Yadav	22.5	6	49	4 —	15.4	4	32	3

AUSTRALIA	O	M	R	W
Hogg	32	6	18	0
Hurst	39	3	93	0
Yardley	44	16	107	4
Higgs	37	9	95	1
Yallop	2	0	6	0

FALL OF WICKETS

	A	I	A
	1st	1st	2nd
1st	21	22	13
2nd	99	61	53
3rd	137	120	62
4th	159	279	—
5th	258	372	—
6th	294	—	—
7th	294	—	—
8th	332	—	—
9th	333	—	—
10th	333	—	—

THIRD TEST MATCH

PLAYED AT KANPUR, 2, 3, 4, 6, 7 OCTOBER

INDIA WON BY 153 RUNS

INDIA

†S. M. Gavaskar	lbw b Dymock	76	c Whatmore b Yardley	12
C. P. S. Chauhan	c & b Hogg	58	c Yardley b Dymock	84
D. B. Vengsarkar	lbw b Hogg	52	c Whatmore b Dymock	20
G. R. Viswanath	c sub (Sleep) b Dymock	44	c Whatmore b Yardley	52
Yashpal Sharma	b Hogg	0	c Wright b Dymock	0
Kapil Dev	c Hughes b Border	5	b Dymock	10
‡S. M. H. Kirmani	c Whatmore b Hogg	4	b Dymock	45
K. D. Ghavri	c Whatmore b Dymock	5	c sub (Sleep) b Hogg	25
S. Yadav	lbw b Dymock		c Whatmore b Dymock	18
S. Venkataraghavan	c Border b Dymock	1	not out	4
D. R. Doshi	not out	0	b Dymock	0
Extras	(B5, LB6, NB15)	26	(B11, LB9, NB21)	41
Total		271		311

AUSTRALIA

A. M. Hilditch	c Chauhan b Ghavri	1	b Doshi	23
B. Yardley	b Yashpal b Ghavri	29	lbw b Dev	5
A. R. Border	c Viswanath b Venkataraghavan	24	b Yadav	8
†K. J. Hughes	b Yadav	50	lbw b Dev	1
G. N. Yallop	hit wkt b Dev	89	c Kirmani b Ghavri	15
‡K. J. Wright	lbw b Dev	6	b Yadav	11
D. F. Whatmore	c Gavaskar b Doshi	14	b Yadav	33
W. M. Darling	c Kirmani b Ghavri	59	lbw b Dev	4
G. Dymock	run out	11	st Kirmani b Yadav	6
R. M. Hogg	b Yadav	10	lbw b Dev	6
J. D. Higgs	not out	3	not out	8
Extras	(LB2, NB6)	8	(B1, LB2, NB2)	5
Total		304		125

BOWLING

AUSTRALIA	O	M	R	W	O	M	R	W
Dymock	35	7	99	5	28.4	5	67	7
Hogg	26	3	66	4	19	4	49	1
Yardley	26	6	54	0	40	15	82	2
Higgs	7	4	23	0	22	7	68	0
Border	3	2	3	1	2	1	4	0
INDIA								
Dev	25	5	78	2	17.2	5	30	4
Ghavri	23.3	5	65	3	11	0	28	1
Venkataraghavan	18	6	56	1	9	4	13	0
Doshi	16	5	32	1	12	5	14	1
Yadav	25	3	65	2	12	0	35	4

FALL OF WICKETS

	I	A	I	A
	1st	1st	2nd	2nd
1st	114	1	24	13
2nd	201	51	48	32
3rd	206	75	161	37
4th	214	168	163	49
5th	231	175	177	74
6th	239	193	256	93
7th	246	246	261	104
8th	246	263	302	106
9th	256	294	311	113
10th	271	304	311	125

FOURTH TEST MATCH

MATCH DRAWN

INDIA

†S. M. Gavaskar lbw b Higgs	115
C. P. S. Chauhan c Whatmore b Dymock	19
D. B. Vengasarkar st Wright b Higgs	26
G. R. Viswanath st Wright b Higgs	131
Yashpal Sharma not out	100
Kapil Dev c Whatmore b Dymock	29
M. V. Narasimha Rao c Wright b Dymock	5
‡S. M. H. Kirmani b Dymock	35
K. D. Ghavri not out	8
S. Yadav did not bat	
D. R. Doshi did not bat	
Extras (B6, LB13, NB23)	42
Total (7 wkts dec)	510

AUSTRALIA

A. M. Hilditch c Kirmani b Yadav	29	c Kirmani b Ghavri	85
W. M. Darling c Kirmani b Dev	19	c Kirmani b Dev	7
A. R. Border c Narasimha b Dev	24	c Narasimha b Ghavri	46
†K. J. Hughes c Kirmani b Dev	18	c & b Ghavri	40
D. F. Whatmore lbw b Yadav	77	lbw b Dev	54
P. R. Sleep c Chauhan b Narasimha	17	c sub (Arunlal) b Chauhan	64
G. N. Yallop c Chauhan b Narasimha	21	b Doshi	25
‡K. J. Wright not out	55	b Yadav	15
G. Dymock c Kirmani b Dev	0	not out	31
R. M. Hogg b Dev	0	run out	0
J. D. Higgs lbw b Doshi	11	c Vengsarkar b Viswanath	7
Extras (B4, LB4, NB19)	27	(B13, LB9, W1, NB16)	39
Total	298		413

BOWLING

AUSTRALIA	O	M	R	W	O	M	R	W	FALL OF WICKETS			
										I	*A*	*A*
Dymock	42.2	8	135	4						*1st*	*1st*	*2nd*
Hogg	33	8	91	0								
Yallop	5	0	21	0					1st	38	32	20
Border	4	2	5	0					2nd	108	72	147
Higgs	47	11	150	3					3rd	267	93	156
Sleep	13	1	66	0					4th	338	116	205
INDIA									5th	395	160	242
Ghavri	20	7	58	0 —	30	8	74	3	6th	415	225	318
Dev	32	7	82	5 —	20	7	49	2	7th	467	228	344
Doshi	13.3	5	29	1 —	34	11	69	1	8th	—	242	395
Yadav	27	10	56	2 —	36	10	100	1	9th	—	246	395
Narasimha	12	1	46	2 —	19	3	50	0	10th	—	298	413
Gavaskar					4	1	10	0				
Chauhan					5	1	11	1				
Viswanath					3.3	0	11	1				

FIFTH TEST MATCH

PLAYED AT CALCUTTA, 26, 27, 28, 30, 31 OCTOBER

MATCH DRAWN

AUSTRALIA

A. M. Hilditch c Kirmani b Dev	0	b Ghavri	29
G. N. Yallop c Gavaskar b Yadav	167	lbw b Dev	4
A. R. Border lbw b Dev	54	st Kirmani b Doshi	6
†K. J. Hughes lbw b Dev	92	not out	64
D. F. Whatmore b Dev	4	c Vengsarkar b Doshi	4
W. M. Darling st Kirmani b Doshi	39	c Gavaskar b Yadav	7
B. Yardley not out	61	c Narasimha b Yadav	12
‡K. J. Wright lbw b Doshi	0	not out	12
G. Dymock lbw b Doshi	3		
R. M. Hogg c Yashpal b Doshi	0		
J. D. Higgs lbw b Dev	1		
Extras (B7, LB7, NB7)	21	(B9, LB4)	13
Total	442	(6 wkts dec)	151

INDIA

†S. M. Gavaskar lbw b Hogg	14	c Hilditch b Dymock	25
C. P. S. Chauhan c Border b Higgs	39	c Wright b Dymock	50
D. B. Vengsarkar c Hughes b Yardley	89	c Wright b Dymock	2
G. R. Viswanath c Wright b Yardley	96	lbw b Dymock	7
Yashpal Sharma c Wright b Hogg	22	not out	85
M. V. Narasimha Rao run out	10	not out	20
‡S. M. H. Kirmani not out	13		
Kapil Dev c Hughes b Dymock	30		
K. D. Ghavri c Wright b Yardley	1		
S. Yadav c Wright b Yardley	0		
D. R. Doshi b Dymock	0		
Extras (B12, LB9, W4, NB8)	33	(B4, LB7)	11
Total	347	(4 wkts)	200

BOWLING

INDIA	O	M	R	W	O	M	R	W
Dev	31.5	8	74	5 —	11	3	33	1
Ghavri	24	3	85	0 —	13.3	5	39	1
Yadav	42	8	135	4 —	11	6	16	2
Narasimha	8	0	24	0 —				
Doshi	43	10	92	4 —	22	6	50	2
Chauhan	4	0	11	0				
AUSTRALIA								
Dymock	26.4	8	56	2 —	25	7	63	4
Hogg	26	2	103	4 —	8.2	1	26	0
Yardley	42	13	91	4 —	13	1	47	0
Higgs	28	12	56	1 —	16	3	51	0
Border	2	0	8	0				
Yallop	1	1	0	0 —	1	0	2	0

FALL OF WICKETS

	A 1st	I 1st	A 2nd	I 2nd
1st	0	15	21	52
2nd	97	132	39	54
3rd	303	256	53	70
4th	311	290	62	123
5th	347	290	81	—
6th	396	305	115	—
7th	396	341	—	—
8th	418	342	—	—
9th	426	346	—	—
10th	442	347	—	—

Note: In India's first innings, Vengsarkar retired hurt at 169–2 and resumed at 290–4.

SIXTH TEST MATCH

INDIA WON BY AN INNINGS AND 100 RUNS

INDIA

†S. M. Gavaskar c Hughes b Border	123
C. P. S. Chauhan b Dymock	73
D. B. Vengsarkar c Whatmore b Border	6
G. R. Viswanath c & b Higgs	10
‡S. M. H. Kirmani not out	101
Yashpal Sharma c Whatmore b Hogg	8
M. Amarnath hit wkt b Hogg	2
Kapil Dev c Whatmore b Higgs	17
K. D. Ghavri c sub b Dymock	86
S. Yadav not out	0
D. R. Doshi did not bat	
Extras (B3, LB12, NB17)	32
Total (8 wkts dec)	458

AUSTRALIA

A. M. Hilditch run out	13	b Dev	9
G. N. Yallop c Dev b Yadav	60	c Amarnath b Ghavri	4
A. R. Border c Vengsarkar b Yadav	23	b Doshi	61
†K. J. Hughes c Vengsarkar b Doshi	14	c Ghavri b Dev	80
D. F. Whatmore lbw b Doshi	6	lbw b Dev	0
W. M. Darling c sub b Yadav	16	retired hurt	0
P. R. Sleep b Yadav	1	c Dev b Doshi	3
‡K. J. Wright not out	11	lbw b Doshi	5
G. Dymock c Chauhan b Doshi	1	c Viswanath b Yadav	7
R. M. Hogg c Amarnath b Doshi	5	b Dev	4
J. D. Higgs b Doshi	0	not out	3
Extras (B1, LB2, NB7)	10	(LB12, NB10)	22
Total	160		198

BOWLING

AUSTRALIA	O	M	R	W	O	M	R	W	FALL OF WICKETS		
										I	*A*	*A*
Dymock	31	5	95	2						*1st*	*1st*	*2nd*
Hogg	28	14	53	2					1st	92	28	11
Higgs	29	4	116	2					2nd	222	77	17
Border	27	7	60	2					3rd	231	110	149
Sleep	28	7	79	0					4th	240	118	154
Whatmore	5	2	11	0					5th	272	124	159
Yallop	1	0	12	0					6th	281	125	176
INDIA									7th	327	144	183
Dev	9	0	26	0 —	14.1	5	39	4	8th	454	145	187
Ghavri	8	1	30	0 —	10	2	28	1	9th	—	158	198
Doshi	19.5	4	43	7 —	25	6	60	3	10th	—	160	—
Yadav	21	7	40	4 —	22	9	48	1				
Amarnath	5	1	11	0 —	2	1	1	0				

Note: In Australia's second innings, Darling retired hurt at 154–4.

FIRST TEST MATCH

PLAYED AT BANGALORE, 21, 22, 24, 25, 26 NOVEMBER

MATCH DRAWN

PAKISTAN

Majid Khan c Kirmani b Ghavri		1	st Kirmani b Doshi	19
Mudassar Nazar c Doshi b Yadav		126	c Dev b Yadav	17
Zaheer Abbas st Kirmani b Doshi		40	not out	31
Javed Miandad lbw b Doshi		76	not out	30
Wasim Raja lbw b Dev		36		
†Asif Iqbal c & b Doshi		55		
Imran Khan c Viswanath b Yadav		6		
‡Wasim Bari not out		49		
Abdul Qadir lbw b Dev		8		
Iqbal Qasim run out		20		
Extras (B1, LB6, NB7)		14	(B4, NB7)	11
Total (9 wkts dec)		431	(2 wkts)	108

INDIA

†S. M. Gavaskar c Javed b Qadir		88
C. P. S. Chauhan c Majid b Imran		13
G. R. Viswanath c Bari b Ehtesamuddin		73
D. B. Vengsarkar b Imran		33
Yashpal Sharma c Javed b Majid		62
R. Binny c Ehtesham b Imran		46
‡S. M. H. Kirmani c Qasim b Ehtesamuddin		37
Kapil Dev b Majid		38
K. D. Ghavri b Majid		2
S. Yadav not out		1
D. R. Doshi b Imran		0
Extras (B13, LB10)		23
Total		416

BOWLING

INDIA	O	M	R	W	O	M	R	W	FALL OF WICKETS			
										P	I	P
Dev	24	4	67	2 —	4	2	6	0		1st	1st	2nd
Ghavri	24	3	83	1 —	8	3	30	0	1st	5	17	41
Binny	10	1	49	0 —	3	2	1	0	2nd	62	122	41
Doshi	52.3	20	102	3 —	12	3	26	1	3rd	196	164	—
Yadav	39	5	116	2 —	11	2	20	1	4th	256	266	—
Viswanath					3	1	6	0	5th	334	307	—
Gavaskar					1	0	8	0	6th	345	347	—
PAKISTAN									7th	348	410	—
Imran	28.4	12	53	4 —					8th	371	414	—
Ehtesamuddin	18	2	52	2 —					9th	431	415	—
Qasim	41	17	75	0 —					10th	—	416	—
Majid	28	9	55	3 —								
Qadir	35	8	114	1 —								
Raja	8	2	30	0 —								
Mudassar	6	1	14	0 —								

SECOND TEST MATCH

PLAYED AT NEW DELHI, 4, 5, 7, 8, 9 DECEMBER
MATCH DRAWN

PAKISTAN

Majid Khan b Dev	0	c Kirmani b Binny	40
Mudassar Nazar c Chauhan b Dev	18	c Kirmani b Dev	12
Zaheer Abbas b Dev	3	c Kirmani b Binny	50
Javed Miandad lbw b Ghavri	34	run out	0
Wasim Raja lbw b Dev	97	c Dev b Doshi	61
†Asif Iqbal c Vengsarkar b Ghavri	64	c Kirmani b Dev	38
Imran Khan lbw b Binny	30	c Chauhan b Doshi	2
‡Wasim Bari b Dev	9	b Ghavri	5
Abdul Qadir b Binny	9	c Vengsarkar b Dev	11
Iqbal Qasim run out	2	not out	5
Sikander Bakht not out	1	lbw b Dev	6
Extras (B2, NB4)	6	(B6, LB4, NB2)	12
Total	273		242

INDIA

†S. M. Gavaskar c Bari b Sikander	31	c Bari b Sikander	21
C. P. S. Chauhan c Bari b Sikander	11	lbw b Sikander	40
D. B. Vengsarkar c Javed b Sikander	1	not out	146
G. R. Viswanath run out	4	b Qasim	34
Yashpal Sharma not out	28	c & b Sikander	60
R. Binny lbw b Sikander	1	c Qadir b Asif	10
‡S. M. H. Kirmani b Sikander	5	not out	11
Kapil Dev b Sikander	15	lbw b Mudassar	21
K. D. Ghavri lbw b Sikander	0		
S. Yadav c Qadir b Sikander	4		
D. R. Doshi c Javed b Asif	10		
Extras (B2, LB5, NB9)	16	(B2, LB5, W1, NB13)	21
Total	126	(6 wkts)	364

BOWLING

INDIA	O	M	R	W	O	M	R	W	FALL OF WICKETS
Dev	23.5	8	58	5 —	23.5	6	63	4	

									P	I	P	I
Ghavri	21	4	58	2 —	17	4	59	1	*1st*	*1st*	*2nd*	*2nd*
Binny	10	0	32	2 —	17	3	56	2	1st	3	19	39	37
Doshi	17	3	51	0 —	19	5	31	2	2nd	13	35	68	92
Yadav	28	2	68	0 —	5	0	21	0	3rd	36	46	68	154
									4th	90	52	143	275
									5th	220	56	201	308
PAKISTAN									6th	224	70	209	343
Imran	7.3	4	11	0 —	1	0	2	0	7th	250	87	210	
Sikander	21	3	69	8 —	38	7	121	3	8th	270	87	230	
Asif	6.2	4	3	1 —	20	7	46	1	9th	271	94	232	
Majid	1	0	12	0 —	4	2	8	0	10th	273	126	242	
Qasim	3	0	7	0 —	21	5	87	1					
Mudassar	3	0	8	0 —	25	8	61	1					
Qadir					11	3	16	0					
Raja					2	1	2	0					

In India's first innings, Imran could not complete his 8th over owing to injury.

THIRD TEST MATCH

PLAYED AT BOMBAY 16, 17, 18, 20 DECEMBER

INDIA WON BY 131 RUNS

INDIA

†S. M. Gavaskar c Qadir b Sikander	4	c Zaheer b Qasim	48
C. P. S. Chauhan c Bari b Imran	5	b Mudassar	0
D. B. Vengsarkar c Majid b Qasim	58	c Bari b Sikander	45
G. R. Viswanath c&b Qasim	47	lbw b Qadir	9
Yashpal Sharma b Qasim	3	c Majid b Qasim	16
R. Binny c Bari b Qasim	0	c&b Sikander	0
‡S. M. H. Kirmani c Asif b Sikander	41	c Asif b Qasim	15
Kapil Dev c Raja b Sikander	69	c Bari b Qasim	3
K. D. Ghavri c Asif b Sikander	36	c Bari b Qasim	1
S. Yadav not out	29	st Bari b Qasim	1
D. R. Doshi c Bari b Sikander	9	not out	1
Extras (B10, LB10, W2, NB11)	33	(B9, LB7, NB5)	21
Total	**334**		**160**

PAKISTAN

Majid Khan c Kirmani b Binny	5	lbw b Ghavri	7
Mudassar Nazar c Gavaskar b Doshi	25	lbw b Ghavri	13
Zaheer Abbas b Binny	2	b Dev	11
Javed Miandad lbw b Binny	16	lbw b Doshi	64
Wasim Raja c Viswanath b Doshi	24	c Vengsarkar b Ghavri	4
†Asif Iqbal c&b Yadav	14	c Viswanath b Doshi	26
Imran Khan c Gavaskar b Doshi	15	c Gavaskar b Ghavri	19
‡Wasim Bari b Yadav	23	lbw b Doshi	3
Abdul Qadir not out	29	c Binny b Yadav	15
Iqbal Qasim c Kirmani b Yadav	0	c Vengsarkar b Yadav	6
Sikander Bakht lbw b Dev	3	not out	1
Extras (B1, LB2, NB14)	17	(B2, LB11, NB8)	21
Total	**173**		**190**

BOWLING

PAKISTAN	O	M	R	W	O	M	R	W	FALL OF WICKETS			
									I	P	I	P
Imran	15	7	35	1					1st	1st	2nd	2nd
Sikander	22.1	5	55	4 —	17	6	30	2				
Qasim	44	15	135	4 —	28.5	14	40	6	1st 13	11	5	16
Majid	23	8	52	0 —	4	1	14	0	2nd 31	15	78	32
Qadir	3	1	16	0 —	11	5	27	1	3rd 111	53	97	41
Mudassar	5	0	7	0 —	8	3	18	1	4th 129	57	132	48
Asif	2	1	1	0					5th 129	83	146	84
Raja					1	0	10	0	6th 154	105	154	145
INDIA									7th 249	116	156	161
Dev	14.3	4	23	1 —	6	1	26	1	8th 250	146	157	178
Ghavri	7	2	17	0 —	18	4	63	4	9th 317	146	157	189
Binny	12	1	53	3 —	2	1	2	0	10th 334	173	160	190
Doshi	27	8	52	3 —	19	4	42	3				
Yadav	8	4	11	3 —	6.4	0	36	2				

FOURTH TEST MATCH

INDIA

†S. M. Gavaskar b Sikander	2	c Mudassar b Ehtesamuddin	81
C. P. S. Chauhan c Zaheer b Sikander	6	c Sadiq b Raja	61
D. B. Vengsarkar c Bari b Sikander	0	not out	16
G. R. Viswanath c Mudassar b Ehtesamuddin	2	not out	17
Yashdal Sharma c Bari b Ehtesamuddin	16		
R. Binny b Sikander	29		
‡S. M. H. Kirmani b Ehtesamuddin	0		
Kapil Dev c Mudassar b Sikander	2		
K. D. Ghavri not out	45		
S. Yadav c Majid b Ehtesamuddin	25		
D. R. Doshi b Ehtesamuddin	20		
Extras (B1, LB1, NB13)	15	(B4, LB1, NB13)	18
Total	**162**	(2 wkts)	**193**

PAKISTAN

Mudassar Nazar c Kirmani b Dev	6
Sadiq Mohammad c Kirmani b Ghavri	47
Zaheer Abbas c Gavaskar b Dev	5
Javed Miandad lbw b Dev	8
Majid Khan lbw b Dev	19
†Asif Iqbal c Viswanath b Doshi	11
Wasim Raja not out	94
‡Wasim Bari b Binny	0
Iqbal Qasim b Dev	32
Sikander Bakht c Kirmani b Dev	4
Ehtesamuddin b Binny	2
Extras (LB11, NB10)	21
Total	**249**

BOWLING

PAKISTAN	O	M	R	W		O	M	R	W
Sikander	24	9	56	5	—	23.2	5	63	0
Ehtesamuddin	26.4	11	47	5	—	26	9	40	1
Mudassar	10	4	22	0	—	3	1	19	0
Asif	8	3	22	0					
Qasim						16	7	28	0
Raja						9	2	25	1

INDIA	O	M	R	W
Dev	28	5	63	6
Ghavri	21	5	42	1
Binny	18.5	2	76	2
Doshi	17	8	26	1
Yadav	5	1	21	0

FALL OF WICKETS

	I	P	I
	1st	1st	2nd
1st	4	12	125
2nd	4	35	168
3rd	11	63	—
4th	17	92	—
5th	58	108	—
6th	67	131	—
7th	69	132	—
8th	69	214	—
9th	117	226	—
10th	162	249	—

FIFTH TEST MATCH

PLAYED AT MADRAS, 15, 16, 17, 19, 20 JANUARY

INDIA WON BY 10 WICKETS

PAKISTAN

Mudassar Nazar c Kirmani b Dev	6	c Vengsarkar b Dev	8
Sadiq Mohammad c Kirmani b Dev	46	c Binny b Dev	0
Majid Khan run out	56	c Patil b Ghavri	11
Zaheer Abbas c Kirmani b Dev	0	c Chauhan b Dev	15
Javed Miandad c Vengsarkar b Dev	45	c Kirmani b Doshi	52
†Asif Iqbal c Kirmani b Ghavri	34	c Kirmani b Dev	5
Wasim Raja c Dev b Doshi	15	c Viswanath b Doshi	57
Imran Khan run out	34	c Doshi b Dev	29
‡Wasim Bari c Binny b Ghavri	13	lbw b Dev	15
Iqbal Qasim not out	3	not out	19
Sikander Bakht c Vengsarkar b Ghavri	1	b Dev	2
Extras (LB3, NB16)	19	(LB3, NB17)	20
Total	**272**		**233**

INDIA

†S. M. Gavaskar c Qasim b Imran	166	not out	29
C. P. S. Chauhan c Qasim b Mudassar	5	not out	46
D. B. Vengsarkar c Javed b Imran	17		
G. R. Viswanath c Mudassar b Qasim	16		
S. R. Patil c Javed b Sikander	15		
Yashdal Sharma b Qasim	46		
‡S. M. H. Kirmani b Imran	2		
Kapil Dev lbw b Imran	84		
R. Binney not out	42		
K. D. Ghavri b Qasim	1		
D. R. Doshi c Javed b Imran	9		
Extras (B1, LB2, NB24)	27	(NB3)	3
Total	**430**	**(0 wkt)**	**78**

BOWLING

INDIA	O	M	R	W		O	M	R	W	FALL OF WICKETS
Dev	19	5	90	4	—	23.4	7	56	7	
Ghavri	18.4	3	73	3	—	14	0	82	1	
Binny	10	1	42	0	—	13	2	33	0	
Doshi	26	6	48	1	—	16	3	42	2	

			P		I		P
			1st		*1st*		*2nd*
	1st		33		30		1
	2nd		79		88		17
	3rd		80		135		33
	4th		151		160		36
	5th		187		265		58
	6th		215		279		147
	7th		225		339		171
	8th		226		412		197
	9th		268		413		229
	10th		272		430		233

PAKISTAN	O	M	R	W		O	M	R	W
Imran	38.2	6	114	5	—	5	1	20	0
Sikander	32	5	105	1	—	6	0	37	0
Mudassar	16	3	54	1	—	2	0	2	0
Qasim	37	13	81	3	—	4	1	12	0
Raja	2	0	19	0					
Majid	9	1	30	0					
Sadiq						1	0	4	0

SIXTH TEST MATCH

PLAYED AT CALCUTTA 29, 30, 31 JANUARY, 2, 3 FEBRUARY

MATCH DRAWN

INDIA

S. M. Gavaskar c Qasim b Imran Khan	44	c Miandad b Imran Khan	15
C. P. S. Chauhan lbw b Ehtesamuddin	18	lbw b Ehtesamuddin	21
R. Binny lbw b Imran Khan	15	c Wasim Raja b Imran Khan	0
*G. R. Viswanath b Ehtasamuddin	13	b Imran Khan	13
S. M. Patil b Imran Khan	62	run out	31
Yashpal Sharma c Bari b Imran Khan	62	b Ehtesamuddin	21
Kapil Dev st Bari b Qasim	16	b Iqbal Qasim	30
†S. M. H. Kirmani c Qasim b Ehtesamuddin	37	c Sadiq b Imran Khan	0
K. D. Ghavri run out	16	not out	37
S, Yadav not out	18	c & b Iqbal Qasim	3
D. Doshi b Ehtesamuddin	3	c Asif b Imran	6
Extras (B3, LB9, NB15)	27	(B9, LB33, NB16)	28
Total	**331**		**205**

PAKISTAN

Sadiq Mohammad lbw b Kapil Dev	5	B Ghavri	8
Taslim Arif c Chauhan b Kapil Dev	90	c & b Binny	46
Majid Khan c Kirmani b Binny	54	b Doshi	11
Javed Miandad lbw b Ghavri	50	c & b Doshi	46
Wasim Raja not out	50	run out	12
*Asif Iqbal not out	5	run out	15
Imran Khan		not out	19
†Wasim Raja		not out	0
Iqbal Qasim			
Sikander Bakht } Did not bat			
Ehtesamuddin			
Extras (B1, LB8, NB9)	18	(B12, LB8, NB2)	22
Total (4 Wkts Dec)	**272**	(6 wkts)	**179**

BOWLING

PAKISTAN	O	M	R	W		O	M	R	W	FALL OF WICKETS			
											I	P	I	P
Imran Khan	33	5	67	4	—	23.5	3	63	5		I	P	I	P
Sikander Bakht	22	5	87	0	—	6	12	18	0	1st	48	20	7	24
Ehtesamuddin	35	7	87	4	—	19	5	44	2	2nd	72	112	10	50
Iqbal Qasim	17	3	53	1	—	21	5	50	2	3rd	91	185	33	86
Majid Khan	2	0	10	0	—	1	0	2	0	4th	99	258	40	111
Wasim Raja										5th	187	—	88	153
INDIA										6th	218	—	92	162
Kapil Dev	26	4	65	2	—	20	7	49	0	7th	252	—	135	—
Ghavri	22.5	3	77	1	—	11	2	32	1	8th	292	—	162	—
Doshi	25	12	38	0	—	20	5	46	2	9th	307	—	173	—
Binny	17	3	35	1	—	8	2	20	1	10th	331	—	205	—
Yadav	10	0	39	0	—	4	3	10	0					

FIRST TEST MATCH

PLAYED AT BRISBANE, 1, 2, 3, 4, 5 DECEMBER
MATCH DRAWN

AUSTRALIA

B. M. Laird c Murray b Garner	92	c sub (Marshall) b Garner		75
R. B. McCosker c Kallicharran b Croft	14	b Holding		33
A. R. Border c Murray b Garner	1	c Richards b Garner		7
†G. S. Chappell c King b Roberts	74	b Croft		124
K. J. Hughes b Croft	3	not out		130
D. W. Hookes c Holding b Croft	43	b Roberts		37
‡R. W. Marsh c Murray b Garner	3	c Kallicharran b King		19
R. J. Bright b Holding	13	not out		2
D. K. Lillee lbw b Garner	0			
R. M. Hogg b Roberts	8			
J. R. Thomson not out	0			
Extras (B1, LB4, NB12)	17	(B2, LB11, W2, NB6)		21
Total	268	(6 wkts dec)		448

WEST INDIES

D. L. Haynes c Marsh b Thomson	42	lbw b Hogg		4
C. G. Greenidge c Marsh b Lillee	34	c McCosker b Thomson		0
I. V. A. Richards c Marsh b Lillee	140			
A. I. Kallicharran c Marsh b Thomson	38	not out		10
L. G. Rowe b Chappell	50	b Hogg		3
C. L. King c Marsh b Lillee	0	not out		8
†‡D. L. Murray c McCosker b Thomson	21			
A. M. E. Roberts run out	7			
J. Garner lbw b Lillee	60			
M. A. Holding b Bright	11			
C. E. H. Croft not out	2			
Extras (B5, LB3, NB28)	36	(B5, W1, NB9)		15
Total	441	(3 wkts)		40

BOWLING

WEST INDIES	O	M	R	W	O	M	R	W
roberts	18.1	5	50	2	—	27	5	70	1
Holding	16	3	53	1	—	30	4	94	1
Croft	25	6	80	3	—	28	3	106	1
Garner	22	5	55	4	—	41	13	75	2
King	5	1	13	0	—	22	6	50	1
Kallicharran					—	18	2	32	0
AUSTRALIA								
Lillee	29.2	8	104	4	—	2	0	3	0
Hogg	25	6	55	0	—	5	2	11	2
Thomson	24	4	90	3	—	3	3	2	1
Bright	32	9	97	1	—	4	3	8	0
Chappell	12	2	25	1	—				
Border	5	1	19	0	—				
Hookes	5	2	15	0	—				

FALL OF WICKETS

	A	WI	A	WI
	1st	1st	2nd	2nd
1st	19	68	40	2
2nd	26	83	55	15
3rd	156	198	179	16
4th	174	317	297	—
5th	228	317	371	—
6th	242	341	442	—
7th	246	365	—	—
8th	252	366	—	—
9th	268	385	—	—
10th	268	441	—	—

SECOND TEST MATCH

PLAYED AT MELBOURNE, 29, 30, 31 DECEMBER, 1 JANUARY
WEST INDIES WON BY 10 WICKETS

AUSTRALIA

J. M. Wiener lbw b Garner	40	c Murray b Croft		24
B. M. Laird c Lloyd b Holding	16	c Garner b Holding		69
A. R. Border c Richards b Garner	17	lbw b Holding		15
†G. S. Chappell c Murray b Garner	19	c Murray b Roberts		22
K. J. Hughes c Rowe b Holding	4	lbw b Roberts		70
P. M. Toohey c Roberts b Holding	10	c Murray b Croft		7
‡R. W. Marsh c Kallicharran b Holding	0	b Croft		7
D. K. Lillee c Lloyd b Croft	12	c&b Roberts		0
G. Dymock c Kallicharran b Croft	7	c Lloyd b Garner		17
R. M. Hogg c Greenidge b Croft	14	c Holding b Garner		11
J. D. Higgs not out	0	not out		0
Extras (B9, LB4, W2, NB2)	17	(B2, LB10, NB5)		17
Total	**156**			**259**

WEST INDIES

G. C. Greenidge c Higgs b Dymock	48	not out	9
D. L. Haynes c Hughes b Lillee	29	not out	9
I. V. A. Richards c Toohey b Dymock	96		
A. I. Kallicharran c Laird b Higgs	39		
L. G. Rowe b Lillee	26		
†C. H. Lloyd c Marsh b Dymock	40		
‡D. L. Murray b Dymock	24		
A. M. E. Roberts lbw b Lillee	54		
J. Garner c Dymock b Higgs	29		
M. A. Holding not out	1		
C. E. H. Croft lbw b Higgs	0		
Extras (LB4, NB7)	11	(LB4)	4
Total	**397**	(0 wkt)	**22**

BOWLING

WEST INDIES	O	M	R	W	O	M	R	W
Roberts	14	1	39	0	21	1	64	3
Holding	14	3	40	4	23	7	61	2
Croft	13.3	4	27	3	22	2	61	3
Garner	15	7	33	3	20.4	2	56	2

AUSTRALIA	O	M	R	W	O	M	R	W
Lillee	36	7	96	3	3	0	9	0
Hogg	6	0	59	0				
Dymock	31	2	106	4	3	0	5	0
Higgs	34.4	4	122	4				
Chappell	5	2	3	0				
Hughes					1	1	0	0
Toohey					0.2	0	4	0

FALL OF WICKETS

	A	WI	A	WI
	1st	1st	2nd	2nd
1st	38	46	43	—
2nd	69	156	88	—
3rd	97	215	121	—
4th	108	226	187	—
5th	112	250	205	—
6th	118	305	228	—
7th	123	320	228	—
8th	133	390	233	—
9th	143	396	258	—
10th	156	397	259	—

THIRD TEST MATCH

PLAYED AT ADELAIDE, 26, 27, 28, 29, 30 JANUARY

WEST INDIES WON BY 408 RUNS

WEST INDIES

C. G. Greenidge lbw b Lillee	6	st Marsh b Mallett	76
D. L. Haynes c Lillee b Mallett	28	c Marsh b Pascoe	27
I. V. A. Richards c Marsh b Lillee	76	b Border	74
A. I. Kallicharran c I. Chappell b Mallett	9	b Mallett	106
L. G. Rowe c Lillee b Dymock	40	c Marsh b Dymock	43
*C.H. Lloyd lbw b Lillee	121	c Marsh b Dymock	40
†D. L. Murray c Marsh b Dymock	4	c G. Chappell b Dymock	28
A. M. E. Roberts b Lillee	9	c Laird b Dymock	8
J. Garner c Hughes b Lillee	16	not out	1
M. A. Holding b Pascoe	9	lbw b Dymock	1
C. E. H. Croft not out	1	c Border b Pascoe	12
Extras (B2, NB7)	9	(B1, LB10, NB21)	32
	—		—
Total	**328**		**448**

AUSTRALIA

J. M. Wiener c Haynes b Holding	3	c Murray b Roberts	8
B. Laird c Garner b Croft	52	lbw b Garner	36
I. M. Chappell c Greenidge b Roberts	2	c Murray b Holding	4
*G. S. Chappell c Garner b Roberts	0	lbw b Croft	31
K. M. Hughes c Lloyd b Croft	34	lbw b Garner	11
A. R. Border b Roberts	54	c Greenidge b Roberts	24
†R. W. Marsh c Murray b Croft	5	not out	23
D. K. Lillee c Haynes b Holding	16	c Kallicharran b Croft	0
G. Dymock c Rowe b Croft	10	c Richards b Holding	2
A. A. Mallett c Rowe b Garner	0	b Holding	12
L. S. Pascoe not out	5	b Holding	5
Extras (B1, LB14, NB7)	22	(LB2, W2, NB5)	9
	—		—
Total	**203**		**165**

BOWLING

AUSTRALIA	O	M	R	W	O	M	R	W	FALL OF WICKETS			
										WI	A	WI	A
Lillee	24	3	78	5	— 26	6	75	0		1st	1st	2nd	2nd
Dymock	25	7	74	2	— 33.5	7	104	5	1st	11	23	48	12
Mallett	27	5	77	2	— 38	7	134	2	2nd	115	26	184	21
Pascoe	15.3	1	90	1	— 25	3	93	2	3rd	115	26	213	71
Border					4	2	10	1	4th	126	83	299	83
									5th	239	110	331	98
WEST INDIES									6th	252	127	398	130
Roberts	16.5	3	43	3	— 15.5	5	30	2	7th	300	165	417	131
Holding	15	5	31	2	— 13	2	14	4	8th	303	188	443	135
Garner	18	4	43	1	— 11	3	39	2	9th	326	189	446	159
Richards	2	0	7	0					10th	328	203	448	165
Croft	22	4	57	4	— 11	1	47	2					

Australia v England 1979—80

FIRST TEST MATCH

PLAYED AT PERTH, 14, 15, 16, 18, 19 DECEMBER
AUSTRALIA WON BY 138 RUNS

AUSTRALIA

J. M. Wiener	run out	11	c Randall b Underwood	58
B. M. Laird	lbw b Botham	0	c Taylor b Underwood	33
A. R. Border	lbw b Botham	4	c Taylor b Willis	115
†G. S. Chappell	c Boycott b Botham	19	st Taylor b Underwood	43
K. J. Hughes	c Brearley b Underwood	99	c Miller b Botham	4
P. M. Toohey	c Underwood b Dilley	19	c Taylor b Botham	3
‡R. W. Marsh	c Taylor b Dilley	42	c Gower b Botham	4
R. J. Bright	c Taylor b Botham	17	b Botham	12
D. K. Lillee	c Taylor b Botham	18	c Willey b Dilley	19
G. Dymock	b Botham	5	not out	20
J. R. Thomson	not out	1	b Botham	8
Extras	(B4, LB3, NB2)	9	(B4, LB5, W2, NB7)	18
Total		**244**		**337**

ENGLAND

D. W. Randall	c Hughes b Lillee	0	lbw b Dymock	1
G. Boycott	lbw b Lillee	0	not out	99
P. Willey	c Chappell b Dymock	9	lbw b Dymock	12
D. I. Gower	c Marsh b Lillee	17	c Thomson b Dymock	23
G. Miller	c Hughes b Thomson	25	c Chappell b Thomson	8
†J. M. Brearley	c Marsh b Lillee	64	c Marsh b Bright	11
I. T. Botham	c Toohey b Thomson	15	c Marsh b Lillee	18
‡R. W. Taylor	b Chappell	14	b Lillee	15
G. R. Dilley	not out	38	c Marsh b Dymock	16
D. L. Underwood	lbw b Dymock	13	c Wiener b Dymock	0
R. G. Willis	b Dymock	11	c Chappell b Dymock	0
Extras	(LB7, NB15)	22	(LB3, W1, NB8)	12
Total		**228**		**215**

BOWLING

ENGLAND	O	M	R	W	O	M	R	W	FALL OF WICKETS			
									A	E	A	E
Dilley	18	1	47	2	18	3	50	1	*1st*	*1st*	*2nd*	*2nd*
Botham	35	9	78	6	45.5	14	98	5	1st	2	0	91	8
Willis	23	7	47	0	26	7	52	1	1st	2	0	91	8
Underwood	13	4	33	1	41	14	82	3	2nd	17	12	100	26
Miller	11	2	30	1	10	0	36	0	3rd	20	14	168	64
Willey					1	0	1	0	4th	88	44	183	75
AUSTRALIA									5th	127	74	191	115
Lillee	28	11	73	4	23	5	74	2	6th	186	90	204	141
Dymock	29.1	14	52	3	17.2	4	34	6	7th	219	123	225	182
Chappell	11	6	5	1	6	4	6	0	8th	219	185	303	211
Thomson	21	3	70	2	11	3	30	1	9th	243	203	323	211
Bright	1	0	6	0	23	11	30	1	10th	244	228	337	215
Wiener					8	3	22	0					
Border					2	0	7	0					

In Australia's second innings, Border retired hurt at 296—7 and resumed at 303—8.

SECOND TEST MATCH

PLAYED AT SYDNEY, 4, 5, 6, 8 JANUARY
AUSTRALIA WON BY 6 WICKETS

ENGLAND

G. A. Gooch b Lillee	18	c G. Chappell b Dymock	4
G. Boycott b Dymock	8	c McCosker b Pascoe	18
D. W. Randall c G. Chappell b Lillee	0	c Marsh b G. Chappell	25
P. Willey c Wiener b Dymock	8	b Pascoe	3
†J. M. Brearley c Pascoe b Dymock	7	c Marsh b Pascoe	19
D. I. Gower b G. Chappell	3	not out	98
I. T. Botham c G. Chappell b Pascoe	27	c Wiener b G. Chappell	0
‡R. W. Taylor c Marsh b Lillee	10	b Lillee	8
G. R. Dilley not out	22	b Dymock	0
R. G. D. Willis c Wiener b Dymock	3	c G. Chappell b Lillee	1
D. L. Underwood c Border b Lillee	12	c Border b Dymock	43
Extras (NB5)	5	(B1, LB10, W1, NB2)	14
Total	**123**		**237**

AUSTRALIA

R. B. McCosker c Gower b Willis	1	c Taylor b Underwood	41
J. M. Wiener run out	22	b Underwood	13
I. M. Chappell c Brearley b Gooch	42	c Botham b Underwood	9
†G. S. Chappell c Taylor b Underwood	18	not out	98
K. J. Hughes c Taylor b Botham	18	c Dilley b Willis	47
A. R. Border c Gooch b Botham	15	not out	2
‡R. W. Marsh c Underwood b Gooch	7		
D. K. Lillee c Brearley b Botham	5		
G. Dymock c Taylor b Botham	4		
L. S. Pascoe not out	10		
J. D. Higgs b Underwood	2		
Extras (B2, LB12, W2)	16	(LB8, W1)	9
Total	**145**	**(4 wkts)**	**219**

BOWLING

AUSTRALIA	O	M	R	W	O	M	R	W	FALL OF WICKETS			
									E	A	E	A
Lillee	13.3	4	40	4	24.3	8	63	3	1st	1st	2nd	2nd
Dymock	17	6	42	4	28	8	48	3				
Pascoe	9	4	14	1	23	3	76	3	1st	10	18	6	31
G. Chappell	4	1	19	1	21	10	36	2	2nd	13	52	21	51
Higgs	1	0	3	0	—				3rd	31	71	29	98
ENGLAND									4th	38	92	77	203
Botham	17	7	29	4	23.3	12	43	0	5th	41	100	105	—
Willis	11	3	30	1	12	2	26	1	6th	74	114	156	—
Underwood	13.2	3	39	2	26	6	71	3	7th	75	121	174	—
Dilley	5	1	13	0	12	0	33	0	8th	90	129	211	—
Willey	1	0	2	0	4	0	17	0	9th	98	132	218	—
Gooch	11	4	16	2	8	2	20	0	10th	123	145	237	—

THIRD TEST MATCH

AUSTRALIA WON BY 8 WICKETS

ENGLAND

G. A. Gooch run out	99	lbw b Mallett	51
G. Boycott c Mallett b Dymock	44	b Lillee	7
W. Larkins c G. Chappell b Pascoe	25	lbw b Pascoe	3
D. I. Gower lbw b Lillee	0	b Lillee	11
P. Willey lbw b Pascoe	1	c Marsh b Lillee	2
I. T. Botham c Marsh b Lillee	8	not out	119
*J. M. Brearley not out	60	c Border b Pascoe	10
†R. W. Taylor b Lillee	23	c Border b Lillee	32
D. L. Underwood c I. Chappell b Lillee	3	b Pascoe	0
J. K. Lever b Lillee	22	c Marsh b Lillee	12
R. G. D. Willis c G. Chappell b Lillee	4	c G. Chappell b Pascoe	2
Extras (B1, LB2, NB14)	17	(B2, LB12, NB10)	24
Total	**306**		**273**

AUSTRALIA

R. B. McCosker c Botham b Underwood	33	lbw b Botham	2
B. M. Laird c Gower b Underwood	74	c Boycott b Underwood	25
I. M. Chappell c & b Underwood	75	not out	26
K. J. Hughes c Underwood b Botham	15		
A. R. Border c & b Botham	63		
*G. S. Chappell c Larkins b Lever	114	not out	40
†R. W. Marsh c Botham b Lever	17		
D. K. Lillee c Willey b Lever	8		
A. A. Mallett lbw b Botham	19	G. Dymock b Botham	19
L. Pascoe not out	1		
Extras (B13, LB12, NB7, W1)	33	(LB8, NB2)	10
Total	**477**	**(2 wkts)**	**103**

BOWLING												
AUSTRALIA	O	M	R	W	—	O	M	R	W	**FALL OF WICKETS**		
											E A	E A
Lillee	33.1	9	60	6	—	33	6	78	5	1st	116 52	25 20
Dymock	28	6	54	1	—	11	2	30	0	2nd	170 179	46 42
Mallett	35	9	104	0	—	14	1	45	1	3rd	175 196	64 —
Pascoe	32	7	71	2	—	29.5	3	80	4	4th	177 219	67 —
Border						4	0	16	0	5th	177 345	88 —
ENGLAND										6th	192 411	92 —
Lever	53	15	111	4	—	7.4	1	18	0	7th	238 421	178 —
Botham	39.5	15	105	3	—	12	5	18	1	8th	242 432	179 —
Willis	21	4	61	0	—	.5	3	8	0	9th	296 465	268 —
Underwood	53	19	131	3	—	14	2	49	1	10th	306 477	273 —
Willey	13	2	36	0								

INDIA v ENGLAND

GOLDEN JUBILEE TEST MATCH

PLAYED AT BOMBAY, 15, 17, 18, 19 FEBRUARY
ENGLAND WON BY 10 WICKETS

INDIA

S. M. Gavaskar c Taylor b Botham	49	c Taylor b Botham	24
R. M. Binny run out	15	lbw b Botham	0
D. B. Vengsarkar c Taylor b Stevenson	34	lbw b Lever	10
*G. R. Viswanath b Lever	11	c Taylor b Botham	5
S. M. Patil c Taylor b Botham	30	lbw b Botham	0
Yashpal Sharma lbw b Botham	21	lbw b Botham	27
Kapil Dev c Taylor b Botham	0	not out	45
†S. M. H. Kirmani not out	40	c Gooch b Botham	5
K. D. Ghavri c Taylor b Stevenson	11	c Brearley b Lever	5
Shivlal Yadav c Taylor b Botham	8	c Taylor b Botham	15
D. R. Doshi c Taylor b Botham	6	c & b Lever	0
Extras (B5, LB3, NB9)	17	(B4, LB8, NB5, W1)	18
Total	**242**		**149**

ENGLAND

G. A. Gooch c Kirmani b Chavri	8	not out	49
G. Boycott c Kirmani b Binny	22	not out	43
W. Larkins lbw b Ghavri	0		
D. I. Gower lbw b Kapil Dev	16		
*J. M. Brearley lbw b Kapil Dev	5		
I. T. Botham lbw b Ghavri	114		
†R. W. Taylor lbw b Kapil Dev	43		
J. E. Emburey c Binny b Ghavri	8		
J. K. Lever b Doshi	21		
G. B. Stevenson not out	27		
D. L. Underwood b Ghavri	1		
Extras (B8, LB9, NB14)	31	(B3, LB1, NB2)	6
Total	**296**	(0 wkt)	**98**

BOWLING

ENGLAND	O	M	R	W	O	M	R	W	FALL OF WICKETS			
									I	*E*	*I*	*E*
Lever	23	3	82	1	20.2	2	65	3				
Botham	22.5	7	58	6	26	7	48	7	1st 56	21	4	—
Stevenson	14	1	59	2	5	1	13	0	2nd 102	21	22	—
Underwood	6	1	23	0	1	0	5	0	3rd 108	45	31	—
Gooch	4	2	3	0					4th 135	57	31	—
INDIA									5th 160	58	56	—
Kapil Dev	29	8	64	3					6th 160	229	68	—
Ghavri	20.1	5	52	5					7th 181	245	102	—
Binny	19	3	70	1					8th 197	262	115	—
Doshi	23	6	57	1					9th 223	283	148	—
Yadav	6	2	22	0					10th 242	296	149	—

Twin blade winner.

The Prudential Cup

ENGLAND v AUSTRALIA AT LORD'S

Australia 159–9 in 60 overs (Hilditch 47)
England 160–4 in 47.1 overs (Gooch 53)
Result: England won by 6 wickets
Man of the Match: G. A. Gooch

NEW ZEALAND v SRI LANKA AT TRENT BRIDGE

Sri Lanka 189 in 56.5 overs (Tennekoon 59)
New Zealand 190–1 in 47.4 overs (Turner 83*, Howarth 63*)
Result: New Zealand won by 9 wickets
Man of the Match: G. P. Howarth

WEST INDIES v INDIA AT EDGBASTON

India 190 in 53.1 overs (Viswanath 75, Holding 4–33)
West Indies 194–1 in 51.3 overs (Greenidge 106*)
Result: West Indies won by 9 wickets
Man of the Match: C. G. Greenidge

PAKISTAN v CANADA AT HEADINGLEY

Canada 139–9 in 60 overs (Sealy 45)
Pakistan 140–2 in 40.1 overs (Sadiq 57*)
Result: Pakistan won by 8 wickets
Man of the Match: Sadiq Mohammad

WEST INDIES v SRI LANKA AT THE OVAL

No play was possible because of rain

NEW ZEALAND v INDIA AT HEADINGLEY

India 182 in 55.5 overs (Gavaskar 55)
New Zealand 183–2 in 57.1 overs (Edgar 84*)
Result: New Zealand won by 8 wickets
Man of the Match: B. A. Edgar

ENGLAND v CANADA AT OLD TRAFFORD

Canada 45 in 40.3 overs (Dennis 21, Willis 4–11, Old 4–8)
England 46–2 in 13.5 overs
Result: England won by 8 wickets
Man of the Match: C. M. Old

PAKISTAN v AUSTRALIA AT TRENT BRIDGE

Pakistan 286–7 in 60 overs (Majid 61, Asif 61)
Australia 197 in 57.1 overs (Hilditch 72)
Result: Pakistan won by 89 runs
Man of the Match: Asif Iqbal

ENGLAND v PAKISTAN AT HEADINGLEY

England 165–9 in 60 overs
Pakistan 151 in 56 overs (Asif 51, Hendrick 4–15)
Result: England won by 14 runs
Man of the Match: M. Hendrick

AUSTRALIA v CANADA AT EDGBASTON

Canada 105 in 33.2 overs (Hurst 5–21)
Australia 106–3 in 26 overs
Result: Australia won by 7 wickets
Man of the Match: A. G. Hurst

INDIA v SRI LANKA AT OLD TRAFFORD

Sri Lanka 238–5 in 60 overs (Wettimuny 67, Mendis 64, Dias 50)
India 191 in 54.1 overs
Result: Sri Lanka won by 47 runs
Man of the Match: L. R. D. Mendis

WEST INDIES v NEW ZEALAND AT TRENT BRIDGE

West Indies 244–7 in 60 overs (Lloyd 73*, Greenidge 65)
New Zealand 212–9 in 60 overs (Hadlee 42)
Result: West Indies won by 32 runs
Man of the Match: C. H. Lloyd

TABLES

GROUP A	*P*	*W*	*L*	*NR*	*Pts*
West Indies	3	2	0	1	10
New Zealand	3	2	1	0	8
Sri Lanka	3	1	1	1	6
India	3	0	3	0	0
GROUP B					
England	3	3	0	0	12
Pakistan	3	2	1	0	8
Australia	3	1	2	0	4
Canada	3	0	3	0	0

SEMI-FINALS

ENGLAND v NEW ZEALAND AT OLD TRAFFORD

England 221–8 in 60 overs (Gooch 71, Brearley 53)
New Zealand 212–9 in 60 overs (Wright 69)
Result: England won by 9 runs
Man of the Match: G. A. Gooch

WEST INDIES v PAKISTAN AT THE OVAL

West Indies 293–6 in 60 overs (Greenidge 73, Haynes 65)
Pakistan 250 in 56.2 overs (Zaheer 93, Majid 81)
Result: West Indies won by 43 runs
Man of the Match: C. G. Greenidge

THE PRUDENTIAL CUP FINAL
ENGLAND v WEST INDIES
Played at Lord's 23 June. West Indies won by 92 runs

WEST INDIES

C. G. Greenidge	run out	9
D. L. Haynes	c Hendrick b Old	20
I. V. A. Richards	not out	138
A. I. Kallicharran	b Hendrick	4
†C. H. Lloyd	c & b Old	13
C. L. King	c Randall b Edmonds	86
‡D. L. Murray	c Gower b Edmonds	5
A. M. E. Roberts	c Brearley b Hendrick	0
J. Garner	c Taylor b Botham	0
M. A. Holding	b Botham	0
C. E. H. Croft	not out	0
Extras	(B11)	11
Total (60 overs)	(9 wkts)	286

ENGLAND

†J. M. Brearley	c King b Holding	64
G. Boycott	c Kallicharran b Holding	57
D. W. Randall	b Croft	15
G. A. Gooch	b Garner	32
D. I. Gower	b Garner	0
I. T. Botham	c Richards b Croft	4
W. Larkins	b Garner	0
P. H. Edmonds	not out	5
C. M. Old	b Garner	0
‡R. W. Taylor	c Murray b Garner	0
M. Hendrick	b Croft	0
Extras	(LB12, W2, NB3)	17
Total (51 overs)		194

Man of the Match: I. V. A. Richards

BOWLING

ENGLAND	O	M	R	W	FALL OF WICKETS		
Botham	12	2	44	2			
Hendrick	12	2	50	2		WI	E
Old	12	0	55	2	1st	22	129
Boycott	6	0	38	0	2nd	36	135
Edmonds	12	2	40	0	3rd	55	183
Gooch	4	0	27	0	4th	99	183
Larkins	2	0	21	0	5th	238	186
WEST INDIES					6th	252	186
Roberts	9	2	33	0	7th	258	188
Holding	8	1	16	2	8th	260	192
Croft	10	1	42	3	9th	272	192
Garner	11	0	38	5	10th	—	194
Richards	10	0	35	0			
King	3	0	13	0			

ONE-DAY INTERNATIONALS 1979—80

Australia v West Indies

Played at Sydney, 27 November.
West Indies 193 (Kallicharran 49, Pascoe 4–29).
Australia 196–5 (G. S. Chappell 74*, Hughes 52).
Australia won by 5 wickets.

England v West Indies

Played at Sydney, 28 November.
England 211–8 in 50 overs (Willey 58*, Garner 3–31).
West Indies 196 (Rowe 60, Underwood 4–44).
England won by 2 runs having set a target of 199 runs (rain).

England v Australia

Played at Melbourne, 8 December.
Australia 207–9 in 50 overs (G. S. Chappell 92, Willey 3–33).
England 209–7 (Boycott 68, Hogg 3–26).
England won by 3 wickets.

Australia v West Indies

Played at Melbourne, 9 December.
West Indies 271–2 in 48.1 overs (Richards 153, Haynes 80).
Australia 191–8 in 48 overs (Border 44).
West Indies won by 80 runs.

England v Australia

Played at Sydney, 11 December.
England 264–7 in 49 overs (Boycott 105, Willey 64, Lilee 4–56)
Australia 192 (Laughlin 74).
England won by 72 runs.

Australia v West Indies

Played at Sydney, 21 December.
Australia 176–6 in 50 overs (I. M. Chappell 63*).
West Indies 169 in 42.5 overs (Richards 62, Lillee 4–28).
Australia won by 7 runs.

Continued on p. 240.

Disposable winner.

ENGLAND v WEST INDIES
1928 to 1976

SERIES BY SERIES

Season		Visiting Captain	P	E W	WI W	D
1928	In England	R. K. Nunes (WI)	3	3	0	0
1929–30	In West Indies	F. S. G. Calthorpe (E)	4	1	1	2
1933	In England	G. C. Grant (WI)	3	2	0	1
1934–35	In West Indies	R. E. S. Wyatt (E)	4	1	2	1
1939	In England	R. S. Grant (WI)	3	1	0	2
1947–48	In West Indies	G. O. Allen (E)	4	0	2	2
1950	In England	J. D. C. Goddard (WI)	4	1	3	0
1953–54	In West Indies	L. Hutton (E)	5	2	2	1
1957	In England	J. D. C. Goddard (WI)	5	3	0	2
1959–60	In West Indies	P. B. H. May (E)	5	1	0	4
1963	In England	F. M. M. Worrell (WI)	5	1	3	1
1966	In England	G. S. Sobers (WI)	5	1	3	1
1967–68	In West Indies	M. C. Cowdrey (E)	5	1	0	4
1969	In England	G. S. Sobers (WI)	3	2	0	1
1973	In England	R. B. Kanhai (WI)	3	0	2	1
1973–74	In West Indies	M. H. Denness (E)	5	1	1	3
1976	In England	C. H. Lloyd (WI)	5	0	3	2
	At Lord's		10	4	2	4
	At Manchester		8	3	3	2
	At The Oval		9	4	4	1
	At Nottingham		4	0	2	2
	At Birmingham		3	1	0	2
	At Leeds		5	2	3	0
	At Bridgetown		7	1	1	5
	At Port of Spain		10	4	2	4
	At Georgetown		7	1	2	4
	At Kingston		8	1	3	4
	In England		39	14	14	11
	In West Indies		32	7	8	17
	Total		71	21	22	28

HIGHEST INDIVIDUAL INNINGS FOR ENGLAND

325	A. Sandham	at Kingston	1929–30
285*	P. B. H. May	at Birmingham	1957
262*	D. L. Amiss	at Kingston	1973–74
258	T. W. Graveney	at Nottingham	1957
205*	E. H. Hendren	at Port of Spain	1929–30
205	L. Hutton	at Kingston	1953–54
203	D. L. Amiss	at The Oval	1976
202*	L. Hutton	at The Oval	1950
196	L. Hutton	at Lord's	1939
174	D. L. Amiss	at Port of Spain	1973–74
169	L. Hutton	at Georgetown	1953–54
165*	L. Hutton	at The Oval	1939
165	T. W. Graveney	at The Oval	1966
164	T. W. Graveney	at The Oval	1957
159	J. B. Hobbs	at The Oval	1928
154	M. C. Cowdrey	at Birmingham	1957
152	A. Sandham	at Bridgetown	1929–30
152	M. C. Cowdrey	at Lord's	1957

A total of 70 centuries has been scored for England.

HIGHEST INDIVIDUAL INNINGS FOR WEST INDIES

302	L. G. Rowe	at Bridgetown	1973–74
291	I. V. A. Richards	at The Oval	1976
270*	G. A. Headley	at Kingston	1934–35
261	F. M. M. Worrell	at Nottingham	1950
232	I. V. A. Richards	at Nottingham	1976
226	G. S. Sobers	at Bridgetown	1959–60
223	G. A. Headley	at Kingston	1929–30
220	C. L. Walcott	at Bridgetown	1953–54
209*	B. F. Butcher	at Nottingham	1966
209	C. A. Roach	at Georgetown	1929–30
206	E. D. Weekes	at Port of Spain	1953–54
197*	F. M. M. Worrell	at Bridgetown	1959–60
191*	F. M. M. Worrell	at Nottingham	1957
182	C. C. Hunte	at Manchester	1963
176	G. A. Headley	at Bridgetown	1929–30
174	G. S. Sobers	at Leeds	1966
169*	G. A. Headley	at Manchester	1933
168*	C. L. Walcott	at Lord's	1950
168	O. G. Smith	at Nottingham	1957
167	F. M. M. Worrell	at Port of Spain	1953–54
166	J. K. Holt	at Bridgetown	1953–54
163*	G. S. Sobers	at Lord's	1966
161	O. G. Smith	at Birmingham	1957
161	G. S. Sobers	at Manchester	1966

A total of 74 centuries has been scored for West Indies.

A CENTURY IN EACH INNINGS OF A MATCH—
WEST INDIES

G. A. Headley	114 & 112 at Georgetown	1929–30
G. A. Headley	106 & 107 at Lord's	1939
C. G. Greenidge	134 & 101 at Manchester	1976

There has been no instance for England.

A CENTURY ON DEBUT IN ENGLAND v WEST INDIES TESTS:
FOR ENGLAND

G. E. Tyldesley	122	at Lord's	1928
A. Sandham	152	at Bridgetown	1929–30
A. H. Bakewell	107	at The Oval	1933
L. Hutton	196	at Lord's	1939
D. C. S. Compton	120	at Lord's	1939
*S. C. Griffith	140	at Port of Spain	1947–48
C. Washbrook	114	at Lord's	1950
W. Watson	116	at Kingston	1953–54
M. C. Cowdrey	154	at Birmingham	1957
K. F. Barrington	128	at Bridgetown	1959–60
E. R. Dexter	136*	at Bridgetown	1959–60
R. Subba Row	100	at Georgetown	1959–60
J. M. Parks	101*	at Port of Spain	1959–60
J. T. Murray	112	at The Oval	1966
*J. H. Hampshire	107	at Lord's	1969
*F. C. Hayes	106*	at The Oval	1973
D. S. Steele	106	at Nottingham	1976

FOR WEST INDIES

*G. A. Headley	176	at Bridgetown	1929–30
*A. G. Ganteaume	112	at Port of Spain	1947–48
O. G. Smith	161	at Birmingham	1957
C. H. Lloyd	118	at Port of Spain	1967–68
I. V. A. Richards	232	at Nottingham	1976

* indicates debut in Test cricket

HIGHEST RUN AGGREGATE IN A TEST RUBBER FOR:

England in England	489 (Av. 97.80)	P. B. H. May	1957
West Indies in England	829 (Av. 118.42)	I. V. A. Richards	1976
England in West Indies	693 (Av. 115.50)	E. H. Hendren	1929–30
West Indies in West Indies	709 (Av. 101.28)	G. S. Sobers	1959–60

HIGHEST INNINGS TOTALS:			LOWEST INNINGS TOTALS:		
England			**England**		
849	at Kingston	1929–30	71	at Manchester	1976
619–6d	at Nottingham	1957	103	at Kingston	1934–35
583–4d	at Birmingham	1957	103	at The Oval	1950
568	at Port of Spain	1967–68	107	at Port of Spain	1934–35
537	at Port of Spain	1953–54	111	at Georgetown	1947–48
527	at The Oval	1966	126	at Manchester	1976
482	at Bridgetown	1959–60	131	at Port of Spain	1973–74
467	at Bridgetown	1929–30	145	at Georgetown	1929–30
	West Indies				
687–8d	at The Oval	1976			
681–8d	at Port of Spain	1953–54		**West Indies**	
652–8d	at Lord's	1973	86	at The Oval	1957
596–6d	at Bridgetown	1973–74	89	at The Oval	1957
583–9d	at Kingston	1973–74	91	at Birmingham	1963
563–8d	at Bridgetown	1959–60	97	at Lord's	1933
558	at Nottingham	1950	100	at The Oval	1933
535–7d	at Kingston	1934–35	102	at Bridgetown	1934–35
526–7d	at Port of Spain	1967–68	112	at Port of Spain	1959–60
503	at The Oval	1950	115	at Manchester	1928
501–6d	at Manchester	1963	127	at Lord's	1957
500–9d	at Leeds	1966	129	at The Oval	1928
498	at The Oval	1939	132	at Leeds	1957
497	at Port of Spain	1947–48	133	at Manchester	1933
494	at Nottingham	1976	139	at at Kingston	1953–54
490	at Kingston	1947–48	142	at Leeds	1957
484	at Manchester	1966	143	at Kingston	1967–68
482–5d	at Nottingham	1966	147	at Manchester	1969

RECORD WICKET PARTNERSHIPS FOR ENGLAND

1st	212	C. Washbrook & R. T. Simpson at Nottingham	1950
2nd	266	P. E. Richardson & T. W. Graveney at Nottingham	1957
3rd	264	L. Hutton & W. R. Hammond at The Oval	1939
4th	411	P. B. H. May & M. C. Cowdrey at Birmingham	1957
5th	130*	C. Milburn & T. W. Graveney at Lord's	1966
6th	163	A. W. Greig & A. P. E. Knott at Bridgetown	1973–74
7th	197	M. J. K. Smith & J. M. Parks at Port of Spain	1959–60
8th	217	T. W. Graveney & J. T. Murray at The Oval	1966
9th	109	G. A. R. Lock & P. I. Pocock at Georgetown	1967–68
10th	128	K. Higgs & J. A. Snow at The Oval	1966

RECORD WICKET PARTNERSHIPS FOR WEST INDIES

1st	206	R. C. Fredericks & L. G. Rowe at Kingston	1973–74
2nd	249	L. G. Rowe & A. I. Kallicharran at Bridgetown	1973–74
3rd	338	E. D. Weekes & F. M. M. Worrell at Port of Spain	1953–54
4th	399	G. S. Sobers & F. M. M. Worrell at Bridgetown	1959–60
5th	265	S. M. Nurse & G. S. Sobers at Leeds	1966
6th	274*	G. S. Sobers & D. A. J. Holford at Lord's	1966
7th	155*†	G. S. Sobers & B. D. Julien at Lord's	1973
8th	99	C. A. McWatt & J. K. Holt at Georgetown	1953–54
9th	63*	G. S. Sobers & W. W. Hall at Port of Spain	1967–68
10th	55	F. M. M. Worrell & S. Ramadhin at Nottingham	1957

† *231 runs were added for this wicket in two separate partnerships: G. S. Sobers retired ill and was replaced by K. D. Boyce when 155 had been added.*

BEST INNINGS BOWLING FIGURES FOR:

England in England	7–44 T. E. Bailey at Lord's	1957
	7–44 F. S. Trueman at Birmingham	1963
West Indies in England	8–92 M. A. Holding at The Oval	1976
England in West Indies	8–86 A. W. Greig at Port of Spain	1973–74
West Indies in West Indies	7–69 W. W. Hall at Kingston	1959–60

TEN OR MORE WICKETS IN A MATCH:

FOR ENGLAND

13–156	A. W. Greig at Port of Spain	1973–74
12–119	F. S. Trueman at Birmingham	1963
11–48	G. A. R. Lock at The Oval	1957
11–96	C. S. Marriott at The Oval	1933
11–98	T. E. Bailey at Lord's	1957
11–149	W. Voce at Port of Spain	1929–30
11–152	F. S. Trueman at Lord's	1963
10–93	A. P. Freeman at Manchester	1928
10–142	J. A. Snow at Georgetown	1967–68
10–195	G. T. S. Stevens at Bridgetown	1929–30

FOR WEST INDIES

14–149	M. A. Holding at The Oval	1976
11–147	K. D. Boyce at The Oval	1973
11–152	S. Ramadhin at Lord's	1950
11–157	L. R. Gibbs at Manchester	1963
11–204	A. L. Valentine at Manchester	1950
11–229	W. Ferguson at Port of Spain	1947–48
10–96	H. H. Johnson at Kingston	1947–48
10–106	L. R. Gibbs at Manchester	1966
10–123	A. M. E. Roberts at Lord's	1976
10–160	A. L. Valentine at The Oval	1950

HIGHEST WICKET AGGREGATE IN A TEST RUBBER:

England in England	F. S. Trueman	34 (Av. 17.47)	1963
West Indies in England	A. L. Valentine	33 (Av. 20.42)	1950
England in West Indies	J. A. Snow	27 (Av. 18.66)	1967–68
West Indies in West Indies	W. Ferguson	23 (Av. 24.65)	1947–48
	S. Ramadhin	23 (Av. 24.30)	1953–54

HIGHEST MATCH AGGREGATE	1815–34 wkts at Kingston, 1929–30
LOWEST MATCH AGGREGATE	309–29 wkts at Bridgetown, 1924–35

SOMERSET

The Gillette Cup at last!

Somerset, who had failed at the last hurdle in 1967, and again in 1978, came back to Lord's for their third Gillette final and, apart from one critical partnership for Northamptonshire between Lamb and Cook ultimately broken by a run-out, Somerset looked likely winners all along. This was one match in which Viv Richards knew full well that he must not fail his adopted county, and this came through very clearly in the early part of his innings when he was more concerned with bedding down than in playing the fluent strokes of which we all know he is capable. Gradually, however, as runs began to flow, the real Richards emerged, and we saw the measure of his brilliance. There wasn't a great deal in the Somerset batting apart from Richards, except that Brian Rose played a captain's innings of 41 at number one, and Joel Garner swished about for an invaluable contribution to the tail of 24. Thus 269 for 8 in the prescribed 60 overs looked good enough to most sound judges of the game (if there is such a thing as a sound judge in one-day cricket!). Jim Watts, the Northants captain, who had won the toss and put Somerset in, was in a very unhappy situation at the end of Somerset's innings. His hope that his bowlers could make some use of whatever the wicket offered at half-past ten in the morning had not been fulfilled, and he knew, though the crowd obviously didn't, that he had broken a finger and would not bat; the position worsened considerably when he lost two wickets for a mere 13.

It was at this point when there was every possibility that Northants chances would begin to ebb away. Garner was in full cry having dismissed both Larkins and Williams (Kent had had good reason to know what Garner is like when his tail is up and he is at full pace for he bowled them out for 60 at Taunton in the quarter-final) but now Cook and Lamb stood in the breach, and how well they did stand. This parlous position of 13-2 grew slowly, and then faster into a partnership of formidable proportions; they hoisted the hundred, then put up the hundred partnership, and at this point the Somerset players must have begun harbouring doubts once again of their capacity to win. With the score 126 for two, came the turning point in the match.

Going for a run which may possibly have been on to anyone in the field less nimble than Roebuck, and with a less accurate arm, they found they had picked the wrong man, and his brilliant pick up and throw into the hands of Jennings at the bowler's end put Cook out – a tragedy for Northants, a match-winning piece of cricket for Somerset.

Lamb continued to bat superbly; he is a fine player bred on the good firm wickets of South Africa which are conducive to driving off the front-foot, and while he was there, if Willey could take the place of Cook in getting runs, Northants were still in with some sort of chance. But Willey failed, and only the most rabid supporter of Northants gave them much of a chance at this stage. When Lamb went to a brilliant piece of stumping by Derek Taylor, the curtain had virtually come down. Somerset were as good as there at their third attempt, and no-one could begrudge them victory for the magnificent cricket they had played all through the competition.

Garner brushed the tail aside to finish with the figures of 10.3-3-29-6, and coupled with his 24 runs, must surely have been the Man of the Match winner on nine occasions out of ten, but Cyril Washbrook, the first Gillette adjudicator to judge the award in 50 matches, felt that without Viv Richards's innings (suppose he had been out for 0) Garner's bowling might not have been able to win the match with a small total to bowl at. Garner's bowling was certainly one of the major contributory factors to Somerset's success from the beginning up to the final. He took two for 28 against Derbyshire in the second round, five for 11 against Kent in the quarter-final, and four for 24 against Middlesex in the semi-final. His aggregate analysis reads; 43-11-92-17. Somerset's four Man of the Match winners were; Brian Rose for his 88 not out against Derbyshire, Joel Garner for his five for 11 against Kent, Peter Denning for his 90 not out against Middlesex, and Viv Richards for his 117 in the final. Richards became only the third batsman to score a century in a Gillette Cup final, and the second West Indian to do so. Geoff Boycott scored 146 for Yorkshire against Surrey in 1965 and Clive Lloyd 126 for Lancashire against Warwickshire in 1972. Joel Garner is the first bowler to take six wickets in a final.

1979 RESULTS
FIRST ROUND—27 JUNE
Buckinghamshire v Suffolk at High Wycombe

Buckinghamshire 133 in 58.5 overs (Cordaroy 44)
Suffolk 137–8 in 38 overs (Rice 45)
Result: Suffolk won by 2 wickets
Man of the Match: P. C. Rice
Adjudicator: J. C. Laker

Durham v Berkshire at Durham City

Durham 221–7 in 60 overs (Greensword 48*, Riddell 44, Jones 4–35)
Berkshire 127–7 in 60 overs
Result: Durham won by 94 runs
Man of the Match: S. Greensword
Adjudicator: C. Washbrook

Glamorgan v Kent at Swansea

Glamorgan 177–9 in 60 overs (Swart 40)
Kent 178–5 in 52 overs (Ealham 85*, Johnson 47)
Result: Kent won by 5 wickets
Man of the Match: A. G. E. Ealham
Adjudicator: K. F. Barrington

Gloucestershire v Hampshire at Bristol

Hampshire 273–6 in 60 overs (Cowley 63*, Turner 58)
Gloucestershire 218 in 55.2 overs (Sadiq Mohammad 62, Jesty 6–46)
Result: Hampshire won by 55 runs
Man of the Match: T. E. Jesty (2)
Adjudicator: W. J. Edrich

Lancashire v Essex at Old Trafford

Lancashire 247–5 in 60 overs (C. H. Lloyd 76, Simmons 54*)
Essex 177 in 53.4 overs
Result: Lancashire won by 70 runs
Man of the Match: J. Simmons
Adjudicator: J. T. Murray

Leicestershire v Devon at Leicester

Devon 111 in 56 overs
Leicestershire 114–1 in 31.4 overs (Steele 76*)
Result: Leicestershire won by 9 wickets
Man of the Match: J. F. Steele (3)
Adjudicator: R. T. Simpson

SECOND ROUND—18 JULY
Durham v Yorkshire at Chester-le-Street
Durham 213–9 in 60 overs (Wasim Raja 52, Cairns 47)
Yorkshire 214–6 in 59.1 overs (Boycott 92, Hampshire 75*)
Result: Yorkshire won by 4 wickets
Man of the Match: G. Boycott (2)
Adjudicator: C. Washbrook

Leicestershire v Worcestershire at Leicester
Leicestershire 326–6 in 60 overs (Dudleston, Davison 78)
Worcestershire 183 in 50 overs (Younis Ahmed 44)
Result: Leicestershire won by 143 runs
Man of the Match: B. Dudleston (2)
Adjudicator: J. D. Robertson

18—19 JULY
Kent v Lancashire at Canterbury
Kent 278–7 in 60 overs (Tavare 87, Asif 61)
Lancashire 260–9 in 60 overs (Wood 116, Asif 4–18)
Result: Kent won by 18 runs
Man of the Match: Asif Iqbal (3)
Adjudicator: J. T. Murray

Middlesex v Hampshire at Lord's
Hampshire 193 in 54.5 overs (Greenidge 87)
Middlesex 196–8 in 58.5 overs (Cowley 4–20)
Result: Middlesex won by 2 wickets
Man of the Match: C. G. Greenidge (3)
Adjudicator: K. F. Barrington

Northamptonshire v Surrey at Northampton
Surrey 238–8 in 60 overs (Smith 61, Roope 43)
Northamptonshire 240–4 in 56 overs (Cook 114*)
Result: Northamptonshire won by 6 wickets
Man of the Match: G. Cook (2)
Adjudicator: R. T. Simpson

Somerset v Derbyshire at Taunton
Derbyshire 224–7 in 60 overs (Steele 81*)
Somerset 226–2 in 56.1 overs (Rose 88*, Richards 73)
Result: Somerset won by 8 wickets
Man of the Match: B. C. Rose (2)
Adjudicator: C. J. Barnett

Sussex v Suffolk at Hove
Suffolk 158 in 55.3 overs
Sussex 159–8 in 49.5 overs
Result: Sussex won by 2 wickets
Man of the Match: Imran Khan (3–1 for Worcestershire)
Adjudicator: W. J. Edrich

Warwickshire v Nottinghamshire at Edgbaston
Nottinghamshire 265 in 60 overs (Todd 105, Hassan 50)
Warwickshire 186 in 51 overs (Whitehouse 41)
Result: Nottinghamshire won by 79 runs
Man of the Match: P. A. Todd
Adjudicator: J. T. Murray

Northamptonshire v Leicestershire at Northampton

Leicestershire 180 in 59.4 overs (Dudleston 59, Williams 3–15)
Northamptonshire 184–2 in 55.4 overs (Larkins 92*, Cook 44)
Result: Northamptonshire won by 8 wickets
Man of the Match: R. G. Williams
Adjudicator: C. Washbrook

Somerset v Kent at Taunton

Somerset 190 in 59.2 overs (Burgess 50*, Richards 44, Woolmer 4–28)
Kent 60 in 28.4 overs (Garner 5–11)
Result: Somerset won by 130 runs
Man of the Match: J. Garner
Adjudicator: J. C. Laker

Sussex v Nottinghamshire at Hove

Nottinghamshire 200 in 56.4 overs (Randall 75, Hassan 53)
Sussex 201–4 in 54.1 overs (Mendis 55)
Result: Sussex won by 6 wickets
Man of the Match: D. W. Randall
Adjudicator: K. F. Barrington

8—9 AUGUST

Middlesex v Yorkshire at Lord's

Middlesex 216 in 60 overs (Brearley 76, Cooper 4–29)
Yorkshire 146 in 54.3 overs
Result: Middlesex won by 70 runs
Man of the Match: J. M. Brearley (3)
Adjudicator: R. T. Simpson

SEMI-FINALS—22 AUGUST

Middlesex v Somerset at Lord's

Middlesex 185 in 57.3 overs (Edmonds 63*, Garner 4–24)
Somerset 190–3 in 50.2 overs (Denning 90*)
Result: Somerset won by 7 wickets
Man of the Match: P. W. Denning (4)
Adjudicator: J. C. Laker

Sussex v Northamptonshire at Hove

Northamptonshire 255–7 in 60 overs (A. J. Lamb 101, Willey 89)
Sussex 218 in 55.2 overs (Mendis 69, T. M. Lamb 4–52)
Result: Northamptonshire won by 37 runs
Man of the Match: P. Willey (4)
Adjudicator: K. F. Barrington

THE GILLETTE CUP FINAL
SOMERSET v NORTHAMPTONSHIRE

SOMERSET

†B. C. Rose	b Watts	41
P. W. Denning	c Sharp b Sarfraz	19
I. V. A. Richards	b Griffiths	117
P. M. Roebuck	b Willey	14
I. T. Botham	b T. Lamb	27
V. J. Marks	b Griffiths	9
G. I. Burgess	c Sharp b Watts	1
D. Breakwell	b T. Lamb	5
J. Garner	not out	24
‡D. J. S. Taylor	not out	1
K. F. Jennings	did not bat	
Extras (B5, LB3, NB3)		11
Total (60 overs) (8 wkts)		269

NORTHAMPTONSHIRE

G. Cook	run out	44
W. Larkins	lbw b Garner	0
R. G. Williams	hit wkt b Garner	8
A. J. Lamb	st Taylor b Richards	78
P. Willey	c Taylor b Garner	5
T. J. Yardley	c Richards b Burgess	20
‡G. Sharp	b Garner	22
Sarfraz Nawaz	not out	16
T. M. Lamb	b Garner	4
B. J. Griffiths	b Garner	0
†P. J. Watts	absent hurt	
Extras (B6, LB9, W5, NB7)		27
Total (56.3 overs)		224

Man of the Match: I. V. A. Richards (3).
Adjudicator: C. Washbrook.

BOWLING

NORTHAMPTONSHIRE	O	M	R	W	FALL OF WICKETS		
Sarfraz	12	3	51	1	1st	34	3
Griffiths	12	1	58	2	2nd	95	13
Watts	12	2	34	2	3rd	145	126
T. Lamb	12	0	70	0	4th	186	138
Willey	12	2	45	1	5th	213	170
SOMERSET					6th	214	186
Garner	10.3	3	29	6	7th	219	218
Botham	10	3	27	0	8th	268	224
Jennings	12	1	29	0	9th	—	224
Burgess	9	1	37	1	10th	—	—
Marks	4	0	22	0			
Richards	9	0	44	1			
Breakwell	2	0	9	0			

GILLETTE CUP
PRINCIPAL RECORDS

Highest innings total: 371–4 off 60 overs, Hampshire v Glamorgan (Southampton) 1975.

Highest innings total by a Minor County: 224–7 off 60 overs, Buckinghamshire v Cambridgeshire (Cambridge) 1972.

Highest innings total by a side batting second: 297–4 off 57.1 overs, Somerset v Warwickshire (Taunton) 1978.

Highest innings total by a side batting first and losing: 292–5 off 60 overs, Warwickshire v Somerset (Taunton) 1978.

Lowest innings total: 41 off 20 overs, Cambridgeshire v Buckinghamshire (Cambridge) 1972; 41 off 19.4 overs, Middlesex v Essex (Westcliff) 1972; 41 off 36.1 overs, Shropshire v Essex (Wellington) 1974.

Lowest innings total by a side batting first and winning: 98 off 56.2 overs, Worcestershire v Durham (Chester-le-Street) 1968.

Highest individual innings: 177 C. G. Greenidge, Hampshire v Glamorgan (Southampton) 1975.

Highest individual innings by a Minor County player: 132 G. Robinson, Lincolnshire v Northumberland (Jesmond) 1971.

Record Wicket Partnerships

1st	227	R. E. Marshall & B. L. Reed, Hampshire v Bedfordshire (Goldington)	1968
2nd	223	M. J. Smith & C. T. Radley, Middlesex v Hampshire (Lord's)	1977
3rd	160	B. Wood & F. C. Hayes, Lancashire v Warwickshire (Birmingham)	1976
4th	234*	D. Lloyd & C. H. Lloyd, Lancashire v Gloucestershire (Manchester)	1978
5th	135	J. F. Harvey & I. R. Buxton, Derbyshire v Worcestershire (Derby)	1972
6th	105	G. S. Sobers & R. A. White, Nottinghamshire v Worcestershire (Worcester)	1974
7th	107	D. R. Shepherd & D. A. Graveney, Gloucestershire v Surrey (Bristol)	1973
8th	69	S. J. Rouse & D. J. Brown, Warwickshire v Middlesex (Lord's)	1977
9th	87	M. A. Nash & A. E. Cordle, Glamorgan v Lincolnshire (Swansea)	1974
10th	45	A. T. Castell & D. W. White, Hampshire v Lancashire (Manchester)	1970
Hat-tricks:		J. D. F. Larter, Northamptonshire v Sussex (Northampton)	1963
		D. A. D. Sydenham, Surrey v Cheshire (Hoylake)	1964
		R. N. S. Hobbs, Essex v Middlesex (Lord's)	1968
		N. M. McVicker, Warwickshire v Lincolnshire (Birmingham)	1971

Seven wickets in an innings: 7–15 A. L. Dixon, Kent v Surrey (The Oval) 1967. P. J. Sainsbury (Hampshire) 7–30 in 1965 and R. D. Jackman (Surrey) 7–33 in 1970 have also achieved this feat.

Most 'Man of the Match' awards: 6 B. L. D'Oliveira (Worcestershire), C. H. Lloyd (Lancashire) and B. Wood (Lancashire); 5 M. C. Cowdrey (Kent), A. W. Greig (Sussex).

86 centuries have been scored in the competition.

THE GILLETTE CUP 1980

FIRST ROUND

Matches to be played on 2 July
Devon v Cornwall at Exeter (County Ground)
Middlesex v Ireland at Lord's
Nottinghamshire v Durham at Trent Bridge
Somerset v Worcestershire at Taunton
Surrey v Northamptonshire at The Oval
Sussex v Suffolk at Hove
Warwickshire v Oxfordshire at Edgbaston

SECOND ROUND

Matches to be played on 16 July
Derbyshire v Hampshire at Derby
Leicestershire v Essex at Leicester
Nottinghamshire or Durham v Middlesex or Ireland
Somerset or Worcestershire v Lancashire
Surrey or Northamptonshire v Gloucestershire
Sussex or Suffolk v Glamorgan
Warwickshire or Oxfordshire v Devon or Cornwall
Yorkshire v Kent at Headingley
**Quarter-finals 30 July; semi-finals 13 August;
final at Lord's 6 September.**

GILLETTE CUP WINNERS

1963	Sussex	1972	Lancashire
1964	Sussex	1973	Gloucestershire
1965	Yorkshire	1974	Kent
1966	Warwickshire	1975	Lancashire
1967	Kent	1976	Northamptonshire
1968	Warwickshire	1977	Middlesex
1969	Yorkshire	1978	Sussex
1970	Lancashire	1979	Somerset
1971	Lancashire		

ESSEX TAKE THE BENSON AND HEDGES CUP

When Essex won the Benson and Hedges Cup by beating Surrey by 35 runs, this success was the first honour of any kind which the county had won since its inception in 1876. When Essex were 172-1 it looked as though they were home and dried, but although they scored 290-6, an almost unassailable total in a 55-over game, Surrey made a very brave fight of it and got within 35 of this formidable target. The Man of the Match – and there was never a moment's doubt about it – was Graham Gooch, whose 120 will rank among the top innings of the season. Surrey, at 45-2, looked on the way out, but Howarth, and the captain, Knight, pulled the innings together, and at 136-2 Surrey were still in the hunt, but time proved to be the cardinal issue, and wickets had to be surrendered in the chase for runs, the tail was brushed aside and Essex had tasted success at last after over one hundred years of trying.

There must have been doubts at Chelmsford in the semi-final whether Essex would ever reach Lord's. Yorkshire's opening pair, Lumb and Hampshire, passed the century mark, but there was some pretty dismal batting to follow and 107 for no wicket collapsed to 173 all out – apart from the openers, the highest score was 13 by Stevenson coming in at number nine. At 68-3 Essex were in trouble once again, but Hardie and Pont in the middle of the batting did enough to ensure ultimate victory.

For Surrey at Derby in the other semi-final it was a close run thing – a matter of 6 runs. Surrey could manage only 166 for 8 in their 55 overs which immediately made Derbyshire clear favourites, but when Kirsten scored 70 out of 160 it indicated the poverty of the Derbyshire batting, Clarke and Wilson taking three wickets apiece and Jackman two.

It was interesting that the two finalists came from the same group in the zonal tables – Group C. The other two first-class counties in that group, Sussex and Northants, met later in the Gillette Cup semi-final, so Group C was a bit of a success story. At the other end of things, Hampshire were the only first-class county to fail to win a single Benson and Hedges game. Kent did little better – they won one.

THE BENSON AND HEDGES CUP FINAL

ESSEX v SURREY

PLAYED AT LORD'S 21 JULY

ESSEX WON BY 35 RUNS

ESSEX

M. H. Denness	c Smith b Wilson	24
G. A. Gooch	b Wilson	120
K. S. McEwan	c Richards b Wilson	72
†K. W. R. Fletcher	b Knight	34
B. R. Hardie	c Intikhab b Wilson	4
K. R. Pont	not out	19
N. Phillip	c Howarth b Jackman	2
S. Turner	not out	1
‡N. Smith		
R. E. East	} did not bat	
J. K. Lever		
Extras (B3, LB8, W1, NB2)		14
Total (55 overs) (6 wkts)		290

SURREY

A. R. Butcher	c Smith b Lever	13
M. A. Lynch	c McEwan b East	17
G. P. Howarth	c Fletcher b Pont	74
†R. D. V. Knight	c Smith b Pont	52
D. M. Smith	b Phillip	24
G. R. J. Roope	not out	39
Intikhab Alam	c Pont b Phillip	1
R. D. Jackman	b East	1
‡C. J. Richards	b Turner	1
P. I. Pocock	b Phillip	7
P. H. L. Wilson	b Lever	0
Extras (B4, LB16, W1, NB5)		26
Total (51.4 overs)		255

SURREY BOWLING	O	M	R	W		FALL OF WICKETS	E	S
Jackman	11	0	69	1	1st		48	21
Wilson	11	1	56	4	2nd		172	45
Knight	11	1	40	1	3rd		239	136
Intikhab	11	0	38	0	4th		261	187
Pocock	11	1	73	0	5th		273	205
ESSEX					6th		276	219
Lever	9.4	2	33	2	7th		—	220
Phillip	10	2	42	3	8th		—	226
East	11	1	40	2	9th		—	255
Turner	11	1	47	1	10th		—	255
Pont	10	0	67	2				

Gold Award: G. A. Gooch (4).

Ajudicator: T. E. Bailey.

BENSON & HEDGES CUP
PRINCIPAL RECORDS

Highest innings total: 350–3 off 55 overs, Essex v Combined Universities (Chelmsford) 1979.

Highest innings total by a side batting second: 282 off 50.5 overs, Gloucestershire v Hampshire (Bristol) 1974.

Highest innings total by a side batting first and losing: 268–5 off 55 overs, Leicestershire v Worcestershire (Worcester) 1976.

Lowest completed innings total: 61 off 26 overs, Sussex v Middlesex (Hove) 1978.

Highest individual innings: 173* C. G. Greenidge, Hampshire v Minor Counties (South) (Amersham) 1973.

62 centuries have been scored in the competition.

Record Wicket Partnerships

1st	223	G. A. Gooch and A. W. Lilley, Essex v Combined Universities (Chelmsford) 1979.
2nd	285*	C. G. Greenidge & D. R. Turner, Hampshire v Minor Counties (South) (Amersham) 1973.
3rd	227	M. E. J. C. Norman & B. F. Davison, Leicestershire v Warwickshire (Coventry) 1972.
	227	D. Lloyd & F. C. Hayes, Lancashire v Minor Counties (North) (Manchester) 1973.
4th	165*	Mushtaq Mohammad & W. Larkins, Northamptonshire v Essex (Chelmsford) 1977.
5th	134	M. Maslin & D. N. F. Slade, Minor Counties (East) v Nottinghamshire (Nottingham) 1976.
6th	114	M. J. Khan & G. P. Ellis, Glamorgan v Gloucestershire (Bristol) 1975.
7th	102	E. W. Jones & M. A. Nash, Glamorgan v Hampshire (Swansea) 1976.
8th	109	R. E. East & N. Smith, Essex v Northamptonshire (Chelmsford) 1977.
9th	81	J. N. Shepherd & D. L. Underwood, Kent v Middlesex (Lord's) 1975.
10th	61	J. M. Rice & A. M. E. Roberts, Hampshire v Gloucestershire (Bristol) 1975.

Note: A higher 1st wicket partnership of 224 occurred between Sadiq Mohammad, A. W. Stovold and Zaheer Abbas for Gloucestershire v Worcestershire (Worcester) 1975, Sadiq retiring hurt after 67 runs had been scored.

Hat-tricks: G. D. McKenzie, Leicestershire v Worcestershire (Worcester) 1972. K. Higgs, Leicestershire v Surrey (Lord's) 1974. A. A. Jones, Middlesex v Essex (Lord's) 1977, M. J. Procter, Gloucestershire v Hampshire (Southampton) 1977.

Seven wickets in an innings: 7–12 W. W. Daniel, Middlesex v Minor Counties (East) (Ipswich) 1978.

Most 'Gold' awards: 10 B. Wood (Lancashire), 9 J. H. Edrich (Surrey).

BENSON & HEDGES CUP WINNERS

1972	Leicestershire	1976	Kent
1973	Kent	1977	Gloucestershire
1974	Surrey	1978	Kent
1975	Leicestershire	1979	Essex

SOMERSET WIN THE JOHN PLAYER LEAGUE

Somerset, against expectations (because it was generally thought that Kent would beat Middlesex at Canterbury on the last day of the season in which case the title would have been theirs) followed up their Gillette Cup win on the Saturday, by beating Notts at Trent Bridge and taking the John Player League as well – a notable double that had proved beyond their reach a year before.

The success of Somerset in the Sunday League is reflected in their attendances at home matches. They took nearly £36,000 from 29,000 paying spectators at their eight home games and as their membership rose from 5,200 to 6,700 it is likely that Somerset have never been watched by more people on Sundays. For the vital Kent match at Taunton on August 26, the receipts were £6,877. There were 377 sixes hit in the John Player League – the third lowest in eleven years. The lowest ever is 343 in 1978.

JOHN PLAYER LEAGUE FINAL TABLE

	P	W	L	NR	Pts	Sixes	Bowling Awards
1 Somerset (2)	16	12	3	1	50	21	1
2 Kent (10)	16	11	3	2	48	16	4
3 Worcestershire (4)	16	9	4	3	42	22	2
4 Middlesex (15)	16	9	5	2	40	27	2
Yorkshire (7)	16	8	4	4	40	29	0
6 Essex (6)	16	8	6	2	36	18	5
Leicestershire (3)	16	7	5	4	36	20	3
8 Gloucestershire (17)	16	7	7	2	32	12	2
Nottinghamshire (13)	16	6	6	4	32	21	2
10 Hampshire (1)	16	7	8	1	30	34	2
Lancashire (5)	16	6	7	3	30	21	2
12 Glamorgan (10)	16	6	10	0	24	21	4
Northants (13)	16	5	9	2	24	20	3
Surrey (5)	16	5	9	2	24	35	3
Sussex (8)	16	6	10	0	24	13	3
16 Derbyshire (8)	16	4	9	3	22	13	3
17 Warwickshire (16)	16	2	13	1	10	34	3

1978 positions in brackets

JOHN PLAYER LEAGUE
PRINCIPAL RECORDS

Highest innings total: 307–4 off 38 overs, Worcestershire v Derbyshire (Worcester) 1975.

Highest innings total by side batting second: 261–8 off 39.1 overs, Warwickshire v Nottinghamshire (Birmingham) 1976.

Highest innings total by side batting first and losing: 260–5 off 40 overs, Nottinghamshire v Warwickshire (Birmingham) 1976.

Lowest completed innings total: 23 off 19.4 overs, Middlesex v Yorkshire (Leeds) 1974.

Highest individual innings: 163* C. G. Greenidge, Hampshire v Warwickshire (Birmingham) 1979.

134 centuries have been scored in the League.

Record Wicket Partnerships

1st	218	A. R. Butcher & G. P. Howarth, Surrey v Gloucestershire (Oval) 1976.
2nd	179	B. W. Luckhurst & M. H. Denness, Kent v Somerset (Canterbury) 1973.
3rd	182	H. Pilling & C. H. Lloyd, Lancashire v Somerset (Manchester) 1970.
4th	175*	M. J. K. Smith & D. L. Amiss, Warwickshire v Yorkshire (Birmingham) 1970.
5th	163	A. G. E. Ealham & B. D. Julien, Kent v Leicestershire (Leicester) 1977.
6th	121	C. P. Wilkins & A. J. Borrington, Derbyshire v Warwickshire (Chesterfield) 1972.
7th	96*	R. Illingworth & J. Birkenshaw, Leicestershire v Somerset (Leicester) 1971.
8th	95*	D. Breakwell & K. F. Jennings, Somerset v Nottinghamshire (Nottingham) 1976.
9th	86	D. P. Hughes & P. Lever, Lancashire v Essex (Leyton) 1973.
10th	57	D. A. Graveney & J. B. Mortimore, Gloucestershire v Lancashire (Tewkesbury) 1973.

Four wickets in four balls: A. Ward, Derbyshire v Sussex (Derby) 1970.

Hat-tricks (excluding above): R. Palmer, Somerset v Gloucestershire (Bristol) 1970, K. D. Boyce, Essex v Somerset (Westcliff) 1971, G. D. McKenzie, Leicestershire v Essex (Leicester) 1972, R. G. D. Willis, Warwickshire v Yorkshire (Birmingham), 1973, W. Blenkiron, Warwickshire v Derbyshire (Buxton), 1974, A. Buss, Sussex v Worcestershire (Hastings) 1974, J. M. Rice, Hampshire v Northamptonshire (Southampton) 1975, M. A. Nash, Glamorgan v Worcestershire (Worcester) 1975, A. Hodgson, Northamptonshire v Sussex (Northampton) 1976, A. E. Cordle, Glamorgan v Hampshire (Portsmouth) 1979, C. J. Tunnicliffe, Derbyshire v Worcestershire (Derby) 1979.

Eight wickets in an innings: 8–26 K. D. Boyce, Essex v Lancashire (Manchester) 1971.

JOHN PLAYER LEAGUE CHAMPIONS

1969 Lancashire	1975 Hampshire
1970 Lancashire	1976 Kent
1971 Worcestershire	1977 Leicestershire
1972 Kent	1978 Hampshire
1973 Kent	1979 Somerset
1974 Leicestershire	

ESSEX ARE CHAMPIONS AT LAST!

Perhaps the most surprising factor about Essex's winning the Schweppes County Championship for the first time, was the ease with which they achieved it. Essex have been on the brink of winning something for years and always seem to have failed at the crucial time, but this time they got away to a flying start and never looked back. It appeared to be all over bar the shouting long before the season ended. Meanwhile, of course, they took the Benson and Hedges Cup to complete a marvellous year after more than a century of trying to accomplish a major success. But after all, Essex had been second last season – a familiar springboard for an assault on the top. The other surprise is the two teams who finished quite a few lengths behind them: Worcestershire, in second place, who in 1978 were fifteenth in the table, and Surrey, in third place – they were sixteenth last season. The biggest fall from grace was Middlesex from third to joint-thirteenth. For many, the disappointment was Yorkshire, whom their followers believed were on the way up at last; they fell, however, from fourth to seventh.

But to return to the champions. Some said that their flying start was due to extraordinary good luck with the foul weather which considerably disrupted the progress of their challengers; but then who were the serious challengers, and who can say that if they had been able to play they would have won their matches as decisively as Essex did? This was impressive form by Essex and if they did have a bit of luck with the weather then it was no more than they deserved, and moreover, it is sometimes said that a good team makes its own luck. For John Lever, their Man of the Season, there was only one minor disappointment for he took 99 Championship wickets instead of the coveted hundred. These, however, cost him only 14.74 apiece and it is a source of good natured banter that his captain, Keith Fletcher, heads him in the bowling averages with 8 wickets for 85, an average of 10.62.

Essex was certainly a team of all-rounders with all the bits and pieces necessary for cricket at the top; Hardie, McEwan and Gooch all had averages above 40, with Fletcher and Denness in the thirties. McEwan hit a not out double century against Warwickshire at Edgbaston and six players altogether hit centuries, while Neil Smith, that highly competent wicket-keeper scored a 90 not out. There was always plenty of bowling of almost endless variety – Turner, Phillip, Acfield, East (the last-named to provide a touch of light humour when the pressure was on in the dressing-room). Between them, these four took 205 wickets.

But Lever's purple patch really carried Essex to the heights almost beyond reach of any rival. In the middle of June in successive matches against Leicestershire and Warwickshire, Lever took 13 wickets in each match, improving his career best innings figures once and match figures twice, and so hoisted Essex into a sixty point lead at the top of the table. At this point – with so much of the season yet to unfold – they were still made 13-8 on favourites to win the Championship by Ladbrokes, and win it they did – in style. But an equally happy place must be the Oval under their new manager Micky Stewart, where there are positive signs of happier days to come.

SCHWEPPES COUNTY CHAMPIONSHIP
FINAL TABLE

		P	W	D	L	Bt	Bw	Pts
1	Essex (2)	22	13	5	4	56	69	281
2	Worcestershire (15)	22	7	11	4	58	62	204
3	Surrey (16)	22	6	13	3	50	70	192
4	Sussex (9)	22	6	12	4	47	65	184
5	Kent (1)	22	6	13	3	49	60	181
6	Leicestershire (6)	22	4	13	5	60	68	176
7	Yorkshire (4)	22	5	14	3	52	63	175
8	Somerset (5)	22	5	16	1	56	55	171
9	Nottinghamshire (7)	22	6	12	4	43	54	169
10	Gloucestershire (10)	22	5	13	4	53	54	167
11	Northamptonshire (17)	22	3	13	6	59	58	153
12	Hampshire (8)	22	3	10	9	39	66	141
13	Lancashire (12)	22	4	14	4	37	55	140
	Middlesex (3)	22	3	16	3	44	60	140
15	Warwickshire (11)	22	3	12	7	46	51	133
16	Derbyshire (14)	22	1	15	6	46	60	118
17	Glamorgan (13)	22	0	12	10	35	58	93

Draws column includes matches where no play was possible.
1978 positions in brackets.

COUNTY CHAMPIONS

1864 Surrey	1896 Yorkshire	1938 Yorkshire
1865 Nottinghamshire	1897 Lancashire	1939 Yorkshire
1866 Middlesex	1898 Yorkshire	1946 Yorkshire
1867 Yorkshire	1899 Surrey	1947 Middlesex
1868 Nottinghamshire	1900 Yorkshire	1948 Glamorgan
1869 { Nottinghamshire / Yorkshire	1901 Yorkshire	1949 { Middlesex / Yorkshire
1870 Yorkshire	1902 Yorkshire	
1871 Nottinghamshire	1903 Middlesex	1950 { Lancashire / Surrey
1872 Nottinghamshire	1904 Lancashire	
1873 { Gloucestershire / Nottinghamshire	1905 Yorkshire	1951 Warwickshire
	1906 Kent	1952 Surrey
1874 Gloucestershire	1907 Nottinghamshire	1953 Surrey
1875 Nottinghamshire	1908 Yorkshire	1954 Surrey
1876 Gloucestershire	1909 Kent	1955 Surrey
1877 Gloucestershire	1910 Kent	1956 Surrey
1878 Undecided	1911 Warwickshire	1957 Surrey
1879 { Nottinghamshire / Lancashire	1912 Yorkshire	1958 Surrey
	1913 Kent	1959 Yorkshire
1880 Nottinghamshire	1914 Surrey	1960 Yorkshire
1881 Lancashire	1919 Yorkshire	1961 Hampshire
1882 { Nottinghamshire / Lancashire	1920 Middlesex	1962 Yorkshire
	1921 Middlesex	1963 Yorkshire
1883 Nottinghamshire	1922 Yorkshire	1964 Worcestershire
1884 Nottinghamshire	1923 Yorkshire	1965 Worcestershire
1885 Nottinghamshire	1924 Yorkshire	1966 Yorkshire
1886 Nottinghamshire	1925 Yorkshire	1967 Yorkshire
1887 Surrey	1926 Lancashire	1968 Yorkshire
1888 Surrey	1927 Lancashire	1969 Glamorgan
1889 { Surrey / Lancashire / Nottinghamshire	1928 Lancashire	1970 Kent
	1929 Nottinghamshire	1971 Surrey
	1930 Lancashire	1972 Warwickshire
1890 Surrey	1931 Yorkshire	1973 Hampshire
1891 Surrey	1932 Yorkshire	1974 Worcestershire
1892 Surrey	1933 Yorkshire	1975 Leicestershire
1893 Yorkshire	1934 Lancashire	1976 Middlesex
1894 Surrey	1935 Yorkshire	1977 { Kent / Middlesex
1895 Surrey	1936 Derbyshire	
	1937 Yorkshire	1978 Kent
		1979 Essex

THE COUNTIES AND
THEIR PLAYERS
Compiled by Michael Fordham

Abbreviations

B	Born	HSC	Highest score for County if different from highest first-class score
RHB	Right-hand bat		
LHB	Left-hand bat		
RF	Right-arm fast	HSGC	Highest score Gillette Cup
RFM	Right-arm fast medium	HSJPL	Highest score John Player League
RM	Right-arm medium		
LF	Left-arm fast	HSBH	Highest score Benson & Hedges Cup
LFM	Left-arm fast medium		
LM	Left-arm medium	BB	Best bowling figures
OB	Off-break	BBUK	Best bowling figures in this country
LB	Leg-break		
LBG	Leg-break and googly	BBTC	Best bowling figures in Test cricket if different from above
SLA	Slow left-arm orthodox		
SLC	Slow left-arm 'chinaman'		
WK	Wicket-keeper	BBC	Best bowling figures for County if different from above
*	Not out or unfinished stand		
HS	Highest score	BBGC	Best bowling figures Gillette Cup
HSUK	Highest score in this country		
		BBJPL	Best bowling figures John Player League
HSTC	Highest score in Test cricket if different from above	BBBH	Best bowling figures Benson & Hedges Cup

When a player is known by a name other than his first name, the name in question has been underlined.

All Test appearances are complete to 4th September 1979.

'Debut' denotes 'first-class debut' and 'Cap' means '1st XI county cap'.

Wisden 1979 indicates that a player was selected as one of *Wisden's* Five Cricketers of the Year for his achievements in 1979.

Owing to the increasing number of privately arranged overseas tours of short duration, only those which may be regarded as major tours have been included.

DERBYSHIRE

Formation of present club: 1870.
Colours: Chocolate, amber, and pale blue.
Badge: Rose and crown.
County Champions: 1936.
Gillette Cup finalists: 1969.
Best final position in John Player League: 3rd in 1970.
Benson & Hedges Cup Finalists: 1978.
Gillette Man of the Match Awards: 15.
Benson & Hedges Gold Awards: 24.

Secretary: D. A. Harrison, County Cricket
Ground: Nottingham Road, Derby, DE2 6DA.
Captain: G. Miller.
Prospects of play Telephone No: Derby (0332) 44849.

DERBYSHIRE

Iain Stuart ANDERSON (Dovecliff GS and Wulfric School, Burton-on-Trent) B Derby 24/4/1960. RHB, OB. Debut 1978. Is studying at University and will not be available for first half of season. HS: 75 v Worcs (Worcester) 1978. HSJPL: 14 v Middlesex (Chesterfield) 1979.

Kim John BARNETT (Leek HS) B Stroke-on-Trent 17/7/1960. RHB, LB. Played for county and Northants 2nd XIs and Staffordshire in 1976 and for Warwickshire 2nd XI in 1977 and 1978. Toured Australia with England under-19 team in 1978–79. Debut 1979. HS: 96 v Lancs (Chesterfield) 1979. HSGC: 22 v Somerset (Taunton) 1979. HSJPL: 43* v Northants (Long Eaton) 1979. HSBH: 16 v Hants (Derby) 1979. BBJPL: 3–39 v Yorks (Chesterfield) 1979.

Anthony John (Tony) BORRINGTON (Spondon Park GS) B Derby 8/12/1948. RHB, LB. Played for MCC Schools at Lord's in 1967. Played in one John Player League match in 1970. Debut 1971. Cap 1977. Benson & Hedges Gold awards: 4. HS: 137 v Yorks (Sheffield) 1978. HSGC: 29 v Somerset (Taunton) 1979. HSJPL: 101 v Somerset (Taunton) 1977. HSBH: 81 v Notts (Nottingham) 1974. Trained as a teacher at Loughborough College of Education.

Harold CARTWRIGHT B Halfway (Derbyshire) 12/5/1951. RHB. Played in John Player and Gillette Cup matches in 1971 and 1972. Debut 1973. Cap 1978. Has become a full-time teacher and is only likely to play in school holidays and one day matches. Benson & Hedges Gold awards: 1. HS: 141* v Warwickshire (Chesterfield) 1977. HSGC: 36 v Somerset (Ilkeston) 1977. HSJPL: 76* v Middlesex (Chesterfield) 1973. HSBH: 56* v Minor Counties (West) (Derby) 1978.

Michael (Mike) HENDRICK B Darley Dale (Derbyshire) 22/10/1948. RHB, RFM. Debut 1969. Cap 1972. Elected Best Young Cricketer of the Year in 1973 by the Cricket Writers Club. *Wisden* 1977. Benefit in 1980. Tests: 25 between 1974 and 1979. Tours: West Indies 1973–74, Australia and New Zealand 1974–75, Pakistan and New Zealand 1977–78, Australia 1978–79, Australia (returned home early through injury) 1979–80. Gillette Man of the Match awards: 1. Benson & Hedges Gold awards: 2. HS: 46 v Essex (Chelmsford) 1973. HSTC: 15 v Australia (Oval) 1977. HSGC: 17 v Middlesex (Derby) 1978. HSJPL: 21 v Warwickshire (Buxton) 1974. HSBH: 32 v Notts (Chesterfield) 1973. BB: 8–45 v Warwickshire (Chesterfield) 1973. BBTC: 4–28 v India (Birmingham) 1974. BBGC: 4–16 v Middlesex (Chesterfield) 1975. BBJPL: 6–7 v Notts (Nottingham) 1972. BBBH: 5–30 v Notts (Chesterfield) 1975 and 5–30 v Lancs (Southport) 1976.

Alan HILL (New Mills GS) B Buxworth (Derbyshire) 29/6/1950. RHB, OB. Joined staff 1970. Debut 1972. Cap 1976. Played for Orange Free State in 1976–77 Currie Cup competition. Gillette Man of the Match awards: 1. Benson & Hedges Gold awards: 1. 1,000 runs (2)—1,303 runs (av 34.28) in 1976 best. HS: 160* v Warwickshire (Coventry) 1976. HSGC: 72 v Middlesex (Derby) 1978. HSJPL: 120 v Northants (Buxton) 1976. HSBH: 102* v Warwickshire (Ilkeston) 1978. BB: 3–5 Orange Free State v Northern Transvaal (Pretoria) 1976–77.

Peter Noel KIRSTEN (South African College School, Cape Town). B Pietermaritzburg, Natal, South Africa 14/5/1955. RHB, OB. Debut for Western Province in Currie Cup 1973–74. Played for Sussex v Australians 1975 as well as playing for county 2nd XI. Played for Derbyshire 2nd XI in 1977 and made debut for county in 1978. Cap 1978. Scored 4 centuries in 4 consecutive innings and 6 in 7 innings including two in match – 173* and 103 Western Province v Eastern Province (Cape Town) 1976–77. 1,000 runs (2)—1,148 runs (av 31.88) in 1979 best. Also scored 1,074 runs (av 76.71) in 1976–77. Benson & Hedges Gold awards: 1. HS: 206* v Glamorgan (Chesterfield) 1978. HSJPL: 102 v Glamorgan (Swansea) 1979. HSBH:

70 v Surrey (Derby) 1979. BB: 4–44 v Middlesex (Derby) 1979. BBJPL: 5–34 v Northants (Long Eaton) 1979.

John Wilton LISTER B Darlington 1/4/1959. RHB, RM. Debut 1978. HS: 48 v Warwickshire (Birmingham) 1978.

Roger John McCURDY B Melbourne, Australia 30/12/1959. RHB, RF. Played for Pudsey St Lawrence in Bradford League and for Shropshire in 1979. Debut 1979. One match v Indians (Derby)

Alan James McLELLAN (Williamstown HS, Melbourne, Australia and Hartshead Secondary School, Ashton-under-Lyne), B Ashton-under-Lyne (Lancashire) 2/9/1958. RHB, WK. Played for both Derbyshire and Lancs 2nd XIs in 1977. Debut 1978. HS: 41 v Hants (Basingstoke) 1979.

Alan John MELLOR (Dovecliff GS). B Burton-on-Trent 4/7/1959. RHB, SLA. Played for 2nd XI since 1976. Debut 1978. HS: 10* v Essex (Southend) 1978. BB: 5–52 v Kent (Maidstone) 1978 (in debut match).

Geoffrey (Geoff) MILLER (Chesterfield GS) B Chesterfield 8/9/1952. RHB, OB. Toured India 1970–71 and West Indies 1972 with England Young Cricketers. Won Sir Frank Worrell Trophy as Outstanding Boy Cricketer of 1972. Debut 1973. Cap 1976. Elected Best Young Cricketer of the Year in 1976 by the Cricket Writers Club. Appointed county captain in 1979. Tests: 23 between 1976 and 1979. Tours: India, Sri Lanka and Australia 1976–77, Pakistan and New Zealand 1977–78, Australia 1978–79, Australia (returned home early through injury) 1979–80. Benson & Hedges Gold awards: 2. HS: 98* England v Pakistan (Lahore) 1977–78. HSUK: 95 v Lancs (Manchester) 1978. HSGC: 59* v Worcs (Worcester) 1978. HSJPL: 44 v Kent (Chesterfield) 1973. HSBH: 75 v Warwickshire (Derby) 1977. BB: 7–54 v Sussex (Hove) 1978. BBTC: 5–44 v Australia (Sydney) 1978–79. BBJPL: 4–22 v Yorks (Huddersfield) 1978. BBBH: 3–23 v Surrey (Derby) 1979.

Stephen (Steve) OLDHAM B High Green, Sheffield 26/7/1948. RHB, RFM. Debut Yorkshire 1974. Benson & Hedges Gold awards: 1. HS: 50 v Sussex (Hove) 1979. HSJPL: 38* v Glamorgan (Cardiff) 1977. BB: 5–40 v Surrey (Oval) 1978. BBGC: 3–45 v Lancs (Leeds) 1974. BBJPL: 4–21 v Notts (Scarborough) 1974. BBBH: 5–32 v Minor Counties (North) (Scunthorpe) 1975. Joined Derbyshire 1980.

Philip Edgar (Phil) RUSSELL (Ilkeston GS) B Ilkeston 9/5/1944. RHB, RM/OB. Debut 1965. Not re-engaged after 1972 season, but rejoined staff in 1974 and is now county coach. Cap 1975. HS: 72 v Glamorgan (Swansea) 1970. HSGC: 27* v Middlesex (Derby) 1978. HSJPL: 47* v Glamorgan (Buxton) 1975. HSBH: 22* v Lancs (Southport) 1976. BB: 7–46 v Yorks (Sheffield) 1976. BBGC: 3–44 v Somerset (Taunton) 1975. BBJPL: 6–10 v Northants (Buxton) 1976. BBBH: 3–28 v Kent (Lord's) 1978.

David Stanley STEELE B Stoke-on-Trent 29/9/1941. Elder brother of J. F. Steele of Leics and cousin of B. S. Crump, former Northants player. Wears glasses. RHB, SLA. Played for Staffordshire from 1958 to 1962. Debut for Northants 1963. Cap 1965. Benefit (£25,500) in 1975. *Wisden* 1975. Transferred to Derbyshire in 1979 as county captain. Relinquished post during season. Cap 1979. Tests: 8 in 1975 and 1976. 1,000 runs (10)—1,756 runs (av 48.77) in 1975 best. Had match double of 100 runs and 10 wkts. (130, 6–36 and 5–39) v Derbyshire (Northampton) 1978. Gillette Man of Match Awards: 1 (for Northants). HS: 140* Northants v Worcs (Worcester) 1971. HSC: 127* v Indians (Derby) 1979. HSTC: 106 v West Indies (Nottingham) 1976. HSGC: 109 Northants v Cambs (March) 1975. HSJPL: 76 Northants v Sussex

71

DERBYSHIRE

(Hove) 1974. HSBH: 69 Northants v Warwickshire (Northampton) 1974. BB: 8–29 Northants v Lancs (Northampton) 1966. BBC: 6–91 v Hants (Basingstoke) 1979. BBJPL: 4–21 v Notts (Derby) 1979.

Robert William (Bob) TAYLOR B Stoke 17/7/1941. RHB, WK. Played for Bignall End (N. Staffs and S. Cheshire League) when only 15 and for Staffordshire from 1958 to 1960. Debut 1960 for Minor Counties v South Africans (Stoke-on-Trent). Debut for county 1961. Cap 1962. Testimonial (£6,672) in 1973. Appointed county captain during 1975 season. Relinquished post during 1976 season. *Wisden* 1976. Tests: 22 between 1970–71 and 1979. Tours: Australia and New Zealand 1970–71, 1974–75, Australia with Rest of the World team 1971–72, West Indies 1973–74, Pakistan and New Zealand 1977–78, Australia 1978–79. Australia and India 1979–80. Withdrew from India, Sri Lanka, and Pakistan tour 1972–73. Dismissed 80 batsmen (77 ct 3 st) in 1962, 83 batsmen (81 ct 2 st) in 1963, and 86 batsmen (79 ct 7 st) in 1965. Dismissed 10 batsmen in match, all caught v Hants (Chesterfield) 1963 and 7 in innings, all caught v Glamorgan (Derby) 1966. Gillette Man of Match awards: 1. Benson & Hedges Gold awards: 2. HS: 97 International Wanderers v South African Invitation XI (Johannesburg) 1975–76 and 97 v Australia (Adelaide) 1978–79. HSUK: 74* v Glamorgan (Derby) 1971. HSGC: 53* v Middlesex (Lord's) 1965. HSJPL: 43* v Glos (Burton-on-Trent) 1969. HSBH: 31* v Hants (Southampton) 1976.

Colin John TUNNICLIFFE B Derby 11/8/1951. RHB, LFM. Debut 1973. Left staff after 1974 season. Re-appeared in 1976. Cap 1977. Hat-trick in John Player League v Worcs (Derby) 1979. HS: 82* v Middlesex (Ilkeston) 1977. HSGC: 13 v Somerset (Ilkeston) 1977. HSJPL: 42 v Yorks (Huddersfield) 1978. HSBH: 28 v Warwickshire (Birmingham) 1979. BB: 4–22 v Middlesex (Ilkeston) 1977. BBJPL: 3–12 v Essex (Chesterfield) 1974. BBBH: 3–16 v Lancs (Manchester) 1978.

John WALTERS B Brampton (Yorks) 7/8/1949. LHB, RFM. Has played in Huddersfield League. Debut 1977. HS: 90 v Yorks (Chesterfield) 1978. HSJPL: 55* v Worcs (Worcester) 1978. HSBH: 12 v Warwickshire (Birmingham) 1979. BB: 4–100 v Worcs (Derby) 1979. BBJPL: 4–14 v Glamorgan (Swansea) 1979.

Robert Colin (Bob) WINCER (Hemsworth GS, Yorkshire) B Portsmouth 2/4/1952. LHB, RFM. Debut 1978. HS: 26 v Kent (Chesterfield) 1979. HSJPL: 11 v Kent (Chesterfield) 1979. BB: 4–42 v Leics (Derby) 1978.

John Geoffrey WRIGHT (Christ's College, Christchurch and Otago University) B Darfield, New Zealand 5/7/1954. LHB, RM. Debut for Northern Districts in Shell Cup in 1975–76. Debut for county 1977. Cap 1977. Tests: 8 for New Zealand between 1977–78 and 1978–79. Tour: New Zealand to England 1978. 1,000 runs (2)—1,249 runs (av 39.03) in 1979 best. Benson & Hedges Gold awards: 2. HS: 164 v Pakistanis (Chesterfield) 1978. HSTC: 88 New Zealand v Pakistan (Napier) 1978–79. HSGC: 87* v Sussex (Hove) 1977. HSJPL: 75 v Glos (Heanor) 1977. HSBH: 102 v Worcs (Chesterfield) 1977.

NB The following player whose particulars appeared in the 1979 Annual has been omitted: F. W. Swarbrook (not re-engaged). His career record will be found elsewhere in this Annual.

COUNTY AVERAGES

Schweppes Championship: Played 21, won 1, drawn 14, lost 6, abandoned 1
All first-class matches: Played 23, won 1, drawn 16, lost 6, abandoned 1

BATTING AND FIELDING

Cap		M	I	NO	Runs	HS	Avge	100	50	Ct	St
1979	D. S. Steele	23	38	8	1190	127*	39.66	2	7	22	—
1977	J. G. Wright	19	35	3	1249	142*	39.03	5	5	9	—
1972	M. Hendrick	10	9	6	99	36	33.00	—	—	9	—
1975	F. W. Swarbrook	6	7	2	163	52	32.60	—	1	4	—
1978	P. N. Kirsten	23	38	2	1148	135*	31.88	2	5	21	—
1976	G. Miller	13	16	4	360	82	30.00	—	2	8	—
1976	A. Hill	19	35	3	887	99	27.71	—	6	8	—
—	K. J. Barnett	23	36	6	752	96	25.06	—	4	13	—
1962	R. W. Taylor	11	12	3	221	43*	24.55	—	—	26	3
1977	A. J. Borrington	19	28	4	563	64	23.45	—	3	9	—
1977	C. J. Tunnicliffe	20	22	4	403	57	22.38	—	2	8	—
—	I. S. Anderson	5	9	3	98	38	16.33	—	—	1	—
—	J. Walters	22	28	7	291	54	13.85	—	1	8	—
—	R. C. Wincer	11	11	4	88	26	12.57	—	—	3	—
—	A. J. McLellan	12	10	3	72	41	10.28	—	—	24	2
—	A. J. Mellor	7	6	4	7	3*	3.50	—	—	4	—
1975	P. E. Russell	5	4	0	8	4	2.00	—	—	1	—

Played in two matches: H. Cartwright 72, 0. J. W. Lister 44, 14, 7, 3.
Played in one match: R. J. McCurdy did not bat.

BOWLING

	Type	O	M	R	W	Avge	Best	5 wI	10 wM
M. Hendrick	RFM	306.4	92	636	29	21.93	4-32	—	—
G. Miller	OB	383.1	115	913	35	26.08	6-53	2	—
D. S. Steele	SLA	503.4	135	1459	48	30.39	6-91	2	—
C. J. Tunnicliffe	LFM	454.5	107	1307	37	35.32	4-35	—	—
R. C. Wincer	RFM	235.5	40	864	24	36.00	4-79	—	—
A. J. Mellor	SLA	97.1	19	311	8	38.87	3-28	—	—
P. N. Kirsten	OB	269.3	65	752	19	39.57	4-44	—	—
J. Walters	RFM	380	80	1209	29	41.86	4-100	—	—
P. E. Russell	RM/OB	121	29	335	6	55.83	3-102	—	—

Also bowled: I. S. Anderson 4-0-13-0; K. J. Barnett 98.5-12-387-4; A. Hill 11-1-61-2; R. J. McCurdy 18-4-50-1; F. W. Swarbrook 41-5-161-0.

County Records

First-class cricket

Highest innings totals:	For —645 v Hampshire (Derby)	1898
	Agst—662 by Yorkshire (Chesterfield)	1898
Lowest innings totals:	For —16 v Nottinghamshire (Nottingham)	1879
	Agst—23 by Hampshire (Burton-on-Trent)	1958
Highest individual innings:	For —274 G. Davidson v Lancashire (Manchester)	1896
	Agst—343*P. A. Perrin for Essex (Chesterfield)	1904
Best bowling in an innings:	For —10-40 W. Bestwick v Glamorgan (Cardiff)	1921
	Agst—10-74 T. F. Smailes for Yorkshire (Sheffield)	1939
Best bowling in a match:	For —16-84 C. Gladwin v Worcs (Stourbridge)	1952
	Agst—16-101 G. Giffen for Australians (Derby)	1886

ESSEX

Most runs in a season: 2165 (av 48.1) D. B. Carr 1959
 runs in a career: 20516 (av 31.41) D. Smith 1927–1952
 100s in a season: 6 by L. F. Townsend 1933
 100s in a career: 30 by D. Smith 1927–1952
 wickets in a season: 168 (av 19.55) T. B. Mitchell 1935
 wickets in a career: 1670 (av 17.11) H. L. Jackson 1947–1963

RECORD WICKET STANDS

1st	322	H. Storer & J. Bowden v Essex (Derby)	1929
2nd	349	C. S. Elliott & J. D. Eggar v Notts (Nottingham)	1947
3rd	246	J. Kelly & D. B. Carr v Leicestershire (Chesterfield)	1957
4th	328	P. Vaulkhard & D. Smith v Notts (Nottingham)	1946
5th	203	C. P. Wilkins & I. R. Buxton v Lancashire (Manchester)	1971
6th	212	G. M. Lee & T. S. Worthington v Essex (Chesterfield)	1932
7th	241*	G. H. Pope & A. E. G. Rhodes v Hampshire (Portsmouth)	1948
8th	182	A. H. M. Jackson & W. Carter v Leicestershire (Leicester)	1922
9th	283	A. R. Warren & J. Chapman v Warwickshire (Blackwell)	1910
10th	93	J. Humphries & J. Horsley v Lancashire (Derby)	1914

One-day cricket

Highest innings totals:	Gillette Cup	250–9 v Hants (Bournemouth)	1963
	John Player League	260–6 v Glos (Derby)	1972
	Benson & Hedges Cup	225–6 v Notts (Nottingham)	1974
Lowest innings totals:	Gillette Cup	79 v Surrey (Oval)	1967
	John Player League	70 v Surrey (Derby)	1972
	Benson & Hedges Cup	102 v Yorks (Bradford)	1975
Highest individual innings:	Gillette Cup	87* J. G. Wright v Sussex (Hove)	1977
	John Player League	120 A. Hill v Northants (Buxton)	1976
	Benson & Hedges Cup	111* P. J. Sharpe v Glamorgan (Chesterfield)	1976
Best bowling figures:	Gillette Cup	6–18 T. J. P. Eyre v Sussex (Chesterfield)	1969
	John Player League	6–7 M. Hendrick v Notts (Nottingham)	1972
	Benson & Hedges Cup	6–33 E. J. Barlow v Glos (Bristol)	1978

ESSEX

Formation of present club: 1876.
Colours: Blue, gold and red.
Badge: Three seaxes with word 'Essex' underneath.
County Champions: 1979.
Gillette Cup semi-finalists: 1978.
John Player League runners-up: (3): 1971, 1976 and 1977.
Benson & Hedges Cup winners: 1979.
Gillette Man of the Match awards: 13.
Benson & Hedges Gold awards: 23.
Secretary: P. J. Edwards, The County Ground, New Writtle Street. Chelmsford CM2 0PG.
Captain: K. W. R. Fletcher.
Prospects of Play telephone no.: Chelmsford matches only. Chelmsford (0245) 66794.

David Laurence ACFIELD (Brentwood School & Cambridge) B Chelmsford 24/7/1947. RHB, OB. Debut 1966. Blue 1967–68. Cap 1970. HS: 42 Cambridge U v Leics (Leicester) 1967. BB: 7–36 v Sussex (Ilford) 1973. BBJPL: 5–14 v Northants (Northampton) 1970. Also obtained Blue for fencing (sabre). Has appeared in internationals in this sport and represented Great Britain in Olympic Games at Mexico City and Munich.

Michael Henry (Mike) DENNESS (Ayr Academy) B Bellshill (Lanarkshire) 1/12/1940. RHB, RM/OB. Debut for Scotland 1959. Debut for Kent 1962. Cap 1964. County captain from 1972 to 1976. Benefit (£19,219) in 1974. *Wisden* 1974. Left county after 1976 season and made debut for Essex in 1977. Cap 1977. Tests: 28 between 1969 and 1975, captaining England in 19 Tests between 1973–74 and 1975. Played in one match against Rest of the World in 1970. Tours: India, Sri Lanka, and Pakistan 1972–73 (vice-captain), West Indies 1973–74 (captain), Australia and New Zealand 1974–75 (captain). Gillette Man of Match awards: 2 (1 for Kent). Benson & Hedges Gold awards: 1 (for Kent), 1,000 runs (14)—1,606 runs (av 31.49) in 1966 best. Scored 1,136 runs (av 54.09) in Australia and New Zealand 1974–75. HS: 195 v Leics (Leicester) 1977. HSTC: 188 England v Australia (Melbourne) 1974–75. HSGC: 85 Kent v Leics (Leicester) 1971. HSJPL: 118* Kent v Yorks (Scarborough) 1976. HSBH: 112* Kent v Surrey (Oval) 1973.

Raymond Eric (Ray) EAST B Manningtree (Essex) 20/6/1947. RHB, SLA. Debut 1965. Cap 1967. Benefit (£29,000) in 1978. Hat-trick: The Rest v MCC Tour XI (Hove) 1973. Benson & Hedges Gold awards: 3. HS: 113 v Hants (Chelmsford) 1976. HSGC: 38* v Glos (Chelmsford) 1973. HSJPL: 25* v Glamorgan (Colchester) 1976. HSBH: 54 v Northants (Chelmsford) 1977. BB: 8–30 v Notts (Ilford) 1977. BBGC: 4–28 v Herts (Hitchin) 1976. BBJPL: 6–18 v Yorks (Hull) 1969. BBBH: 5–33 v Kent (Chelmsford) 1975.

Keith William Robert FLETCHER B. Worcester 20/5/1944. RHB, LB. Debut 1962. Cap 1963. Appointed county vice-captain in 1971 and county captain in 1974. Benefit (£13,000) in 1973. *Wisden* 1973. Tests: 52 between 1968 and 1976–77. Also played in 4 matches v Rest of the World in 1970. Tours: Pakistan 1966–67, Ceylon and Pakistan 1968–69, Australia and New Zealand, 1970–71, 1974–75, India, Sri Lanka and Pakistan 1972–73, West Indies 1973–74, India, Sri Lanka and Australia 1976–77. 1,000 runs (15)—1,890 runs (av 41.08) in 1968 best. Scored two centuries in match (111 and 102*) v Notts (Nottingham) 1976. Gillette Man of Match awards: 1. Benson & Hedges Gold awards: 3. HS: 228* v Sussex (Hastings) 1968. HSTC: 216 v New Zealand (Auckland) 1974–75. HSGC: 74 v Notts (Nottingham) 1969. HSJPL: 99* v Notts (Ilford) 1974. HSBH: 90 v Surrey (Oval) 1974. BB: 5–41 v Middlesex (Colchester) 1979.

Graham Alan GOOCH (Norlington Junior HS, Leyton) B Leytonstone 23/7/1953. Cousin of G. J. Saville, former Essex player and assistant secretary of club. RHB, RM. Toured West Indies with England Young Cricketers 1972. Debut 1973. Cap 1975. *Wisden* 1979. Tests: 17 between 1975 and 1979. Tours: Australia 1978–79, Australia and India 1979–80. 1,000 runs (3)—1,273 runs (av 42.43) in 1976 best. Shared in 2nd wicket partnership record for county, 321 with K. S. McEwan v Northants (Ilford) 1978. Scored record aggregate of runs in limited overs competitions in 1979—1,137 runs (av.54-14). Benson & Hedges Gold awards: 4. HS: 136 v Worcs (Westcliff) 1976. HSTC: 91* v New Zealand (Oval) 1978. HSGC: 61 v Somerset (Taunton) 1978. HSJPL: 90* v Middlesex (Lord's) 1978. HSBH: 138 v Warwickshire (Chelmsford) 1979. BB: 5–40 v West Indians (Chelmsford) 1976. BBJPL: 3–14 v Derbyshire (Derby) 1978.

ESSEX

Brian Ross HARDIE (Larbert HS) B Stenhousemuir 14/1/1950. RHB, RM. Has played for Stenhousemuir in East of Scotland League. Debut for Scotland 1970. His father and elder brother K. M. Hardie have also played for Scotland. Debut for Essex by special registration in 1973. Cap 1974. 1,000 runs (4)—1,522 runs (av 43.48) in 1975 best. Scored two centuries in match for Scotland v MCC, Aberdeen 1971, a match not regarded as first-class. HS: 162 v Warwickshire (Birmingham) 1975. HSGC: 83 v Staffs (Stone) 1976. HSJPL: 94 v Northants (Northampton) 1973. HSBH: 42* v Cambridge U (Cambridge) 1974.

Reuben HERBERT (Barstaple Comprehensive School, Basildon) B Cape Town 1/12/1957. RHB, OB. Debut 1976. Did not play in 1978 or 1979. HS: 12 v Cambridge U (Cambridge) 1977.

John Kenneth LEVER B Ilford 24/2/1949. RHB, LFM. Debut 1967. Cap 1970. *Wisden* 1978. Benefit in 1980. Tests: 15 between 1976–77 and 1979. Tours: India, Sri Lanka and Australia 1976–77. Pakistan and New Zealand 1977–78. Australia 1978–79, Australia and India 1979–80. 100 wkts (2) – 106 wkts (av 15.18) in 1978 and 106 wkts (av. 17.30) in 1979. Gillette Man of Match awards: 3. Benson & Hedges Gold awards: 1. HS: 91 v Glamorgan (Cardiff) 1970. HSTC: 53 v India (Delhi) 1976–77 (on debut). HSJPL: 23 v Worcs (Worcester) 1974. HSBH: 12* v Warwickshire (Birmingham) 1975. BB: 8–49 (13–87 match) v Warwickshire (Birmingham) 1979. BBTC: 7–46 v India (Delhi) 1976–77 (on debut). BBGC: 5–8 v Middlesex (Westcliff) 1972. BBJPL: 5–13 v Glamorgan (Ebbw Vale) 1975. BBBH: 5–16 v Middlesex (Chelmsford) 1976.

Alan William LILLEY (Caterham Secondary High School, Ilford) B Ilford 8/5/1959. RHB, WK. Debut 1978. Scored century in second innings of debut match v Notts (Nottingham). Benson & Hedges Gold Awards: 1. HS: 100* v Notts (Nottingham) 1978. HJPL: 54 v Surrey (Southend) 1978. HSBH: 119 v Combined Universities (Chelmsford) 1979.

Michael Stephen Anthony McEVOY (Colchester RGS) B Jorhat Assam, India 25/1/1956. RHB, RM. Debut 1976. HS: 67* v Yorks (Middlesbrough) 1977. Trained as a teacher at Borough Road College of Education.

Kenneth Scott (Ken) McEWAN (Queen's College, Queenstown) B Bedford, Cape Province, South Africa 16/7/1952. RHB, OB. Debut for Eastern Province in 1972–73 Currie Cup competition. Played for T. N. Pearce's XI v West Indians (Scarborough) 1973. Debut for county and cap 1974. *Wisden* 1977. Played for Western Australia in 1979–80. 1,000 runs (6)—1,821 runs (av 49.21) in 1976 best. Scored 4 consecutive centuries in 1977 including two centuries in match (102 and 116) v Warwickshire (Birmingham). Shared in 2nd wicket partnership record for county, 321 with G. A. Gooch v Northants (Ilford) 1978. Benson & Hedges Gold awards: 4. HS: 218 v Sussex (Chelmsford) 1977. HSGC: 63 v Somerset (Westcliff) 1974. HSJPL: 123 v Warwickshire (Ilford) 1976. HSBH: 133 v Notts (Chelmsford) 1978.

Norbert PHILLIP (Dominica GS Roseau) B Bioche, Dominica 12/6/1948 RHB, RFM. Debut 1969–70 for Windward Islands v Glamorgan and has played subsequently for Combined Islands in Shell Shield competition. Debut for county and cap 1978. Tests: 9 for West Indies between 1977–78 and 1978–79. Tour: West Indies to India and Sri Lanka 1978–79. Had match double of 100 runs and 10 wickets (160 and 10–130), Combined Islands v Guyana (Georgetown) 1977–78. HS: 134 v Glos (Gloucester) 1978. HSTC: 47 West Indies v India (Calcutta) 1978–79. HSGC: 24* v Leics (Leicester) 1978. HSJPL: 17* v Warwickshire (Colchester) 1978. HSBH: 14 v Surrey (Oval) 1979. BB: 6–33 v Pakistanis (Chelmsford) 1978. BBTC: 4–48 West Indies v India (Madras) 1978–79. BBJPL: 4–23 v Kent (Chelmsford) 1979. BBBH: 3–42 v Surrey (Lord's) 1979.

Keith Rupert PONT B Wanstead 16/1/1953. RHB., RM. Debut 1970. Cap 1976. Benson & Hedges Gold awards: 2. HS: 113 v Warwickshire (Birmingham) 1973. HSGC: 39 v Somerset (Taunton) 1978. HSJPL: 52 v Glamorgan (Chelmsford) 1979. HSBH: 60* v Notts (Ilford) 1970. BB: 4–100 v Middlesex (Southend) 1977. BBJPL: 4–24 v Derbyshire (Chelmsford) 1979.

Derek Raymond PRINGLE (Felsted School and Cambridge). B Nairobi, Kenya 18/9/1958. 6 ft 4½ ins. tall. Son of late Donald Pringle who played for East Africa in 1975 Prudential Cup. RHB, RM. Toured India with England Schools C.A. 1977–78. Debut 1978. Did not play for county in 1979. Blue 1979. HS: 103* Cambridge U. v Oxford U. (Lord's) 1979. HSBH: 58 Combined Universities v Essex (Chelmsford) 1979. BB: 4–43 Cambridge U. V Yorks (Cambridge) 1979.

Gary Edward SAINSBURY (Beal HS, Ilford) B Wanstead 17/1/1958. RHB, LM. Played for 2nd XI since 1977. Debut 1979. One match v Northants (Chelmsford). Obtained degree in Statistics at University of Bath.

Neil SMITH (Ossett GS) B Dewsbury 1/4/1949. RHB, WK. Debut for Yorks 1970. Debut for county by special registration in 1973. Cap 1975. HS: 126 v Somerset (Leyton) 1976. HSGC: 12 v Leics (Southend) 1977. HSJPL: 32 v Glamorgan (Chelmsford) 1979. HSBH: 61 v Northants (Chelmsford) 1977.

Stuart TURNER B Chester 18/7/1943. RHB, RFM. Debut 1965. Cap 1970. Played for Natal in 1976–77 and 1977–78 Currie Cup competition. Benefit in 1979. Hat-trick: v Surrey (Oval) 1971. HS: 121 v Somerset (Taunton) 1970. HSGC: 50 v Lancs (Chelmsford) 1971. HSJPL: 87 v Worcs (Chelmsford) 1975. HSBH: 41* v Minor Counties (East) (Chelmsford) 1977. BB: 6–26 v Northants (Northampton) 1977. BBGC: 3–16 v Glamorgan (Ilford) 1971. BBJPL: 5–35 v Hants (Chelmsford) 1978. BBBH: 4–22 v Minor Counties (South) (Bedford) 1975.

NB: The following player whose particulars appeared in the 1979 Annual has been omitted: S. J. Malone has joined Hampshire and his particulars will be found under that county.

COUNTY AVERAGES

Schweppes Championship: Played 21, won 13, drawn 4, lost 4, abandoned 1.
All first-class matches: Played 23, won 13, drawn 6, lost 4, abandoned 1.

BATTING AND FIELDING

Cap		M	I	NO	Runs	HS	Avge	100	50	Ct	St
1974	K. S. McEwan	23	35	2	1387	208*	42.03	3	6	19	—
1974	B. R. Hardie	23	34	5	1170	146*	40.34	3	5	30	—
1975	G. A. Gooch	12	18	2	614	109	38.37	1	4	20	—
1963	K. W. R. Fletcher	23	34	4	1006	140*	33.53	1	8	19	—
1977	M. H. Denness	21	35	2	1032	136	31.27	2	4	8	—
1970	S. Turner	23	30	4	561	102	21.57	1	1	14	—
1976	K. R. Pont	13	20	3	346	77	20.35	—	2	6	—
1967	R. E. East	20	26	5	401	70	19.09	—	1	8	—
1975	N. Smith	23	29	7	417	90*	18.95	—	3	51	3
1978	N. Phillip	22	30	5	425	66	17.00	—	2	6	—
—	A. W. Lilley	4	5	0	76	35	15.20	—	—	1	—
—	M. S. A. McEvoy	7	12	0	108	28	9.00	—	—	11	—
1970	J. K. Lever	19	14	5	73	14	8.11	—	—	3	—
1970	D. L. Acfield	19	16	9	55	12*	7.85	—	—	5	—

Played in one match: G. E. Sainsbury did not bat (1 ct).

ESSEX

BOWLING	Type	O	M	R	W	avge	Best	5 wI	10 wM
K. W. R. Fletcher	LB	34.3	5	134	9	14.88	5–41	1	—
J. K. Lever	LFM	635.1	150	1631	104	15.68	8–49	8	2
S. Turner	RFM	576.3	164	1285	61	21.06	5–35	4	1
N. Phillip	RFM	548.1	128	1506	70	21.51	5–23	1	—
D. L. Acfield	OB	489.2	143	1048	41	25.56	6–56	3	—
K. R. Pont	RM	96	18	251	9	27.88	3–34	—	—
R. E. East	SLA	561.3	168	1290	43	30.00	5–56	1	—

Also bowled: G. A. Gooch 43–9–119–3; B. R. Hardie 5–0–39–2; G. E. Sainsbury 23–2–79–1.

County Records

First-class cricket

Highest innings totals:	For —692 v Somerset (Taunton)		1895
	Agst—803–4 by Kent (Brentwood)		1934
Lowest innings totals:	For —30 v Yorkshire (Leyton)		1901
	Agst—31 by Derbyshire (Derby) and by Yorkshire (Huddersfield)		1914 & 1935
Highest individual innings:	For —343* P. A. Perrin v Derbyshire (Chesterfield)		1904
	Agst—332 W. H. Ashdown for Kent (Brentwood)		1934
Best bowling in an innings:	For —10–32 H. Pickett v Leicestershire (Leyton)		1895
	Agst—10–40 G. Dennett for Gloucestershire (Bristol)		1906
Best bowling in a match:	For —17–119 W. Mead v Hampshire (Southampton)		1895
	Agst—17–56 C. W. L. Parker for Gloucestershire (Gloucester)		1925
Most runs in a season:	2308 (av 56.29) J. O'Connor		1934
runs in a career:	29162 (av. 36.18) P. A. Perrin		1896–1928
100s in a season:	9 by J. O'Connor and D. J. Insole		1934 & 1955
100s in a career:	71 by J. O'Connor		1921–1939
wickets in a season:	172 (av 27.13) T. P. B. Smith		1947
wickets in a career:	1611 (av 26.26) T. P. B. Smith		1929–1951

RECORD WICKET STANDS

1st	270	A. V. Avery & T. C. Dodds v Surrey (The Oval)	1946
2nd	321	G. A. Gooch & K. S. McEwan v Northamptonshire (Ilford)	1978
3rd	343	P. A. Gibb & R. Horsfall v Kent (Blackheath)	1951
4th	298	A. V. Avery & R. Horsfall v Worcestershire (Clacton)	1948
5th	287	C. T. Ashton & J. O'Connor v Surrey (Brentwood)	1934
6th	206	J. W. H. T. Douglas & J. O'Connor v Gloucestershire (Cheltenham)	1923
		B. R. Knight & R. A. G. Luckin v Middlesex (Brentwood)	1962
7th	261	J. W. H. T. Douglas & J. Freeman v Lancashire (Leyton)	1914
8th	263	D. R. Wilcox & R. M. Taylor v Warwickshire (Southend)	1946
9th	251	J. W. H. T. Douglas & S. N. Hare v Derbyshire (Leyton)	1921
10th	218	F. H. Vigar & T. P. B. Smith v Derbyshire (Chesterfield)	1947

One-day cricket

Highest innings totals:	Gillette Cup	316–6 v Staffordshire (Stone)	1976
	John Player League	283–6 v Gloucestershire (Cheltenham)	1975
	Benson & Hedges Cup	350–3 v Combined Universities (Chelmsford)	1979
Lowest innings totals:	Gillette Cup	100 v Derbyshire (Brentwood)	1965
	John Player League	69 v Derbyshire (Chesterfield)	1974
	Benson & Hedges Cup	123 v Kent (Canterbury)	1973
Highest individual innings:	Gillette Cup	101 B. Ward v Bedfordshire (Chelmsford)	1971
	John Player League	123 K. S. McEwan v Warwickshire (Ilford)	1976
	Benson & Hedges Cup	138 G. A. Gooch v Warwickshire (Chelmsford)	1979
Best bowling figures:	Gillette Cup	5–8 J. K. Lever v Middlesex (Westcliff)	1972
	John Player League	8–26 K. D. Boyce v Lancs (Manchester)	1971
	Benson & Hedges Cup	5–16 J. K. Lever v Middlesex (Chelmsford)	1976

GLAMORGAN

Formation of present club: 1888.
Colours: Blue and gold.
Badge: Gold daffodil.
County Champions (2): 1948 and 1969.
Gillette Cup finalists: 1977
Best final position in John Player League: 8th in 1977.
Benson & Hedges Cup quarter-finalists (5): 1972, 1973, 1977, 1978 and 1979.
Gillette Man of the Match awards: 13.
Benson & Hedges Gold awards: 18.
Secretary: P. B. Clift, 6 High Street, Cardiff CF1 2PW
Cricket Manager: T. W. Cartwright
Captain: R. N. S. Hobbs
Prospects of Play telephone nos.: Cardiff (0222) 29956 or 387367
Swansea (0792) 466321

Anthony Elton (Tony) CORDLE B St Michael, Barbados 21/9/1940. RHB, RFM. Debut 1963. Cap 1967. Benefit (£8,000) in 1977. Hat-trick in John Player League v Hants (Portsmouth) 1979. HS: 81 v Cambridge U (Swansea) 1972. HSGC: 36 v Lincs (Swansea) 1974. HSJPL: 87 v Notts (Nottingham) 1971. HSBH: 27* v Hants (Swansea) 1976. BB: 9–49 (13–100 match) v Leics (Colwyn Bay) 1969. BBGC: 4–42 v Worcs (Worcester) 1977. BBJPL: 5–24 v Hants (Portsmouth) 1979. BBBH: 4–14 v Hants (Swansea) 1973.

Terry DAVIES B St Albans (Herts) 25/10/1960. 5 ft 4 ins. tall. RHB, WK. Played for 2nd XI in 1978. Debut 1979. One match v Sri Lankans (Swansea).

David Arthur FRANCIS (Cwmtawe Comprehensive School, Pontardawe) B Clydach (Glamorgan) 29/11/1953. RHB, OB. Debut 1973 after playing for 2nd XI in 1971 and 1972. HS: 110 v Warwickshire (Nuneaton) 1977. HSGC: 62* v Worcs (Worcester) 1977. HSJPL: 50 v Surrey (Byfleet) 1976. HSBH: 59 v Warwickshire (Birmingham) 1977.

GLAMORGAN

Robin Nicholas Stuart HOBBS (Raine's Foundation School, Stepney), B Chippenham (Wilts.) 8/5/1942. RHB, LBG. Debut for Essex 1961. Cap 1964. Benefit (£13,500) in 1974. Retired at end of 1975 season. Played for Suffolk from 1976 to 1978. Debut for county in 1979 being appointed as County Captain. Cap 1979. Tests: 7 between 1967 and 1971. Tours: South Africa 1964–65, Pakistan 1966–67, West Indies 1967–68, Ceylon and Pakistan 1968–69. 100 wkts. (2) – 102 wkts. (av. 21.40) in 1970 best. Hat-trick: Essex v. Middlesex (Lord's) 1968 in Gillette Cup. Benson & Hedges Gold Awards: 1 (for Essex). HS: 100 Essex v. Glamorgan (Ilford) 1968 and 100 Essex v. Australians (Chelmsford) 1975 in 44 minutes. HSC: 29 v. Leics (Leicester) 1979. HSTC: 15* v India (Birmingham) 1967. HSGC: 34 Essex v. Lancs (Chelmsford) 1971. HSJPL: 54* Essex v Yorks (Colchester) 1970. HSBH: 40 Essex v Middlesex (Lord's) 1972. BB: 8–63 (13–164 match) Essex v. Glamorgan (Swansea) 1966. BBC: 3–21 v Oxford U. (Oxford) 1979. BBTC: 3–25 v India (Birmingham) 1967. BBGC: 4–55 Essex v Wilts (Chelmsford) 1969. BBJPL: 6–22 Essex v Hants (Harlow) 1973. BBBH: 3–41 v Derbyshire (Cardiff) 1979.

Geoffrey Clark HOLMES (West Denton HS, Newcastle-upon-Tyne) B Newcastle-upon-Tyne 16/9/1958. RHB, RM. Debut 1978. HS: 100* v Glos (Bristol) 1979. HSJPL: 43* v Hants (Portsmouth) 1979. BB: 4–78 v Sri Lankans (Swansea) 1979.

John Anthony HOPKINS B Maesteg 16/6/1953. Younger brother of J. D. Hopkins, formerly on staff and who appeared for Middlesex. RHB, WK. Debut 1970. Cap 1977. 1,000 runs (3)–1,371 runs (av. 33.43) in 1978 best. Gillette Man of the Match awards: 1. Benson & Hedges Gold awards: 2. HS: 230 v Worcs (Worcester) 1977 – the fourth highest score for the county. HSGC: 63 v Leics (Swansea) 1977. HSJPL: 62* v Northants (Northampton) 1979. HSBH: 81 v Worcs (Swansea) 1977. Trained as a teacher at Trinity College of Education, Carmarthen.

JAVED MIANDAD KHAN B Karachi 12/6/1957. RHB, LBG. Debut 1973–74 for Karachi Whites in Patron Trophy tournament aged 16 years 5 months. Has subsequently played for various Karachi, Sind and Habib Bank sides. Vice-captain of Pakistan Under-19 side in England 1974 and Captain of Under-19 side in Sri Lanka 1974–75. Scored 227 for Sussex 2nd XI v Hants (Hove) 1975 whilst qualifying for county. Debut for Sussex 1976. Cap 1977. Left county after end of 1979 season and has joined Glamorgan for 1980. Tests: 21 for Pakistan between 1976–77 and 1978–79. Tours: Pakistan to Australia and West Indies 1976–77, England 1978, New Zealand and Australia 1978–79, India 1979–80. Scored 1,326 runs (av 40.18) in 1977. Scored 163 for Pakistan v New Zealand (Lahore) 1976–77 on Test debut and 206 v New Zealand (Karachi) in third Test becoming youngest double-century maker in Test cricket at age of 19 years 141 days. Gillette Man of Match awards: 1. HS: 311 Karachi Whites v National Bank (Karachi) 1974–75. HSUK: 162 Sussex v Kent (Canterbury) 1976. HSTC: 206 Pakistan v New Zealand (Karachi) 1976–77. HSGC: 75 Sussex v Lancs (Hove) 1978. HSJPL: 98* Sussex v Lancs (Hastings) 1979. HSBH: 76 Sussex v Surrey (Oval) 1977. BB: 6–93 Sind v Railways (Lahore) 1974–75. BBUK: 4–10 Sussex v Northants (Northampton) 1977. BBTC: 3–74 Pakistan v New Zealand (Hyderabad) 1976–77.

Alan JONES B Swansea 4/11/1938. LHB, OB. Joined staff in 1955. Debut 1957. Cap 1962. Played for Western Australia in 1963–64, for Northern Transvaal in 1975–76 and for Natal in 1976–77. Benefit (£10,000) in 1972. County captain from 1976 to 1978. *Wisden* 1977. Testimonial in 1980. Played one match v Rest of World 1970. 1,000 runs (19)–1,865 runs (av 34.53) in 1966 and 1,862 runs (av 38.00) in 1968 best. Scored two centuries in match (187* and 105*) v Somerset (Glastonbury) 1963, (132 and 156*) v Yorks (Middlesbrough) 1976 and (147 and 100) v Hants (Swansea) 1978. Shared in record partnership for any wicket for county, 330 for 1st wkt with R. C. Fredericks v Northants (Swansea) 1972. Shared in 2nd wkt partnership record for county, 238 with A. R. Lewis v Sussex (Hastings) 1962. Has scored more runs and centuries for county than any other player. Gillette Man of the Match awards: 2. Benson & Hedges Gold awards: 1. HS: 187* v Somerset (Glastonbury) 1963. HSGC: 124* v Warwickshire (Birmingham) 1976. HSJPL: 110* v Glos (Cardiff) 1978. HSBH: 89 v Worcs (Cardiff) 1979. BBJPL: 3–21 v Northants (Wellingborough) 1975.

Alan Lewis JONES (Ystalyfera GS and Cwmtawe Comprehensive School) B Alltwen (Glamorgan) 1/6/1957. No relation to A. and E. W. Jones. LHB. Played for 2nd XI in 1972. Debut 1973 at age of 16 years 99 days. Toured West Indies with England Young Cricketers 1976. HS: 83 v Worcs (Worcester) 1979. HSGC: 11 v Hants (Southampton) 1975. HSJPL: 62 v Hants (Cardiff) 1975. HSBH: 36 v Worcs (Cardiff) 1979.

Eifion Wyn JONES B Velindre (Glamorgan) 25/6/1942. Brother of A. Jones. RHB, WK. Debut 1961. Cap 1967. Benefit (£17,000) in 1975. Dismissed 94 batsmen (85 ct 9 st) in 1970. Dismissed 7 batsmen (6 ct 1 st) in innings v Cambridge U (Cambridge) 1970. Benson & Hedges Gold awards: 1. HS: 146* v Sussex (Hove) 1968. HSGC: 67* v Herts (Swansea) 1969. HSJPL: 48 v Hants (Cardiff) 1971. HSBH: 39* v Minor Counties (West) (Amersham) 1977.

Michael John (Mike) LLEWELLYN B Clydach (Glamorgan) 27/11/1953. LHB, OB. Debut 1970 at age of 16 years 202 days. Cap 1977. Gillette Man of the Match awards: 1. Benson & Hedges Gold awards: 2. HS: 129* v Oxford U (Oxford) 1977. HSGC: 62 v Middlesex (Lord's) 1977. HSJPL: 79* v Glos (Bristol) 1977. HSBH: 63 v Hants (Swansea) 1973. BB: 4–35 v Oxford U (Oxford) 1970.

Barry John LLOYD B Neath 6/9/1953. RHB, OB. Formerly on MCC groundstaff. Debut 1972. HS: 45* v Hants (Portsmouth) 1973. HSJPL: 13 v Derbyshire (Swansea) 1976 and 13 v Leics (Leicester) 1979. BB: 4–49 v Hants (Portsmouth) 1973. BBJPL: 3–32 v Lancs (Cardiff) 1979. Trained as a teacher at Bangor Normal College.

Andrew James (Andy) MACK B Aylsham (Norfolk) 14/1/1956. 6ft 5in tall. LHB, LM. Joined Surrey staff 1973. Played in five John Player League matches in 1975. Debut for Surrey 1976. Left county after 1977 season and made debut for Glamorgan in 1978. HS: 18 v Indians (Swansea) 1979. HSJPL: 16 Surrey v Hants (Southampton) 1977. BB: 4–28 v Worcs (Worcester) 1978. BBJPL: 3–48 Surrey v Hants (Southampton) 1977. BBBH: 3–34 Surrey v Combined Universities (Oval) 1976.

Malcolm Andrew NASH (Wells Cathedral School) B Abergavenny (Monmouthshire) 9/5/1945. LHB, LM. Debut 1966. Cap 1969. Benefit (£18,000) in 1978. Benson & Hedges Gold awards: 3. Hat-trick in John Player League v Worcs (Worcester) 1975. HS: 130 v Surrey (Oval) 1976. HSGC: 51 v Lincs (Swansea) 1974. HSJPL: 68 v Essex (Purfleet) 1972. HSBH: 103* v Hants (Swansea) 1976. BB: 9–56 (14–137 match) v Hants (Basingstoke) 1975. BBGC: 3–14 v Staffs (Stoke) 1971. BBJPL: 6–29 v Worcs (Worcester) 1975. BBBH: 4–12 v Surrey (Cardiff) 1975.

Rodney Craig ONTONG (Selborne College, East London) B Johannesburg, South Africa 9/9/1955. RHB, RFM. Debut 1972–73 for Border in Currie Cup competition. Debut for county 1975 after being on MCC staff. Transferred to Transvaal for 1976–77 season. Cap 1979. Scored 1,157 runs (av 34.02) in 1979. Benson and Hedges Gold awards: 1. HS: 135* v Warwickshire (Birmingham) 1979. HSGC: 64 v Somerset (Cardiff) 1978. HSJPL: 55 v Lancs (Cardiff) 1979. HSBH: 50* v Glos (Swansea) 1979. BB: 7–60 Border v Northern Transvaal (Pretoria) 1975–76. BBUK: 5–40 v Glos (Cardiff) 1979. BBJPL: 4–31 v Middlesex (Lord's) 1979. BBBH: 4–28 v Worcs (Cardiff) 1979.

GLAMORGAN

PARVEZ JAMIL MIR B Dacca, East Pakistan 24/9/1953. 5ft 6ins tall. RHB, RM. Debut 1970–71 for Rawalpindi Blues. Member of 1975 Pakistan Prudential Cup side. Debut for Derbyshire in 1975. One match v Oxford University. Has played subsequently as a league professional. Debut for county 1979. One match v Sri Lankans (Cardiff). HS: 155 Punjab v Sind (Lahore) 1977–78. HSUK: 57* Derbyshire v Oxford U (Burton-on-Trent) 1975. BB: 6–39 Lahore A v Sargodha (Lahore) 1975–76.

Neil James PERRY B Sutton (Surrey) 27/5/1958. RHB, SLA. On Surrey staff 1977. Joined county 1978. Debut 1979. BB: 3–51 v Indians (Swansea) 1979.

Gwyn RICHARDS B Maesteg 29/11/1951. RHB, OB. Formerly on MCC staff. Debut 1971. Cap 1976. Benson & Hedges Gold awards: 2. HS: 102* v Yorks (Middlesbrough) 1976. HSGC: 18 v Surrey (Cardiff) 1977 and 18 v Kent (Swansea) 1979. HSJPL: 73 v Glos (Cardiff) 1978. HSBH: 52 v Hants (Swansea) 1975. BB: 5–55 v Somerset (Taunton) 1978. BBJPL: 5–29 v Lancs (Swansea) 1977.

John Gregory THOMAS (Cwmtawe School, Swansea) B Garnswllt (Glamorgan) 12/8/1960. 6ft 3ins tall. RHB, RM. Debut 1979. One match v Sri Lankans (Swansea) HS: 34 v Sri Lankans (Swansea) 1979. Training as a teacher at Cardiff College of Education.

Alan Haydn WILKINS (Whitchurch HS, Cardiff) B Cardiff 22/8/1953. RHB, LM. Played in two John Player League matches in 1975. Debut 1976. HS: 70 v Notts (Worksop) 1977. HSGC: 18* v Somerset (Cardiff) 1978. BB: 6–79 v Hants (Southampton) 1979. BBJPL: 5–23 v Warwickshire (Birmingham) 1978. BBBH: 5–17 v Worcs (Worcester) 1978. Trained as a teacher at Loughborough College of Education.

N.B. The following player whose particulars appeared in the 1979 Annual has been omitted: P. D. Swart (returned to league cricket). His career record will be found elsewhere in this Annual.

In addition C. L. Smith who made his debut for the county in 1979 has joined Hampshire and his particulars will be found under that county.

COUNTY AVERAGES

Schweppes Championship: Played 21, won 0, drawn 11, lost 10, abandoned 1
All first-class matches: Played 24, won 1, drawn 12, lost 11, abandoned 1

BATTING AND FIELDING

Cap		M	I	NO	Runs	HS	Avge	100	50	Ct	St
1979	R. C. Ontong	23	41	7	1157	135*	34.02	3	7	8	—
1962	A, Jones	22	40	0	1198	115	29.95	2	8	12	—
1979	P. D. Swart	21	36	5	918	122	29.61	1	4	15	—
1977	J. A. Hopkins	23	42	1	1174	94	28.63	—	8	18	—
—	D. A. Francis	15	26	7	446	56*	23.47	—	1	3	—
—	G. C. Holmes	10	14	3	246	100*	22.36	1	—	1	—
—	A. L. Jones	15	27	3	498	83	20.75	—	4	10	—
1977	M. J. Llewellyn	10	15	1	285	106*	20.35	1	1	4	—
—	B. J. Lloyd	15	26	6	293	43	15.42	—	—	13	—
1967	A. E. Cordle	22	28	6	316	51	14.36	—	1	12	—
1967	E. W. Jones	21	34	6	368	108	13.14	1	—	39	3
1976	G. Richards	10	13	1	155	34	12.91	—	3	5	—
1969	M. A. Nash	9	11	0	123	41	11.18	—	—	5	—
—	A. H. Wilkins	10	12	2	81	43	8.10	—	1	1	—
1979	R. N. S. Hobbs	19	21	7	111	29	7.92	—	—	12	—
—	A. J. Mack	8	12	4	35	18	4.37	—	2	2	—
—	N. J. Perry	6	6	3	8	5*	2.66	—	—	1	—

Played in one match: T. Davies did not bat (3 ct); Parvez Mir 10, 6; C.L. Smith 67, 14* (1 ct); J. G. Thomas 34.

BOWLING	Type	O	M	R	W	Avge	Best	5 wl	10 wM
G. Richards	OB	57	15	164	9	18.22	3–14	—	—
A. H. Wilkins	LM	248.5	56	717	30	23.90	6–79	3	—
A. E. Cordle	RFM	609.3	133	1604	58	27.65	6–49	1	—
G. C. Holmes	RM	41.9	9	201	7	28.71	4–78	—	—
R. C. Ontong	RFM	302	62	927	32	28.96	5–40	2	—
P. D. Swart	RM	234.3	48	673	21	32.04	4–61	—	—
R. N. S. Hobbs	LBG	269.3	77	805	22	36.59	3–21	—	—
M. A. Nash	LM	226.3	66	619	16	38.68	4–50	—	—
A. J. Mack	LM	176.3	27	552	14	40.85	4–62	—	—
B. J. Lloyd	OB	396.1	89	1102	26	42.38	4–55	—	—
N. J. Perry	SLA	174.4	39	563	13	43.30	3–51	—	—

Also bowled: Parvez Mir 4–0–21–0; J. G. Thomas 25–4–132–1.

Details of Featherstone and Jones will be found on page 240.

County Records

First-class cricket

Highest innings totals:	For —587–8d v Derbyshire (Cardiff)		1951
	Agst—653–6d by Gloucestershire (Bristol)		1928
Lowest innings totals:	For —22 v Lancashire (Liverpool)		1924
	Agst—33 by Leicestershire (Ebbw Vale)		1965
Highest individual innings:	For —287* E. Davies v Gloucestershire (Newport)		1939
	Agst—302* W. R. Hammond for Gloucs (Bristol)		1934
	302 W. R. Hammond for Gloucs (Newport)		1939
Best bowling in an innings	For —10–51 J. Mercer v Worcs (Worcester)		1936
	Agst—10–18 G. Geary for Leics (Pontypridd)		1929
Best bowling in a match:	For —17–212 J. C. Clay v Worcs (Swansea)		1937
	Agst—16–96 G. Geary for Leics (Pontypridd)		1929
Most runs in a season:	2071 (av 49.30) W. G. A. Parkhouse		1959
runs in a career:	28,921 (av 32.72) A. Jones		1957–1979
100s in a season:	7 by W. G. A. Parkhouse		1950
100s in a career:	44 by A. Jones		1957–1979
wickets in a season:	176 (av 17.34) J. C. Clay		1937
wickets in a career:	2174 (av 20.95) D. J. Shepherd		1950–1972

RECORD WICKET STANDS

1st	330	A. Jones & R. C. Fredericks v Northamptonshire (Swansea)	1972
2nd	238	A. Jones & A. R. Lewis v Sussex (Hastings)	1962
3rd	313	E. Davies & W. E. Jones v Essex (Brentwood)	1948
4th	263	G. Lavis & C. Smart v Worcestershire (Cardiff)	1934
5th	264	M. Robinson & S. W. Montgomery v Hampshire (Bournemouth)	1949
6th	230	W. E. Jones & B. L. Muncer v Worcestershire (Worcester)	1953
7th	195*	W. Wooller & W. E. Jones v Lancashire (Liverpool)	1947
8th	202	D. Davies & J. J. Hills v Sussex (Eastbourne)	1928
9th	203*	J. J. Hills & J. C. Clay v Worcestershire (Swansea)	1929
10th	131*	C. Smart & W. D. Hughes v South Africans (Cardiff)	1935

GLOUCESTER

One-day cricket

Highest innings totals:	Gillette Cup	283–3 v Warwickshire (Birmingham)	1976
	John Player League	266–6 v Northants (Wellingborough)	1975
	Benson & Hedges Cup	245–7 v Hampshire (Swansea)	1976
Lowest innings totals:	Gillette Cup	76 v Northants (Northampton)	1968
	John Player League	42 v Derbyshire (Swansea)	1979
	Benson & Hedges Cup	68 v Lancs (Manchester)	1973
Highest individual innings:	Gillette Cup	124* A. Jones v Warwickshire (Birmingham)	1976
	John Player League:	110* A. Jones v Glos. (Cardiff)	1978
	Benson & Hedges Cup	103* M. A. Nash v Hants (Swansea)	1976
Best bowling figures:	Gillette Cup	5–21 P. M. Walker v Cornwall (Truro)	1970
	John Player League	6–29 M. A. Nash v Worcs (Worcester)	1975
	Benson & Hedges Cup	5–17 A. H. Wilkins v Worcestershire (Worcester)	1978

GLOUCESTERSHIRE

Formation of present club: 1871.
Colours: Blue, gold, brown, silver, green and red.
Badge: Coat of Arms of the City and County of Bristol.
County Champions: (3) 1874, 1876 and 1877.
Joint Champions: 1873.
Gillette Cup Winners: 1973.
Best Position in John Player League: 6th in 1969, 1973 and 1977.
Benson & Hedges Cup Winners: 1977.
Gillette Man of the Match awards: 17.
Benson & Hedges Gold awards: 19.

Secretary: A. S. Brown, County Ground, Nevil Road, Bristol, BS7 9EJ.
Captain: M. J. Procter.
Prospects of Play telephone Nos.: Bristol (0272) 48461
Cheltenham (0242) 22000.

Philip BAINBRIDGE (Hanley HS and Stoke-on-Trent Sixth Form College) B Stoke-on-Trent 16/4/1958. RHB, RM, Played for four 2nd XI's in 1976 – Derbyshire, Glos, Northants and Warwickshire. Debut 1977. HS: 81* v Indians (Bristol) 1979. HSJPL: 20 v Warwickshire (Birmingham) 1978. BBJPL: 3–15 v Surrey (Cheltenham) 1979. Trained as a teacher at Borough Road College of Education.

Brian Maurice BRAIN (King's School, Worcester), B Worcester 13/9/1940. RHB, RFM. Debut for Worcs 1959. Left staff in 1960. Rejoined staff in 1963 and reappeared in 1964. Cap 1966. Left staff in 1971, but rejoined in 1973. Not re-engaged after 1975 season and joined Glos in 1976. Cap 1977. Gillette Man of the Match awards: 1 (for Worcs). HS: 57 v Essex (Cheltenham) 1976. HSGC: 21* Worcs v Sussex (Worcester) 1967. HSJPL: 33 v Kent (Canterbury) 1978. HSBH: 16 v Warwickshire (Bristol) 1978. BB: 8–55 Worcs v Essex (Worcester) 1975. BBGC: 7–51 v Australians (Bristol) 1977. BBGC: 4–13 Worcs v Durham (Chester-le-Street) 1968. BBJPL: 4–27 Worcs v Somerset (Taunton) 1970. BBBH: 4–30 v Somerset (Bristol) 1977.

Andrew James (Andy) BRASSINGTON B Bagnall (Staffordshire) 9/8/1954. RHB, WK. Debut 1974. Cap 1978. HS: 28 v Glamorgan (Cardiff) 1975. HSGC: 20 v Hants (Bristol) 1979. Plays soccer as a goalkeeper.

Brian Christopher (Chris) BROAD (Colston's School, Bristol) B Bristol 29/9/1957. 6ft 4ins tall. LHB, RM. Played for 2nd XI since 1976. Debut 1979. Shared in first wkt. partnerships of 126 and 89 with S. J. Windaybank in their debut match v Cambridge U. (Cambridge). HS: 129 v Northants (Bristol) 1979. HSJPL: 22 v Derbyshire (Bristol) 1979. HSBH: 39 v Glamorgan (Swansea) 1979. Trained as a teacher at St Paul's College, Cheltenham.

John Henry CHILDS B Plymouth 15/8/1951. LHB, SLA. Played for Devon 1973–74. Debut 1975. Cap 1977. HS: 12 v Derbyshire (Ilkeston) 1977. HSJPL: 11* v Essex (Cheltenham) 1975. HSBH: 10 v Somerset (Bristol) 1979. BB: 8–34 v Hants (Basingstoke) 1978. BBJPL: 4–15 v Northants (Northampton) 1976.

David Anthony GRAVENEY (Millfield School) B Bristol 2/1/1953. Son of J. K. R. Graveney, RHB, SLA. Debut 1972. Cap 1976. HS: 92 v Warwickshire (Birmingham) 1978. HSGC: 44 v Surrey (Bristol) 1973. HSJPL: 44 v Essex (Cheltenham) 1975. HSBH: 21 v Somerset (Street) 1975. BB: 8–85 v Notts (Cheltenham) 1974. BBGC: 3–67 v Leics (Leicester) 1975. BBJPL: 4–22 v Hants (Lydney) 1974. BBBH: 3–32 v Middlesex (Bristol) 1977.

Alastair James HIGNELL (Denstone College and Cambridge) B Cambridge 4/9/1955. RHB, LB. Scored 117* and 78* for England Schools v All India Schools (Birmingham) 1973 and 133 for England Young Cricketers v West Indies Young Cricketers (Arundel) 1974. Debut 1974. Cap 1977. Blue 1975–76–77–78. Captain in last two years. 1,000 runs (2)—1,140 runs (av 30.81) in 1976 best. Scored two centuries in match (108 and 145) for Cambridge U v Surrey (Cambridge) 1978. Benson & Hedges Gold awards: 1 (for Combined Universities). HS: 149 Cambridge U v Glamorgan (Cambridge) 1977 and 149* v Northants (Bristol) 1979. HSGC: 85* v Northants (Bristol) 1977. HSJPL: 51 v Northants (Northampton) 1976. HSBH: 63 Combined Universities v Worcs (Worcester) 1978. Blue for rugby 1974–75 (captain)–76–77 (captain). Plays for Bristol. Toured Australia with England Rugby team 1975. 14 caps for England between 1975 and 1978–79.

Martin David PARTRIDGE (Marling School, Stroud) B Birdlip (Glos) 25/10/1954. LHB, RM. Debut 1976. HS: 90 v Notts (Nottingham) 1979. HSJPL: 33 v Warwickshire (Moreton-in-Marsh) 1978. HSBH: 27 v Warwickshire (Bristol) 1978. BB: 5–29 v Worcs (Worcester) 1979. BBJPL: 5–47 v Kent (Cheltenham) 1977. Studied civil engineering at Bradford University.

GLOUCESTER

Michael John (Mike) PROCTER (Hilton College, Natal) B Durban 15/9/1946. RHB, RF/OB. Vice-captain of South African Schools team to England 1963. Debut for county 1965 in one match v South Africans. Returned home to make debut for Natal in 1965–66 Currie Cup competition. Joined staff in 1968. Cap 1968. *Wisden* 1969. Transferred to Western Province for 1969–70 Currie Cup competition, Rhodesia in 1970–71 and Natal 1976–77. Appointed county captain in 1977. Benefit (£15,500) in 1976. Tests: 7 for South Africa v Australia 1966–67 and 1969–70. Played in 5 matches for Rest of World v England in 1970. 1,000 runs (8)—1,786 runs (av 45.79) in 1971 best. 100 wkts (2)—109 wkts (av 18.04) in 1977 best. Scored 6 centuries in 6 consecutive innings for Rhodesia 1970–71 to equal world record. Scored two centuries in match (114 and 131) for Rhodesia v International Wanderers (Salisbury) 1972–73. Hat-tricks (4): v Essex (Westcliff) 1972—all lbw—and also scored a century in the match, v Essex (Southend) 1977, v Leics (Bristol) 1979 and also scored a century, and in next match v Yorks (Cheltenham) 1979 – all lbw. Also v Hants (Southampton) in Benson & Hedges Cup, 1977. Had match double of 100 runs and 10 wkts (108 and 13–73) v Worcs (Cheltenham) 1977. Gillette Man of the Match awards: 2. Benson & Hedges Gold awards: 6. HS: 254 Rhodesia v Western Province (Salisbury) 1970–71. HSUK: 203 v Essex (Gloucester) 1978. HSTC: 48 South Africa v Australia (Cape Town) 1969–70. HSGC: 107 v Sussex (Hove) 1971. HSJPL: 109 v Warwickshire (Cheltenham) 1972. HSBH: 154* v Somerset (Taunton) 1972. BB: 9–71 Rhodesia v Transvaal (Bulawayo) 1972–73. BBUK: 8–30 v Worcs (Worcester) 1978. BBTC: 6–73 South Africa v Australia (Port Elizabeth) 1969–70. BBGC: 4–21 v Yorks (Leeds) 1977. BBJPL: 5–8 v Middlesex (Gloucester) 1977. BBBH: 6–13 v Hants (Southampton) 1977.

SADIQ MOHAMMAD B Junagadh (India) 3/5/1945. LHB, LBG. Youngest of family of five cricket-playing brothers which includes Hanif and Mushtaq Mohammad. Debut in Pakistan 1959–60 at age of 14 years 9 months and has played subsequently for various Karachi sides, Pakistan International Airways and United Bank. Played for Northants 2nd XI in 1967 and 1968, for Nelson in Lancs League in 1968, and subsequently for Poloc, Glasgow in Scottish Western Union. Played for D. H. Robins' XI v Oxford U 1969 and for Essex v Jamaica XI in 1970. Debut for county 1972. Cap 1973. Played for Tasmania against MCC in 1974–75. Tests: 35 for Pakistan between 1969–70 and 1978–79. Tours: Pakistan to England 1971, 1974 and 1978. Australia and New Zealand 1972–73, Australia and West Indies 1976–77, India 1979–80, 1,000 runs (6)—1,759 runs (av 47.54) in 1976 best. Scored 1,169 runs (av 41.75) in Australia and New Zealand 1972–73. Scored 4 centuries in 4 consecutive innings in 1976 including two centuries in match (163* and 150) v Derbyshire (Bristol). Also scored two centuries in match (171 and 103) v Glamorgan (Bristol) 1979. Gillette Man of Match awards: 1. Benson & Hedges Gold awards: 3. HS: 184* v New Zealanders (Bristol) 1973. HSTC: 166 Pakistan v New Zealand (Wellington) 1972–73. HSGC: 122 v Lancs (Manchester) 1975. HSJPL: 131 v Somerset (Imperial Ground, Bristol) 1975. HSBH: 128 v Minor Counties (South) (Bristol) 1974. BB: 7–34 United Bank v Universities (Peshawar) 1978–79. BBUK: 5–37 v Kent (Bristol) 1973. BBGC: 3–19 v Oxfordshire (Bristol) 1975. BBJPL: 3–27 v Hants (Bristol) 1972. BBBH: 3–20 v Minor Counties (South) (Bristol) 1972.

Brian Keith SHANTRY (Whitefield Fishponds Comprehensive School) B Bristol 26/5/1955. 6ft 3ins. tall. LHB, LFM. Played for county 2nd XI in 1976 and Warwickshire 2nd XI in 1977. Debut 1978. Played in one match and three John Player league matches in 1979 before having operation for brain tumour.

Andrew Willis STOVOLD (Filton HS) B Bristol 19/3/1953. RHB, WK. Toured West Indies with England Young Cricketers 1972. Played for 2nd XI since 1971. Debut 1973. Cap 1976. Played for Orange Free State in 1974–75 and 1975–76.

Currie Cup competition. 1,000 runs (3)—1,388 runs (av 36.52) in 1979 best. Benson & Hedges Gold awards: 4. HS: 196 v Notts (Nottingham) 1977. HSGC: 45 v Lancs (Manchester) 1978. HSJPL: 98* v Kent (Cheltenham) 1977. HSBH: 104 v Leics (Leicester) 1977.

Martin Willis STOVOLD (Thornbury GS) B Bristol 28/12/1955. Younger brother of A. W. Stovold. LHB. Played in one John Player League match v Essex (Gloucester) 1978. Debut 1979. HS: 27 v Worcs (Worcester) 1979. Trained as a teacher at Loughborough College.

Stephen James WINDAYBANK (Cotham GS) B Pinner (Middlesex) 20/10/1956. RHB: Played for 2nd XI in 1978. Debut 1979. Two matches. Shared in first wkt. partnership of 126 and 89 with B. C. Broad in their debut match v Cambridge U (Cambridge). HS: 53 v Cambridge U (Cambridge) 1979.

Syed ZAHEER ABBAS B Sialkot (Pakistan) 24/7/1947. RHB, OB. Wears glasses. Debut for Karachi Whites 1965–66. subsequently playing for Pakistan International Airways. *Wisden* 1971. Debut for county 1972. Cap 1975. Tests: 33 for Pakistan between 1969–70 and 1978–79. Played in 5 matches for Rest of the World v Australia 1971–72. Tours: Pakistan to England 1971 and 1974, Australia and New Zealand 1972–73, Australia and West Indies 1976–77, New Zealand and Australia 1978–79, India 1979–80. Rest of World to Australia 1971–72. 1,000 runs (8)—2,554 runs (av 75.11) in 1976 best. Scored 1,597 runs (av 84.05) in Pakistan 1973–74—the record aggregate for a Pakistan season. Scored 4 centuries in 4 consecutive innings in 1970–71. Scored two centuries in a match twice in 1976–216* and 156* v Surrey (Oval) and 230* and 104* v Kent (Canterbury) and once in 1977—205* and 108* v Sussex (Cheltenham) to create record of being only player ever to score a double-century and a century in a match on three occasions. Was dismissed, hit the ball twice, for Pakistan International Airways v Karachi Blues (Karachi) 1969–70. Gillette Man of Match awards: 4. HS: 274 Pakistan v England (Birmingham) 1971. HSC: 230* v Kent (Canterbury) 1977. HSGC: 131* v Leics (Leicester) 1975. HSJPL: 114* v Hants (Bristol) 1976. HSBH: 98 v Surrey (Oval) 1975. BB: 5–15 Dawood Club v Railways (Lahore) 1975–76.

N.B. The following players whose particulars appeared in the 1979 Annual have been omitted: J. Davey (retired), N. H. Finan (not re-engaged), J. C. Foat (not re-engaged), T. M. G. Hansell, D. R. Shepherd (retired) and S. Williams. In addition M. A. Garnham has joined Leicestershire and his particulars will be found under that county.

The career records of Finan, Foat, Garnham and Shepherd will be found elsewhere in this Annual.

COUNTY AVERAGES

Schweppes Championship: Played 20, won 5, drawn 11, lost 4, abandoned 2
All first-class matches: Played 23, won 6, drawn 13, lost 4, abandoned 2

BATTING AND FIELDING

Cap		M	I	NO	Runs	HS	Avge	100	50	Ct	St
1973	Sadiq Mohammad	17	30	2	1595	171	56.96	8	5	16	—
1975	Zaheer Abbas	17	30	2	1304	151*	46.57	3	8	9	—
1968	M. J. Procter	21	36	4	1241	122	38.78	3	7	11	—
—	B. C. Broad	9	16	2	512	129	36.57	1	2	3	—
1976	A. W. Stovold	22	39	1	1388	156	36.52	1	10	18	—
1977	A. J. Hignell	16	27	6	736	149*	35.04	2	3	19	—
—	M. D. Partridge	23	31	10	717	90	34.14	—	6	8	—
1979	J. C. Foat	10	17	2	463	126	30.86	2	1	5	—
1969	D. R. Shepherd	8	10	2	223	70	27.87	—	1	—	—
—	M. A. Garnham	3	4	2	50	21	25.00	—	2	2	—
1976	D. A. Graveney	22	27	10	301	56*	17.70	—	1	5	—
—	P. Bainbridge	8	14	2	149	81*	12.41	—	1	1	—
—	M. W. Stovold	7	10	1	84	27	9.33	—	1	1	—
1977	J. H. Childs	21	15	9	47	9	7.83	—	—	5	—
1977	B. M. Brain	23	18	0	123	24	6.83	—	—	3	—
1978	A. J. Brassington	20	21	8	74	17	5.69	—	—	17	4
—	N. H. Finan	3	1	1	4	4*	—	—	—	—	—

Played in two matches: S. J. Windaybank 53, 35, 13.
Played in one match: B. K. Shantry did not bat.

BOWLING

	Type	O	M	R	W	Avge	Best	5 wI	10 wM
M. J. Procter	RF/OB	574.5	140	1532	81	18.91	8–30	7	1
B. M. Brain	RFM	495.5	125	1355	49	27.65	5–33	2	—
D. A. Graveney	SLA	417	98	1311	39	33.61	5–39	3	1
P. Bainbridge	RM	72	19	240	7	34.28	2–30	—	—
J. H. Childs	SLA	658.3	195	1861	48	38.77	5–118	1	—
M. D. Partridge	RM	296.4	51	1072	21	51.04	5–29	1	—

Also bowled: N. H. Finan 16–4–61–0; J. C. Foat 4–0–17–0; A. J. Hignell 1–0–4–0
Sadiq Mohammad 48–7–180–4; A. W. Stovold. 13.4–4–39–1; Zaheer Abbas 2–0–2–0.

County Records

First-class cricket

Highest innings totals:	For —653–6d v Glamorgan (Bristol)	1928
	Agst—774–7d by Australians (Bristol)	1948
Lowest innings totals:	For —17 v Australians (Cheltenham)	1896
	Agst—12 by Northamptonshire (Gloucester)	1907
Highest individual innings:	For —318* W. G. Grace v Yorkshire (Cheltenham)	1876
	Agst—296 A. O. Jones for Notts (Nottingham)	1903
Best bowling in an innings:	For —10–40 G. Dennett v Essex (Bristol)	1906
	Agst—10–66 A. A. Mailey for Aust (Cheltenham)	1921
	and K. Smales for Notts (Stroud)	1956
Best bowling in a match:	For —17–56 C. W. L. Parker v Essex (Gloucester)	1925
	Agst—15–87 A. J. Conway for Worcestershire (Moreton-in-Marsh)	1914

Most runs in a season:	2860 (av 69.75) W. R. Hammond	1933
runs in a career:	33664 (av 57.05) W. R. Hammond	1920–1951
100s in a season:	13 by W. R. Hammond	1938
100s in a career:	113 by W. R. Hammond	1920–1951
wickets in a season:	222 (av 16.80 & 16.37)	
100s in a career:	113 by W. R. Hammond	1920–1951
wickets in a season:	222 (av 16.80 & 16.37)	
	T. W. J. Goddard	1937 & 1947
wickets in a career:	3171 (Av 19.43) C. W. L. Parker	1903–1935

RECORD WICKET STANDS

1st	395	D. M. Young & R. B. Nicholls v Oxford U (Oxford)	1962
2nd	256	C. T. M. Pugh & T. W. Graveney v Derbyshire (Chesterfield)	1960
3rd	336	W. R. Hammond & B. H. Lyon v Leicestershire	
		(Leicester)	1933
4th	321	W. R. Hammond & W. L. Neale v Leicestershire	
		(Gloucester)	1937
5th	261	W. G. Grace & W. O. Moberley v Yorkshire (Cheltenham)	1876
6th	320	G. L. Jessop & J. H. Board v Sussex (Hove)	1902
7th	248	W. G. Grace & E. L. Thomas v Sussex (Hove)	1896
8th	239	W. R. Hammond & A. E. Wilson v Lancashire (Bristol)	1938
9th	193	W. G. Grace & S. A. Kitcat v Sussex (Bristol)	1896
10th	131	W. R. Gouldsworthy & J. G. Bessant v Somerset (Bristol)	1923

One-day cricket

Highest innings totals:	Gillette Cup	327–7 v Berkshire (Reading)	1966
	John Player League	255 v Somerset (Imperial Ground, Bristol)	1975
	Benson & Hedges Cup	282 v Hants (Bristol)	1974
Lowest innings totals:	Gillette Cup	86 v Sussex (Hove)	1969
	John Player League	49 v Middlesex (Bristol)	1978
	Benson & Hedges Cup	62 v Hants (Bristol)	1975
Highest individual innings:	Gillette Cup	131* Zaheer Abbas v Leics (Leicester)	1975
	John Player League	131 Sadiq Mohammad v Somerset (Imperial Ground, Bristol)	1975
	Benson & Hedges Cup	154* M. J. Procter v Somerset (Taunton)	1972
Best bowling figures:	Gillette Cup	5–39 R. D. V. Knight v Surrey (Bristol)	1971
	John Player League	5–8 M. J. Procter v Middlesex (Gloucester)	1977
	Benson & Hedges Cup	6–13 M. J. Procter v Hampshire (Southampton	1977

HAMPSHIRE

Formation of present club: 1863.
Colours: Blue, gold, and white.
Badge: Tudor rose and crown.
County Champions (2): 1961 and 1973.
Gillette Cup semi-finalists (2): 1966 and 1976.
John Player League Champions (2): 1975 and 1978.
Benson & Hedges Cup semi-finalists: 1975 and 1977.
Fenner Trophy Winners (3): 1975, 1976 and 1977.
Gillette Man of the Match awards: 24.
Benson & Hedges Gold awards: 22.

Secretary: A. K. James, County Cricket Ground,
   Northlands Road, Southampton, SO9, 2TY.

Captain: N. E. J. Pocock.,

Prospects of play telephone nos.: Southampton (0703) 24155, Bournemouth (0202)
25872, Basingstoke (0256) 3646.

   Michael John BAILEY (Cheltenham GS) B Cheltenham 1/8/1954. LHB, OB.
Played for Glos 2nd XI 1974 and for county 2nd XI in 1978. Debut 1979. HS: 24 v
Surrey (Portsmouth) 1979.

   Nigel Geoffrey COWLEY B Shaftesbury (Dorset) 1/3/1953. RHB, OB. Debut
1974. Cap 1978. HS: 109* v Somerset (Taunton) 1977. HSGC: 63* v Glos (Bristol)
1979. HSJPL: 47 v Notts (Nottingham) 1978. HSBH: 59 v Glos (Southampton)
1977. BB: 5–44 v Derbyshire (Basingstoke) 1979. HBGC: 4–20 v Middlesex
(Lord's) 1979. BBJPL: 3–19 v Glos (Cheltenham) 1978.

   Cuthbert Gordon GREENIDGE B St Peter, Barbados 1/5/1951. RHB, RM.
Debut 1970. Cap 1972. Has subsequently played for Barbados. *Wisden* 1976 Tests:
19 for West Indies between 1974–75 and 1977–78. Tours: West Indies to India, Sri
Lanka and Pakistan 1974–75, Australia 1975–76, England 1976, Australia and New
Zealand 1979–80. 1,000 runs (9)—1,952 runs (av 55.77) in 1976 best. Scored two
centuries in match (134 and 101) West Indies v England (Manchester) 1976, and
(136 and 120) v Kent (Bournemouth) 1978. Gillette Man of Match awards: 3.
Benson & Hedges Gold awards: 4. HS: 273* D. H. Robins' XI v Pakistan (Eastbourne) 1974. HSC: 259 v Sussex (Southampton) 1975. HSTC: 134 West Indies v
England (Manchester) 1976. HSGC: 177 v Glamorgan (Southampton)
1975—record for all one day competitions. HSJPL: 163* v Warwickshire (Birmingham) 1979—record for competition. HSBH: 173* v Minor Counties (South) (Amersham) 1973—record for competition—and shared in partnership of 285* for second
wicket with D. R. Turner—the record partnership for all one-day competitons. BB:
5–49 v Surrey (Southampton) 1971.

   Richard Edward HAYWARD B Hillingdon (Middlesex) 15/2/1954. RHB. Played
for Buckinghamshire in 1978 and 1979. Debut 1979 for Minor Counties v Indians
(Wellington). Has joined Hants for 1980.

   Trevor Edward JESTY B Gosport 2/6/1948. RHB, RM. Debut 1966. Cap 1971.
Played for Border in 1973–74 and Griqualand West in 1974–75 and 1975–76 Currie
Cup competitions. 1,000 runs (4)—1,288 runs (av 35.77) in 1976 best. Gillette Man
of Match awards: 2. Benson & Hedges Gold awards: 5. Took 3 wkts in 4 balls v
Somerset (Portsmouth) 1969. HS: 159* v Somerset (Bournemouth) 1976. HSGC:
69 v Yorks (Bournemouth) 1977. HSJPL: 107 v Surrey (Southampton) 1977.
HSBH: 105 v Glamorgan (Swansea) 1977. BB: 7–75 v Worcs (Southampton) 1976.
BBGC: 6–46 v Glos (Bristol) 1979. BBJPL: 6–20 v Glamorgan (Cardiff) 1975.
BBBH: 4–28 v Somerset (Taunton) 1974.

Steven John MALONE (King's School, Ely) B Chelmsford 19/10/1953. RHB, RM. Debut for Essex 1975 playing in one match v Cambridge U (Cambridge). Re-appeared in corresponding match in 1978. Did not play in 1979 and has joined Hants for 1980.

Malcolm Denzil MARSHALL (Parkinson Comprehensive School, Barbados), B St. Michael, Barbados 18/4/1958. RHB, RFM. Debut for Barbados 1977–78 in last match of Shell Shield competition. Debut for county 1979. Tests: 3 in 1978–79 Tours: West Indies to India and Sri Lanka 1978–79, Australia and New Zealand 1979–80. HS: 59 West Indians v West Zone (Baroda) 1978–79. HSUK: 38 v Surrey (Oval) 1979. HSTC: 5 West Indies v India (Bangalore) 1978–79. HSGC: 21* v Middlesex (Lord's) 1979. HSJPL: 20 v Middlesex (Lord's) 1979. HSBH: 15 v Derbyshire (Derby) 1979. BB: 6–42 West Indians v Karnataka (Ahmedabad) 1978–79. BBUK: 5–56 v Glos (Southampton) 1979. BBJPL: 5–13 v Glamorgan (Portsmouth) 1979.

Mark Charles Jefford NICHOLAS (Bradfield College) B London 29/9/1957. RHB, RFM. Debut 1978. HS: 105* v Oxford U (Oxford) 1979. HSJPL: 33* v Somerset (Taunton) 1979.

Nicholas Edward Julian (Nick) POCOCK (Shrewsbury School) B Maracaibo, Venezuela 15/12/1951. RHB, LM. Debut 1976. Appointed county captain for 1980. HS: 143* v Middlesex (Portsmouth) 1979. HSGC: 33 v Glos (Bristol) 1979. HSJPL: 52* v Glos (Basingstoke) 1979.

John Michael RICE (Brockley CGS, London) B Chandler's Ford (Hants) 23/10/1949. RHB, RM. On Surrey staff 1970, but not re-engaged. Debut 1971. Cap 1975. Hat-trick in John Player League v Northants (Southampton) 1975. Gillette Man of the Match awards: 1. Benson & Hedges Gold awards: 1. HS: 96* v Somerset (Weston-super-Mare) 1975. HSGC: 40 v Glos (Bristol) 1979. HSJPL: 91 v Yorks (Leeds) 1979. HSBH: 43 v Lancs (Southampton) 1977. BB: 7–48 v Worcs (Worcester) 1977. BBGC: 5–35 v Yorks (Bournemeth) 1977. BBJPL: 5–14 v Northants (Southampton) 1975, BBBH: 3–20 v Somerset (Bournemouth) 1975.

David John ROCK (Portsmouth GS) B Southsea 20/4/1957. RHB, RM. Debut 1976. HS: 114 v Leics (Leicester) 1977. HSGC: 50 v Middlesex (Lord's) 1977. HSJPL: 68 v Glos (Portsmouth) 1977. HSBH: 49 v Leics (Southampton) 1979.

Christopher Lyall (Kippy) SMITH (Northlands HS, Durban) B Durban, South Africa 15/10/1958. RHB, OB. Debut for Natal B 1977–78. One match v Rhodesia B (Pinetown). Did not play in 1978–79. Debut for Glamorgan 1979. One match v Sri Lankans (Swansea). Has joined Hants for 1980 on one-year contract. HS: 67 Glamorgan v Sri Lankans (Swansea) 1979.

John William SOUTHERN (The William Ellis School, Highgate) B King's Cross, London 2/9/1952. 6ft 3¾in tall. RHB, SLA. Debut 1975. Cap 1978. HS: 61* v Yorks (Bradford) 1979. BB: 6–46 v Glos (Bournemouth) 1975. Obtained BSc degree in Chemistry at Southampton University.

George Robert (Bob) STEPHENSON (Derby School) B Derby 19/11/1942. RHB, WK. Debut for Derbyshire 1967 following injury to R. W. Taylor. Joined Hants by special registration in 1969 following resignation of B. S. V. Timms. Cap 1969. Benefit in 1979. County captain in 1979. Benson & Hedges Gold awards: 1. Dismissed 80 batsmen (73st and 7ct) in 1970. HS: 100* v Somerset (Taunton) 1976. HSGC: 29 v Notts (Nottingham) 1972. HSJPL: 30 v Worcs (Worcester) 1976. HSBH: 29* v Somerset (Taunton) 1974. Soccer for Derby County, Shrewsbury Town and Rochdale.

HAMPSHIRE

Keith STEVENSON (Bemrose GS, Derby) B Derby 6/10/1950. RHB, RFM. Debut for Derbyshire 1974. Left county after 1977 season and made debut for Hants in 1978, cap 1979. HS: 33 Derbyshire v Northants (Chesterfield) 1974. HSC: 24 v Yorks (Bradford) 1979. HSGC: 14 Derbyshire v Surrey (Ilkeston) 1976. BB: 7–22 v Oxford U (Oxford) 1979. BBGC: 4–21 Derbyshire v Surrey (Ilkeston) 1976. BBJPL: 3–29 Derbyshire v Surrey (Chesterfield) 1975.

Michael Norman Somerset (Mike) TAYLOR (Amersham College) B Amersham (Bucks) 12/11/1942. Twin brother of D. J. S. Taylor of Somerset. RHB, RM. Played for Buckinghamshire in 1961–62. Debut for Notts 1964. Cap 1967. Not re-engaged after 1972 season and made debut for Hants in 1973. Cap 1973. Took 99 wkts (av 21.00) in 1968. Hat-trick Notts v Kent (Dover) 1965. Gillette Man of Match awards: 1. Benson & Hedges Gold awards: 1 (for Notts). HS: 105 Notts v Lancs (Nottingham) 1967. HSC: 103* v Glamorgan (Southampton) 1978. HSGC: 58 Notts v Hants (Nottingham) 1972. HSJPL: 57* v Notts (Nottingham) 1978. HSBH: 41 v Minor Counties (South) (Portsmouth) 1974. BB: 7–23 v Notts (Basingstoke) 1977. BBGC: 4–31 Notts v Lancs (Nottingham) 1968. BBJPL: 4–20 Notts v Surrey (Nottingham) 1969. BBBH: 3–15 v Somerset (Taunton) 1974.

Vivian Paul TERRY (Millfield School) B Osnabruck, West Germany 14/1/1959. RHB, RM. Played for 2nd XI since 1976. Debut 1978. HS: 21 v Warwickshire (Nuneaton) 1979. HSGC: 11 v Middlesex (Lord's) 1979. HSJPL: 33 v Glos (Basingstoke) 1979.

Timothy Maurice (Tim) TREMLET (Richard Taunton College, Southampton) B Wellington (Somerset) 26/7/1956. Son of M. F. Tremlett, former Somerset player. RHB, RM. Debut 1976. HS: 50 v Glos (Basingstoke) 1978. HSBH: 15* v Derbyshire (Derby) 1979. BBJPL: 3–19 v Kent (Canterbury) 1979. BBBH: 3–21 v Combined Universities (Cambridge) 1978.

David Roy TURNER B Chippenham (Wilts) 5/2/1949. LHB, RN. Played for Wiltshire in 1965. Debut 1966. Cap 1970. Played for Western Province in 1977–78 Currie Cup competition. 1,000 runs (6)—1,269 runs (av 36.25) in 1976 best. Gillette Man of Match awards: 1. Benson & Hedges Gold awards: 3. HS: 181* v Surrey (Oval) 1969. HSGC: 86 v Northants (Southampton) 1976. HSJPL: 99* v Glos (Bristol) 1972. HSBH: 123* v Minor Counties (South) (Amersham) 1973.

NB The following player whose particulars appeared in the 1979 annual has been omitted: A. J. Murtagh.

COUNTY AVERAGES

Schweppes Championship: Played 21, won 3, drawn 9, lost 9, abandoned 1
All first-class matches: Played 23, won 3, drawn 11, lost 9, abandoned 1

BATTING AND FIELDING

Cap		M	I	NO	Runs	HS	Avge	100	50	Ct	St
1972	C. G. Greenidge	17	30	2	1404	145	50.14	3	8	27	—
1971	T. E. Jesty	19	35	3	1100	76	34.37	—	10	16	—
1975	J. M. Rice	23	41	3	927	84*	24.39	—	4	16	—
—	M. C. J. Nicholas	4	7	1	133	105*	22.16	—	1	1	—
1970	D. R. Turner	22	39	1	815	129	21.44	1	3	3	—
1978	J. W. Southern	16	21	9	247	61*	20.58	—	1	5	—
—	N. E. J. Pocock	12	22	2	393	143*	19.65	1	—	14	—
1978	N. G. Cowley	23	39	6	611	85	18.51	—	2	7	—
1973	M. N. S. Taylor	21	30	3	495	75	18.33	—	3	9	—
—	D. J. Rock	16	27	1	473	104	18.19	1	1	8	—
—	M. J. Bailey	4	6	1	76	24	15.20	—	—	1	—
—	V. P. Terry	5	7	0	86	21	12.28	—	—	4	—
1969	G. R. Stephenson	23	33	3	333	43	11.10	—	—	31	4
—	M. D. Marshall	19	25	2	197	38	8.56	—	—	12	—
1979	K. Stevenson	23	28	15	96	24	7.38	—	—	6	—
—	T. M. Tremlett	6	11	2	51	18	5.66	—	—	3	—

BOWLING

	Type	O	M	R	W	Avge	Best	5 wI	10 wM
M. D. Marshall	RFM	467	146	1051	47	22.36	5-56	1	—
K. Stevenson	RFM	548.3	133	1567	69	22.71	7-22	4	—
M. N. S. Taylor	RM	265.5	70	746	27	27.62	5-33	1	—
T. M. Tremlett	RM	89.2	21	248	8	31.00	2-9	—	—
J. M. Rice	RM	270.4	58	760	24	31.66	5-17	1	—
J. W. Southern	SLA	370.2	120	951	29	32.79	6-81	1	—
N. G. Cowley	OB	507.4	146	1306	37	35.29	5-44	1	—

Also bowled: M. J. Bailey 50.4–9–151–3; T. E. Jesty 44–12–140–3; M. C. J. Nicholas 0.1–0–1–0; N. E. J. Pocock 7–3–25–1; G. R. Stephenson 1–1–0–0; D. R. Turner 15.2–5–66–3.

County Records

First-class cricket

Highest innings totals:	For —672–7d v Somerset (Taunton)	1899
	Agst—742 by Surrey (The Oval)	1909
Lowest innings totals:	For —15 v Warwickshire (Birmingham)	1922
	Agst—23 by Yorkshire (Middlesbrough)	1965
Highest individual innings:	For —316 R. H. Moore v Warwickshire (Bournemouth)	1937
	Agst—302* P. Holmes for Yorkshire (Portsmouth)	1920
Best bowling in an innings:	For —9–25 R. M. H. Cottam v Lancs (Manchester)	1965
	Agst—9–21 L. B. Richmond for Notts (Nottingham)	1921
Best bowling in a match:	For —16–88 J. A. Newman v Somerset (Weston super-Mare)	1927
	Agst—17–119 W. Mead for Essex (Southampton)	1895

HAMPSHIRE

Most runs in a season:	2854	(av 79.27)	C. P. Mead	1928
runs in a career:	48892	(av 48.84)	C. P. Mead	1905–1936
100s in a season:	12		by C. P. Mead	1928
100s in a career:	138		by C. P. Mead	1905–1936
wickets in a season:	190	(av 15.61)	A. S. Kennedy	1922
wickets in a career:	2669	(av 18.22)	D. Shackleton	1948–1969

RECORD WICKET STANDS

1st	249	R. E. Marshall & J. R. Gray v Middlesex (Portsmouth)	1960
2nd	321	G. Brown & E. I. M. Barrett v Gloucestershire (Southampton)	1920
3rd	344	C. P. Mead & G. Brown v Yorkshire (Portsmouth)	1927
4th	263	R. E. Marshall & D. A. Livingstone v Middlesex (Lord's)	1970
5th	235	G. Hill & D. F. Walker v Sussex (Portsmouth)	1937
6th	411	R. M. Poore & E. G. Wynyard v Somerset (Taunton)	1899
7th	325	G. Brown & C. H. Abercombie v Essex (Leyton)	1913
8th	178	C. P. Mead & C. P. Brutton v Worcestershire (Bournemouth)	1925
9th	230	D. A. Livingstone & A. T. Castell v Surrey (Southampton)	1962
10th	192	A. Bowell & W. H. Livsey v Worcestershire (Bournemouth)	1921

NB   A partnership of 334 for the first wicket by B. A. Richards, C. G. Greenidge and D. R. Turner occurred against Kent at Southampton in 1973. Richards retired hurt after 241 runs had been scored and in the absence of any official ruling on the matter, it is a matter of opinion as to whether it should be regarded as the first-wicket record for the county.

One-day cricket

Highest innings totals:	Gillette Cup	371–4 v Glamorgan (Southampton)	1975
	John Player League	288–5 v Somerset (Weston-super-Mare)	1975
	Benson & Hedges Cup	321–1 v Minor Counties (South) (Amersham)	1973
Lowest innings totals:	Gillette Cup	98 v Lancashire (Manchester)	1975
	John Player League	43 v Essex (Basingstoke)	1972
	Benson & Hedges Cup	94 v Glamorgan (Swansea)	1973
Highest individual innings:	Gillette Cup	177 C. G. Greenidge v Glamorgan (Southampton)	1975
	John Player League	163* C. G. Greenidge v Warwickshire (Birmingham)	1979
	Benson & Hedges Cup	173* C. G. Greenidge v Minor Counties (South) (Amersham)	1973
Best bowling figures:	Gillette Cup	7–30 P. J. Sainsbury v Norfolk (Southampton)	1965
	John Player League	6–20 T. E. Jesty v Glamorgan (Cardiff)	1975
	Benson & Hedges Cup	5–24 R. S. Herman v Gloucestershire (Bristol)	1975

KENT

Formation of present club: 1859, re-organised 1870.
Colours: Red and white.
Badge: White horse.
County Champions (6): 1906, 1909, 1910, 1913,
1970 and 1978.
Joint Champions: 1977.
Gillette Cup winners (2): 1967 and 1974.
Gillette Cup finalists: 1971.
John Player League Champions (3): 1972, 1973
and 1976.
Benson & Hedges Cup winners (3): 1973, 1976 and 1978.
Benson & Hedges Cup finalists: 1977.
Fenner Trophy winners (2): 1971 and 1973.
Gillette Man of the Match awards: 23.
Benson & Hedges Gold awards: 29.

Secretary: M. D. Fenner, St Lawrence Ground, Canterbury, CT1 3NZ.
Cricket Manager: J. C. T. Page
Captain: A. G. E. Ealham.

ASIF IQBAL RAZVI (Osmania University, Hyderabad, India) B Hyderabad 6/6/1943. Nephew of Ghulam Ahmed, former Indian off-break bowler and Test cricketer. RHB, RM. Debut 1959–60 for Hyderabad in Ranji Trophy. Migrated to Pakistan in 1961 and has since appeared for various Karachi teams, Pakistan International Airways and National Bank. Captained Pakistan under-25 v England under-25 in 1966–67. Debut for county and cap 1968. *Wisden* 1967. County captain in 1977. Tests: 52 for Pakistan between 1964–65 and 1978–79. Tours: Pakistan to Australia and New Zealand 1964–65, 1972–73 (vice-captain), England 1967, 1971 (vice-captain) and 1974 (vice-captain) Australia and West Indies 1976–77, India 1979–80 (captain). Pakistan Eaglets to England 1963, Pakistan 'A' to Ceylon 1964, Pakistan International Airways to East Africa 1964. 1,000 runs (6)—1,379 runs (av 39.40) in 1970 best. Scored 1,029 runs (av 41.16) in Australia and New Zealand 1972–73. Scored two centuries in match (104 and 110*) Pakistan International Airways v Habib Bank (Lahore) 1979–80. Scored 146 v England (Oval) 1967 sharing in 9th wkt partnership of 190 with Intikhab Alam after Pakistan were 65–8—record 9th wkt stand in Test cricket. Gillette Man of Match awards: 3. Benson & Hedges Gold awards: 4. HS: 196 National Bank v Pakistan International Airways (Lahore) 1976–77. HSTC: 175 Pakistan v New Zealand (Dunedin) 1972–73. HSUK: 171 v Glos (Folkestone) 1978. HSGC: 89 v Lancs (Lord's) 1971. HSJPL: 106 v Glos (Maidstone) 1976. HSBH: 75 v Middlesex (Canterbury) 1973. BB: 6–45 Pakistan Eaglets v Cambridge U (Cambridge) 1963. BBTC: 5–48 Pakistan v New Zealand (Wellington) 1964–65. BBC: 4–11 v Lancs (Canterbury) 1968. BBGC: 4–18 v Lancs (Canterbury) 1979. BBJPL: 3–3 v Northants (Tring) 1977. BBBH: 4–43 v Worcs (Lord's) 1973.

Christopher Stuart (Chris) COWDREY (Tonbridge School) B Farnborough (Kent) 20/10/1957. Eldest son of M. C. Cowdrey. RHB, RM. Played for 2nd XI at age of 15. Captain of England Young Cricketers team to West Indies 1976. Played in one John Player League match in 1976. Debut 1977. Cap 1979. Benson & Hedges Gold awards: 1. HS: 101* v Glamorgan (Swansea) 1977. HSGC: 23* v Lancs (Canterbury) 1979. HSJPL: 74 v Worcs (Worcester) 1978. HSBH: 114 v Sussex (Canterbury) 1977. BB: 3–40 v Warwickshire (Birmingham) 1979.

KENT

Graham Roy DILLEY B Dartford 18/5/1959. 6ft 3ins tall. LHB, RFM. Debut 1977. Tour: Australia and India 1979–80. HS: 81 v Northants (Northampton) 1979. BB: 6–66 v Middlesex (Lord's) 1979. BBJPL: 3–13 v Surrey (Oval) 1978.

Paul Rupert DOWNTON (Sevenoaks School) B Farnborough (Kent) 4/4/1957. Son of G. Downton, former Kent player. RHB, WK. Played for 2nd XI at age of 16. Vice-captain of England Young Cricketers team to West Indies 1976. Debut 1977. Cap 1979. Tour: Pakistan and New Zealand 1977–78. HS: 31* v Surrey (Maidstone) 1977 and 31 v Sussex (Hove) 1978. HSJPL: 19* v Worcs (Canterbury) 1979. Is studying law at Exeter University.

Alan George Ernest EALHAM B Ashford (Kent) 30/8/1944. RHB, OB. Debut 1966. Cap 1970. Appointed county captain in 1978. 1,000 runs (3)— 1,363 runs (av 34.94) in 1971 best. Held 5 catches in innings v Glos (Folkestone) 1966, all in outfield off D. L. Underwood. Gillette Man of Match awards: 1. Benson & Hedges Gold awards: 4. HS: 153 v Worcs (Canterbury) 1979. HSGC: 85* v Glamorgan (Swansea) 1979. HSJPL: 83 v Leics (Leicester) 1977. HSBH: 94* v Sussex (Canterbury) 1977.

Richard William HILLS B Borough Green (Kent) 8/1/1951. RHB, RM. Debut 1973. Cap 1977. Benson & Hedges Gold awards: 1. HS: 45 v Hants (Canterbury) 1975. HSJPL: 26 v Somerset (Maidstone) 1978, HSBH: 34 v Surrey (Canterbury) 1977. BB: 6–64 v Glos (Folkestone) 1978. BBJPL: 4–21 v Glamorgan (Cardiff) 1979. BBBH: 5–28 v Combined Universities (Oxford) 1976.

Kevin Bertram Sidney JARVIS (Springhead School, Northfleet) B Dartford 23/4/1953. 6ft 3in tall. RHB, RFM. Debut 1975. Cap 1977. Benson & Hedges Gold awards: 1. HS: 12* v Cambridge U (Canterbury) 1977 and 12 v Sussex (Hove) 1978. BB: 8–97 v Worcs (Worcester) 1978. BBGC: 3–53 v Sussex (Canterbury) 1979. BBJPL: 4–27 v Surrey (Maidstone) 1977. BBBH: 4–34 v Worcs (Lord's) 1976.

Graham William JOHNSON (Shooters Hill GS) B Beckenham 8/11/1946. RHB OB. Debut 1965. Cap 1970. 1,000 runs (3)—1,438 runs (av 31.26) in 1973 and 1,438 runs (av 35.95) in 1975 best. Gillette Man of Match awards: 1. Benson & Hedges Gold awards: 3. HS: 168 v Surrey (Oval) 1976. HSGC: 120* v Bucks (Canterbury) 1974. HSJPL: 89 v Sussex (Hove) 1976. HSBH: 85* v Minor Counties (South) (Canterbury) 1975. BB: 6–32 v Surrey (Tunbridge Wells) 1978. BBJPL: 5–26 v Surrey (Oval) 1974. Studied at London School of Economics.

Nicholas John (Nick) KEMP (Tonbridge School) B Bromley 16/12/1956. RHB, RM. Played for 2nd XI since 1974. Toured West Indies with England Young Cricketers 1976. Debut 1977. HS: 10 v Sri Lankans (Canterbury) 1979. BB: 3–83 v Pakistanis (Canterbury) 1978.

Alan Philip Eric KNOTT B Belvedere 9/4/1946. RHB, WK. Can bowl OB. Debut 1964. Cap 1965. Elected Best Young Cricketer of the Year in 1965 by Cricket Writers Club. *Wisden* 1969. Played for Tasmania 1969–70 whilst coaching there. Benefit (£27,037) in 1976. Tests: 89 between 1967 and 1977. Played in 5 matches against Rest of World in 1970. Tours: Pakistan 1966–67, West Indies 1967–68 and 1973–74, Ceylon and Pakistan 1968–69, Australia and New Zealand 1970–71, 1974–75, India, Sri Lanka and Pakistan 1972–73, India, Sri Lanka and Australia 1976–77. 1,000 runs (2)—1,209 runs (av 41.68) in 1971 best. Scored two centuries in match (127* and 118*) v Surrey (Maidstone) 1972. Gillette Man of Match awards: 2. Benson & Hedges Gold awards: 1. HS; 156 MCC v South Zone (Bangalore) 1972–73. HSUK: 144 v Sussex (Canterbury) 1976. HSTC: 135 v Australia (Nottingham) 1977. HSGC: 46 v Notts (Nottingham) 1975. HSJPL: 60 v Hants (Canterbury) 1969. HSBH: 65 v Combined Universities (Oxford) 1976. Dismissed 84 batsmen (74 ct 10 st) in 1965. 81 batsmen (73 ct 8 st) in 1966, and 98 batsmen (90 ct 8 st) in 1967. Dismissed 7 batsmen (7 ct) on debut in Test cricket v Pakistan (Nottingham) 1967. Holds record for most dismissals in Test cricket.

David NICHOLLS (Gravesend GS) B East Dereham (Norfolk) 8/12/1943. LHB, reserve WK. LB. Debut 1960. Cap 1969. Scored 1,000 runs (av 32.25) in 1971. Did not play in 1978 or 1979. Benefit in 1980. HS: 211 v Derbyshire (Folkestone) 1963. HSGC: 43 v Warwickshire (Canterbury) 1971. HSJPL: 64 v Glos (Gillingham) 1971. HSBH: 51 v Essex (Chelmsford) 1972.

Charles James Castell ROWE (King's School, Canterbury) B Hong Kong 27/11/1951. RHB, OB. Debut 1974. Cap 1977. Scored 1,065 runs (av 35.50) in 1978. HS: 147* v Sussex (Canterbury) 1979. HSGC: 18* v Somerset (Canterbury) 1978. HSJPL: 78* v Notts (Canterbury) 1977. HSBH: 40 v Combined Universities (Canterbury) 1977. BB: 6–46 v Derbyshire (Dover) 1976. BBJPL: 5–32 v Worcs (Worcester) 1976.

John Neil SHEPHERD (Alleyn's School, Barbados) B St Andrew, Barbados 9/11/1943. RHB, RM. Debut 1964–65 in one match for Barbados v Cavaliers and has played subsequently for Barbados in Shell Shield competition. Debut for county 1966. Cap 1967. Played for Rhodesia in 1975–76 Currie Cup competition. *Wisden* 1978. Benefit in 1979. Tests: 5 for West Indies in 1969 and 1970–71. Tour: West Indies to England 1969. Scored 1,157 runs (av 29.66) and took 96 wkts (av 18.72) in 1968. Gillette Man of Match awards: 1. Benson & Hedges Gold awards: 2. HS: 170 v Northants (Folkestone) 1968. HSTC: 32 West Indies v England (Lord's) 1969. HSGC: 101 v Middlesex (Canterbury) 1977. HSJPL: 94 v Hants (Southampton) 1978. HSBH: 96 v Middlesex (Lord's) 1975. BB: 8–40 West Indians v Glos. (Bristol) 1969. BBTC: 5–104 West Indies v England (Manchester) 1969. BBC: 8–83 v Lancs (Tunbridge Wells) 1977. BBGC: 4–23 v Essex (Leyton) 1972. BBJPL: 4–17 v Middlesex (Lord's) 1978. BBBH: 4–25 v Derbyshire (Lord's) 1978.

Guy Dennis SPELMAN (Sevenoaks School) B Westminster 18/10/1958. 6ft 3½ins tall. LHB, RM. Played in three John Player League matches in 1978. Has yet to appear in first-class cricket. BBJPL: 3–39 v Derbyshire (Canterbury) 1978. Is studying at Nottingham University.

Christopher James (Chris) TAVARE (Sevenoaks School and Oxford) B Orpington 27/10/1954. RHB, RM. Scored 124* for England Schools v All-India Schools (Birmingham) 1973. Debut 1974. Blue 1975–76–77. Cap 1978. 1,000 runs (3)—1,534 runs (av 45.11) in 1978 best. Benson & Hedges Gold awards: 3 (2 for Combined Universities). HS: 150* v Essex (Tunbridge Wells) 1979. HSGC: 87 v Lancs (Canterbury) 1979. HSJPL: 136* v Glos (Canterbury) 1978. HSBH: 89 Combined Universities v Surrey (Oval) 1976.

Neil TAYLOR (Cray Technical School) B Orpington 21/7/1959. RHB, OB. Played for 2nd XI since 1977. Debut 1979. One match v Sri Lankans (Canterbury) scoring 110 in first innings. HS: 110 as above.

Derek Leslie UNDERWOOD (Beckenham and Penge GS) B Bromley 8/6/1945. RHB, LM. Debut 1963, taking 100 wkts and being the youngest player ever to do so in debut season. Cap 1964 (second youngest Kent player to have received this award). Elected Best Young Cricketer of the Year in 1966 by the Cricket Writers' Club. *Wisden* 1968. Benefit (£24,114) in 1975. Took 1,000th wkt in first-class cricket in New Zealand 1970–71 at age of 25 years 264 days—only W. Rhodes (in 1902) and G. A. Lohmann (in 1890) have achieved the feat at a younger age. Took 200th wkt in Test cricket against Australia in 1975. Tests: 74 between 1966 and 1977. Played in 3 matches against Rest of World in 1970. Tours: Pakistan 1966–67, Ceylon and Pakistan 1968–69, Australia and New Zealand 1970–71, 1974–75, India, Sri Lanka and Pakistan 1972–73. West Indies 1973–74, India, Sri Lanka and Australia 1976–77, Australia and India 1979–80. 100 wkts (9)—157 wkts (av 13.80)

KENT

in 1966 best. Hat-trick v Sussex (Hove) 1977. HS: 80 v Lancs (Manchester) 1969. HSTC: 45* v Australia (Leeds) 1968. HSGC: 28 v Sussex (Tunbridge Wells) 1963. HSJPL: 22 v Worcs (Dudley) 1969. HSBH: 17 v Essex (Canterbury) 1973. BB: 9–28 v Sussex (Hastings) 1964 and 9–32 v Surrey (Oval) 1978. BBTC: 8–51 v Pakistan (Lord's) 1974. BBGC: 4–57 v Leics (Canterbury) 1974. BBJPL: 5–19 v Glos (Maidstone) 1972. BBBH: 5–35 v Surrey (Oval) 1976.

Robert Andrew (Bob) WOOLMER (Skinners' School, Tunbridge Wells) B Kanpur (India) 14/5/1948. RHB, RM. Debut 1968. Cap 1970. *Wisden* 1975. Played for Natal between 1973–74 and 1975–76 in Currie Cup competition. Tests: 15 between 1975 and 1977. Tour: India, Sri Lanka and Australia 1976–77. 1,000 runs (5)—1,749 runs (av 47.27) in 1976 best. Hat-trick for MCC v Australians (Lord's) 1975. Gillette Man of Match awards: 2. Benson & Hedges Gold awards: 3. HS: 169 v Yorks (Canterbury) 1979. HSTC: 149 England v Australia (Oval) 1975. HSGC: 78 v Notts (Nottingham) 1979. HSJPL: 64 v Lancs (Manchester) 1976. HSBH: 79 v Derbyshire (Lord's) 1978. BB: 7–47 v Sussex (Canterbury) 1969. BBGC: 4–28 v Somerset (Taunton) 1979. BBJPL: 6–9 v Derbyshire (Chesterfield) 1979. BBBH: 4–14 v Sussex (Tunbridge Wells) 1972.

COUNTY AVERAGES
Schweppes Championship: Played 22, Won 6, drawn 13, lost 3
All first-class matches: Played 24, won 6, drawn 15, lost 3

BATTING AND FIELDING

Cap		M	I	NO	Runs	HS	Avge	100	50	Ct	St
1970	R. A. Woolmer	24	39	5	1382	169	40.64	4	5	12	—
1978	C. J. Tavare	23	36	5	1239	150*	39.96	3	6	21	—
1968	Asif Iqbal	10	16	1	506	152	33.73	1	—	3	—
1970	G. W. Johnson	24	31	7	726	82	30.25	—	5	17	—
1977	C. J. C. Rowe	23	39	5	945	147*	27.79	3	3	7	—
1965	A. P. E. Knott	10	11	2	243	63	27.00	—	1	15	1
1979	C. S. Cowdrey	21	30	4	692	83	26.61	—	4	12	—
1970	A. G. E. Ealham	24	33	4	760	153	26.20	1	3	13	—
—	G. R. Dilley	21	23	10	262	81	20.15	—	1	16	—
1967	J. N. Shepherd	16	20	1	370	86	19.47	—	1	9	—
1964	D. L. Underwood	23	24	5	210	45	11.05	—	—	17	—
1977	R. W. Hills	10	11	4	73	27	10.42	—	—	4	—
1979	P. R. Downton	14	18	1	162	29	9.52	—	—	26	4
1977	K. B. S. Jarvis	19	15	5	38	8	3.80	—	—	3	—

Played in one match: N. J. Kemp 10, 2; N. R. Taylor 110, 11.

BOWLING

	Type	O	M	R	W	Avge	Best	5 wI	10 wM
D. L. Underwood	LM	799.2	335	1575	106	14.85	8–28	10	4
G. R. Dilley	RFM	446.4	110	1151	49	23.48	6–66	1	—
C. J. C. Rowe	OB	53	17	150	6	25.00	4–4	—	—
R. W. Hills	RM	151	34	437	14	31.21	4–58	—	—
J. N. Shepherd	RM	418.3	114	1075	34	31.61	4–55	—	—
K. B. S. Jarvis	RFM	414.2	104	1275	38	33.55	4–42	—	—
G. W. Johnson	OB	448	143	1087	24	45.29	5–12	1	—

Also bowled: Asif Iqbal 17–3–71–1; C. S. Cowdrey 13.4–2–72–4; A. G. E. Ealham 8.3–2–49–1; N. J. Kemp 22–2–102–2; C. J. Tavare 9.5–2–39–1; R. A. Woolmer 107–20–301–3.

County Records

First-class cricket

Highest innings totals:	For —803–4d v Essex (Brentwood)	1934
	Agst—676 by Australians (Canterbury)	1921
Lowest innings totals:	For —18 v Sussex (Gravesend)	1867
	Agst—16 by Warwickshire (Tonbridge)	1913
Highest individual innings:	For —332 W. H. Ashdown v Essex (Brentwood)	1934
	Agst—344 W. G. Grace for MCC (Canterbury)	1876
Best bowling in an innings:	For —10–30 C. Blythe v Northamptonshire (Northampton)	1907
	Agst—10–48 C. H. G. Bland for Sussex (Tonbridge)	1899
Best bowling in a match:	For —17–48 C. Blythe v Northamptonshire (Northampton)	1907
	Agst—17–106 T. W. J. Goddard for Gloucestershire (Bristol)	1939

Most runs in a season:	2894 (av 59.06) F. E. Woolley	1928
runs in a career:	48483 (av 42.05) F. E. Wolley	1906–1938
100s in a season:	10 by F. E. Woolley	1928 & 1934
100s in a career:	112 by F. E. Woolley	1906–1938
wickets in a season:	262 (av 14.74) A. P. Freeman	1933
wickets in a career:	3359 (av 14.45) A.P. Freeman	1914–1936

RECORD WICKET STANDS

1st	283	A. E. Fagg & P. R. Sunnucks v Essex (Colchester)	1938
2nd	352	W. H. Ashdown & F. E. Woolley v Essex (Brentwood)	1934
3rd	321	A. Hearne & J. R. Mason v Nottinghamshire (Nottingham)	1899
4th	297	H. T. W. Hardinge & A. P. F. Chapman v Hampshire (Southampton)	1926
5th	277	F. E. Woolley & L. E. G. Ames v New Zealanders (Canterbury)	1931
6th	284	A. P. F. Chapman & G. B. Legge v Lancashire (Maidstone)	1927
7th	248	A. P. Day & E. Humphreys v Somerset (Taunton)	1908
8th	157	A. L. Hilder & C. Wright v Essex (Gravesend)	1924
9th	161	B. R. Edrich & F. Ridgway v Sussex (Tunbridge Wells)	1949
10th	235	F. E. Woolley & A. Fielder v Worcestershire (Stourbridge)	1909

LANCASHIRE

One-day cricket

Highest innings totals:	Gillette Cup	297–3 v Worcestershire (Canterbury)	1970
	John Player League	278–5 v Gloucestershire (Maidstone)	1976
	Benson & Hedges Cup	280–3 v Surrey (Oval)	1976
Lowest innings totals:	Gillette Cup	60 v Somerset (Taunton)	1979
	John Player League	84 v Gloucestershire (Folkestone)	1969
	Benson & Hedges Cup	73 v Middlesex (Canterbury)	1979
Highest individual innings:	Gillette Cup	129 B. W. Luckhurst v Durham (Canterbury)	1974
	John Player League	142 B. W. Luckhurst v Somerset (Weston-super-Mare)	1970
	Benson & Hedges Cup	114 C. S. Cowdrey v Sussex (Canterbury)	1977
Best bowling figures:	Gillette Cup	7–15 A. L. Dixon v Surrey (Oval)	1967
	John Player League	6–9 R. A. Woolmer v Derbyshire (Chesterfield)	1979
	Benson & Hedges Cup	5–21 B. D. Julien v Surrey (Oval)	1973

LANCASHIRE

Formation of present club: 1864.
Colours: Red, green and blue.
Badge: Red Rose.
County Champions (8): 1881, 1897, 1904, 1926, 1927, 1928, 1930 and 1934.
Joint Champions (4): 1879, 1889 and 1950.
Gillette Cup Winners (4): 1970, 1971, 1972 and 1975.
Gillette Cup Finalists (2): 1974 and 1976.
John Player League Champions (2): 1969 and 1970.
Benson & Hedges Cup semi-finalists (2): 1973 and 1974.
Gillette Man of the Match awards: 35.
Benson & Hedges Gold awards: 21.

Secretary: C. D. Hassell, Old Trafford, Manchester, M16 0PX.
Cricket Manager: J. D. Bond.
Captain: F. C. Hayes.
Prospects of play Telephone No.: 061 872 0261.

John ABRAHAMS (Heywood GS) B Cape Town, South Africa 21/7/1952. LHB, OB. Son of Cecil J. Abrahams, former professional for Milnrow and Radcliffe in Central Lancashire League. Has lived in this country since 1962. Debut 1973. HS: 126 v Cambridge U (Cambridge) 1978. HSGC: 46 v Northants (Lord's) 1976. HSJPL: 59 v Hants (Manchester) 1979. HSBH: 22 v Hants (Southampton) 1977.

Paul John Walter ALLOTT (Altrincham County Grammar School for Boys) B Altrincham (Cheshire) 14/9/1956. 6ft 4ins tall. RHB, RFM. Played for Cheshire in 1976 and for county 2nd XI in 1977. Debut 1978. HS: 14 v Warwickshire (Manchester) 1979. HSJPL: 22* v Middlesex (Manchester) 1979. BB: 5–39 v Worcs (Southport) 1979. BBJPL: 3–15 v Warwickshire (Birmingham) 1979. Studied at Durham University.

Ian COCKBAIN (Bootle GS) B Bootle 19/4/1958. RHB, SLA. Played for 2nd XI since 1976. Debut 1979 in last match of season. HS: 23 v Leics (Manchester) 1979.

Graeme FOWLER (Accrington GS) B Accrington 20/4/1957. RHB, RM. Played for 2nd XI since 1973. Played in one John Player League match v Derbyshire (Chesterfield) 1978. Debut 1979 (two matches). HS: 20 v Cambridge U (Cambridge) 1979. Studied at Durham University.

Frank Charles HAYES (De La Salle College, Salford) B Preston 6/12/1946. RHB, RM, Debut 1970 scoring 94 and 99 in first two matches after scoring 203* for 2nd XI v Warwickshire 2nd XI (Birmingham) Cap 1972. Appointed county captain in 1978. Tests: 9 between 1973 and 1976. Tour: West Indies 1973–74. 1,000 runs (5)—1,311 runs (av 35.43) in 1974 best. Scored 34 in one over (6 4 6 6 6 6) off M. A. Nash v Glamorgan (Swansea) 1977. Gillette Man of Match awards: 1. Benson & Hedges Gold awards: 2. HS: 187 v Indians (Manchester) 1974. HSTC: 106* v West Indies (Oval) 1973 in second innings on Test debut. HSGC: 93 v Warwickshire (Birmingham) 1976. HSJPL: 70 v Worcs (Worcester) 1978. HSBH: 102 v Minor Counties (North) (Manchester) 1973. Amateur soccer player. Studied at Sheffield University.

Kevin Anthony HAYES (Queen Elizabeth's GS, Blackburn) B Thurnscoe (Yorks) 26/9/1962. No relation to F. C. Hayes. Has lived in Lancs since 1969. RHB, RM. Played for 2nd XI in 1979. Plays for East Lancashire in Lancashire League. Has not yet appeared in first-class cricket.

William (Willis) HOGG (Ulverston Comprehensive School) B Ulverston 12/7/1955. RHB, RFM. Debut 1976 after playing as professional for Preston in Northern League. HS: 19 v Middlesex (Lord's) 1978. BB: 7–84 v Warwickshire (Manchester) 1978. BBJPL: 4–23 v Essex (Ilford) 1979. BBBH: 4–35 v Hants (Manchester) 1979.

David Paul HUGHES (Newton-le-Willows GS) B Newton-le-Willows (Lancs) 13/5/1947. RHB, SLA. Debut 1967. Cap 1970. Played for Tasmania in 1975–76 and 1976–77 whilst coaching there. Gillette Man of Match awards: 1. HS: 101 v Cambridge U (Cambridge) 1975. HSGC: 42* v Middlesex (Lord's) 1974. HSJPL: 84 v Essex (Leyton) 1973. HSBH: 42* v Minor Counties (West) (Watford) 1978. BB: 7–24 v Oxford U (Oxford) 1970. BBGC: 4–61 v Somerset (Manchester) 1972. BBJPL: 6–29 v Somerset (Manchester) 1977. BBBH: 5–23 v Minor Counties (West) (Watford) 1978.

Andrew KENNEDY (Nelson GS) B Blackburn 4/11/1949. LHB, RM. Debut 1970. Cap 1975. Elected Best Young Cricketer of the Year in 1975 by the Cricket Writers' Club. Scored 1,022 runs (av 42.58) in 1975. Gillette Man of Match awards: 1. HS: 176* v Leics (Leicester) 1974. HSGC: 131 v Middlesex (Manchester) 1978. HSJPL: 89 v Yorks (Manchester) 1978. HSBH: 51 v Hants (Manchester) 1979.

LANCASHIRE

Geoffrey Francis (Geoff) LAWSON. B in Australia 7/12/1957. RHB, RFM. Debut for New South Wales 1977–78. Debut for county 1979. One match v Cambridge U (Cambridge). Played for Heywood in Central Lancs League in 1979. Tour: Australia to India 1979–80 (flown out as replacement for A. G. Hurst). HS: 39 New South Wales v Western Australia (Perth) 1978–79. HSUK: 17 v Cambridge U (Cambridge) 1979. BB: 4–71 New South Wales v South Australia (Adelaide) 1978–79. BBUK: 4–81 v Cambridge U (Cambridge) 1979.

Peter Granville LEE B Arthingworth (Northants) 27/8/1945. RHB, RFM. Debut for Northants 1967. Joined Lancs in 1972. Cap 1972. *Wisden* 1975. 100 wkts (2)—112 wkts (av 18.45) in 1975 best. HS: 26 Northants v Glos (Northampton) 1969. HSGC: 10* v Middlesex (Lord's) 1974. HSJPL: 27* Northants v Derbyshire (Chesterfield) 1971. BB: 8–53 v Sussex (Hove) 1973. BBGC: 4–7 v Cornwall (Truro) 1977. BBJPL: 4–17 v Derbyshire (Chesterfield) 1972. BBBH: 4–32 v Worcs (Manchester) 1973.

Clive Hubert LLOYD (Chatham HS, Georgetown) B Georgetown, British Guiana 31/8/1944. 6ft 3½ins tall. Cousin of L. R. Gibbs. LHB, RM. Wears glasses. Debut 1963–64 for Guyana (then British Guiana). Played for Haslingden in Lancashire League in 1967 and also for Rest of World XI in 1967 and 1968. Debut for county v Australians 1968. Cap 1969. *Wisden* 1970. Appointed county vice-captain in 1973. Testimonial (£27,199) in 1977. Tests: 65 for West Indies between 1966–67 and 1977–78, captaining West Indies in 30 Tests. Played in 5 matches for Rest of World 1970 and 2 in 1971–72. Scored 118 on debut v England (Port of Spain) 1967–68, 129 on debut v Australia (Brisbane) 1968–69, and 82 and 78* on debut v India (Bombay) 1966–67. Tours: West Indies to India and Ceylon 1966–67, Australia and New Zealand 1968–69, England 1969, 1973 and 1976 (captain). Rest of World to Australia 1971–72 (returning early owing to back injury), India, Sri Lanka and Pakistan 1974–75 (captain), Australia 1975–76 (captain), 1979–80 (captain) 1,000 runs (8)—1,603 runs (av 47.14) in 1970 best. Also scored 1,000 runs in Australia and New Zealand 1968–69 and in India, Sri Lanka and Pakistan 1974–75. Scored 201* in 120 minutes for West Indians v Glamorgan (Swansea) 1976 to equal record for fastest double century in first-class cricket. Gillette Man of Match awards: 6. HS: 242* West Indies v India (Bombay) 1974–75. HSUK: 217* v Warwickshire (Manchester) 1971. HSGC: 126 v Warwickshire (Lord's) 1972. HSJPL: 134* v Somerset (Manchester) 1970. HSBH: 73 v Notts (Manchester) 1974. BB: 4–48 v Leics (Manchester) 1970. BBGC: 3–39 v Somerset (Taunton) 1970. BBJPL: 4–33 v Middlesex (Lord's) 1971. BBBH: 3–23 v Derbyshire (Manchester) 1974.

David LLOYD (Accrington Secondary TS) B Accrington 18/3/1947. LHB, SLA. Debut 1965. Cap 1968. County captain from 1973 to 1977. Testimonial (£40,171) in 1978. Tests: 9 in 1974 and 1974–75. Tour: Australia and New Zealand 1974–75. 1,000 runs (9)—1,510 runs (av 47.18) in 1972 best. Scored two centuries in match (116 and 104*) v Worcs (Southport) 1979. Gillette Man of Match awards: 3. HS: 214* England v India (Birmingham) 1974. HSC: 195 v Glos (Manchester) 1973. HSGC: 121* v Glos (Manchester) 1978. HSJPL: 103* v Northants (Bedford) 1971. HSBH: 113 v Minor Counties (North) (Manchester) 1973. BB: 7–38 v Glos (Lydney) 1966.

Michael Francis (Mick) MALONE (Scarborough HS, Perth) B Perth, Australia 9/10/1950. RHB, RFM. Debut for Western Australia 1974–75. Played for Haslingden in Lancashire League in 1979. Debut for county as special overseas registration in 1979 playing in three matches and two John Player League Matches. Tests: 1 for Australia in 1977. Tour: Australia to England 1977. HS: 46 Australia v England (Oval) 1977. BB: 7–88 v Notts (Blackpool) 1979. BBTC: 5–63 Australia v England (Oval) 1977.

Harry PILLING (Ashton TS) B Ashton-under-Lyne (Lancs) 23/2/1943. 5 ft 3 ins tall. RHB, OB. Debut 1962. Cap 1965. Testimonial (£9,500) in 1974. Played in only one match and one Benson and Hedges match in 1979. 1,000 (8)—1,606 runs (av 36.50) in 1967 best. Scored two centuries in match (119* and 104*) v Warwickshire (Manchester) 1970. Gillette Man of Match awards: 3. Benson & Hedges Gold awards: 3. HS: 149* v Glamorgan (Liverpool) 1976. HSGC: 90 v Middlesex (Lord's) 1973. HSJPL: 85 v Sussex (Hove) 1970. HSBH: 109* v Glamorgan (Manchester) 1973.

Robert Malcolm (Bob) RATCLIFFE B Accrington 29/11/1951. RHB, RM. Joined staff 1971. Debut 1972. Cap 1976, Gillette Man of Match awards: 1. Shared in 8th wicket partnership record for county, 158 with J. Lyon v Warwickshire (Manchester) 1979. HS: 101* v Warwickshire (Manchester) 1979. HSGC: 17 v Cornwall (Truro) 1977. HSJPL: 28 v Essex (Manchester) 1976, HSBH; 14 v Derbyshire (Southport) 1976. BB: 7–58 v Hants (Bournemouth) 1978. BBGC: 4–25 v Hants (Manchester) 1975. BBJPL: 4–17 v Somerset (Manchester) 1975. BBBH: 3–33 v Warwickshire (Birmingham) 1976.

Bernard Wilfrid REIDY (St Mary's College, Blackburn) B Bramley Meade, Whalley (Lancs) 18/9/1953. LHB, LM. Toured West Indies with England Young Cricketers 1972. Played for 2nd XI since 1971. Debut 1973. Benson & Hedges Gold Awards: 1. HS: 131* v Derbyshire (Chesterfield) 1979. HSGC: 18 v Glos (Manchester) 1975. HSJPL: 58* v Somerset (Manchester) 1975. HSBH: 65* v Leics (Leicester) 1979. BB: 5–61 v Worcs (Worcester) 1979. BBJPL: 3–33 v Surrey (Manchester) 1978.

Christopher John SCOTT (Ellesmere Park HS) B Swinton, Manchester 16/9/1959. LHB, WK. Played for 2nd XI since 1975. Debut 1977 aged 17 years 8 months. HS: 16 v Cambridge U (Cambridge) 1979.

Jack SIMMONS (Accrington Secondary TS and Blackburn TS) B Clayton-le-Moors (Lancs) 28/3/1941. RHB, OB. Debut for 2nd XI 1959. Played for Blackpool in Northern League as professional. Debut 1968. Cap 1971. Played for Tasmania from 1972–73 to 1978–79 whilst coaching there. Testimonial in 1980. Hat-trick v Notts (Liverpool) 1977. Gillette Man of Match awards: 1. Benson & Hedges Gold awards: 2. HS: 112 v Sussex (Hove) 1970. HSGC: 54* v Essex (Manchester) 1979. HSBH: 64 v Derbyshire (Manchester) 1978. BB: 7–59 Tasmania v Queensland (Brisbane) 1978–79. BBUK: 7–64 v Hants (Southport) 1973. BBGC: 5–49 v Worcs (Worcester) 1974. BBJPL: 5–28 v Northants (Peterborough) 1972. BBBH: 4–31 v Yorks (Manchester) 1975. Has played soccer in Lancs Combination.

Geoffrey Edward TRIM B Openshaw, Manchester 6/4/1956. RHB, LB. Joined staff 1974. Played in last John Player League match of 1975 season. Debut 1976. HS: 91 v Derbyshire (Chesterfield) 1979. HSJPL: 18 v Middlesex (Manchester) 1979.

LANCASHIRE

NB   The following players whose particulars appeared in the 1979 Annual have been omitted: R. Arrowsmith (not re-engaged), P. A. Robinson (not re-engaged), J. Lyon (left staff), R. J. Sutcliffe, A. Worsick and B. Wood.

The career records of Arrowsmith, Lyon and Robinson will be found elsewhere in this Annual.

COUNTY AVERAGES

Schweppes County Championship: Played 22, Won 4, Drawn 14, Lost 4
All First-class Matches: Played 24, Won 4, Drawn 16, Lost 4

BATTING AND FIELDING

Cap		M	I	NO	Runs	HS	Avge	100	50	Ct	St
1969	C. H. Lloyd	17	22	4	880	104*	48.88	3	3	11	—
1972	F. C. Hayes	18	22	5	747	88	43.94	—	6	8	—
1968	B. Wood	22	35	7	1144	135*	40.85	2	6	12	—
1968	D. Lloyd	22	34	3	1078	135*	34.77	4	4	14	—
—	B. W. Reidy	18	26	6	547	131*	27.35	1	1	6	—
—	J. Abrahams	15	25	1	633	79	26.37	—	6	12	—
1976	R. M. Ratcliffe	17	16	5	285	101*	25.90	1	—	3	—
—	R. Arrowsmith	8	7	4	73	39	24.33	—	—	3	—
1971	J. Simmons	23	25	5	469	74*	23.45	—	1	17	—
1975	J. Lyon	21	22	8	313	123	22.35	1	—	30	2
—	G. E. Trim	8	13	0	258	91	19.84	—	1	9	—
1970	D. P. Hughes	15	14	3	188	60*	17.09	—	1	14	—
1975	A. Kennedy	9	11	3	135	21	16.87	—	—	4	—
1972	P. G. Lee	16	14	7	68	19	9.71	—	—	3	—
—	C. J. Scott	3	4	1	24	16	8.00	—	—	10	1
—	P. J. W. Allott	12	6	2	19	14	4.75	—	—	4	—
—	W. Hogg	11	8	1	33	11	4.71	—	—	4	—
—	M. F. Malone	3	2	0	0	0	0.00	—	—	—	—

Played in two matches: G. Fowler 2, 2, 20, 0.
Played in one match: I. Cockbain 23; G. F. Lawson 17, 2; H. Pilling did not bat; P. A. Robinson 15.

BOWLING	Type	O	M	R	W	Avge	Best	5 wI	10 wM
M. F. Malone	RFM	102.3	32	230	19	12.10	7–88	3	1
D. Lloyd	SLA	59.3	19	164	11	14.90	6–60	2	—
G. F. Lawson	RFM	30	6	88	5	17.60	4–81	—	—
J. Simmons	OB	454	112	1231	51	24.13	7–86	1	—
W. Hogg	RFM	212.4	45	704	25	28.16	4–26	—	—
B. Wood	RM	161.2	30	513	18	28.50	4–58	—	—
R. M. Ratcliffe	RM	450.5	131	1103	38	29.02	6–84	3	1
B. W. Reidy	LM	148.4	22	468	16	29.25	5–61	1	—
R. Arrowsmith	SLA	96.1	22	316	10	31.60	2–22	—	—
P. G. Lee	RFM	288.5	61	901	23	39.17	3–50	—	—
D. P. Hughes	SLA	226.2	56	646	15	43.06	4–77	—	—
P. J. W. Allott	RFM	223.2	41	609	13	46.84	5–39	1	—

Also bowled: J. Abrahams 2–1–3–0; G. E. Trim 2–0–13–0; P. A. Robinson 19.5–4–58–?

County Records

First-class cricket

Highest innings totals:	For —801 v Somerset (Taunton)	1895
	Agst—634 v Surrey (The Oval)	1898
Lowest innings totals:	For —25 v Derbyshire (Manchester)	1871
	Agst—22 by Glamorgan (Liverpool)	1924
Highest individual innings:	For —424 A. C. MacLaren v Somerset (Taunton)	1895
	Agst—315* T. W. Hayward for Surrey (The Oval)	1898
Best bowling in innings:	For —10–55 J. Briggs v Worcestershire (Manchester)	1900
	Agst—10–40 G. O. Allen for Middlesex (Lord's)	1929
Best bowling in a match:	For —17–91 H. Dean v Yorkshire (Liverpool)	1913
	Agst—16–65 G. Giffen for Australians (Manchester)	1886
Most runs in a season:	2633 (av 56.02) J. T. Tyldesley	1901
runs in a career:	34222 (av 45.02) G. E. Tyldesley	1909–1936
100s in a season:	11 by C. Hallows	1928
100s in a career:	90 by G. E. Tyldesley	1909–1936
wickets in a season:	198 (av 18.55) E. A. McDonald	1925
wickets in a career:	1816 (av 15.12) J. B. Statham	1950–1968

RECORD WICKET STANDS

1st	368	A. C. MacLaren & R. H. Spooner v Gloucestershire (Liverpool)	1903
2nd	371	F. Watson & G. E. Tyldesley v Surrey (Manchester)	1928
3rd	306	E. Paynter & N. Oldfield v Hampshire (Southampton)	1938
4th	324	A. C. MacLaren & J. T. Tyldesley v Nottinghamshire (Nottingham)	1904
5th	249	B. Wood & A. Kennedy v Warwickshire (Birmingham)	1975
6th	278	J. Iddon & H. R. W. Butterworth v Sussex (Manchester)	1932
7th	245	A. H. Hornby & J. Sharp v Leicestershire (Manchester)	1912
8th	158	J. Lyon & R. M. Ratcliffe v Warwickshire (Manchester)	1979
9th	142	L. O. S. Poidevin & A. Kermode v Sussex (Eastbourne)	1907
10th	173	J. Briggs & R. Pilling v Surrey (Liverpool)	1885

One-day cricket

Highest innings totals:	Gillette Cup	304–9 v Leicestershire (Manchester)	1963
	John Player League	255–5 v Somerset (Manchester)	1970
	Benson & Hedges Cup	275–5 v Minor Counties (North) (Manchester)	1973
Lowest innings totals:	Gillette Cup	59 v Worcestershire (Worcester)	1963
	John Player League	76 v Somerset (Manchester)	1972
	Benson & Hedges Cup	82 v Yorks (Bradford)	1972
Highest individual innings:	Gillette Cup	131 A. Kennedy v Middlesex (Manchester)	1978
	John Player League	134* C. H. Lloyd v Somerset (Manchester)	1970
	Benson & Hedges Cup	113 D. Lloyd v Minor Counties (North) (Manchester)	1973
Best bowling figures:	Gillette Cup	5–28 J. B. Statham v Leics (Manchester)	1963
	John Player League	6–29 D. P. Hughes v Somerset (Manchester)	1977
	Benson & Hedges Cup	5–12 B. Wood v Derbyshire (Southport)	1976

LEICESTERSHIRE

Formation of present club: 1879.
Colours: Scarlet and dark green.
Badge: Running fox (gold) on green background.
County Champions: 1975.
Gillette Cup semi-finalists: 1977.
John Player League Champions (2): 1974 and 1977.
Benson & Hedges Cup Winners (2): 1972 and 1975.
Benson & Hedges Cup finalists: 1974.
Fenner Trophy Winners: 1979.
Gillette Man of the Match awards: 15.
Benson & Hedges Gold awards: 29.

Secretary: F. M. Turner, County Ground, Grace Road, Leicester, LE2 8AD.
Captain: B. F. Davison.
Prospects of play Telephone No.: Leicester (0533) 832128, 831880.

Jonathan Philip AGNEW (Uppingham School) B Macclesfield (Cheshire) 4/4/1960. 6ft 3½ins tall. RHB, RF. Played for Surrey 2nd XI in 1976 and 1977. Debut 1978. BB: 3–51 v Northants (Leicester) 1978.

John Christopher (Chris) BALDERSTONE B Huddersfield 16/11/1940. RHB, SLA. Played for Yorks from 1961 to 1970. Specially registered and made debut for Leics in 1971. Cap 1973. Tests: 2 in 1976. 1,000 runs (5)—1,409 runs (av 33.54) in 1976 best. Hat-trick v Sussex (Eastbourne) 1976. Gillette Man of Match awards: 2. Benson & Hedges Gold awards: 5. HS: 178* v Notts (Nottingham) 1977. HSTC: 35 v West Indies (Leeds) 1976. HSGC: 119* v Somerset (Taunton) 1973. HSJPL: 96 v Northants (Leicester) 1976. HSBH: 101* v Hants (Leicester) 1975. BB: 6–25 v

106

Hants (Southampton) 1978. BBGC: 4–33 v Herts (Leicester) 1977. BBJPL: 3–29 v Worcs (Leicester) 1971. Soccer for Huddersfield Town, Carlisle United, Doncaster Rovers and Queen of the South.

Jack BIRKENSHAW (Rothwell GS) B Rothwell (Yorks) 13/11/1940. LHB, OB. Played for Yorks 1958 to 1960. Specially registered and made debut for Leics in 1961. Cap 1965. Benefit (£13,100) in 1974. Tests: 5 in 1972–73 and 1973–74. Tours: India Pakistan and Sri Lanka 1972–73, West Indies 1973–74. 100 wkts (2)—111 wkts (av 21.41) in 1967 best. Hat-tricks (2) v Worcs (Worcester) 1967 and v Cambridge U (Cambridge) 1968. Shared in 7th wkt partnership record for county, 206 with B Dudleston v Kent (Canterbury) 1969. Gillette Man of Match awards: 1. HS: 131 v Surrey (Guildford) 1969. HSTC: 64 v India (Kanpur) 1972–73. HSGC: 101* v Hants (Leicester) 1976. HSJPL: 79 v Yorks (Leicester) 1978. HSBH: 35* v Worcs (Worcester) 1972. BB: 8–94 v Somerset (Taunton) 1972. BBGC: 3–19 v Somerset (Leicester) 1968. BBJPL: 5–20 v Essex (Leicester) 1975.

Peter BOOTH (Whitcliffe Mount GS, Cleckheaton) B Shipley (Yorks) 2/11/1952. RHB, RFM. Played for MCC Schools at Lord's 1970 and 1971. Toured West Indies with England Youth Team 1972. Debut 1972. Cap 1976. HS: 58* v Lancs (Leicester) 1976. HSGC: 40* v Glamorgan (Swansea) 1977. HSJPL: 22* v Derbyshire (Leicester) 1976. HSBH: 29* v Derbyshire (Leicester) 1979. BB: 6–93 v Glamorgan (Swansea) 1978. BBGC: 5–33 v Northants (Northampton) 1977. BBJPL: 4–20 v Warwickshire (Leicester) 1977. BBBH: 3–27 v Hants (Leicester) 1975. Trained as a teacher at Loughborough College.

Nigel Edwin BRIERS (Lutterworth GS) B Leicester 15/1/1955. RHB, Cousin of N. Briers who played once for county in 1967. Debut 1971 at age of 16 years 103 days. Youngest player ever to appear for county. Shared in 5th wicket partnership record for county, 235 with R. W. Tolchard v Somerset (Leicester) 1979. Benson & Hedges Gold awards: 1. HS: 119 v Warwickshire (Birmingham) 1979. HSGC: 20 v Worcs (Leicester) 1979. HSJPL: 81 v Worcs (Worcester) 1978. HSBH: 71* v Hants (Southampton) 1979.

Ian Paul BUTCHER (John Ruskin HS, Croydon) B Farnborough (Kent) 1/7/1962. RHB, WK. Brother of A. R. Butcher of Surrey. Played in last two John Player League matches of 1979. Has not yet appeared in first-class cricket. HSJPL: 16 v Surrey (Leicester) 1979.

Patrick Bernard (Paddy) CLIFT (St George's College, Salisbury) B Salisbury, Rhodesia 14/7/1953. RHB, RM. Debut for Rhodesia 1971–72. Debut for county 1975. Cap 1976. Hat-trick v Yorks (Leicester) 1976. HS: 88* v Oxford U (Oxford) 1979. HSGC: 48* v Worcs (Leicester) 1979. HSJPL: 51* v Somerset (Leicester) 1979. HSBH: 58 v Worcs (Worcester) 1976. BB: 8–17 v MCC (Lord's) 1976. BBGC: 3–36 v Worcs (Leicester) 1979. BBJPL: 4–14 v Lancs (Leicester) 1978. BBBH: 4–13 v Minor Counties (East) (Amersham) 1978.

Nicholas Grant Billson COOK (Lutterworth GS) B Leicester 17/6/1956. RHB, SLA. Played for 2nd XI since 1974. Debut 1978. HS: 31 v Northants (Leicester) 1978. HSJPL· 13* v Kent (Leicester) 1979. BB: 6–57 v Essex (Leicester) 1979.

LEICESTERSHIRE

Brian Fettes DAVISON (Gifford Technical HS, Rhodesia) B Bulawayo, Rhodesia 21/12/1946. RHB, RM. Debut for Rhodesia 1967–68 in Currie Cup competition. Debut for county 1970 after having played for International Cavaliers. Cap 1971. Played for Tasmania in 1979–80. 1,000 runs (9)—1,818 runs (av 56.81) in 1976 best. Gillette Man of Match awards: 1. Benson & Hedges Gold awards: 6. HS: 189 v Australians (Leicester) 1975. HSGC: 99 v Essex (Southend) 1977. HSJPL: 85* v Glamorgan (Cardiff) 1974. HSBH: 158* v Warwickshire (Coventry) 1972. BB: 5–52 Rhodesia v Griqualand West (Bulawayo) 1967–68. BBUK: 4–99 v Northants (Leicester) 1970. BBJPL: 4–29 v Glamorgan (Neath) 1971. Has played hockey for Rhodesia.

Barry DUDLESTON (Stockport School) B Bebington (Cheshire) 16/7/1945. RHB, SLA. Debut 1966. Cap 1969. Played for Rhodesia from 1976–77 to 1979–80 in Currie Cup competitions. Benefit in 1980. 1,000 runs (8)—1,374 runs (av 31.22) in 1970 best. Shared in 1st wkt partnership record for county, 390 with J. F. Steele v Derbyshire (Leicester) 1979. Also shared in 7th wkt partnership record for county, 206 with J. Birkenshaw v Kent (Canterbury) 1969. Gillette Man of Match awards: 2. Benson & Hedges Gold awards: 4. HS: 202 v Derbyshire (Leicester) 1979. HSGC: 125 v Worcs (Leicester) 1979. HSJPL: 152 v Lancs (Manchester) 1975. HSBH: 90 v Warwickshire (Leicester) 1973. BB: 4–6 v Surrey (Leicester) 1972.

Michael Anthony (Mike) GARNHAM (Camberwell GS, Melbourne, Scotch College, Perth, Australia, Park School, Barnstaple) B Johannesburg 20/8/1960. RHB, WK. Played for Devon and Glos 2nd XI since 1976. Toured India with English Schools Cricket Association in 1977. Played for Glos in last John Player League match of 1978 v Warwickshire (Birmingham). Debut for Glos 1979 playing in three matches and two John Player league matches. Has joined Leics for 1980. HS: 21 Glos v Northants (Bristol) 1979. HSJPL: 18 Glos v Warwickshire (Moreton-in-Marsh) 1979. Is studying at East Anglia University.

David Ivon GOWER (King's School, Canterbury) B Tunbridge Wells 1/4/1957. LHB, OB. Toured South Africa with English Schools XI 1974–75 and West Indies with England Young Cricketers 1976. Debut 1975. Cap 1977. *Wisden* 1978. Elected Best Young Cricketer of the Year in 1978 by Cricket Writers Club. Tests: 15 between 1978 and 1979. Tours: Australia 1978–79, Australia and India 1979–80. Scored 1,098 runs (av 37.86) in 1978. Gillette Man of Match awards: 1. HS: 200* England v India (Birmingham) 1979. HSC: 144* v Hants (Leicester) 1977. HSGC: 117* v Herts (Leicester) 1977. HSJPL: 135* v Warwickshire (Leicester) 1977. HSBH: 49 v Middlesex (Lord's) 1978. BB: 3–47 v Essex (Leicester) 1977.

Kenneth (Ken) HIGGS B Sandyford (Staffordshire) 14/1/1937. LHB, RM. Played for Staffordshire 1957. Debut for Lancs 1958. Cap 1959. *Wisden* 1967. Benefit (£8,390) in 1968. Retired after 1969 season. Reappeared for Leics in 1972. Cap 1972. Appointed county vice-captain in 1973 and county captain in 1979. Tests: 15 between 1965 and 1968. Shared in 10th wkt partnership of 128 with J. A. Snow v WI (Oval) 1966—2 runs short of then record 10th wkt partnership in Test cricket. Also shared in 10th wkt partnership record for county, 228 with R. Illingworth v Northants (Leicester) 1977. Tours: Australia and New Zealand 1965–66. West Indies 1967–68. 100 wkts (5)—132 wkts (av 19.42) in 1960 best. Hat-tricks (3): Lancs v Essex (Blackpool) 1960. Lancs v Yorks (Leeds) 1968 and v Hants (Leicester) 1977. Hat-trick also in Benson & Hedges Cup Final v Surrey (Lord's) 1974. Benson & Hedges Gold awards: 1. HS: 98 v Northants (Leicester) 1977. HSTC: 63 England v West Indies (Oval) 1966. HSGC: 25 Lancs v Somerset (Taunton) 1966. HSJPL: 17* v Notts (Nottingham) 1975. BB: 7–19 Lancs v Leics (Manchester) 1965. BBTC: 6–91 v West Indies (Lord's) 1966. BB: 7–44 v Middlesex (Lord's) 1978. BBGC: 6–20 v Staffs (Longton) 1975. BBJPL: 6–17 v Glamorgan (Leicester) 1973. BBBH: 4–10 v Surrey (Lord's) 1974. Soccer for Port Vale.

Gordon James PARSONS B Slough (Bucks) 17/10/1959. LHB, RM. Played for county 2nd XI since 1976 and also for Buckinghamshire in 1977. Debut 1978. HS: 17 v Worcs (Leicester) 1979. BB: 4–43 v Oxford U (Oxford) 1979.

Martin SCHEPENS (Rawlins School, Quorn) B Barrow-upon-Soar (Leics) 12/8/1955. RHB, LB. Played for 2nd XI since 1971. Debut 1973 aged 17 years 8 months. HS: 57 v Glamorgan (Leicester) 1979. HSJPL: 24 v Warwickshire (Birmingham) 1979.

Kenneth (Ken) SHUTTLEWORTH B St Helens 13/11/1944. RHB, RFM. Debut for Lancs 1964. Cap 1968. Joint testimonial (£12,500) with J. Sullivan in 1975. Did not play in 1976. Not re-engaged at end of season and made debut for county in 1977. Cap 1977. Tests: 5 in 1970–71 and 1971. Played in one match v Rest of World 1970. Tour: Australia and New Zealand 1970–71. Hat-trick v Surrey (Oval) 1977. HS: 71 Lancs v Glos (Cheltenham) 1967. HSTC: 21 v Pakistan (Birmingham) 1971. HSC: 44 v Glamorgan (Cardiff) 1979. HSGC: 23 Lancs v Somerset (Manchester) 1967. HSJPL: 24* v Hants (Portsmouth) 1979. HSBH: 12* Lancs v Derbyshire (Manchester) 1972. BB: 7–41 Lancs v Essex (Leyton) 1968. BBTC: 5–47 v Australia (Brisbane) 1970–71. BBC: 6–17 v Essex (Leicester) 1977. BBGC: 4–26 Lancs v Essex (Chelmsford) 1971. BBJPL: 5–13 Lancs v Notts (Nottingham) 1972. BBBH: 3–15 Lancs v Notts (Manchester) 1972.

John Frederick STEELE B Stafford 23/7/1946. Younger brother of D. S. Steele of Derbys. RHB, SLA. Debut 1970. Was 12th man for England v Rest of World (Lord's) a month after making debut. Cap 1971. Played for Natal in 1973–74 and 1977–78 Currie cup competition. 1,000 runs (6)—1,347 runs (av 31.32) in 1972 best. Shared in 1st wkt partnership record for county, 390 with B. Dudleston v Derbyshire (Leicester) 1979. Gillette Man of Match awards: 3. Benson & Hedges Gold awards: 4. HS: 195 v Derbyshire (Leicester) 1971. HSGC: 108* v Staffs (Longton) 1975. HSJPL: 92 v Essex (Leicester) 1973. HSBH: 91 v Somerset (Leicester) 1974. BB: 7–29 Natal B v Griqualand West (Umzinto) 1973–74. BBUK: 6–33 v Northants (Northampton) 1975. BBGC: 5–19 v Essex (Southend) 1971. BBJPL: 5–22 v Glamorgan (Leicester) 1979. BBBH: 3–17 v Cambridge U (Leicester) 1972.

Leslie Brian TAYLOR (Heathfield HS, Earl Shilton) B Earl Shilton (Leics) 25/10/1953. 6ft 3½ins tall, RHB, RFM. Debut 1977. Hat-trick v Middlesex (Leicester) 1979. HS: 15 v Kent (Canterbury) 1978. BB: 6–61 v Essex (Ilford) 1979. BBGC: 3–11 v Hants (Leicester) 1978. BBJPL: 5–23 v Notts (Nottingham) 1978.

Roger William TOLCHARD (Malvern College) B Torquay 15/6/1946. RHB, WK. Played for Devon in 1963 and 1964. Also played for Hants 2nd XI and Public Schools v Combined Services (Lord's) in 1964. Debut 1965. Cap 1966. Appointed vice-captain in 1970. Relinquished appointment in 1973. Tests: 4 in 1976–77. Tours: India, Pakistan, and Sri Lanka 1972–73, India, Sri Lanka and Australia 1976–77, Australia 1978–79. Scored 998 runs (av 30.24) in 1970. Shared in 5th wicket partnership record for county, 235 with N. E. Briers v Somerset (Leicester) 1979. Benson & Hedges Gold awards: 4. HS: 126* v Cambridge U (Cambridge) 1970. HSGC: 86* v Glos (Leicester) 1975. HSJPL: 103 v Middlesex (Lord's) 1972 and was dismissed obstructing the field. HSBH: 92* v Worcs (Worcester) 1976. Had soccer trial for Leicester City.

N. B. The following player whose particulars appeared in the 1979 annual has been ommitted: A. Ward (left staff before start of season).

COUNTY AVERAGES

**Schweppes County Championship: Played 21, won 4, drawn 12, lost 5, abandoned 1
All first-class matches: Played 24, won 5, drawn 14, lost 5, abandoned 2**

BATTING AND FIELDING

Cap		M	I	NO	Runs	HS	Avge	100	50	Ct	St
1973	J. C. Balderstone	24	41	7	1393	122*	40.97	1	11	15	—
1971	J. F. Steele	23	38	5	1301	187	39.42	3	6	21	—
1969	B. Dudleston	21	35	0	1258	202	35.94	2	8	17	1
1977	D. I. Gower	12	21	3	602	98	33.44	—	6	5	—
1971	B. F. Davison	24	39	0	1245	84	31.92	—	8	16	—
1976	P. B. Clift	24	34	10	741	88*	30.87	—	3	7	—
1966	R. W. Tolchard	20	30	7	688	109	29.91	1	2	43	3
—	M. Schepens	5	7	2	132	57	26.40	—	1	6	—
1977	K. Shuttleworth	19	20	9	279	44	25.36	—	—	17	—
1965	J. Birkenshaw	9	10	5	119	33*	23.80	—	—	7	—
—	N. E. Briers	19	32	2	620	119	20.66	2	1	9	—
1976	P. Booth	10	8	3	64	20	12.80	—	—	4	—
—	N. G. B. Cook	14	12	5	74	18*	10.57	—	—	3	—
—	G. J. Parsons	3	4	1	21	17	7.00	—	—	1	—
—	L. B. Taylor	15	9	5	25	11*	6.25	—	—	3	—
1972	K. Higgs	19	13	6	42	19	6.00	—	—	19	—
—	J. P. Agnew	3	2	0	10	9	5.00	—	—	—	—

BOWLING

	Type	O	M	R	W	Avge	Best	5 wI	10 wM
B. Dudleston	SLA	55	25	104	6	17.33	3–25	—	—
K. Higgs	RFM	404.5	133	872	47	18.55	6–33	4	—
G. J. Parsons	RM	54	17	179	9	19.88	4–43	—	—
L. B. Taylor	RFM	352.3	77	958	44	21.77	6–61	2	—
N. G. B. Cook	SLA	359.5	119	870	36	24.16	6–57	2	—
J. F. Steele	SLA	272.4	91	654	27	24.22	6–36	1	—
P. B. Clift	RM	560.1	151	1412	50	28.24	5–57	1	—
K. Shuttleworth	RFM	444	101	1273	45	28.28	4–59	—	—
J. P. Agnew	RF	69	16	199	7	28.42	2–33	—	—
J. C. Balderstone	SLA	265.5	80	681	23	29.60	3–38	—	—
J. Birkenshaw	OB	151.3	40	381	12	31.75	3–20	—	—
P. Booth	RFM	111	28	379	10	37.90	3–46	—	—

Also bowled: N. E. Briers 3–2–1–0; B. F. Davison 0.5–0–7–0

County Records
First-class cricket

Highest innings totals:	For	—701–4d v Worcestershire (Worcester)	1906
	Agst	—739–7d by Nottinghamshire (Nottingham)	1903
Lowest innings totals:	For	—25 v Kent (Leicester)	1912
	Agst	—24 by Glamorgan (Leicester)	1971
Highest individual innings:	For	—252* S. Coe v Northants (Leicester)	1914
	Agst	—341 G. H. Hirst for Yorkshire (Leicester)	1905
Best bowling in an innings:	For	—10–18 G. Geary v Glamorgan (Pontypridd)	1929
	Agst	—10–32 H. Pickett for Essex (Leyton)	1958
Best bowling in a match:	For	—16–96 G. Geary v Glamorgan (Pontypridd)	1929
	Agst	—16–102 C. Blythe for Kent (Leicester)	1909

Most runs in a season:	2446 (av 52.04) G. L. Berry	1937
runs in a career:	30143 (av 30.32) G. L. Berry	1924–1951
100s in a season:	7 by G. L. Berry and	
	W. Watson 1937 and 1959	
100s in a career:	45 by G. L. Berry	1924–1951
Wickets in a season:	170 (av 18.96) J. E. Walsh	1948
Wickets in a career:	2130 (av 23.19) W. E. Astill	1906–1939

RECORD WICKET STANDS

1st	390	B. Dudleston & J. F. Steele v Derbyshire (Leicester)	1979
2nd	287	W. Watson & A. Wharton v Lancashire (Leicester)	1961
3rd	316*	W. Watson & A. Wharton v Somerset (Taunton)	1961
4th	270	C. S. Dempster & G. S. Watson v Yorkshire (Hull)	1937
5th	235	N. E. Briers & R. W. Tolchard v Somerset (Leicester)	1979
6th	262	A. T. Sharpe & G. H. S. Fowke v Derbyshire (Chesterfield)	1911
7th	206	B. Dudleston & J. Birkenshaw v Kent (Canterbury)	1969
8th	164	M. R. Hallam & C. T. Spencer v Essex (Leicester)	1964
9th	160	W. W. Odell & R. T. Crawford v Worcestershire (Leicester)	1902
10th	228	R. Illingworth & K. Higgs v Northamptonshire (Leicester)	1977

One-day cricket

Highest innings totals	Gillette Cup	326–6 v Worcestershire (Leicester)	1979
	John Player League	262–6 v Somerset (Frome)	1970
	Benson & Hedges Cup	327–4 v Warwickshire (Coventry)	1972
Lowest innings totals:	Gillette Cup	56 v Northamptonshire (Leicester)	1964
	John Player League	36 v Sussex (Leicester)	1973
	Benson & Hedges Cup	82 v Hampshire (Leicester)	1973
Highest individual innings:	Gillette Cup	125 B. Dudleston v Worcestershire (Leicester)	1979
	John Player League	152 B. Dudleston v Lancs (Manchester)	1975
	Benson & Hedges Cup	158* B. F. Davison v Warwicks (Coventry)	1972
Best bowling figures:	Gillette Cup	6–20 K. Higgs v Staffs (Longton)	1975
	John Player League	6–17 K. Higgs v Glamorgan (Leicester)	1973
	Benson & Hedges Cup	5–20 R. Illingworth v Somerset (Leicester)	1974

MIDDLESEX

Formation of present club: 1863.
Colours: Blue.
Badge: Three seaxes.
County Champions (6): 1866, 1903, 1920, 1921, 1947 and 1976.
Joint Champions (2): 1949 and 1977.
Gillette Cup Winners: 1977.
Gillette Cup finalists: 1975.
Best position in John Player League: 3rd in 1977.
Benson & Hedges Cup finalists: 1975.
Gillette Man of the Match awards: 22.
Benson & Hedges Gold awards: 16.

Secretary: A. J. Burridge, Lord's Cricket Ground, St John's Wood Road, London NW8 8QN.
Captain: J. M. Brearley, OBE.

Prospects of play Telephone No.: (01) 286 8011.

 Graham Derek BARLOW (Ealing GS) B Folkestone 26/3/1950. LHB, RM. Played in MCC Schools matches at Lord's 1968. Debut 1969. Cap 1976. Tests: 3 in 1976–77 and 1977. Tour: India, Sri Lanka and Australia 1976–77. 1,000 runs (3)—1,478 runs (av 49.26) in 1976 best. Gillette Man of Match awards: 1. Benson & Hedges Gold awards: 1. HS: 160* v Derbyshire (Lord's) 1976. HSTC: 7* v India (Calcutta) 1976–77. HSGC: 76* v Warwickshire (Birmingham) 1975. HSJPL: 114 v Warwickshire (Lord's) 1979. HSBH: 129 v Northants (Northampton) 1977. Studied at Loughborough College for whom he played rugby.

 John Michael (Mike) BREARLEY (City of London School and Cambridge) B Harrow 28/4/1942. RHB. Occasional WK. Debut 1961 scoring 1,222 runs (av 35.94) in first season. Blue 1961–62–63–64 (capt 1963–64). Cap 1964. Elected Best Young Cricketer of the Year in 1964 by the Cricket Writers' Club. Did not play in 1966 or 1967, but reappeared in latter half of each season between 1968 and 1970. Appointed county captain in 1971. *Wisden* 1976. Awarded OBE in 1978 New Year Honours List. Benefit (£31,000) in 1978. Tests: 31 between 1976 and 1979, captaining England in 23 tests between 1977 and 1979. Tours: South Africa 1964–65, Pakistan 1966–67 (captain), India, Sri Lanka and Australia (vice-captain) 1976–77, Pakistan and New Zealand 1977–78 (captain). Returned home early owing to injury, Australia 1978–79 (captain), Australia and India 1979–80 (captain). 1,000 runs (8)—2,178 runs (av 44.44) in 1964 best. Holds record for most runs scored for Cambridge University (4,310 runs, av 38.48). Gillette Man of Match awards: 3. Benson & Hedges Gold awards: 2. HS: 312* MCC under-25 v North Zone (Peshawar) 1966–67. HSUK: 173* v Glamorgan (Cardiff) 1974. HSTC: 91 v India (Bombay) 1976–77. HSGC: 124* v Bucks (Lord's) 1975. HSJPL: 75* v Glamorgan (Lord's) 1974. HSBH: 88 v Notts (Newark) 1976.

 Roland Orlando BUTCHER B East Point, St. Philip, Barbados 14/10/1953. RHB, RM. Debut 1974. Played for Barbados in 1974–75 Shell Shield competition. Cap 1979. HS: 142 v Glos (Bristol) 1978. HSJPL: 94 v Surrey (Oval) 1979.

Wayne Wendell DANIEL B St Philip, Barbados 16/1/1956. RHB, RF. Toured England with West Indies Schoolboys team 1974. Played for 2nd XI in 1975. Debut for Barbados 1975–76. Debut for county and cap 1977. Tests: 5 for West Indies in 1975–76 and 1976. Tour: West Indies to England 1976. Gillette Man of Match awards: 1. Benson & Hedges Gold awards: 2. HS: 30 West Indians v Sussex (Hove) 1976 and 30* v Notts (Lord's) 1978. HSTC: 11 West Indies v India (Kingston) 1975–76. HSBH: 20* v Derbyshire (Derby) 1978. BB: 6–21 West Indians v Yorks (Sheffield) 1976. BBC: 6–33 v Sussex (Lord's) 1977. BBTC: 4–53 West Indies v England (Nottingham) 1976. BBGC: 4–24 v Somerset (Lord's) 1977. BBJPL: 4–13 v Derbyshire (Chesterfield) 1979. BBBH: 7–12 v Minor Counties (East) (Ipswich) 1978 – record for competition.

Phillippe Henri (Phil) EDMONDS (Gilbert Rennie HS, Lusaka, Skinner's School, Tunbridge Wells, Cranbrook School and Cambridge) B Lusaka, Northern Rhodesia (now Zambia) 8/3/1951. RHB, SLA. Debut for Cambridge U and county 1971. Blue 1971–73 (capt in 1973). Cap 1974. Elected Best Young Cricketer of the Year in 1974 by the Cricket Writers' Club. Played for Eastern Province in 1975–76 Currie Cup competition. Tests: 18 between 1975 and 1979. Tours: Pakistan and New Zealand 1977–78, Australia 1978–79. HS: 141* v Glamorgan (Lord's) 1979. HSTC: 50 v New Zealand (Christchurch) 1977–78. HSGC: 63* v Somerset (Lord's) 1979. HSJPL: 43 v Leics (Lord's) 1977. HSBH: 44* v Notts (Newark) 1976. BB: 8–132 (14–150 match) v Glos (Lord's) 1977. BBTC: 7–66 v Pakistan (Karachi) 1977–78. BBGC: 3–28 v Yorks (Lord's) 1979. BBJPL: 3–19 v Leics (Lord's) 1973. BBBH: 4–11 v Kent (Lord's) 1975. Has also played rugby for University and narrowly missed obtaining Blue.

John Ernest EMBUREY B Peckham 20/8/1952. RHB, OB. Played for Surrey Young Cricketers 1969–70. Joined county staff. Debut 1973. Cap 1977. Tests: 5 in 1978 and 1978–79. Tours: Australia 1978–79, Australia and India 1979–80 (as replacement for G. Miller). HS: 91* v Surrey (Oval) 1979. HSTC: 42 v Australia (Adelaide) 1978–79. HSGC: 36* v Lancs (Manchester) 1978. HSJPL: 30 v Lancs (Lord's) 1978. HSBH: 10 v Yorks (Lord's) 1979. BB: 7–36 v Cambridge U (Cambridge) 1977. BBTC: 4–46 v Australia (Sydney) 1978–79. BBJPL: 4–43 v Worcs (Worcester) 1976.

Paul Bernard FISHER (St Ignatius College, Enfield and Oxford). B Edmonton, 19/12/1954. RHB, WK. Debut for Oxford U 1974. Blue 1975–76–77–78. Played for county in one Fenner Trophy match and in last John Player League Match in 1978. Debut for county in last two championship matches of 1979. HS: 42 Oxford U v Warwickshire (Oxford) 1975.

Michael William (Mike) GATTING (John Kelly Boys HS, Cricklewood) B Kingsbury (Middlesex) 6/6/1957. RHB, RM. Represented England Young Cricketers 1974. Debut 1975. Toured West Indies with England Young Cricketers 1976. Cap 1977. Tests: 2 in 1977–78. Tour: Pakistan and New Zealand 1977–78. 1,000 runs (2)— 1,166 runs (av 33.31) in 1978 best. Benson & Hedges Gold awards: 2. HS: 128 v Derbyshire (Lord's) 1978. HSTC: 6 v Pakistan (Karachi) 1977–78. HSGC: 62 v Kent (Canterbury) 1977 and 62 v Lancs (Manchester) 1978. HSJPL: 85 v Notts (Lord's) 1976. HSBH: 67 v Kent (Canterbury) 1979. BB: 5–59 v Leics (Lord's) 1978. BBJPL: 4–32 v Kent (Lord's) 1978. BBBH: 3–35 v Minor Counties (East) (Lord's) 1976.

Ian James GOULD B Slough (Bucks) 19/8/1957. LHB, WK. Joined staff 1972. Debut 1975. Toured West Indies with England Young Cricketers 1976. Cap 1977. HS: 128 v Worcs (Worcester) 1978. HSGC: 58 v Derbyshire (Derby) 1978. HSJPL: 36* v Yorks (Lord's) 1975. HSBH: 32 v Notts (Nottingham) 1979.

MIDDLESEX

William Gerald (Bill) MERRY B Newbury (Berks) 8/8/1955. RHB, RM. Played for Leics 2nd XI in 1976 and for Hertfordshire between 1976 and 1978. Debut 1979. HS: 4* v Leics (Leicester) 1979. BB: 3–46 v Kent (Tunbridge Wells) 1979. BBJPL: 3–29 v Lancs (Manchester) 1979.

Roger Peter MOULDING (Haberdashers' Aske's School, Elstree and Oxford) B Enfield 3/1/1958. RHB, LB. Debut 1977. Blue 1978–79. University Secretary in 1979. Did not play for county in 1978 or 1979. HS: 77* Oxford U v Worcs (Worcester) 1978. HSC: 26* v Cambridge U (Cambridge) 1977.

· **Clive Thornton RADLEY** (King Edward VI GS, Norwich) B Hertford 13/5/1944. RHB, LB. Debut 1964. Cap 1967. Benefit (£26,000) in 1977. *Wisden* 1978. Tests: 8 in 1977–78 and 1978. Tours: Pakistan and New Zealand 1977–78 (as replacement for J. M. Brearley), Australia 1978–79. 1,000 runs (12)—1,414 runs (av 38.21) in 1969 and 1,413 runs (av 41.55) in 1972 best. Shared in 6th wkt partnership record for county, 227 with F. J. Titmus v South Africans (Lord's) 1965. Gillette Man of Match awards: 2. Benson & Hedges Gold awards: 2. HS: 171 v Cambridge U (Cambridge) 1976. HSTC: 158 v New Zealand (Auckland) 1977–78. HSGC: 105* v Worcs (Worcester) 1975. HSJPL: 133* v Glamorgan (Lord's) 1969. HSBH: 121* v Minor Counties (East) (Lord's) 1976.

Michael Walter Williams (Mike) SELVEY (Battersea GS and Manchester and Cambridge Universities) B Chiswick 25/4/1948. RHB, RFM. Debut for Surrey 1968. Debut for Cambridge U and Blue 1971. Debut for Middlesex 1972. Cap 1973. Played for Orange Free State in 1973–74 Currie Cup competition. Tests: 3 in 1976 and 1976–77. Tour: India, Sri Lanka and Australia 1976–77. Took 101 wkts (av 19.09) in 1978. Benson & Hedges Gold awards: 1. HS: 45 v Essex (Colchester) 1979. HSGC: 14 v Derbyshire (Derby) 1978. HSJPL: 38 v Essex (Southend) 1977 and 38* v Essex (Chelmsford) 1979. HSBH: 27* v Surrey (Lord's) 1973. BB: 7–20 v Glos (Gloucester) 1976. BBTC: 4–41 v West Indies (Manchester) 1976. BBGC: 3–32 v Somerset (Lord's) 1977. BBJPL: 5–18 v Glamorgan (Cardiff) 1975. BBBH: 5–39 v Glos (Lord's) 1972. Played soccer for University.

Wilfred Norris SLACK B Troumaca, St. Vincent, 12/12/1954. LHB, RM. Played for Buckinghamshire in 1976. Debut 1977. HS: 66 v Notts (Nottingham) 1979. HSJPL: 57 v Kent (Lord's) 1978.

Michael John (Mike) SMITH (Enfield GS) B Enfield 4/1/1942. RHB, SLA. Debut 1959. Cap 1967. Benefit (£20,000) in 1976. 1,000 runs (11)—1,705 runs (av 39.65) in 1970 best. Gillette Man of Match awards: 2. Benson & Hedges Gold awards: 1. HS: 181 v Lancs (Manchester) 1967. HSGC: 123 v Hants (Lord's) 1977. HSJPL: 101 v Lancs (Lord's) 1971. HSBH: 105 v Minor Counties (East) (Lord's) 1976. BB: 4–13 v Glos (Lord's) 1961.

Keith Patrick TOMLINS (St. Benedict's School, Ealing) B Kingston-upon-Thames 23/10/1957. RHB, RM. Debut 1977. HS: 94 v Worcs (Worcester) 1978. HSJPL: 15 v Sussex (Hove) 1978. BBJPL: 4–24 v Notts (Lord's) 1978. Is studying at Durham University.

N.B. The following players whose particulars appeared in the 1979 annual have been omitted: R. Herkes, A. S. Patel and S. J. Poulter. In addition F. J. Titmus who re-appeared in two matches has not been included.
The career records of Herkes and Titmus will be found elsewhere in this annual.

COUNTY AVERAGES

Schweppes County Championships: Played 20, Won 3, Drawn 14, Lost 3, Abandoned 2.
All First-class Matches: As above.

BATTING AND FIELDING

Cap		M	I	NO	Runs	HS	Avge	100	50	Ct	St
1974	P. H. Edmonds	10	12	5	398	141*	56.85	1	1	9	—
1976	G. D. Barlow	20	33	9	1000	133	41.66	1	5	9	—
1967	C. T. Radley	20	35	6	1128	118*	38.89	2	8	23	—
1964	J. M. Brearley	8	13	2	415	148*	37.72	1	1	10	—
1967	M. J. Smith	19	34	4	1109	137	36.96	5	1	12	—
1977	M. W. Gatting	14	21	4	557	93*	32.76	—	2	11	—
1977	J. E. Emburey	18	20	5	437	91*	29.13	—	1	20	—
1971	N. G. Featherstone	10	14	3	260	59*	23.63	—	1	10	—
1979	R. O. Butcher	14	22	0	513	106	23.31	1	2	13	—
—	W. N. Slack	6	12	0	236	66	19.66	—	1	2	—
1977	I. J. Gould	18	21	1	347	89	17.35	—	2	24	2
1973	M. W. W. Selvey	20	18	1	237	45	13.94	—	—	7	—
1977	W. W. Daniel	17	13	6	72	18	10.28	—	—	5	—
1976	A. A. Jones	11	8	3	29	12	5.80	—	—	3	—
—	W. G. Merry	8	6	4	7	4*	3.50	—	—	1	—

Played in two matches: P. B. Fisher 6, 0 (ct 5); R. Herkes 0, 0*, 0*, 0; F. J. Titmus
25, 5 (ct 1).

Played in one match: K. P. Tomlins 4 (ct 1).

BOWLING

	Type	O	M	R	W	Avge	Best	5 wI	10 wM
R. Herkes	RM	25.4	2	84	6	14.00	6–60	1	—
W. W. Daniel	RF	429.2	100	1170	52	22.50	6–38	2	—
N. G. Featherstone	OB	191.1	40	568	23	24.69	4–28	—	—
J. E. Emburey	OB	681.2	206	1457	57	25.56	4–31	—	—
M. W. W. Selvey	RFM	578.3	177	1443	56	25.76	5–42	3	—
P. H. Edmonds	SLA	387.4	121	878	32	27.43	4–30	—	—
A. A. Jones	RFM	221.2	49	646	17	38.00	3–39	—	—
W. G. Merry	RM	150	36	431	10	43.10	3–46	—	—

Also bowled: G. D. Barlow 2–1–1–0; R. O. Butcher 1–0–4–0; M. W. Gatting
34.4–7–106–1; C. T. Radley 2–0–9–1; W. N. Slack 6–3–3–0; M. J. Smith 5–0–22–0;
F. J. Titmus 76–16–177–3; K. P. Tomlins 2–0–13–0.

County Records

Highest innings totals:	For —642–3d v Hampshire (Southampton)	1923
	Agst—665 by West Indians (Lord's)	1939
Lowest innings totals:	For —20 v MCC (Lord's)	1864
	Agst—31 by Gloucestershire (Bristol)	1924
Highest individual innings:	For —331* J. D. Robertson v Worcs (Worcester)	1949
	Agst—316* J. B. Hobbs for Surrey (Lord's)	1926
Best bowling in an innings:	For —10–40 G. O. Allen v Lancs (Lord's)	1929
	Agst—9–38 R. C. Robertson-Glasgow for Somerset (Lord's)	1924

Best bowling in a match:

For—16–114 { G. Burton v Yorks (Sheffield) 1888
              { J. T. Hearne v Lancs (Manchester) 1898

Agst—16–109 C. W. L. Parker for Glos (Cheltenham) 1930

Most runs in a season:	2650 (av 85.48) W. J. Edrich	1947
runs in a career:	40302 (av 49.81) E. H. Hendren	1907–1937
100s in a season:	13 by D. C. S. Compton	1947
100s in a career:	119 by E. H. Hendren	1907–1937
wickets in a season:	158 (av 14.63) F. J. Titmus	1955
wickets in a career:	2346 (av 21.23) F. J. Titmus	1949–1976

RECORD WICKET STANDS

1st	310	W. E. Russell & M. J. Harris v Pakistanis (Lord's)	1967
2nd	380	F. A. Tarrant & J. W. Hearne v Lancashire (Lord's)	1914
3rd	424*	W. J. Edrich & D. C. S. Compton v Somerset (Lord's)	1948
4th	325	J. W. Hearne & E. H. Hendren v Hampshire (Lord's)	1919
5th	338	R. S. Lucas & T. C. O'Brien v Sussex (Hove)	1895
6th	227	C. T. Radley & F. J. Titmus v South Africans (Lord's)	1965
7th	271*	E. H. Hendren & F. T. Mann v Nottinghamshire (Nottingham)	1925
8th	182*	M. H. C. Doll & H. R. Murrell v Nottinghamshire (Lord's)	1913
9th	160*	E. H. Hendren & T. J. Durston v Essex (Leyton)	1927
10th	230	R. W. Nicholls & W. Roche v Kent (Lord's)	1899

One-day cricket

Highest innings totals:	Gillette Cup	280–8 v Sussex (Lord's)	1965
	John Player League	256–9 v Worcestershire (Worcester)	1976
	Benson & Hedges Cup	303–7 v Northants (Northampton)	1977
Lowest innings totals:	Gillette Cup	41 v Essex (Westcliff)	1972
	John Player League	23 v Yorkshire (Leeds)	1974
	Benson & Hedges Cup	97 v Northamptonshire (Lord's)	1976
Highest individual innings:	Gillette Cup	124* J. M. Brearley v Buckinghamshire (Lord's)	1975
	John Player League	133* C. T. Radley v Glamorgan (Lord's)	1969
	Benson & Hedges Cup	129 G. D. Barlow v Northants (Northampton)	1977
Best bowling figures:	Gillette Cup	6–28 K. V. Jones v Lancashire (Lord's)	1974
	John Player League	6–6 R. W. Hooker v Surrey (Lord's)	1969
	Benson & Hedges Cup	7–12 W. W. Daniel v Minor Counties (East) (Ipswich)	1978

NORTHAMPTONSHIRE

Formation of present club: 1820, reorganised 1878
Colours: Maroon.
Badge: Tudor Rose.
County Championship runners-up (4):
1912, 1957, 1965 and 1976.
Gillette Cup winners: 1976.
Gillette Cup finalists: 1979.
Best final position in John Player League: 4th in 1974.
Benson & Hedges Cup semi-finalists: 1977.
Fenner Trophy Winners: 1977.
Gillette Man of the Match awards: 17.
Benson & Hedges Gold awards: 10.

Secretary: K. C. Turner, County Ground, Wantage Rd, Northampton, NN1 4TJ.
Captain: P. J. Watts.

Prospects of play Telephone No: Northampton (0604) 32697.

Robert Michael CARTER B King's Lynn 25/5/1960. RHB, RM. Played for 2nd XI since 1976. Debut 1978. HS: 26* v Glos (Northampton) 1979. HSJPL: 21* v Surrey (Oval) 1979. BBJPL: 3–35 v Worcs (Milton Keynes) 1978. Has played soccer for Norwich City.

Geoffrey (Geoff) Cook (Middlesbrough HS) B Middlesbrough 9/10/1951. RHB, SLA. Debut 1971. Cap 1975. Played for Eastern Province in 1978–79 Currie Cup competition. 1,000 runs (5)—1,241 runs (av 35.45) in 1979 best. Gillette Man of Match awards: 2. Benson & Hedges Gold awards: 1. HS: 155. 172 Eastern Province v Northern Transvaal (Port Elizabeth) 1979–80. HS: UK 155 v Derbyshire (Northampton) 1978. HSGC: 114* v Surrey (Northampton) 1978. HSJPL: 85 v Leics (Leicester) 1976. HSBH: 96 v Minor Counties (East) (Northampton) 1978.

Vincent Anthony FLYNN (Aylesbury GS) B Aylesbury (Bucks) 3/10/1955, RHB, WK. Debut 1978. Did not play in 1979. HS: 15 v Yorks (Northampton) 1978. Studied at Leeds University.

Brian James (Jim) GRIFFITHS B Wellingborough 13/6/1949. RHB, RFM. Debut 1974. Cap 1978. HS: 11 v Middlesex (Lord's) 1978. BB: 5–66 v Surrey (Northampton) 1978. BBGC: 3–39 v Leics (Northampton) 1978. BBJPL: 4–22 v Somerset (Weston-super-Mare) 1977. BBBH: 5–43 v Sussex (Eastbourne) 1979.

Allan Joseph LAMB (Wynberg Boys' High School) B Langebaanweg, Cape Province, South Africa 20/6/1954. RHB, RM. Debut for Western Province in Currie Cup 1972–73. Debut for county and cap 1978. Scored 1,747 runs (av 67.19) in 1979. Benson & Hedges Gold awards: 1. HS: 178 v Leics (Leicester) 1979. HSGC: 101 v Sussex (Hove) 1979. HSJPL: 77 v Warwickshire (Northampton) 1979. HSBH: 77 v Essex (Northampton) 1979.

Hon. Timothy Michael LAMB (Shrewsbury School and Oxford) B Hartford (Cheshire) 24/3/1953. Younger son of Lord Rochester. RHB, RM. Debut for Oxford U 1973. Blue 1973–74. Debut for Middlesex 1974. Left county and made debut for Northants in 1978. Cap 1978. HS: 77 Middlesex v Notts (Lord's) 1976. HSC: 33 v Notts (Northampton) 1978. HSGC: 11* Middlesex v Lancs (Lord's) 1975. HSJPL: 27 Middlesex v Hants (Basingstoke) 1976. BB: 6–49 Middlesex v Surrey (Lord's) 1975. BBC: 6–71 v Warwickshire (Northampton) 1978. BBGC: 4–52 v Sussex (Hove) 1979. BBJPL: 5–13 v Notts (Northampton) 1979. BBBH: 5–44 Middlesex v Yorks (Lord's) 1975.

NORTHAMPTONSHIRE

Wayne Larkins B Roxton (Beds) 22/11/1953. RHB, RM. Joined staff 1969. Debut 1972. Cap 1976.Tour: Australia and India 1979–80. 1,000 runs (2)—1,448 runs (av 37.12) in 1978 best. Benson & Hedges Gold awards: 1. HS: 170* v Worcs (Northampton) 1978. HSGC: 92* v Leics (Northampton) 1979. HSJPL: 111 v Leics (Wellingborough) 1979. HSBH: 73* v Essex (Chelmsford) 1977. BB: 3–34 v Somerset (Northamptom) 1976. BBJPL: 5–32 v Essex (Ilford) 1978. BBBH: 3–13 v Essex (Chelmsford) 1977.

Leslie McFARLANE B Portland, Jamaica, 19/8/1952. RHB, RM. Played for 2nd XI since 1974. Debut 1979. BB: 3–83 v Glos (Northampton) 1979.

Ian Michael RICHARDS (Grangefield GS and Stockton VIth Form College) B Stockton-on-Tees 9/12/1957. LHB, RM. Debut 1976. HS: 50 v Notts (Northampton) 1976. HSJPL: 18 v Worcs (Milton Keynes) 1978. BB: 4–57 v Warwickshire (Birmingham) 1978.

Sarfraz NAWAZ (Government College, Lahore) B Lahore, Pakistan 1/12/1948. RHB, RFM. Debut 1967–68 for West Pakistan Governor's XI v Punjab University at Lahore and subsequently played for various Lahore sides and United Bank. Debut for county 1969. Not re-engaged after 1971 season, but rejoined staff in 1974. Cap 1975. Tests: 34 for Pakistan between 1968–69 and 1978–79. Tours: Pakistan to England 1971, 1974 and 1978, Australia and New Zealand 1972–73, Australia and West Indies 1976–77. New Zealand and Australia 1978–79. Took 101 wkts (av 20.30) in 1975, Gillette Man of Match awards: 1. Benson & Hedges Gold awards: 1. HS: 86 v Essex (Chelmsford) 1975. HSTC: 53 Pakistant v England (Leeds) 1974. HSGC: 22 v Cambs (March) 1975. HSJPL: 43* v Lancs (Manchester) 1975. HSBH: 50 v Kent (Northampton) 1977. BB: 9–86 Pakistan v Australia (Melbourne) 1978–79. BBUK: 8–27 Pakistanis v Notts (Nottingham) 1974. BBC: 7–37 v Somerset (Weston-super-Mare) 1974. BBGC: 4–17 v Herts (Northampton) 1976. BBJPL: 5–15 v Yorks (Northampton) 1975. BBBH: 3–11 v Minor Counties (East) (Horton) 1977.

George SHARP B West Hartlepool 12/3/1950. RHB, WK. Can also bowl LM. Debut 1968. Cap 1973. HS: 85 v Warwickshire (Birmingham) 1976. HSGC: 35* v Durham (Northampton) 1977. HSJPL: 47 v Sussex (Hove) 1974 and 47* v Worcs (Milton Keynes) 1978. HSBH: 43 v Surrey (Northampton) 1979.

Robert Michael TINDALL (Harrow School) B Harrow-on-the-Hill 16/6/1959. Son of M. Tindall of Cambridge U and Middlesex. LHB, SLA. Played for 2nd XI in 1978. Played in last John Player League match of 1979. Has not yet appeared in first-class cricket. HSJPL: 14* v Hants (Bournemouth) 1979.

Patrick James (Jim) WATTS (Stratton School, Biggleswade) B Henlow (Beds) 16/6/1940. Brother of P. D. Watts who also played for county. LHB, RM. Debut 1959, scoring 1,118 runs (av 28.66) in his first season. Cap 1962. Left staff after 1966 season, but rejoined staff in 1970. County captain from 1971 to 1974. Benefit (£6,351) in 1974. Left staff after 1974 season to train as a teacher. Played occasionally in 1975, but did not appear in 1976 and 1977. Re-appointed county captain in 1978. 1,000 runs (7)—1,798 runs (av 43.85) in 1962 best. Benson & Hedges Gold awards: 1. HS: 145 v Hants (Bournemouth) 1962. HSGC: 40 v Glamorgan (Northampton) 1972. HSJPL: 83 v Lancs (Bedford) 1971. HSBH: 40 v Middlesex (Lord's) 1974. BB: 6–18 v Somerset (Taunton) 1965. BBGC: 4–58 v Warwickshire (Northampton) 1964. BBJPL: 5–24 v Notts (Peterborough) 1971. BBBH: 4–11 v Middlesex (Lord's) 1974.

Peter WILLEY B Sedgefield (County Durham) 6/12/1949. RHB, OB. Debut 1966 aged 16 years 180 days scoring 78 in second innings of first match v Cambridge U (Cambridge). Cap 1971. Tests: 3 between 1976 and 1979. Tour: Australia and India 1979–80. 1,000 runs (2)—1,115 runs (av 41.29) in 1976 best. Shared in 4th wkt partnership record for county, 370 with R. T. Virgin v Somerset (Northampton) 1976. Gillette Man of Match awards: 4'. HS: 227 v Somerset (Northampton) 1976. HSTC: 52 v India (Oval) 1979. HSGC: 89 v Sussex (Hove) 1979. HSJPL: 107 v Warwickshire (Birmingham) 1975 and 107 v Hants (Tring) 1976. HSBH: 58 v Warwickshire (Northampton) 1974. BB: 7–37 v Oxford U (Oxford) 1975. BBGC: 3–37 v Cambs (March) 1975. BBJPL: 4–59 v Kent (Northampton) 1971. BBBH: 3–12 v Minor Counties (East) (Horton) 1977.

Richard Grenville WILLIAMS (Ellesmere Port GS) B Bangor (Caernarvonshire) 10/8/1957. RHB, OB. 5ft 6½ins tall. Debut for 2nd XI in 1972, aged 14 years 11 months. Debut 1974 aged 16 years 313 days. Toured West Indies with England Young Cricketers 1976. Cap 1979. Scored 1,057 runs (av 33.03) in 1979. Scored two centuries in match (109 and 151*) v Warwickshire (Northampton) 1979. Gillette Man of Match awards: 1. HS: 151* v Warwickshire (Northampton) 1979. HSGC: 51 v Durham (Northampton) 1977. HSJPL: 65* v Glamorgan (Cardiff) 1976. HSBH: 10* v Minor Counties (East) (Longton) 1976. BB: 5–57 v Sussex (Northampton) 1979. BBGC: 3–15 v Leics (Northampton) 1979. BBJPL: 4–32 v Derbyshire (Long Eaton) 1979.

Thomas James (Jim) YARDLEY (King Charles I GS Kidderminster) B Chaddesley Corbett (Worcs) 27/10/1946. LHB, RM. Occasional WK. Debut for Worcs. 1967. Capt 1972. Not re-engaged after 1975 season and made debut for Northants in 1976. Cap 1978. Scored 1,066 runs (av 30.45) in 1971. HS: 135 Worcs v Notts (Worcester) 1973. HSC: 97 v Middlesex (Lord's) 1978. HSGC: 52 Worcs v Warwickshire (Birmingham) 1972 and 52* Worcs v Warwickshire (Birmingham) 1973. HSJPL: 66* v Middlesex (Lord's) 1977. HSBH: 75* Worcs v Warwickshire (Worcester) 1972.

NB The following player whose particulars appeared in the 1979 Annual has been omitted: A. Hodgson.
His career record will be found elsewhere in this Annual.

COUNTY AVERAGES

Schweppes County Championship: Played 21, won 3, drawn 12, lost 6, abandoned 1.
All First-class matches: Played 22, won 3, drawn 13, lost 6, abandoned 1.

BATTING AND FIELDING

Cap		M	I	NO	Runs	HS	Avge	100	50	Ct	St
1978	A. J. Lamb	21	34	8	1747	178	67.19	4	11	19	—
1976	W. Larkins	14	24	1	1036	136	45.04	3	7	11	—
1971	P. Willey	20	31	7	986	131	41.08	2	5	10	—
1975	G. Cook	22	37	2	1241	130	35.45	3	4	17	—
1979	R. G. Williams	22	35	3	1057	151*	33.03	4	3	7	—
1978	T. J. Yardley	19	29	6	623	66*	27.08	—	4	17	—
—	I. M. Richards	11	15	1	312	47	22.28	—	—	3	—
1962	P. J. Watts	18	24	7	323	42*	19.00	—	11	—	—
1975	Sarfraz Nawaz	13	15	2	220	46	16.92	—	7	3	—
1973	G. Sharp	22	26	2	386	51	16.08	—	1	34	6
—	R. M. Carter	10	10	3	94	26*	13.42	—	—	6	—
1978	T. M. Lamb	17	17	7	72	14	7.20	—	—	4	—
1976	A. Hodgson	11	11	3	39	10	4.87	—	—	4	—
1978	B. J. Griffiths	14	14	6	36	10*	4.50	—	—	3	—
—	L. McFarlane	8	2	0	0	0	0.00	—	—	—	—

NORTHAMPTONSHIRE

BOWLING	Type	O	M	R	W	Avge	Best	5 wI	10 wM
Sarfraz Nawaz	RFM	407.5	130	913	45	20.28	6–60	2	—
B. J. Griffiths	RFM	422.5	89	1222	50	24.44	5–76	1	—
P. Willey	OB	641.2	169	1527	47	32.48	5–46	3	—
R. G. Williams	OB	430	119	1184	36	32.88	5–57	1	—
R. M. Carter	RM	99	26	316	8	39.50	2–12	—	—
T. M. Lamb	RM	329.5	94	997	24	41.54	4–58	—	—
P. J. Watts	RM	107	24	304	7	43.42	2–10	—	—
L. McFarlane	RM	181	34	569	13	43.76	3–83	—	—
A. Hodgson	RFM	234	39	819	18	45.50	3–41	—	—

Also bowled: G. Cook 11.3–4–31–0; A. J. Lamb 6–1–15–1; W. Larkins
30–8–107–3; I. M. Richards 5–2–25–0; T. J. Yardley 0.3–0–3–0.

County Records

First-class cricket

Highest innings totals:	For —557–6d v Sussex (Hove)	1914
	Agst—670–9d by Sussex (Hove)	1921
Lowest innings totals:	For —12 v Gloucestershire (Gloucester)	1907
	Agst—43 by Leicestershire (Peterborough)	1968
Highest individual innings	For —300 R. Subba Row v Surrey (The Oval)	1958
	Agst—333 K. S. Duleepsinhji for Sussex (Hove)	1930
Best bowling in an innings:	For —10–127 V. W. C. Jupp v Kent (Tunbridge Wells)	1932
	Agst—10–30 C. Blythe for Kent (Northampton)	1907
Best bowling in a match:	For —15–31 G. E. Tribe v Yorkshire (Northampton)	1958
	Agst—17–48 C. Blythe for Kent (Northampton)	1907
Most runs in a season:	2198 (av 51.11) D. Brookes	1952
runs in a career:	28980 (av 36.13) D. Brookes	1934–1959
100s in a season:	8 by R. Haywood	1921
100s in a career:	67 by D. Brookes	1934–1959
wickets in a season:	175 (av 18.70) G. E. Tribe	1955
wickets in a career:	1097 (av 21.31) E. W. Clark	1922–1947

RECORD WICKET STANDS

1st	361	N. Oldfield & V. Broderick v Scotland (Peterborough)	1953
2nd	299*	T. L. Livingston & D. Barrick v Sussex (Northampton)†	1953
3rd	320	T. L. Livingston & F. Jakeman v South Africans (Northampton)	1951
4th	370	R. T. Virgin & P. Willey v Somerset (Northampton)	1976
5th	347	D. Brookes & D. Barrick v Essex (Northampton)	1952
6th	376	R. Subba Row & A. Lightfoot v Surrey (The Oval)	1958
7th	229	W. W. Timms & F. A. Walden v Warwickshire (Northampton)	1926
8th	155	F. R. Brown & A. E. Nutter v Glamorgan (Northampton)	1952
9th	156	R. Subba Row & S. Starkie v Lancashire (Northampton)	1955
10th	148	R. Bellamy & V. Murdin v Glamorgan (Northampton)	1925

†307 *runs in all were added for this wicket, N. Oldfield*
retiring hurt after 8 runs had been scored.

One-day cricket

Highest innings totals:	Gillette Cup	275–5 v Nottinghamshire (Nottingham)	1976
	John Player League	259 v Warwickshire (Northampton)	1979
	Benson & Hedges Cup	249–3 v Warwickshire (Northampton)	1974
Lowest innings totals:	Gillette Cup	62 v Leics (Leicester)	1974
	John Player League	41 v Middlesex (Northampton)	1972
	Benson & Hedges Cup	85 v Sussex (Northampton)	1978
Highest individual innings:	Gillette Cup	109 D. S. Steele v Cambs (March)	1975
	John Player League	115* H. M. Ackerman v Kent (Dover)	1970
	Benson & Hedges Cup	131 Mushtaq Mohammad v Minor Counties (East) (Longton)	1976
Best bowling figures:	Gillette Cup	5–24 J. D. F. Larter v Leicestershire (Leicester)	1964
	John Player League	7–39 A. Hodgson v Somerset (Northampton)	1976
	Benson & Hedges Cup	5–30 J. C. J. Dye v Worcestershire (Northampton)	1975

NOTTINGHAMSHIRE

Formation of present club: 1841, reorganized 1866.
Colours: Green and gold.
Badge: County Badge of Nottinghamshire.
County Champions (12): 1865, 1868, 1871, 1872, 1875, 1880, 1883, 1884, 1885, 1886, 1907 and 1929.
Joint Champions (5): 1869, 1873, 1879, 1882 and 1889.
Gillette Cup semi-finalists: 1969.
Best final position in John Player League: 5th in 1975.
Benson & Hedges Cup quarter-finalists (3): 1973, 1976 and 1978.
Gillette Man of Match awards: 13.
Benson & Hedges Gold awards: 17.
Chief Executive: P. G. Carling, County Cricket Ground, Trent Bridge, Nottingham, NG2 6AG.
Cricket Manager: K. Taylor.
Captain: C. E. B. Rice.
Prospects of play Telephone No.: Nottingham (0602) 869681.

Mark Edward ALLBROOK (Tonbridge School and Cambridge) B Frimley (Surrey) 15/11/1954. RHB, OB. Played for Kent 2nd XI 1974–75. Debut for Cambridge U 1975. Blue 1975–76–77–78. Debut for county 1976. Did not play in 1979. HS: 39 Cambridge U v Yorks (Cambridge) 1976. HSC: 13 v Yorks (Bradford) 1976. BB: 7–79 Cambridge U v Notts (Cambridge) 1978. BBC: 4–106 v Northants (Northampton) 1976.

NOTTINGHAMSHIRE

John Dennis BIRCH B Nottingham 18/6/1955. RHB, RM. Debut 1973. Benson and Hedges gold awards: 1. HS: 94* v Yorks (Worksop) 1979. HSGC: 32 v Yorks (Bradford) 1978. HSJPL: 71 v Yorks (Scarborough) 1978. HSBH: 85 v Minor Counties (North) (Nottingham) 1979. BB: 6–64 v Hants (Bournemouth) 1975. BBJPL: 3–29 v Glamorgan (Swansea) 1976.

Michael Kenneth (Mike) BORE B Hull 2/6/1947, RHB, LM. Debut for Yorks 1969. Left county after 1978 season and made debut for Notts in 1979. HS: 37* Yorks v Notts (Bradford) 1973. HSC: 13* v Lancs (Blackpool) 1979. HSJPL: 28* v Northants (Northampton) 1979. BB: 8–89 v Kent (Folkestone) 1979. BBGC: 3–35 Yorks v Kent (Canterbury) 1971. BBJPL: 4–21 Yorks v Sussex (Middlesbrough) 1970 and 4–21 Yorks v Worcs (Worcester) 1974. BBBH: 3–29 Yorks v Minor Counties (North) (Leeds) 1974.

Kevin Edward COOPER B Hucknall (Notts) 27/12/1957. LHB, RFM. Debut 1976. HS: 19 v Cambridge U (Cambridge) 1978. HSJPL: 12 v Northants (Northampton) 1978. BB: 6–32 v Derbyshire (Derby) 1978. BBJPL: 4–25 v Hants (Nottingham) 1976. BBBH: 4–23 v Kent (Canterbury) 1979.

Christopher Colin CURZON B Lenton, Nottingham 22/12/1958. RHB, WK. Played for 2nd XI since 1976. Debut 1978. HS: 26 v Glos (Cheltenham) 1978. HSJPL: 18* v Yorks (Scarborough) 1978.

Roy Evatt DEXTER (Nottingham High School) B Nottingham 13/4/1955. RHB. Debut 1976. HS: 48 v Derbyshire (Ilkeston) 1977.

Bruce Nicholas FRENCH (The Meden Comprehensive School, Warsop) B Warsop (Notts) 13/8/1959. RHB, WK. Debut 1976 aged 16 years 287 days. HS: 66 v Cambridge U (Cambridge) 1978. HSJPL: 25 v Northants (Nottingham) 1978.

Peter John HACKER B Lenton Abbey, Nottingham 16/7/1952. RHB, LFM. Debut 1974. HS: 35 v Kent (Canterbury) 1977. BB: 4–46 v Glos (Nottingham) 1979. BBGC: 3–27 v Warwickshire (Birmingham) 1979. BBJPL: 3–35 v Sussex (Nottingham) 1979.

Richard John HADLEE (Christchurch Boys' High School). B Christchurch, New Zealand 3/7/1951. Youngest son of W. A. Hadlee, former New Zealand Test cricketer, and brother of D. R. Hadlee. LHB, RFM. Debut for Canterbury 1971–72 in Plunket Shield Competition. Debut for county and cap 1978. Played for Tasmania in 1979–80. Tests: 26 for New Zealand between 1972–73 and 1978–79. Tours: New Zealand to England 1973 and 1978. Australia 1973–74, Pakistan and India 1976–77. HS: 101* v Derbyshire (Nottingham) 1978. HSTC: 87 New Zealand v Pakistan (Karachi) 1976–77. HSGC: 12* v Warwickshire (Birmingham) 1979. HSJPL: 25* v Leics (Leicester) 1979. HSBH: 41 v Kent (Canterbury) 1978. BB: 7–23 New Zealand v India (Wellington) 1975–76 and 7–23 v Sussex (Nottingham) 1979. BBJPL: 5–21 v Leics (Leicester) 1979. BBBH: 3–30 v Minor Counties (North) (Nottingham) 1979.

Michael John (Mike, Pasty) HARRIS B St Just-in-Roseland (Cornwall) 25/5/1944. RHB, WK. Can bowl LBG. Debut for Middlesex 1964. Cap 1967. Left staff after 1968 season and joined Notts by special registration in 1969. Cap 1970. Played for Eastern Province in 1971–72 Currie Cup competition. Played for Wellington in New Zealand Shell Shield competition in 1975–76. Benefit in 1977. 1,000 runs (11)—2,238 runs (av 50.86) in 1971 best. Scored 9 centuries in 1971 to equal county record. Scored two centuries in match twice in 1971, 118 and 123 v Leics (Leicester) and 107 and 131* v Essex (Chelmsford) and also in 1979, 133* and 102 v

122

Northants (Nottingham). Shared in 1st wkt partnership record for Middlesex, 312 with W. E. Russell v Pakistanis (Lord's) 1967. Benson & Hedges Gold awards: 2. HS: 201* v Glamorgan (Nottingham) 1973. HSGC: 101 v Somerset (Nottingham) 1970. HSJPL: 104* v Hants (Nottingham) 1970. HSBH: 101 v Yorks (Hull) 1973. BB: 4–16 v Warwickshire (Nottingham) 1969.

Basharat HASSAN (City HS, Nairobi) B Nairobi (Kenya) 24/3/1944. RHB, RM, occasional WK. Debut for East Africa Invitation XI v MCC 1963–64. Played for Coast Invitation XI v Pakistan International Airways 1964. Also played for Kenya against these and other touring sides. Debut for county 1966. Cap 1970. Benefit in 1978. 1,000 runs (5)—1,395 runs (av 32.44) in 1970 best. Scored century with aid of a runner v Kent (Canterbury) 1977—a rare achievement in first-class cricket. HS: 182* v Glos (Nottingham) 1977. HSGC: 79 v Hants (Southampton) 1977. HSJPL: 111v Surrey (Oval) 1977. HSBH: 98* v Minor Counties (North) (Nottingham) 1973. BB: 3–33 v Lancs (Manchester) 1976. BBGC: 3–20 v Durham (Chester-le-Street) 1967.

Edward Ernest (Eddie) HEMMINGS (Campion School, Leamington Spa) B Leamington Spa 20/2/1949. RHB, OB. Debut for Warwickshire 1966. Cap 1974. Left staff after 1978 season and made debut for Notts in 1979. Hat-trick Warwickshire v Worcs (Birmingham) 1977. HS: 85 Warwickshire v Essex (Birmingham) 1977 and 85* v Hants (Bournemouth) 1979. HSGC: 20 Warwickshire v Worcs (Birmingham) 1973. HSJPL: 44* Warwickshire v Kent (Birmingham) 1971. HSBH: 61* Warwickshire v Leics (Birmingham) 1974. BB: 7–33 (12–64 match) Warwickshire v Cambridge U (Cambridge) 1975. BBC: 5–74 v Warwickshire (Birmingham) 1979. BBJPL: 5–22 Warwickshire v Northants (Birmingham) 1974. BBBH: 3–18 Warwickshire v Oxford and Cambridge Universities (Coventry) 1975.

Kevin Scott MACKINTOSH (Kingston-Upon-Thames GS) B Surbiton (Surrey) 30/8/1957. RHB, RM. On Surrey staff from 1975 to 1977. Debut for County 1978. HS: 23* v Essex (Nottingham) 1978. HSJPL: 12* v Lancs (Nottingham) 1978. BB: 4–49 v Surrey (Oval) 1978. BBJPL: 4–26 v Glos (Nottingham) 1979.

Nirmal NANAN B Preysal Village, Couva, Trinidad 19/8/1951. RHB, LBG. Toured England with West Indian schoolboy team 1970. Debut 1969–70 for South Trinidad v North Trinidad (Pointe-a-Pierre). Debut for county 1971. Has not played since 1977, but is still on staff and scored over 1,000 runs for 2nd XI in 1977 and again in 1978. HS: 72 v Oxford U (Oxford) 1971. HSGC: 16 v Hants (Southampton) 1977. HSJPL: 58 v Somerset (Torquay) 1972. BB: 3–12 v Oxford U (Oxford) 1971.

Derek William RANDALL B Retford 24/2/1951. RHB, RM. Played in one John Player League match in 1971. Debut 1972. Cap 1973. *Wisden* 1979. Tests: 25 between 1976–77 and 1979. Tours: India, Sri Lanka and Australia 1976–77, Pakistan and New Zealand 1977–78. Australia 1978–79, Australia and India 1979–80. 1,000 runs (5)—1,546 runs (av 42.94) in 1976 best. Scored two centuries in match (209 and 146) v Middlesex (Nottingham) 1979. Gillette Man of Match awards: 1. Benson & Hedges Gold awards: 3. HS: 209 v Middlesex (Nottingham) 1979. HSTC: 174 v Australia (Melbourne) 1976–77. HSGC: 75 v Sussex (Hove) 1979. HSJPL: 107* v Middlesex (Lord's) 1976. HSBH: 103* v Minor Counties (North) (Nottingham) 1979.

Clive Edward Butler RICE (St John's College, Johannesburg) B Johannesburg 23/7/1949. RHB, RFM. Debut for Transvaal 1969–70. Professional for Ramsbottom in Lancashire League in 1973. Played for D. H. Robins' XI v West Indians 1973 and Pakistanis 1974. Debut for county and cap 1975. Appointed county captain for 1978, but was relieved of appointment when his signing for World Series Cricket was

123

NOTTINGHAMSHIRE

announced. Re-appointed county captain during 1979 season. 1,000 runs (5)—1,871 runs (av 66.82) in 1978 best. Benson & Hedges Gold awards: 2. HS: 246 v Sussex (Hove) 1976. HSGC: 71 v Yorks (Bradford) 1978. Scored 157 for Transvaal v Orange Free State (Bloemfontein) 1975–76 in South African Gillette Cup competition. HSJPL: 120* v Glamorgan (Swansea) 1978. HSBH: 94 v Middlesex (Newark) 1976. BB: 7–62 Transvaal v Western Province (Johannesburg) 1975–76. BBUK: 6–16 v Worcs (Worcester) 1977. BBGC: 3–29 v Sussex (Nottingham) 1975. BBJPL: 4–23 v Glamorgan (Nottingham) 1975. BBBH: 4–9 v Combined Universities (Nottingham) 1977.

Robert Timothy (Tim) ROBINSON (High Pavement College, Nottingham). B Sutton-in-Ashfield (Notts) 21/11/1958. RHB, RM. Played for Northants 2nd XI in 1974 and 1975 and for county 2nd XI in 1977. Debut 1978. HS: 40 v Middlesex (Nottingham) 1979. HSJPL: 35 v Somerset (Nottingham) 1979. Is studying at Sheffield University.

Kevin SAXELBY (Magnus GS, Newark) B Worksop 23/2/1959. RHB, RM. Debut 1978. Played in two matches and two John Player League matches in 1978. Did not play in 1979.

Paul Adrian TODD B Morton (Notts) 12/3/1953. RHB, RM. Debut 1972. Cap 1977. Gillette Man of Match awards: 1. Benson & Hedges Gold awards: 1. 1,000 runs (3).—1,181 runs (av 29.52) in 1978 best. HS: 178 v Glos (Nottingham) 1975. HSGC: 105 v Warwickshire (Birmingham) 1979. HSJPL: 79 v Hants (Nottingham) 1978. HSBH: 59 v Kent (Canterbury) 1979.

Howard Trevor TUNNICLIFFE (Malvern College) B Derby 4/3/1950. RHB, RM. Debut 1973. HS: 97 v Glamorgan (Nottingham) 1979. HSGC: 53* v Yorks (Bradford) 1974. HSJPL: 52* v Somerset (Nottingham) 1978. HSBH: 32 v Kent (Canterbury) 1976. BB: 4–30 v Sri Lankans (Nottingham) 1979. BBJPL: 3–17 v Sussex (Nottingham) 1975.

William Kenneth (Ken) WATSON (Dale College, Kingwilliamstown) B Port Elizabeth 21/5/1955. RHB, RFM. Debut for Border 1974–75. Played for Northern T. ansvaal 1975–76 and for Eastern Province from 1976–77. Debut for county 1976. HS: 28* v Cambridge U (Cambridge) 1978. BB: 6–51 v Derbyshire (Nottingham) 1979. BBJPL: 3–20 v Hants (Bournemouth) 1977.

Neil Ivan WEIGHTMAN (Magnus GS, Newark) B Normanton-on-Trent 5/10/1960. LHB, OB. Played for 2nd XI since 1977. Has yet to appear in first class cricket.

Robert Arthur (Bob) WHITE (Chiswick GS) B Fulham 6/10/1936. LHB, OB. Debut for Middlesex 1958. Cap 1963. Debut for Notts after special registration in 1966 and developed into useful off-break bowler. Cap 1966. Benefit (£11,000) in 1974. Did not play in 1979. Scored 1,355 runs (av 33.87) in 1963. HS: 116* v Surrey (Oval) 1967, sharing in 7th wkt partnership record for county, 204 with M. J. Smedley. HSGC: 39 v Worcs (Worcester) 1966. HSJPL: 86* v Surrey (Guildford) 1973. HSBH: 52* v Worcs (Worcester) 1973. BB: 7–41 v Derbyshire (Ilkeston) 1971. BBGC: 3–43 v Worcs (Worcester) 1968. BBJPL: 4–15 v Somerset (Bath) 1975. BBBH: 3–27 v Northants (Northampton) 1976.

NB The following players whose particulars appeared in the 1979 annual have been omitted: D. E. Coote, J. T. Curzon and M. J. Smedley (left staff).
The career record of Smedley will be found elsewhere in this annual.

COUNTY AVERAGES

Schweppes County Championship: Played 19, won 6, drawn 9, lost 4, abandoned 3
All first-class matches: Played 22, won 8, drawn 10, lost 4, abandoned 3

BATTING AND FIELDING

Cap		M	I	NO	Runs	HS	Avge	100	50	Ct	St
1973	D. W. Randall	11	22	1	1055	209	50.23	3	4	8	—
1975	C. E. B. Rice	21	34	3	1297	129	41.83	1	10	22	—
1970	M. J. Harris	21	38	4	1368	133*	40.23	2	10	9	—
1977	P. A. Todd	19	34	2	1164	176	36.37	2	4	14	—
—	C. C. Curzon	3	4	3	36	18*	36.00	—	—	3	1
—	H. T. Tunnicliffe	22	39	12	883	97	32.70	—	6	16	—
—	J. D. Birch	13	21	5	440	94*	27.50	—	2	12	—
1966	M. J. Smedley	12	16	1	351	91	23.40	—	1	12	—
—	E. E. Hemmings	21	31	6	453	85*	18.12	—	2	9	—
—	W. K. Watson	10	10	5	89	25	17.80	—	—	7	—
1970	B. Hassan	11	16	1	257	49	17.13	—	—	7	—
1978	R. J. Hadlee	12	16	4	193	41	16.08	—	—	5	—
—	K. E. Cooper	12	9	4	79	18*	15.80	—	—	3	—
—	B. N. French	19	20	5	223	41	14.86	—	—	38	4
—	M. K. Bore	22	17	8	45	13*	5.00	—	—	5	—
—	P. J. Hacker	10	11	3	40	9	5.00	—	—	2	—

Played in one match: R. E. Dexter 1; K. S. Mackintosh 8, 8 (2 ct); R. T. Robinson 28, 40.

BOWLING	Type	O	M	R	W	Avge	Best	5 wI	10 wM
R. J. Hadlee	RFM	317	103	753	47	16.02	7–23	2	—
C. E. B. Rice	RFM	448	134	1139	58	19.63	6–49	3	—
W. K. Watson	RFM	213.5	69	560	20	28.00	6–51	1	—
E. E. Hemmings	OB	738	226	1770	62	28.54	5–74	2	—
M. K. Bore	LM	731	226	1885	61	30.90	8–89	3	—
K. E. Cooper	RM	177.4	45	536	15	35.73	4–42	—	—
H. T. Tunnicliffe	RM	166.2	50	511	13	39.30	4–30	—	—
P. J. Hacker	LFM	177	42	639	15	42.60	4–46	—	—

Also bowled: J. D. Birch 25–6–76–1; M. J. Harris 10–2–31–0; K. S. Mackintosh 10–3–23–0.

County Records

First-class Cricket .

Highest innings totals:	For —739–7d v Leicestershire (Nottingham)	1903
	Agst—706–4d by Surrey (Nottingham)	1947
Lowest innings totals:	For —13 v Yorkshire (Nottingham)	1901
	Agst—16 by Derbyshire (Nottingham) and Surrey (The Oval)	1879 & 1880
Highest individual innings:	For —312* W. W. Keeton v Middlesex (The Oval)	1939
	Agst—345 C. G. Macartney for Australians (Nottingham)	1921
Best bowling in an innings:	For —10–66 K. Smales v Gloucestershire (Stroud)	1956
	Agst—10–10 H. Verity for Yorkshire (Leeds)	1932
Best bowling in a match:	For —17–89 F. C. L. Mathews v Northants (Nottingham)	1923
	Agst—17–89 W. G. Grace for Glos (Cheltenham)	1877

NOTTINGHAMSHIRE

Most runs in a season:	2620	(av 53.46) W. W. Whysall	1929
runs in a career:	31327	(av 36.71) G. Gunn	1902–1932
100s in a season:	9	by W. W. Whysall	1928
		and M. J. Harris	1971
100s in a career:	62	by J. Hardstaff	1930–1955
wickets in a season:	181	(av 14.96) B. Dooland	1954
wickets in a career:	1653	(av 20.40) T. Wass	1896–1914

RECORD WICKET STANDS

1st	391	A. O. Jones & A. Shrewsbury v Gloucestershire (Bristol)	1899
2nd	398	W. Gunn & A. Shrewsbury v Sussex (Nottingham)	1890
3rd	369	J. Gunn & W. Gunn v Leicestershire (Nottingham)	1903
4th	361	A. O. Jones & J. Gunn v Essex (Leyton)	1905
5th	266	A. Shrewsbury & W. Gunn v Sussex (Hove)	1884
6th	303*	H. Winrow & P. F. Harvey v Derbyshire (Nottingham)	1947
7th	204	M. J. Smedley & R. A. White v Surrey (Oval)	1967
8th	220	G. F. H. Heane & R. Winrow v Somerset (Nottingham)	1933
9th	167	W. McIntyre & G. Wootton v Kent (Nottingham)	1869
10th	152	E. Alletson & W. Riley v Sussex (Hove)	1911

One-day cricket

Highest innings totals:	Gillette Cup	271 v Gloucestershire (Nottingham)	1968
	John Player League	260–5 v Warwickshire (Birmingham)	1976
	Benson & Hedges Cup	245–7 v Essex (Ilford)	1976
Lowest innings totals:	Gillette Cup	123 v Yorkshire (Scarborough)	1969
	John Player League	66 v Yorks (Bradford)	1969
	Benson & Hedges Cup	94 v Lancashire (Nottingham)	1975
Highest individual innings:	Gillette Cup	107 M. Hill v Somerset (Taunton)	1964
	John Player League	120* C. E. B. Rice v Glamorgan (Swansea)	1978
	Benson & Hedges Cup	103* D. W. Randall v Minor Counties (North) (Nottingham)	1979
Best bowling figures:	Gillette Cup	5–44 B. Stead v Worcestershire (Worcester)	1974
	John Player League	5–21 R. J. Hadlee v Leicestershire (Leicester)	1979
	Benson & Hedges Cup	5–26 B. Stead v Minor Counties (North) (Newark)	1975

SOMERSET

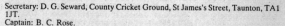

Formation of present club: 1875, reorganised 1885.
Colours: Black, white and maroon.
Badge: Wessex Wyvern.
Best final position in Championship: Third (4):
1892, 1958, 1963, and 1966.
Gillette Cup winners: 1979.
Gillette Cup finalists (2): 1967 and 1978.
John Player League Champions: 1979.
Benson & Hedges Cup semi-finalists (2): 1974 and
1978.
Gillette Man of the Match awards: 26.
Benson & Hedges Gold awards: 20.

Secretary: D. G. Seward, County Cricket Ground, St James's Street, Taunton, TA1
1JT.
Captain: B. C. Rose.
Prospects of play Telephone No.: Taunton (0823) 2946.

Ian Terrence BOTHAM B Heswall (Cheshire) 24/11/1955. RHB, RFM. Played
for 2nd XI in 1971. On MCC staff 1972–73. Played for county in last two John Player
League matches of 1973. Debut 1974. Cap 1976. Elected Best Young Cricketer of
the Year in 1977 by the Cricket Writers' Club. *Wisden* 1977. Tests: 21 between 1977
and 1979. Tours: Pakistan and New Zealand 1977–78, Australia 1978–79, Australia
and India 1979–80. Scored 1,022 runs (av 34.06) in 1976. Took 100 wkts (av 16.40)
in 1978. Became first player ever to score a century and take 8 wkts in innings in a Test
match, v Pakistan (Lord's) 1978. Took 100th wkt in Test cricket in 1979 in record
time of 2 years 9 days. Achieved double of 1,000 runs and 100 wkts in Tests in 1979 to
create records of fewest Tests (21), shortest time (2 years 33 days) and at youngest
age (23 years 279 days). Hat-trick for MCC v Middlesex (Lord's) 1978. Gillette Man
of Match awards: 1. Benson & Hedges Gold awards: 3. HS: 167* v Notts (Nottingham) 1976. HSTC: 137 v India (Leeds) 1979. HSGC: 91* v Northumberland
(Taunton) 1977. HSJPL: 69 v Hants (Street) 1977. HSBH: 54 v Sussex (Hove)
1978. BB: 8–34 v Pakistan (Lord's) 1978. BBC: 7–61 v Glamorgan (Cardiff) 1978.
BBGC: 3–15 v Kent (Taunton) 1979. BBJPL: 4–10 v Yorks (Scarborough) 1979.
BBBH: 4–16 v Combined Universities (Taunton) 1978. Has played soccer in Somerset Senior League.

Dennis BREAKWELL (Ounsdale Comprehensive School, Wombourne, Wol-
verhampton) B Brierley Hill (Staffs) 2/7/1948. LHB, SLA. Debut for Northants
1969 after being on staff for some years. Left county after 1972 season and joined
Somerset by special registration in 1973. Cap 1976. HS: 100* v New Zealanders
(Taunton) 1978. HSGC: 19* v Essex (Westcliff) 1974. HSJPL: 44* v Notts (Notting-
ham) 1976. HSBH: 36* v Glamorgan (Taunton) 1979. BB: 8–39 Northants v Kent
(Dover) 1970. BBC: 6–41 v Glamorgan (Swansea) 1979. BBJPL: 4–10 Northants v
Derbyshire (Northampton) 1970.

Peter William (Pete) DENNING (Millfield School) B Chewton Mendip (Somerset)
16/12/1949. LHB, OB. Debut 1969. Cap 1973. 1,000 runs (4)—1,222 runs (av
42.13) in 1979 best. Scored two centuries in match (122 and 107) v Glos (Taunton)
1977. Gillette Man of Match awards: 4. Benson & Hedges Gold awards: 2. HS: 122 v
Glos (Taunton) 1977. HSGC: 145 v Glamorgan (Cardiff) 1978. HSJPL: 100 v
Northants (Brackley) 1974. HSBH: 87 v Glos (Taunton) 1974. Trained as a teacher
at St Luke's College, Exeter

SOMERSET

Colin Herbert DREDGE B Frome 4/8/1954. LHB, RM. 6ft, 5in. tall. Debut 1976. Cap 1978, Gillette Man of Match awards: 1. HS: 56* Yorks (Harrogate) 1977. HSJPL: : 14 v Essex (Taunton) 1978. HSBH: 10* v Worcs (Taunton) 1978. BB: 5–53 v Kent (Taunton) 1978. BBGC: 4–23 v Kent (Canterbury) 1978.BBJPL: 3–19 v Middlesex (Taunton) 1978. Played soccer for Bristol City Reserves.

Trevor GARD (Huish Episcopi School, Langport) B West Lambrook, near South Petheron (Somerset) 2/6/1957. RHB, WK. Played for 2nd XI since 1972. Debut 1976. HS: 51* v Indians (Taunton) 1979.

Joel GARNER B Barbados 16/12/1952. RHB, RFM. 6ft. 8ins. tall. Debut for Barbados in Shell Shield competition 1975–76. Debut for county 1977 plays in mid-week matches whilst playing as a professional for Littleborough in Central Lancashire League. Cap 1979. *Wisden* 1979. Tests: 7 for West Indies in 1976–77 and 1977–78. Tour: West Indies to Australia and New Zealand 1979–80. Gillette Man of Match awards: 1. HS: 60 West Indies v Australia (Brisbane) 1979–80. HSUK: 53 v Yorks (Harrogate) 1979. HSGC: 24* v Northants (Lord's) 1979. HSJPL: 32 v Kent (Taunton) 1979. HSBH: 17 v Sussex (Hove) 1978. BB: 8–31 v Glamorgan (Cardiff) 1977. BBTC: 4–48 West Indies v Pakistan (Georgetown) 1976–77. BBGC: 6–29 v Northants (Lord's) 1979. BBJPL: 3–16 v Notts (Nottingham) 1979. BBBH: 3–23 v Glamorgan (Taunton) 1979.

David Roberts GURR (Aylesbury GS and Oxford) B Whitchurch (Bucks) 27/3/1956. RHB, RFM. 6ft 3½ins tall. Played for Middlesex 2nd XI in 1974. Debut for both Oxford U and county in 1976. Blue 1976–77. HS: 46* Oxford U v Cambridge U (Lord's) 1977. HSC: 21 v Glos (Bristol) 1976. HSBH: 29* Combined Universities v Sussex (Oxford) 1977. BB: 6–82 Oxford U v Warwickshire (Birmingham) 1976. BBC: 5–30 v Lancs (Weston-super-Mare) 1977. BBBH: 3–42 Combined Universities v Kent (Oxford) 1976.

Keith Francis JENNINGS B Wellington (Somerset) 5/10/1953. RHB, RM. Formerly on MCC staff. Debut 1975. Cap 1978, Benson & Hedges Gold awards: 1. HS: 49 v West Indians (Taunton) 1976. HSJPL: 51* v Notts (Nottingham) 1976. BB: 5–18 v Sussex (Hove) 1978. BBGC: 3–31 v Derbyshire (Taunton) 1979. BBJPL: 4–33 v Hants (Portsmouth) 1976. BBBH: 4–11 v Minor Counties (South) (Taunton) 1979.

Jeremy William LLOYDS (Blundell's School) B Penang, Malaya 17/11/1954. LHB,RM. Played for 2nd XI from 1973 to 1977. Played for Hants, Middlesex and Worcs 2nd XIs in 1978. Debut 1979. HS: 43 v Sussex (Hove) 1979.

Victor James (Vic) MARKS (Blundell's School and Oxford) B Middle Chinnock (Somerset) 25/6/1955. RHB, OB. Debut for both Oxford U and county 1975. Blue 1975–76–77–78 (captain in 1976–77). Cap 1979. Benson & Hedges Gold awards: 1. Scored 215 for Oxford U v Army (Aldershot) in non-first class match. HS: 105 Oxford U v Worcs (Oxford) 1976. HSC: 98 v Essex (Leyton) 1976. HSGC: 33* v Essex (Taunton) 1978. HSJPL: 32* v Hants (Weston-super-Mare) 1975. HSBH: 59 Combined Universities v Glamorgan (Oxford) 1978. BB: 6–33 v Northants (Taunton) 1979. BBJPL: 3–19 v Derbyshire (Taunton) 1979. Half blue for Rugby Fives.

Hallam Reynold MOSELEY B Christchurch, Barbados 28/5/1948. RHB, RFM. Toured England with Barbados team in 1969 and made debut v Notts (Nottingham). Subsequently played for Barbados in Shell Shield. Joined county in 1970 and made debut in 1971. Cap 1972. Testimonial in 1979. HS: 67 v Leices (Taunton) 1972. HSGC: 15 v Lancs (Manchester) 1972. HSJPL: 24 v Notts (Torquay) 1972 and 24 v Hants (Weston-super-Mare) 1975. HSBH: 33 v Hants (Bournemouth) 1973. BB: 6–34 v Derbyshire (Bath) 1975 and 6–35 v Glos (Taunton) 1978. BBGC: 4–31 v Surrey (Taunton) 1974. BBJPL: 5–30 v Middlesex (Lord's) 1973. BBBH: 3–17 v Leics (Taunton) 1977.

Martin OLIVE (Millfield School) B Watford (Herts) 18/4/1958. RHB, RM. Played for 2nd XI since 1974. Debut 1977. Played in one match in 1978 and one match in 1979. HS: 39 v Cambridge U (Bath) 1979.

Nigel Francis Mark POPPLEWELL (Radley College and Cambridge) B Chislehurst (Kent) 8/8/1957. Son of O. B. Popplewell, Q.C., former Cambridge Blue. RHB, RM. Played for Buckinghamshire in 1975 and 1978 and for Hants 2nd XI in 1976 and 1977. Debut for Cambridge U 1977. Blue 1977–78–79 (secretary). Debut for county 1979. HS: 92 Cambridge U v Lancs (Cambridge) 1979. HSC: 37 v Indians (Taunton) 1979. HSBH: 22* Combined Universities v Sussex (Oxford) 1979. BB: 3–18 Cambridge U v Somerset (Bath) 1979. BBC: 3–43 v Lancs (Manchester) 1979.

Isaac Vivian Alexander (Viv) RICHARDS (Antigua Grammar School) B St John's Antigua 7/3/1952. RHB, OB. Debut 1971–72 for Leeward Islands v Windward Islands and subsequently played for Combined Islands in Shell Shield tournament. Debut for county and cap 1974. *Wisden* 1976. Played for Queensland 1976–77 Sheffield Shield competition. Tests: 28 for West Indies between 1974–75 and 1977–78. Tours: West Indies to India, Sri Lanka and Pakistan 1974–75, Australia 1975–76, England 1976, Australia and New Zealand 1979–80. 1,000 runs (6)—2,161 runs (av 65.48) in 1977 best. Also scored 1,267 runs (av 60.33) on 1974–75 tour and 1,107 runs (av 58.26) on 1975–76 tour. Scored 1,710 in 11 Test matches in 1976 including 829 runs in 4 Tests against England – record aggregate for a year and fourth highest aggregate for a Test Series. Shared in 4th wkt partnership record for county, 251 with P. M. Roebuck v Surrey (Weston-super-Mare) 1977. Scored 99 and 110 v Leics (Taunton) 1978. Gillette Man of Match awards: 3. Benson & Hedges Gold awards: 3. HS: 291 West Indies v England (Oval) 1976. HSC: 241* v Glos (Bristol) 1977. HSGC: 139* v Warwickshire (Taunton) 1978. HSJPL: 126* v Glos (Bristol, Imperial Ground) 1975. HSBH: 85 v Glamorgan (Cardiff) 1978. BB: 3–15 v Surrey (Weston-super-Mare) 1977. BBJPL: 3–32 v Glos (Bristol) 1978.

Peter Michael ROEBUCK (Millfield School and Cambridge) B Oxford 6/3/1956. RHB, OB. Played for 2nd XI in 1969 at age of 13. Debut 1974. Blue 1975–76–77. Cap 1978. Scored 1,273 runs (av 47.14) in 1979. Shared in 4th wkt partnership record for county, 251 with I. V. A. Richards v Surrey (Weston-super-Mare) 1977. Benson & Hedges Gold awards: 1. HS: 158 Cambridge U v Oxford U (Lord's) 1975. HSC: 131* v New Zealanders (Taunton) 1978. HSGC: 57 v Essex (Taunton) 1977. HSJPL: 50 v Notts (Nottingham) 1979. HSBH: 48 Combined Universities v Kent (Oxford) 1976. BB: 6–50 Cambridge U. v Kent (Canterbury) 1977.

Brian Charles ROSE (Weston-super-Mare GS) B Dartford (Kent) 4/6/1950. LHB, LM. Played for English Schools CA at Lord's 1968. Debut 1969. Cap 1975. Appointed county captain in 1978. *Wisden* 1979. Tests: 5 in 1977–78. Tour: Pakistan and New Zealand 1977–78. 1,000 runs (5)—1,624 runs (av 46.40) in 1976 best. Gillette Man of Match awards: 2. HS: 205 v Northants (Weston-super-Mare) 1977. HSTC: 27 v Pakistan (Hyderabad) 1977–78. HSGC: 128 v Derbyshire (Ilkeston) 1977. HSJPL: 81* v Yorks (Scarborough) 1979. HSBH: 68 v Glos (Street) 1975. BB: 3–9 v Glos (Taunton) 1975. BBJPL: 3–25 v Lancs (Manchester) 1975. Trained as a teacher at Borough Road College, Isleworth.

SOMERSET

Neil RUSSOM (Huish's GS, Taunton and Cambridge) B Finchley, London 3/12/1958. RHB, RM. Played for 2nd XI since 1975. Played in one Fenner Trophy match v Northants (Scarborough) 1978. Debut for Cambridge U, 1979. Has yet to appear for county in first-class cricket. HS: 12 Cambridge U v Sussex (Cambridge) 1979.

Philip Anthony (Phil) SLOCOMBE (Weston-super-Mare GS and Millfield School) B Weston-super-Mare 6/9/1954. RHB, RM. Played for 2nd XI in 1969 at age of 14. Joined staff 1974. Debut 1975. Cap 1978. 1,000 runs (2)—1,221 runs (av 38.15) in 1978 best. Scored 106* & 98 v Worcs (Worcester) 1978. HS: 132 v Notts (Taunton) 1975. HSGC: 42 v Surrey (Oval) 1975. HSJPL: 39 v Glamorgan (Yeovil) 1977. HSBH: 11 v Minor Counties (West) (Chippenham) 1976. Plays soccer for Weston-super-Mare in Western League.

Derek John Somerset TAYLOR (Amersham College) B Amersham (Bucks) 12/11/1942. Twin brother of M. N. S. Taylor of Hants. RHB, WK. Debut for Surrey 1966. Cap 1969. Left staff after 1969 season and made debut for Somerset in 1970. Cap 1971. Testimonial (£20,764) in 1978. Played for Griqualand West in Currie Cup competition 1970–71 and 1971–72. Scored 1,121 runs (av 28.02) in 1975. HS: 179 v Glamorgan (Swansea) 1974. HSGC: 49 v Kent (Canterbury) 1974. HSJPL: 93 v Surrey (Guildford) 1975. HSBH: 83* v Glos (Street) 1975. Has played soccer for Corinthian Casuals.

NB. The following players whose particulars appeared in the 1979 Annual have been omitted: G. I. Burgess (retired), M. J. Kitchen (retired) and P. J. Robinson. The career records of Burgess and Kitchen will be found elsewhere in this Annual.

COUNTY AVERAGES

Schweppes County Championship: Played 21, won 5, drawn 15, lost 1, abandoned 1
All first-class matches: Played 24, won 6, drawn 17, lost 1, abandoned 1

BATTING AND FIELDING

Cap		M	I	NO	Runs	HS	Avge	100	50	Ct	St
1978	P. M. Roebuck	23	37	10	1273	89	47.14	—	11	22	—
1973	P. W. Denning	22	35	6	1222	106	42.13	2	7	18	—
1975	B. C. Rose	21	33	1	1317	133	41.15	2	8	12	—
1974	I. V. A. Richards	16	26	0	1043	156	40.11	3	4	13	—
1979	V. J. Marks	24	33	9	894	93	37.25	—	7	8	—
1978	C. H. Dredge	11	11	5	215	55	35.83	—	1	5	—
1976	I. T. Botham	11	15	1	487	120	34.78	1	1	11	—
1971	D. J. S. Taylor	20	20	10	318	50*	31.80	—	1	29	10
1978	P. A. Slocombe	23	38	3	956	103*	27.31	1	6	8	—
1976	D. Breakwell	24	31	9	510	54*	23.18	—	2	9	—
1979	J. Garner	14	10	4	106	53	17.66	—	1	4	—
—	J. W. Lloyds	4	7	0	117	43	16.71	—	—	2	—
1966	M. J. Kitchen	7	10	0	146	36	14.60	—	—	8	—
—	N. F. M. Popplewell	7	10	1	119	37	13.22	—	1	5	—
1972	H. R. Moseley	8	5	2	25	15	8.33	—	—	1	—
1978	K. F. Jennings	19	11	5	19	11*	3.16	—	—	9	—

Played in four matches: T. Gard 5*, 8, 51*, 0*, 7* (6 ct 3 st); D. R. Gurr 11*, 20*.
Played in one match: G. I. Burgess 9, 11; M. Olive 39, 38.

BOWLING	Type	O	M	R	W	Avge	Best	5 wI	10 wM
J. Garner	RFM	393.1	127	761	55	13.83	6-80	4	—
H. R. Moseley	RFM	196.4	50	495	31	15.96	6-52	2	1
V. J. Marks	OB	568.4	153	1581	57	27.73	6-33	4	—
D. Breakwell	SLA	567.3	193	1311	47	27.89	6-41	1	—
C. H. Dredge	RM	251	60	759	25	30.36	4-40	—	—
K. F. Jennings	RM	245.3	78	620	20	31.00	4-25	—	—
I. T. Botham	RFM	257.4	62	846	26	32.53	6-81	1	—
N. F. M. Popplewell	RM	102	33	271	6	45.16	3-43	—	—
I. V. A. Richards	OB	77.3	11	270	5	54.00	2-47	—	—

Also bowled: G. I. Burgess 5–3–8–0; D. R. Gurr 71–17–189–2; J. W. Lloyds 6–3–14–0; P. M. Roebuck 6–0–22–1; B. C. Rose 5–0–14–0.

County Records

First-class cricket

Highest innings totals:	For —675-9d v Hampshire (Bath)	1924
	Agst—811 by Surrey (The Oval)	1899
Lowest innings totals:	For —25 v Gloucestershire (Bristol)	1947
	Agst—22 by Gloucestershire (Bristol)	1920
Highest individual innings:	For —310 H. Gimblett v Sussex (Eastbourne)	1948
	Agst—424 A. C. MacLaren for Lancs (Taunton)	1895
Best bowling in an innings:	For —10-49 E. J. Tyler v Surrey (Taunton)	1895
	Agst—10-35 A. Drake for Yorkshire (Weston-super-Mare)	1914
Best bowling in a match:	For —16-83 J. C. White v Worcestershire (Bath)	1919
	Agst—17-137 W. Brearley for Lancashire (Manchester)	1905
Most runs in a season:	2761 (av 56.82) W. E. Alley	1961
runs in a career:	21108 (av 37.09) H. Gimblett	1935–1954
100s in a season:	10 by W. E. Alley	1961
100s in a career:	49 by H. Gimblett	1935–1954
wickets in a season:	169 (av 19.24) A. W. Wellard	1938
wickets in a career:	2153 (av 18.10) J. C. White	1909–1937

RECORD WICKET STANDS

1st	346	H. T. Hewett & L. C. H. Palairet v Yorkshire (Taunton)	1892
2nd	286	J. C. W. MacBryan & M. D. Lyon v Derbyshire (Buxton)	1924
3rd	300	G. Atkinson & P. B. Wight v Glamorgan (Bath)	1960
4th	251	I. V. A. Richards & P. M. Roebuck v Surrey (Weston-super-Mare)	1977
5th	235	J. C. White & C. C. C. Case v Gloucestershire (Taunton)	1927
6th	265	W. E. Alley & K. E. Palmer v Northamptonshire (Northampton)	1961
7th	240	S. M. J. Woods & V. T. Hill v Kent (Taunton)	1898
8th	143*	E. F. Longrigg & C. J. P. Barnwell v Gloucestershire (Bristol)	1938
9th	183	C. Greetham & H. W. Stephenson v Leicestershire (Weston-super-Mare)	1963
10th	143	J. J. Bridges & H. Gibbs v Surrey (Weston-super-Mare)	1919

SURREY

One-day cricket

Highest innings totals:	Gillette Cup	330–4 v Glamorgan (Cardiff)	1978
	John Player League	270–4 v Gloucestershire (Bristol, Imperial)	1975
	Benson & Hedges Cup	265–8 v Gloucestershire (Taunton)	1974
Lowest innings totals:	Gillette Cup	59 v Middlesex (Lord's)	1977
	John Player League	58 v Essex (Chelmsford)	1977
	Benson & Hedges Cup	105 v Hampshire (Bournemouth)	1975
Highest individual innings:	Gillette Cup	145 B. C. Rose v Glamorgan (Cardiff)	1978
	John Player League	131 D. B. Close v Yorkshire (Bath)	1974
	Benson & Hedges Cup	95 R. C. Cooper v Minor Counties South (Plymouth)	1972
Best bowling figures:	Gillette Cup	6–29 J. Garner v Northamptonshire (Lord's)	1979
	John Player League	6–25 G. I. Burgess v Glamorgan (Glastonbury)	1972
	Benson & Hedges Cup	4–11 K. F. Jennings v Minor Counties (South) (Taunton)	1979

SURREY

Formation of present club: 1845.
Colours: Chocolate.
Badge: Prince of Wales' Feathers.
County Champions (18): 1864, 1887, 1888, 1890, 1891, 1892, 1894, 1895, 1899, 1914, 1952, 1953, 1954, 1955, 1956, 1957, 1958 and 1971.
Joint Champions (2): 1889 and 1950.
Gillette Cup finalist: 1965.
Best final position in John Player League: 5th in 1969.
Benson & Hedges Cup winners: 1974.
Benson & Hedges Cup finalists: 1979.
Gillette Man of the Match awards: 14.
Benson & Hedges Gold awards: 23.

Secretary: I. F. B. Scott-Browne, Kennington Oval, London, SE11 5SS.
Cricket manager: M. J. Stewart.
Captain: R. D. V. Knight.
Prospects of play Telephone No.: (01) 735 2424.

Alan Raymond BUTCHER (Heath Clark GS, Croydon) B Croydon 7/1/1954. LHB, SLA. Played in two John Player League matches in 1971. Debut 1972. Cap 1975. Tests: 1 in 1979. Scored 1,398 runs (av 37.78) in 1979. Benson & Hedges Gold awards: 4. HS: 188 v Sussex (Hove) 1978. HSTC: 20 v India (Oval) 1979. HSGC: 51 v Derbyshire (Ilkeston) 1976. HSJPL: 113* v Warwickshire (Birmingham) 1978. HSBH: 61 v Kent (Canterbury) 1976. BB: 6–48 v Hants (Guildford) 1972. BBJPL: 5–19 v Glos (Bristol) 1975. BBBH: 3–11 v Lancs (Manchester) 1974.

Robert Giles Lenthall CHEATLE (Stowe School) B London 31/7/1953. LHB, SLA. Debut Sussex 1974. HS: 34 v Kent (Hove) 1977. HSJPL: 18* v Warwickshire (Hove) 1979. HSBH: 10* v Surrey (Hove) 1979. BB: 6–32 v Yorks (Hove) 1979. BBJPL: 4–33 v Glamorgan (Eastbourne) 1977. Joined Surrey 1980.

Sylvester Theophilus CLARKE B Christchurch, Barbados 11/12/1954. RHB, RFM. Debut for Barbados 1977–78. Debut for county 1979. Tests: 6 for West Indies between 1977–78 and 1978–79. Tour: West Indies to India and Sri Lanka 1978–79. HS: 25 v Hants (Oval) 1979. HSTC: 15 West Indies v India (Delhi) 1978–79. HSJPL: 30 v Lancs (Oval) 1979. BB: 6–39 Barbados v Trinidad (Bridgetown) 1977–78. BBUK: 6–61 v Glamorgan (Cardiff) 1979. BBTC: 5–126 West Indies v India (Bangalore) 1978–79. BBJPL: 3–26 v Lancs (Oval) 1979. BBBH: 4–23 v Essex (Oval) 1979.

Grahame Selvey CLINTON (Chislehurst and Sidcup GS) B Sidcup 5/5/1953. LHB, RM. Toured West Indies v England Young Cricketers 1972. Debut for Kent 1974. Left county after 1978 season and made debut for Surrey in 1979. Scored 1,082 runs (av 32.78) in 1979. Benson & Hedges Gold awards: 1. (for Kent). HS: 134 v Kent (Oval) 1979. HSJPL: 34 v Notts (Nottingham) 1979. HSBH: 66 Kent v Surrey (Canterbury) 1976.

Geoffrey Philip (Geoff) HOWARTH (Auckland GS) B Auckland 29/3/1951. Younger brother of H. J. Howarth, New Zealand Test cricketer. RHB, OB. Debut for New Zealand under-23 XI v Auckland (Auckland) 1968–69. Joined Surrey staff 1969. Debut 1971. Cap 1974. Tests: 17 for New Zealand between 1974–75 and 1978–79. Tours: New Zealand to Pakistan and India 1976–77, England 1978. 1,000 runs (3)—1,554 runs (av 37.90) in 1976 best. Scored two centuries in match (122 and 102) New Zealand v England (Auckland) 1977–78. Benson & Hedges Gold awards: 1. HS: 183 v Hants (Oval) 1979. HSTC: 123 New Zealand v England (Lord's) 1978. HSGC: 34 v Lancs (Manchester) 1977 and 34 v Northants (Northampton) 1979. HSJPL: 122 v Glos (Oval) 1976. HSBH: 80 v Yorks (Oval) 1974. BB: 5–32 Auckland v Central Districts (Auckland) 1973–74. BBUK: 3–20 v Northants (Northampton) 1976. BBJPL: 4–16 v Warwickshire (Byfleet) 1979.

INTIKHAB ALAM B Hoshiarpur, India 28/12/1941. RHB, LBG. Debut for Karachi 1957–58 aged 16 years 9 months and has played continuously for various Karachi sides and Pakistan International Airways since. Professional for West of Scotland Club in Scottish Western Union for some seasons. Debut for county and cap 1969. Benefit (£20,000) in 1978. Tests: 47 for Pakistan between 1959–60 and 1976–77, captaining country in 17 Tests: Played in 5 matches for Rest of World in 1970 and 5 in 1971–72. Took wkt of C. C. McDonald with first ball he bowled in Test cricket. Tours: Pakistan to India 1960–61, England 1962, 1967, 1971 and 1974 (captain on last two tours), Ceylon 1964. Australia and New Zealand 1964–65, 1972–73 (captain), Australia and West Indies 1976–77, Pakistan Eaglets to England 1963, Pakistan International Airways to East Africa 1964, Rest of World to Australia 1971–72 (vice-captain). Took 104 wkts (av 28.36) in 1971. Hat-trick v Yorks (Oval) 1972. Benson & Hedges Gold awards: 1. HS: 182 Karachi Blues v Pakistan International Airways B (Karachi) 1970–71. HSUK: 139 v Glos (Oval) 1973. HSTC: 138 Pakistan v England (Hyderabad) 1972–73. HSGC: 50 v Somerset (Oval) 1975. HSJPL: 62 v Northants (Tolworth) 1973. HSBH: 32 v Middlesex (Lord's) 1973. BB: 8–54 Pakistanis v Tasmania (Hobart) 1972–73. BBUK: 8–61 Pakistanis v Minor Counties (Swindon) 1967. BBTC: 7–52 Pakistan v New Zealand (Dunedin) 1972–73. BBC: 8–74 v Middlesex (Oval) 1970. BBJPL: 6–25 v Derbyshire (Oval) 1974. BBBH: 3–42 v Essex (Chelmsford) 1973.

SURREY

Robin David JACKMAN (St Edmund's School, Canterbury) B Simla (India) 13/8/1945. RHB, RFM. Debut 1964. Cap 1970. Played for Western Province in 1971–72 and Rhodesia from 1972–73 to 1976–77 in Currie Cup competition. Hat-tricks (3): v Kent (Canterbury) 1971, Western Province v Natal (Pietermaritzburg) 1971–72 and v Yorks (Leeds) 1973. Gillette Man of Match awards: 1. HS: 92* v Kent (Oval) 1974. HSGC: 18* v Glamorgan (Cardiff) 1977. HSJPL: 43 v Kent (Maidstone) 1977. HSBH: 36 v Leics (Lord's) 1974. BB: 8–40 Rhodesia v Natal (Durban) 1972–73. BBUK: 8–64 v Lancs (Oval) 1979. BBGC: 7–33 v Yorks (Harrogate) 1970. BBJPL: 6–34 v Derbyshire (Derby) 1973. BBBH: 4–31 v Kent (Canterbury) 1973.

Roger David Verdon KNIGHT (Dulwich College and Cambridge) B Streatham 6/9/1946. LHB, RM. Debut for Cambridge U 1967. Blue 1967-68-69-70. Debut for Surrey 1968. Left county after 1970 season and made debut for Glos by special registration 1971. Cap 1971. Left county after 1975 season and made debut for Sussex in 1976. Cap 1976. Left county after 1977 season and rejoined Surrey for 1978 as county captain. Cap 1978. 1,000 runs (8)—1,350 runs (av 38.57) in 1974 best. Gillette Man of Match awards: 3 (for Glos). Benson & Hedges Gold awards: 4 (1 for Sussex, 2 for Glos). HS: 165* Sussex v Middlesex (Hove) 1976. HSC: 128 v Lancs (Oval) 1978. HSGC: 75 Glos v Glamorgan (Cardiff) 1973. HSJPL: 127 Sussex v Hants (Hove) 1976. HSBH: 117 Sussex v Surrey (Oval) 1977. BB: 6–44 Glos v Northants (Northampton) 1974. BBC: 5–44 v Glos (Cheltenham) 1979. BBGC: 5–39 Glos v Surrey (Bristol) 1971. BBJPL: 5–42 Sussex v Notts (Nottingham) 1977. BBBH: 3–19 Sussex v Surrey (Oval) 1977.

Monte Alan LYNCH (Ryden's School, Walton-on-Thames) B Georgetown, British Guiana 21/5/1958. RHB, RM/OB. Debut 1977. HS: 101 v Pakistanis (Oval) 1978. HSJPL: 52 v Leics (Leicester) 1979. HSBH: 67 v Worcs (Worcester) 1979.

Andrew NEEDHAM (Paisley GS and Watford GS) B Calow (Derbyshire) 23/3/1957. RHB, OB. Debut 1977. HS: 21 v Sussex (Hove) 1978. HSJPL: 18 v Lancs (Oval) 1979. BB: 3–25 v Oxford U (Oxford) 1977.

Duncan Brian PAULINE (Bishop Fox School, Molesey) B Aberdeen 15/12/1960. RHB, RM. Played for 2nd XI since 1977. Toured Australia with England under-19 side in 1978–79. Debut 1979. One match v Oxford U (Oxford).

Ian Roger PAYNE (Emanuel School) B Lambeth Hospital, Kennington 9/5/1958. RHB, RM. Debut 1977. Played in one John Player League match only in 1979. HS: 29 v Kent (Oval) 1977. HSJPL: 20 v Kent (Maidstone) 1977. BBJPL: 4–31 v Northants (Guildford) 1977.

Patrick Ian (Pat) POCOCK (Wimbledon Technical School) B Bangor (Caernarvonshire) 24/9/1946. RHB, OB. Debut 1964. Benefit (£18,500) in 1977. Played for Northern transvaal in 1971–72 Currie Cup competition. Tests: 17 between 1967–68 and 1976. Tours: Pakistan 1966–67, West Indies 1967–68 and 1973–74, Ceylon and Pakistan 1968–69, India, Pakistan and Sri Lanka 1972–73. Took 112 wkts (av 18.22) in 1967. Took 4 wkts in 4 balls, 5 in 6, 6 in 9, and 7 in 11 (the last two being first-class records) v Sussex (Eastbourne) 1972. Hat-tricks (2): as above and v Worcs (Guildford) 1971. Benson & Hedges Gold awards: 2. HS: 75* v Notts (Oval) 1968. HSTC: 33 v Pakistan (Hyderabad) 1972–73. HSGC: 14 v Essex (Colchester) 1978. HSJPL: 22 v Notts (Nottingham) 1971. HSBH: 19 v Middlesex (Oval) 1972. BB: 9–57 v Glamorgan (Cardiff) 1979. BBTC: 6–79 v Australia (Manchester) 1968. BBGC: 3–34 v Somerset (Oval) 1975. BBJPL: 4–27 v Essex (Chelmsford) 1974. BBBH: 4–11 v Yorks (Barnsley) 1978.

Clifton James (Jack) RICHARDS (Humphrey Davy GS, Penzance) B Penzance 10/8/1958. RHB, WK. Debut 1976. Cap 1978. HS: 50 v Notts (Oval) 1978. HSGC: 14 v Essex (Colchester) 1978. HSJPL: 18* v Glos (Cheltenham) 1977. HSBH: 25* v Derbyshire (Derby) 1979.

Graham Richard James ROOPE (Bradfield College) B Fareham (Hants) 12/7/1946. RHB, RM. Played for Public Schools XI v Comb. Services (Lord's) 1963 and 1964. Played for Berkshire 1963 scoring century against Wiltshire. Joined county staff and debut 1964. Cap 1969. Played for Griqualand West in 1973–74 Currie Cup competition. Benefit in 1980. Tests: 21 between 1972–73 and 1978. Tours: India, Pakistan and Sri Lanka 1972–73, Pakistan and New Zealand 1977–78. 1,000 runs (8)—1,641 runs (av 44.35) in 1971 best. Scored two centuries in match (109 and 103*) v Leics (Leicester) 1971. Held 59 catches in 1971. Benson & Hedges Gold awards: 3. HS: 171 v Yorks (Oval) 1971. HSTC: 77 v Australia (Oval) 1975. HSGC: 66 v Somerset (Oval) 1975. HSJPL: 120* v Worcs (Byfleet) 1973. HSBH: 115* v Essex (Chelmsford) 1973. BB: 5–14 v West Indians (Oval) 1969. BBGC: 5–23 v Derbyshire (Oval) 1967. BBJPL: 4–31 v Glamorgan (Oval) 1974. BBBH: 3–31 v Essex (Chelmsford) 1978. Soccer (goalkeeper) for Corinthian Casuals, Wimbledon, and Guildford City.

David Mark SMITH (Battersea GS) B Balham 9/1/1956. LHB, RM. Played for 2nd XI in 1972. Debut 1973 aged 17 years 4 months, whilst still at school. HS: 115 v Hants (Portsmouth) 1978. HSGC: 61 v Northants (Northampton) 1979. HSJPL: 45 v Middlesex (Oval) 1979. HSBH: 45* v Northants (Northampton) 1979. BB: 3–40 v Sussex (Oval) 1976. BBGC: 3–39 v Derbyshire (Ilkeston) 1976.

Stuart Spicer SURRIDGE (Westminster School) B Westminster 28/10/1951. Son of W. S. Surridge. RHB, WK. Has played for county 2nd XI since 1971 and for Derbyshire 2nd XI in 1976. Debut 1978. One match v Pakistanis (Oval). Did not play in 1979.

David James THOMAS (Licensed Victuallers School, Slough) B Solihull (Warwickshire) 30/6/1959. LHB, LM. Debut 1977. HS: 15* v Worcs (Guildford) 1979. BB: 6–84 v Derbyshire (Oval) 1979. BBJPL: 4–13 v Sussex (Oval) 1978.

Peter Hugh L'Estrange WILSON (Wellington College) B Guildford 17/8/1958. 6ft 5ins tall. RHB, RFM. Played for Hants 2nd XI 1976–77. Debut 1978. Played for Northern Transvaal in 1979–80 Currie Cup competition. HS: 29 Northern Transvaal v Transvaal (Pretoria) 1979–80. HSUK: 15 v Worcs (Guildford) 1979. HSJPL: 18* v Worcs (Oval) 1979. BB: 4–39 v Warwickshire (Oval) 1979. BBGC: 3–59 v Essex (Colchester) 1978. BBJPL: 4–32 v Middlesex (Oval) 1979. BBBH: 5–21 v Combined Universities (Oval) 1979.

NB The following player whose particulars appeared in the 1979 annual has been omitted: J. H. Edrich (retired).

COUNTY AVERAGES

Schweppes County Championship: Played 21, won 6, drawn 12, lost 3, abandoned 1
All first-class matches: Played 23, won 7, drawn 13, lost 3, abandoned 1

BATTING AND FIELDING

Cap		M	I	NO	Runs	HS	Avge	100	50	Ct	St
1974	G. P. Howarth	19	30	4	1238	183	47.61	4	7	12	—
1975	A. R. Butcher	23	40	5	1364	169	38.97	4	6	14	—
—	D. M. Smith	19	23	7	555	79	34.68	—	4	8	—
1978	R. D. V. Knight	22	33	5	946	117*	33.78	2	4	15	—
1969	G. R. J. Roope	23	35	7	939	114	33.53	1	5	41	—
—	G. S. Clinton	22	38	5	1082	134	32.78	2	6	13	—
1969	Intikhab Alam	15	21	4	345	52	20.29	—	2	8	—
1970	R. D. Jackman	21	25	8	287	82	16.88	—	1	12	—
—	M. A. Lynch	7	12	2	153	45	15.30	—	—	3	—
—	P. H. L. Wilson	17	11	7	48	15	12.00	—	—	3	—
—	S. T. Clarke	11	11	3	90	25	11.25	—	—	6	—
1967	P. I. Pocock	22	19	7	131	20	10.91	—	—	5	—
1978	C. J. Richards	23	20	1	183	29	9.63	—	—	50	8
—	D. J. Thomas	7	8	2	48	15*	8.00	—	—	2	—

Played in one match: A. Needham 2 (2 ct); D. Pauline did not bat (1 ct).

BOWLING

	Type	O	M	R	W	Avge	Best	5 wI	10 wM
R. D. Jackman	RFM	628.1	173	1595	93	17.15	8–64	8	—
S. T. Clarke	RFM	320.1	106	757	43	17.60	6–61	3	—
P. I. Pocock	OB	595.5	189	1435	70	20.50	9–57	4	1
R. D. V. Knight	RM	260	66	728	29	25.10	5–44	2	—
P. H. L. Wilson	RFM	284.5	63	861	30	28.70	4–39	—	—
G. R. J. Roope	RM	40.4	6	167	5	33.40	2–5	—	—
D. J. Thomas	LM	169	32	556	13	42.76	6–84	1	—
Intikham Alam	LBG	345.1	100	959	18	53.27	3–44	—	—

Also bowled: A. R. Butcher 27–8–114–1; G. P. Howarth 20–6–46–1; D. M. Smith 12–1–55–0.

County Records

First-class cricket

Highest innings	For	—811 v Somerset (The Oval)	1899
totals:	Agst	—705-8d by Sussex (Hastings	1902
Lowest innings	For	—16 v Nottinghamshire (The Oval)	1880
totals:	Agst	—15 by MCC (Lord's)	1839
Highest Indi-	For	—357* R. Abel v Somerset (The Oval)	1899
vidual innings:	Agst	—300* F. Watson for Lancashire (Manchester)	1928
		300 R. Subba Row for Northamptonshire	
		(The Oval)	1958
Best bowling	For	—10–43 T. Rushby v Somerset (Taunton)	1921
in an innings:	Agst	—10–28 W. P. Howell for Australians (The Oval)	1899
Best bowling	For	—16–83 G. A. R. Lock v Kent (Blackheath)	1956
in a match:	Agst	—15–57 W. P. Howell for Australians (The Oval)	1899

Most runs in a season:	3246 (av 72.13) T. W. Hayward	1906
runs in a career:	43703 (av 49.77) J. B. Hobbs	1905–1934
100s in a season:	13 by T. W. Hayward	1906
	J. B. Hobbs	1925
100s in a career:	144 by J. B. Hobbs	1905–1934
wickets in a season:	250 (av 14.06) T. Richardson	1895
wickets in a career:	1775 (av 17.91) T. Richardson	1892–1905

RECORD WICKET STANDS

1st	428	J. B. Hobbs & A. Sandham v Oxford U (The Oval)	1926
2nd	371	J. B. Hobbs & E. G. Hayes v Hampshire (The Oval)	1909
3rd	353	A. Ducat & E. G. Hayes v Hampshire (Southampton)	1919
4th	448	R. Abel & T. W. Hayward v Yorkshire (The Oval)	1899
5th	308	J. N. Crawford & F. C. Holland v Somerset (The Oval)	1908
6th	298	A. Sandham & H. S. Harrison v Sussex (The Oval)	1913
7th	200	T. F. Shepherd & J. W. Hitch v Kent (Blackheath)	1921
8th	204	T. W. Hayward & L. C. Braund v Lancashire (The Oval)	1898
9th	168	E. R. T. Holmes & E. W. J. Brooks v Hampshire (The Oval)	1936
10th	173	A. Ducat & A. Sandham v Essex (Leyton)	1921

One-day cricket

Highest innings totals:	Gillette Cup	280–5 v Middlesex (Oval)	1970
	John Player League	248–2 v Gloucestershire (Oval)	1976
	Benson & Hedges Cup	264 v Kent (Oval)	1976
Lowest innings totals:	Gillette Cup	74 v Kent (Oval)	1967
	John Player League	64 v Worcestershire (Worcester)	1978
	Benson & Hedges Cup	125 v Sussex (Hove)	1972
Highest individual innings:	Gillette Cup	101 M. J. Stewart v Durham (Chester-le-Street)	1972
	John Player League	122 G. P. Howarth v Gloucestershire (Oval)	1976
	Benson & Hedges Cup	115 G. R. J. Roope v Essex (Chelmsford)	1973
Best bowling figures:	Gillette Cup	7–33 R. D. Jackman v Yorkshire (Harrogate)	1970
	John Player League	6–25 Intikhab Alam v Derbyshire (Oval)	1974
	Benson & Hedges Cup	5–21 P. H. L. Wilson v Combined Universities (Oval)	1979

SUSSEX

Formation of present club: 1839, reorganised 1857,
Colours: Dark blue, light blue, and gold.
Badge: County Arms of six martlets (in shape of
    inverted pyramid).
County Championship runners-up (6): 1902,
    1903, 1932, 1933, 1934, and 1953.
Gillette Cup winners (3): 1963, 1964, and 1978.
Gillette Cup finalists (3): 1968, 1970, and 1973.
John Player League runners-up: 1976.
Benson & Hedges Cup quarter-finalists (2): 1972
    and 1977.
Gillette Man of the Match awards: 27
Benson & Hedges Gold awards: 19.

Secretary: R. Stevens, County Ground, Eaton Road, Hove, BN3 3AN.
Cricket Manager: A. Buss.
Captain: A. Long.
Prospects of play Telephone No.: Hove (0273) 772766,

    Geoffrey Graham (Geoff) ARNOLD B Earlsfield (Surrey) 3/9/1944. RHB, RFM.
Debut for Surrey 1963. Cap 1967. *Wisden* 1971. Benefit (£15,000) in 1976. Played
for Orange Free State in 1976–77 Currie Cup competition. Left county after 1977
season and made debut for Sussex in 1978. Cap 1979. Tests: 34 between 1967 and
1975. Tours: Pakistan 1966–67, India, Pakistan, and Sri Lanka 1972–73, West
Indies 1973–74, Australia and New Zealand 1974–75. Took 109 wkts (av 18.22) in
1967. Hat-trick v Leics (Leicester) 1974. Gillette Man of Match awards: 3 (2 for
Surrey). HS: 73 MCC under-25 v Central Zone (Sahiwal) 1966–67. HSUK: 63
Surrey v Warwickshire (Birmingham) 1968. HSC: 51 v Leics (Leicester) 1979.
HSTC: 59 v Pakistan (Oval) 1967. HSGC: 18* v Northants (Hove) 1979. HSJPL:
24* Surrey v Notts (Nottingham) 1971. HSBH: 12* Surrey v Combined Universities
(Oval) 1976. BB: 8–41 (13–128 match) Surrey v Glos (Oval) 1967. BBC: 7–44 v
Lancs (Manchester) 1978. BBTC: 6–45 v India (Delhi) 1972–73. BBGC: 5–9
Surrey v Derbyshire (Oval) 1967. BBJPL: 5–11 Surrey v Glamorgan (Oval) 1969.
BBBH: 3–19 Surrey v Yorks (Bradford) 1976. Soccer for Corinthian Casuals.

    John Robert Troutbeck BARCLAY (Eton College) B Bonn, West Germany
22/1/1954. RHB, OB. Debut 1970 aged 16 years 205 days, whilst still at school. Was
in XI at school from age of 14 and scored the record number of runs for school in a
season in 1970. Played in MCC Schools matches at Lord's in 1969–71. Vice-captain
of English Schools Cricket Association team to India 1970–71. Captain of England
Young Cricketers team to West Indies 1972. Cap 1976. Played for Orange Free
State in 1978–79 Castle Bowl Competition. 1,000 runs (4)—1,093 runs (av 32.14) in
1979 best. Benson & Hedges Gold awards: 2. HS: 112 v Warwickshire (Hove) 1977.
HSGC: 44 v Derbyshire (Hove) 1977, and 44 v Somerset (Lord's) 1978. HSJPL: 48
v Derbyshire (Derby) 1974. HSBH: 93* v Surrey (Oval) 1976. BB: 6–61 v Sri
Lankans (Horsham) 1979. BBGC: 3–27 v Lancs (Hove) 1978. BBJPL: 3–11 v
Worcs (Eastbourne) 1978. BBBH: 5–43 v Combined Universities (Oxford) 1979.

    Christopher David Bryan (Chris) FLETCHER (Torquay GS) B Harrogate
10/12/1957. LHB, RFM. Played for Devon in 1976 and for county 2nd XI in 1978.
Debut 1979. One match v Oxford U. (Pagham) 1979.

138

Peter John GRAVES (Hove Manor School) B Hove 19/5/1946. LHB, SLA. Close field. Debut 1965. Cap 1969. Is vice-captain of county. Benefit (£35,000) in 1978. Played for Orange Free State in 1969-70, 1970-71 (captain), 1973-74 to 1976-77 Currie Cup competition whist appointed as coach. 1,000 runs (5)—1,282 runs (av 38.84) in 1974 best. Scored two centuries in match (119 and 136*) for Orange Free State v Border (Bloemfontein) 1976-77. Gillette Man of Match awards: 1. Benson & Hedges Gold awards: 2. HS: 145* v Glos (Gloucester) 1974. HSGC: 84* v Derbyshire (Chesterfield) 1973. HSJPL: 101* v Middlesex (Eastbourne) 1972. HSBH: 114* v Cambridge U (Hove) 1974. BB: 3-69 Orange Free State v Australians (Bloemfontein) 1969-70. BBUK: 3-75 v Glos (Cheltenham) 1965. Soccer player.

Allan Michael GREEN B Pulborough (Sussex) 28/5/1960. RHB. Joined staff 1979. Has yet to appear in first-class cricket.

Ian Alexander GREIG (Queen's College, Queenstown and Cambridge) B Queenstown, South Africa 8/12/1955. RHB, RM. Younger brother of A. W. Greig. Debut for Border in 1974-75 Currie Cup competition. Played for Griqualand West in 1975-76. Has played for county 2nd XI since 1976. Debut for Cambridge U 1977. Blue 1977-78-79 (captain). Appeared in one John Player League match for county in 1979. Re-appeared for Border in 1979-80 Castle Bowl competition. HS: 96 Cambridge U v Kent (Canterbury) 1977. HSBH: 37 Combined Universities v Surrey (Oval) 1979. BB: 4-76 Cambridge U v Glamorgan (Cambridge) 1977. BBBH: 3-51 Combined Universities v Glamorgan (Oxford) 1978. Blues for rugby 1977-78.

Timothy John (Tim) HEAD (Lancing College) B Hammersmith 22/9/1957. RHB, WK. Debut 1976. HS: 31 v Oxford U (Oxford) 1978. HSJPL: 12* v Yorks (Hove) 1979. Held 7 catches in his debut match v Oxford U (Pagham).

IMRAN KHAN NIAZI (Aitchison College and Cathedral School, Lahore, Worcester RGS and Oxford) B Lahore, Pakistan 25/11/1952. RHB, RF. Cousin of Majid Jahangir Khan. Debut for Lahore A 1969-70 and has played subsequently for various Lahore teams. Debut for Worcs 1971. Blue 1973-74-75 (capt in 1974). Cap 1976. Left Worcs in 1977 and joined Sussex by special registration. Cap 1978. Tests: 22 for Pakistan between 1971 and 1978-79. Tours: Pakistan to England 1971 and 1974, Australia and West Indies 1976-77, New Zealand and Australia 1978-79, India 1979-80. 1,000 runs (3)—1,339 runs (av 41,84) in 1978 best. Scored two centuries in match (117* and 106), Oxford U v Notts (Oxford) 1974. Had match double of 111* and 13-99 (7-53 & 6-46) v Lancs (Worcester) 1976. Gillette Man of Match awards: 3 (1 for Worcs). Benson & Hedges Gold awards: 5 (1 for Oxford and Cambridge Universities, 1 for Worcs). HS: 170 Oxford U v Northants (Oxford) 1974. HSC: 167 v Glos (Hove) 1978. HSTC: 59 Pakistan v New Zealand (Karachi) 1976-77. HSGC: 55* Worcs v Essex (Worcester) 1976. HSJPL: 75 Worcs v Warwickshire (Worcester) 1976. HSBH: 72 Worcs v Warwickshire (Birmingham) 1976. BB: 7-52 v Glos (Bristol) 1978. BBTC: 6-63 (12-165 match) Pakistan v Australia (Sydney) 1976-77. BBGC: 4-27 v Staffs (Stone) 1975. BBJPL: 5-29 Worcs v Leics (Leicester) 1973. BBBH: 5-8 v Northants (Northampton) 1978.

Garth Stirling LE ROUX (Wynberg Boys High School) B Cape Town 4/9/1955. 6ft 3ins tall. RHB, RF. Debut for Western Province B in 1975-78 Currie Cup competition. Played for Derbyshire 2nd XI in 1977. Debut for county 1978. One match v New Zealanders (Hove). Joined staff in 1979 and is available for competitive matches in 1980. HS: 47* Western Province v Transvaal (Cape Town) 1977-78. HSUK: 17* v New Zealanders (Hove) 1978. BB: 7-40 Western Province v Eastern Province (Port Elizabeth) 1977-78.

SUSSEX

Arnold LONG (Wallington CGS) B Cheam 18/12/1940. LBH, WK. Debut for Surrey 1960. Cap 1962. Benefit (£10,353) in 1971. Appointed county vice-captain in 1973. Left staff after 1975 season and made debut for Sussex in 1976. Cap 1976. Appointed county captain in 1978. Dismissed 7 batsmen in innings and 11 in match (all ct) v Sussex (Hove) 1964, world record for most catches in match and only one short of record for most dismissals in match. Dismissed 89 batsmen (72 ct 17 st) in 1962. HS: 92 Surrey v Leics (Leicester) 1970. HSC: 60 v Hants (Basingstoke) 1976. HSGC: 42 Surrey v Sussex (Oval) 1970. HSJPL: 71 Surrey v Warwickshire (Birmingham) 1971. HSBH: 46 Surrey v Kent (Oval) 1973. Soccer for Corinthian Casuals.

Gehan Dixon MENDIS (St Thomas College, Colombo and Brighton, Hove and Sussex GS) B Colombo, Ceylon 20/4/1955. RHB, WK. Played for 2nd XI since 1971. Played in one John Player League match in 1973. Debut 1974. Scored 979 runs (av 30,39) in 1978. HS: 128 v Essex (Hove) 1978. HSGC: 69 v Northants (Hove) 1979. HSJPL: 56 v Glos (Bristol) 1978. HSBH: 39 v Northants (Eastbourne) 1979.

Paul William Giles PARKER (Collyers' GS, Horsham and Cambridge) B Bulawayo, Rhodesia 15/1/1956. RHB, RM. Debut for both Cambridge U and county 1976. Blue 1976–77–78. University Secretary for 1977 and 1978. Cap 1979. Elected Best Young Cricketer for the Year in 1979 by Cricket Writers' Club. 1,000 runs (2)—1,330 runs (av 44.33) in 1979 best. Gillette Man of Match awards: 2. HS: 215 Cambridge U v Essex (Cambridge) 1976. HSC: 112 v Glamorgan (Swansea) 1978. HSGC: 69 v Lancs (Hove) 1978. HSJPL: 57 v Glos (Hove) 1979. HSBH: 36* Combined Universities v Sussex (Cambridge) 1976. Selected for University rugby match in 1977, but had to withdraw through injury.

Christopher Paul PHILLIPSON (Ardingly College) B Brindaban, India 10/2/1952. RHB, RM. Debut 1970. Benson & Hedges Gold awards: 1. HS: 70 v Oxford U (Oxford) 1978. HSGC: 34 v Lancs (Hove) 1978. HSJPL: 71 v Lancs (Hastings) 1979. HSBH: 38* v Essex (Chelmsford) 1979. BB: 6–56 v Notts (Hove) 1972. BBJPL: 4–25 v Middlesex (Eastbourne) 1972. BBBH: 5–32 v Combined Universities (Oxford) 1977. Trained as a teacher at Loughborough College of Education.

Anthony Charles Shackleton (Tony) PIGOTT (Harrow School) B London 4/6/1958. RHB, RFM. Played for 2nd XI since 1975. Debut 1978. Hat-trick v Surrey (Hove) 1978. HS: 55 v Yorks (Hove) 1979. HSGC: 30 v Northants (Hove) 1979. HSJPL: 49 v Warwickshire (Hove) 1979. BB: 4–40 v Cambridge U (Cambridge) 1979. BBGC: 3–43 v Notts (Hove) 1979.

John SPENCER (Brighton, Hove and Sussex GS, and Cambridge) B Brighton 6/10/1949. RHB, RM. Debut 1969. Blues 1970–71–72, Cap 1973, Benson & Hedges Gold awards: 3. HS: 79 v Hants (Southampton) 1975. HSGC: 14 v Glos (Hove) 1971. HSJPL: 35 v Northants (Northampton) 1977. HSBH: 18 Cambridge U v Warwickshire (Birmingham) 1972. BB: 6–19 v Glos (Gloucester) 1974. BBGC: 4–25 v Derbyshire (Chesterfield) 1973. BBJPL: 4–16 v Somerset (Hove) 1975. BBBH: 4–19 v Minor Counties (South) (Hove) 1975.

Christopher Edward (Chris) WALLER B Guildford 3/10/1948. RHB, SLA. Debut for Surrey 1967. Cap 1972. Left staff after 1973 season and made debut for Sussex in 1974. Cap 1976. HS: 47 Surrey v Pakistanis (Oval) 1971. HSC: 38 v Worcs (Worcester) 1975. HSGC: 14* v Notts (Nottingham) 1975. HSJPL: 18* v Glamorgan (Hove) 1975. HSBH: 11* v Essex (Chelmsford) 1975. BB: 7–64 Surrey v Sussex

140

(Oval) 1971. BBC: 6–40 v Surrey (Hove) 1975. BBJPL: 4–28 v Essex (Hove) 1976. BBBH: 4–25 v Minor Counties (South) (Hove) 1975.

Colin Mark WELLS (Tideway School, Newhaven) B Newhaven 3/3/1960. RHB, RM. Played in three John Player League matches in 1978. Debut 1979. HS: 29 v Hants (Bournemouth) 1979. HSJPL: 27 v Middlesex (Lord's) 1979. BB: 4–23 v Oxford U (Pāgham) 1979.

Kepler Christoffel WESSELS (Greys College, Bloemfontein) B Bloemfontain, South Africa 14/9/1957. LHB, OB. Debut for Orange Free State 1973–74 in Currie Cup competition, aged 16 years 4 months. Debut for county 1976. Cap 1977. Played for Queensland in 1979–80 Sheffield Shield competition. Scored 1,800 runs (av 52.94) in 1979. Benson & Hedges Gold awards: 2. HS: 187 v Kent (Eastbourne) 1979. HSGC: 43 v Staffs (Stone) 1978. HSJPL: 88 v Notts (Nottingham) 1977. HSBH: 106 v Notts (Hove) 1977.

NB.   The following players whose particulars appeared in the 1979 Annual have been omitted: K. B. Smith (not re-engaged) and S. J. Storey (appointed coach). In addition Javed Miandad has joined Glamorgan and his particulars will be found under that county.

COUNTY AVERAGES

Schweppes County Championship: **Played 20, won 6, lost 4, drawn 10, abandoned 2**
All first-class matches: **Played 23, won 7, lost 4, drawn 12, abandoned 2**

BATTING AND FIELDING

Cap		M	I	NO	Runs	HS	Avge	100	50	Ct	St
1977	K. C. Wessels	21	36	2	1800	187	52.94	6	11	21	—
1979	P. W. G. Parker	21	34	6	1203	103	42.96	3	5	14	—
1976	Imran Khan	16	25	5	700	154*	35.00	1	6	6	—
1976	J. R. T. Barclay	23	39	5	1093	104*	32.14	2	7	18	—
1976	A. Long	16	17	10	200	35*	28.57	—	—	36	5
—	G. D. Mendis	22	37	4	929	118	28.15	1	6	24	—
1969	P. J. Graves	17	24	2	501	59	22.77	—	1	5	—
—	A. C. S. Pigott	14	20	3	328	55	19.29	—	1	6	—
1977	Javed Miandad	3	6	2	76	30*	19.00	—	—	4	—
—	C. P. Phillipson	23	31	6	460	47	18.40	—	1	19	—
—	T. J. Head	7	6	2	70	22	17.50	—	—	21	1
—	S. P. Hoadley	5	7	0	97	23	13.85	—	1	—	—
—	C. M. Wells	5	6	1	60	29	12.00	—	—	1	—
1976	C. E. Waller	16	13	7	69	18*	11.50	—	—	12	—
1973	J. Spencer	17	16	3	145	35	11.15	—	3	—	—
1979	G. G. Arnold	18	19	2	163	51	9.58	—	1	5	—
—	R. G. L. Cheatle	8	5	1	38	15	9.50	—	—	11	—

Played in one match: C. D. B. Fletcher did not bat.

BOWLING	Type	O	M	R	W	Avge	Best	5 wI	10 wM
C. M. Wells	RM	73.1	30	137	10	13.70	4–23	—	—
Imran Khan	RF	415.4	106	1091	73	14.94	6–37	7	—
G. G. Arnold	RFM	435.5	147	950	52	18.26	6–41	2	—
R. G. L. Cheatle	SLA	185.1	49	467	21	22.23	6–32	2	—
C. P. Phillipson	RM	203.5	53	477	20	23.85	4–24	—	—
J. R. T. Barclay	OB	412.4	85	1250	52	24.03	6–61	2	—
J. Spencer	RM	365.1	107	888	33	26.90	6–40	2	—
C. E. Waller	SLA	487.1	126	1262	39	32.35	4–18	—	—
A. C. S. Pigott	RFM	269	48	917	28	32.75	4–40	—	—

Also bowled: C. D. B. Fletcher 19–4–51–1; Javed Miandad 24–4–73–1; P. W. G. Parker 28–4–117–1; K. C. Wessels 1–0–4–0.

County Records

First-class cricket

Highest innings totals:	For —705–8d v Surrey (Hastings)	1902
	Agst—726 by Nottinghamshire (Nottingham)	1895
Lowest innings totals:	For —19 v Surrey (Godalming)	1830
	19 v Nottinghamshire (Hove)	1873
	Agst—18 by Kent (Gravesend)	1867
Highest individual innings:	For —333 K. S. Duleepsinhji v Northants (Hove)	1930
	Agst—322 E. Paynter for Lancashire (Hove)	1937
Best bowling in an innings:	For —10–48 C. H. G. Bland v Kent (Tonbridge)	1899
	Agst—9–11 A. P. Freeman for Kent (Hove)	1922
Best bowling in a match:	For —17–106 G. R. Cox v Warwicks (Horsham)	1926
	Agst—17–67 A. P. Freeman for Kent (Hove)	1922
Most runs in a season:	2850 (av 64.77) John Langridge	1949
runs in a career:	34152 (av 37.69) John Langridge	1928–1955
100s in a season:	12 by John Langridge	1949
100s in a career:	76 by John Langridge	1928–1955
wickets in a season:	198 (av 13.45) M. W. Tate	1925
wickets in a career:	2223 (av 16.34) M. W. Tate	1912–1937

RECORD WICKET STANDS

1st	490	E. H. Bowley & John Langridge v Middlesex (Hove)	1933
2nd	385	E. H. Bowley & M. W. Tate v Northamptonshire (Hove)	1921
3rd	298	K. S. Ranjitsinhji & E. H. Killick v Lancashire (Hove)	1901
4th	326*	G. Cox & James Langridge v Yorkshire (Leeds)	1949
5th	297	J. H. Parks & H. W. Parks v Hampshire (Portsmouth)	1937
6th	255	K. S. Duleepsinhji & M. W. Tate v Northamptonshire (Hove)	1930
7th	344	K. S. Ranjitsinhji & W. Newham v Essex (Leyton)	1902
8th	229*	C. L. A. Smith & G. Brann v Kent (Hove)	1902
9th	178	H. W. Parks & A. F. Wensley v Derbyshire (Horsham)	1930
10th	156	G. R. Cox & H. R. Butt v Cambridge U (Cambridge)	1908

One-day cricket

Highest innings totals:	Gillette Cup	314–7 v Kent (Tunbridge Wells)	1963
	John Player League	288–6 v Middlesex (Hove)	1969
	Benson & Hedges Cup	280–5 v Cambridge U (Hove)	1974
Lowest innings totals:	Gillette Cup	49 v Derbyshire (Chesterfield)	1969
	John Player League	61 v Derbyshire (Derby)	1978
	Benson & Hedges Cup	61 v Middlesex (Hove)	1978
Highest individual innings:	Gillette Cup	115 E. R. Dexter v Northamptonshire (Northampton)	1963
	John Player League	129 A. W. Greig v Yorkshire (Scarborough)	1976
	Benson & Hedges Cup	114* P. J. Graves v Cambridge U (Hove)	1974
Best bowling figures:	Gillette Cup	6–30 D. L. Bates v Gloucestershire (Hove)	1968
	John Player League	6–14 M. A. Buss v Lancashire (Hove)	1973
	Benson & Hedges Cup	5–8 Imran Khan v Northamptonshire (Northampton)	1978

WARWICKSHIRE

Formation of present club: 1884.
Colours: Blue, gold, and silver.
Badge: Bear and ragged staff.
County Champions (3): 1911, 1951 and 1972.
Gillette Cup winners (2): 1966 and 1968.
Gillette Cup finalists (2): 1964 and 1972.
Best final position in John Player League: 5th in 1970 and 1975.
Benson & Hedges Cup semi-finalists (4): 1972, 1975, 1976 and 1978.
Gillette Man of the Match awards: 20.
Benson & Hedges Gold awards: 23.

Secretary: A. C. Smith, County Ground, Edgbaston, Birmingham, B5 7QU.
Cricket Manager: D. J. Brown.
Captain: R. G. D. Willis.
Prospects of play Telephone No.: (021) 440 3624,

Robert **Neal** ABBERLEY (Saltley GS) B Birmingham 22/4/1944. RHB, OB. Debut 1964. Cap 1966. Benefit in 1979. Tour: Pakistan 1966–67 (returning home early owing to injury). 1,000 runs (3)—1,315 runs (av 28.58) in 1966 best. Benson & Hedges Gold awards: 1. HS: 117* v Essex (Birmingham) 1966. HSGC: 47 v Lincs (Birmingham) 1971. HSJPL: 76 v Glamorgan (Birmingham) 1974. HSBH: 113* v Hants (Bournemouth) 1976.

Dennis Leslie AMISS B Birmingham 7/4/1943. RHB, SLC. Joined county staff 1958. Debut 1960. Cap 1965. *Wisden* 1974. Benefit (£34,947) in 1975. Tests: 50 between 1966 and 1977. Played in one match v Rest of World in 1970. Tours: Pakistan 1966–67, India, Pakistan, and Sri Lanka 1972–73, West Indies 1973–74, Australia and New Zealand 1974–75, India, Sri Lanka and Australia 1976–77.

1,000 runs (15)—2,110 runs (av 65.93) in 1976 best. Also scored 1,120 runs (av 74.66) in West Indies 1973–74. Scored two centuries in match (155* and 112) v Worcs (Birmingham) 1978. Gillette Man of Match awards: 2. Benson & Hedges Gold awards: 2. HS: 262* England v West Indies (Kingston) 1973–74. HSUK: 232* v Glos (Bristol) 1979. HSGC: 113 v Glamorgan (Swansea) 1966. HSJPL: 110 v Surrey (Birmingham) 1974. HSBH: 73* v Minor Counties (West) (Coventry) 1977. BB: 3–21 v Middlesex (Lord's) 1970.

David John (Dave) BROWN (Queen Mary GS, Walsall) B Walsall 30/1/1942. RHB, RFM. 6ft 4ins tall. Debut 1961. Cap 1964. Benefit (£21,109) in 1973. County captain from 1975 to 1977. Appointed cricket manager and unlikely to play regularly in future. Tests: 26 between 1965 and 1969. Played in 2 matches v Rest of World 1970. Tours: South Africa 1964–65, Australia and New Zealand 1965–66, Pakistan 1966–67 (vice-captain), West Indies 1967–68, Ceylon and Pakistan 1968–69. Gillette Man of Match awards: 1. Benson & Hedges Gold awards: 1. HS: 79 v Derbyshire (Birmingham) 1972. HSTC: 44 v New Zealand (Christchurch) 1965–66 and 44* v Pakistan (Lahore) 1968–69. HSUK: 41 v Middlesex (Lord's) 1977. HSJPL: 38* v Worcs (Birmingham) 1972. HSBH: 20* v Northants (Coventry) 1973. BB: 8–60 b Middlesex (Lord's) 1975. BBTC: 5–42 v Australia (Lord's) 1968. BBGC: 5–18 v Glamorgan (Swansea) 1966. BBJPL: 5–13 v Worcs (Birmingham) 1970. BBBH: 3–17 v Lancs (Coventry) 1978.

Neville John BULPITT (Caludon Castle Comprehensive School, Coventry) B Coventry 15/4/1957. RHB, RM. Played for 2nd XI since 1975. Played in last three John Player League matches in 1979. Has yet to appear in first-class cricket. HSJPL: 11 v Yorks (Birmingham) 1979.

John Alan CLAUGHTON (King's Edward's School, Birmingham and Oxford) B Leeds 17/9/1956. RHB, SLA. Played for 2nd XI since 1974. Debut for Oxford U 1976, scoring 51 and 112 in debut match v Glos (Oxford). Blue 1976–77–78 (captain)–79. Debut for county 1979 (two matches). HS: 130 Oxford U v Sussex (Oxford) 1978. HSC: 12 v Hants (Nuneaton) 1979. HSBH: 15 Oxford and Cambridge Universities v Hants (Cambridge) 1978.

Christopher Craven (Chris) CLIFFORD (Malton GS) B Hoveringham (Yorks) 5/7/1942. RHB, OB. Played for Yorks 2nd XI in 1963 and made debut for county in 1972. Did not play again until making debut for Warwickshire in 1978. HS: 26 v Surrey (Oval) 1979. BB: 6–89 v Somerset (Weston-super-Mare) 1978.

Anthonie Michal (Yogi) FERREIRA (Hillview High School, Pretoria) B Pretoria 13/4/1955. RHB, RM. Debut for Northern Transvaal 1974–75. Played for D. H. Robin's XI v both Oxford and Cambridge Universities at Eastbourne in 1978. Debut for county 1979. HS: 84 Northern Transvaal v Griqualand West (Pretoria) 1978–79. HSUK: 57 v Yorks (Birmingham) 1979. HSJPL: 36* v Middlesex (Lord's) 1979. HSBH: 13* v Lancs (Southport) and 13 v Essex (Chelmsford) 1979. BB: 8–38 Northern Transvaal v Transvaal B (Pretoria) 1977–78. BBUK: 5–66 v Somerset (Birmingham) 1979. BBGC: 4–50 v Notts (Birmingham) 1979. BBJPL: 3–32 v Kent (Maidstone) 1979.

David Charles HOPKINS (Moseley GS) B Birmingham 11/2/1957. RHB, RM. 6ft 6½ins tall. Played for 2nd XI since 1975. Debut 1977. HS: 34* v Essex (Birmingham) 1979. HSJPL: 13* v Sussex (Hove) 1979. BB: 6–67 v Somerset (Taunton) 1979. BBJPL: 3–26 v Lancs (Birmingham) 1979.

Geoffrey William (Geoff) HUMPAGE (Golden Hillock Comprehensive School, Birmingham) B Birmingham 24/4/1954. RHB, WK, RM. Debut 1974. Cap 1976. 1,000 runs (2)—1,329 runs (av 44.30) in 1976 best. HS: 125* v Sussex (Birmingham) 1976. HSGC: 58 v Somerset (Taunton) 1978. HSJPL: 58 v Yorks (Birmingham) 1979. HSBH: 78 v Derbyshire (Derby) 1978. BBJPL: 4–53 v Glos (Moreton-in-Marsh) 1979.

Alvin Isaac (Kalli) KALLICHARRAN B Port Mourant, Berbice, Guyana 21/3/1949. LHB, OB. 5ft 4 ins tall. Debut 1966–67 for Guyana in Shell Shield competition. Debut for county 1971. Cap 1972. Played for Queensland in 1977–78 Sheffield Shield competition. Tests: 51 for West Indies between 1971–72 and 1978–79, scoring 100* and 101 in first two innings in Tests v New Zealand and captaining country in 9 Tests. Tours: West Indies to England 1973 and 1976. India, Sri Lanka and Pakistan 1974–75, Australia 1975–76, India and Sri Lanka 1978–79 (captain), Australia and New Zealand 1979–80. 1,000 runs (6)—1,343 runs (av 41.96) in 1977 best. Also scored 1,249 runs (av 56.77) on 1974–75 tour. Benson & Hedges Gold awards: 2. HS: 197 Guyana v Jamaica (Kingston) 1973–74. HSUK: 170* v Northants (Northampton) 1979. HSTC: 187 West Indies v India (Bombay) 1978–79. HSGC: 88 v Glamorgan (Birmingham) 1972. HSJPL: 101* v Derbyshire (Chesterfield) 1972 and 101 v Glos (Moreton-in-Marsh) 1979. HSBH: 109 v Glos (Bristol) 1978. BB: 4–48 v Derbyshire (Birmingham) 1978.

Timothy Andrew (Andy) LLOYD (Oswestry Boys' HS) B Oswestry (Shropshire) 5/11/1956. LHB, RM. Played for both Shropshire and county 2nd XI in 1975. Appeared in one John Player League match in 1976, v Yorks (Leeds). Debut 1977. Played for Orange Free State in 1978–79 and 1979–80 Castle Bowl competitions. HS: 104 v Notts (Birmingham) 1979. HSJPL: 54* v Middlesex (Birmingham) 1978. HSBH: 35* v Glamorgan (Birmingham) 1978.

Gordon John LORD (Warwick School) B Warwick 25/4/1961. LHB, SLA. Toured Australia 1979 and West Indies 1980 with England Young Cricketers. Has joined staff for 1980. Has yet to appear in first class cricket.

Robert Keith MAGUIRE (Smiths Wood School, Chelmsley Wood, Birmingham) B Birmingham 20/3/1961. RHB, RM. Has joined staff for 1980. Has yet to appear in first class cricket.

Christopher (Chris) MAYNARD (Bishop Vesey's GS, Sutton Coldfield) B Haslemere (Surrey) 8/4/1958. RHB, WK. Played for 2nd XI since 1976. Debut 1978. HS: 85 v Kent (Birmingham) 1979. HSJPL: 35 v Essex (Birmingham) 1979.

Philip Robert OLIVER B West Bromwich (Staffs) 9/5/1956. RHB, OB. Played for Shropshire 1972–74. Debut 1975. HS: 83 v Yorks (Birmingham) 1979. HSGC: 22 v Notts (Birmingham) 1979. HSJPL: 78* v Hants (Southampton) 1978. HSBH: 46 v Essex (Chelmsford) 1979. BBJPL: 3–36 v Middlesex (Lord's) 1977. Plays soccer for Telford in Southern League.

Stephen Peter (Steve) PERRYMAN (Sheldon Heath Comprehensive School) B Yardley, Birmingham 22/10/1955. RHB, RM. Debut 1974. Cap 1977. Benson & Hedges Gold awards: 1. HS: 43 v Somerset (Birmingham) 1977. HSJPL: 17* v Worcs (Birmingham) 1975. HSBH: 18 v Essex (Chelmsford) 1979. BB: 7–49 v Hants (Bournemouth) 1978. BBGC: 3–35 v Middlesex (Lord's) 1977. BBJPL: 4–19 v Surrey (Oval) 1975. BBBH: 4–17 v Minor Counties (West) (Birmingham) 1978.

WARWICKSHIRE

Stephen John (Mic) ROUSE (Moseley County School) B Merthyr Tydfil (Glamorgan) 20/1/1949. LHB, LFM. Debut 1970. Cap 1974. Benson & Hedges Gold awards: 2. HS: 93 v Hants (Bournemouth) 1976. HSGC: 34 v Middlesex (Lord's) 1977. HSJPL: 36 v Somerset (Weston-super-Mare) 1978. HSBH: 34* v Glamorgan (Birmingham) 1978. BB: 6–34 v Leics (Leicester) 1976. BBGC: 4–27 v Sussex (Hove) 1976. BBJPL: 5–20 v Kent (Canterbury) 1976. BBBH: 5–21 v Worcs (Worcester) 1974.

Charles Alpheus (Alphie) SAM (Emmanuel HS, St Vincent) B St Vincent 7/5/1953. LHB, RM. 5ft 5ins tall. Has lived in Warwickshire since 1969. Played in last two John Player League matches in 1979. Has yet to appear in first-class cricket. HSJPL: 31 v Yorks (Birmingham) 1979.

Richard Le Quesne SAVAGE (Marlborough College and Oxford) B Waterloo, London 10/12/1955. RHB, RM/OB. Played for county 2nd XI since 1974. Debut for both county and University 1976. Blue 1976–77–78. HS: 22* Oxford U v Worcs (Oxford) 1977. HSC: 15* v Somerset (Taunton) 1979. BB: 7–50 v Glamorgan (Nuneaton) 1977. BBJPL: 3–19 v Worcs (Birmingham) 1979.

Gladstone Cleopthas SMALL (Moseley School, Birmingham) B Barbados 18/10/1961. RHB, RFM. Has joined staff for 1980. Has yet to appear in first class cricket.

Kenneth David SMITH (Heaton GS, Newcastle upon Tyne) B Jesmond, Newcastle upon Tyne 9/7/1956. RHB. Son of Kenneth D. Smith, former Nortumberland and Leics player. Played for 2nd XI 1972, Debut 1973, Cap 1978. 1,000 runs (2)—1,187 runs (av 33.91) in 1978 best. Benson & Hedges Gold awards: 1. HS: 135 v Lancs (Manchester) 1977. HSGC: 28 v Somerset (Taunton) 1978. HSJPL: 60 v Glamorgan (Swansea) 1979. HSBH: 68 v Hants (Bournemouth) 1979.

Richard Anthony (Tony) SMITH (Heaton School, Newcastle upon Tyne) B Newcastle upon Tyne 13/4/1959. LHB, RM. Younger brother of K. D. Smith. Played for 2nd XI since 1978. Has yet to appear in first class cricket.

Gary Philip THOMAS (George Dixon GS, Birmingham) B Birmingham 8/11/1958. RHB, RM. Played for 2nd XI since 1975. Debut 1978. Played in one Championship match only in 1979. HSJPL: 16 v Lancs (Manchester) 1978.

John WHITEHOUSE (King Edward VI School, Nuneaton and Bristol University) B Nuneaton 8/4/1949. RHB, OB. Played for county against Scotland in 1970, a match no longer counted as first-class. Debut 1971, scoring 173 v Oxford U (Oxford) in first innings of debut match, in 167 minutes with 35 4's. Elected Best Young Cricketer of the Year in 1971 by Cricket Writers' Club. Cap 1973. Appointed county captain in 1978. Relinquished appointment after 1979 season. 1,000 runs (3)—1,543 runs (av 42.86) in 1977 best. HS: as above. HSGC: 109 v Glamorgan (Birmingham) 1976. HSJPL: 92 v Surrey (Birmingham) 1976. HSBH: 71* v Lancashire (Birmingham) 1976.

Robert George Dylan (Bob) WILLIS (Guildford RGS) B Sunderland 30/5/1949. RHB, RF. Debut for Surrey 1969. Left staff after 1971 season and made debut for Warwickshire in 1972. Cap 1972. *Wisden* 1977. Appointed county captain for 1980. Tests: 50 between 1970–71 and 1979. Tours: Australia and New Zealand 1970–71 (flown out as replacement for A. Ward) and 1974–75, West Indies 1973–74, India, Sri Lanka and Australia 1976–77, Pakistan and New Zealand 1977–78, Australia 1978–79 (vice-captain), Australia and India 1979–80 (vice-captain). Hat-tricks (2) v Derbyshire (Birmingham) 1972 and v West Indians (Birmingham) 1976. Also in John Player League v Yorks (Birmingham) 1973. Gillette Man of Match awards: 1

(for Surrey). Benson & Hedges Gold awards: 3. HS: 43 v Middlesex (Birmingham) 1976. HSTC: 24 v India (Manchester) 1974, 24* v Australia (Oval) 1977 and 24 v Australia (Adelaide) 1978–79. HSGC: 12* Surrey v Sussex (Oval) 1970. HSJPL: 52* v Derbyshire (Birmingham) 1975. HSBH: 25* v Northants (Northampton) 1977. BB: 8–32 v Glos (Bristol) 1977. BBTC: 7–78 v Australia (Lord's) 1977. BBGC: 6–49 Surrey v Middlesex (Oval) 1970. BBJPL: 4–12 v Middlesex (Lord's) 1973. BBBH: 5–27 v Lancs (Birmingham) 1976. Played soccer (goalkeeper) for Guildford City.

NB. The following player whose particulars appeared in the 1979 Annual has been omitted: R. W. Flower.

COUNTY AVERAGES

Schweppes County Championship: Played 21, won 3, drawn 11, lost 7, abandoned 1
All first-class matches: Played 22, won 4, drawn 11, lost 7, abandoned 1

BATTING AND FIELDING

Cap		M	I	NO	Runs	HS	Avge	100	50	Ct	St
1972	A. I. Kallicharran	17	26	5	1098	170*	52.28	4	6	14	—
1965	D. L. Amiss	22	37	3	1672	232*	49.17	6	6	15	—
—	C. Maynard	12	12	3	310	85	34.44	—	2	27	1
1976	G. W. Humpage	17	24	2	755	96	34.31	—	2	21	2
—	T. A. Lloyd	15	26	5	613	104	29.19	1	1	16	—
1972	R. G. D. Willis	9	6	3	84	42*	28.00	—	1	—	—
—	P. R. Oliver	16	18	3	394	83	26.26	—	2	9	—
1978	K. D. Smith	20	34	3	739	71	23.83	—	7	9	—
1973	J. Whitehouse	21	34	4	624	98	20.80	—	3	10	—
—	A. M. Ferreira	16	17	6	219	57	19.90	—	1	7	—
1964	D. J. Brown	9	7	1	103	33	17.16	—	2	—	—
—	R. L. Savage	7	8	5	39	15*	13.00	—	—	3	—
1966	R. N. Abberley	6	9	2	79	22*	11.28	—	—	3	—
—	D. C. Hopkins	12	14	2	103	34*	8.58	—	—	3	—
1977	S. P. Perryman	19	13	4	68	12	7.55	—	—	6	—
—	C. C. Clifford	20	17	5	88	26	7.33	—	—	4	—

Playeed in two matches: J. A. Claughton 0, 12 (1 ct).
Played in one match: S. J. Rouse 21 (1 ct); G. P. Thomas 9.

BOWLING

	Type	O	M	R	W	Avge	Best	5 wI	10 wM
S. J. Rouse	LFM	20.3	3	80	6	13.33	4–41	—	—
D. J. Brown	RFM	243.4	60	653	21	31.09	7–73	2	—
S. P. Perryman	RM	671	224	1662	51	32.58	6–69	4	1
D. C. Hopkins	RM	275	59	886	27	32.81	6–67	1	—
R. G. D. Willis	RF	159	45	401	11	36.45	5–41	1	—
A. M. Ferreira	RM	426	102	1210	31	39.03	5–66	1	—
C. C. Clifford	OB	682.4	154	2166	49	44.20	5–37	3	—
R. L. Savage	RM/OB	177.4	39	566	11	51.45	4–83	—	—
A. I. Kallicharran	LB	119.1	20	403	6	67.16	2–13	—	—
P. R. Oliver	OB	141	27	482	7	68.85	2–50	—	—

Also bowled: R. N. Abberley 3–1–9–1; G. W. Humpage 16–1–96–0; T. A. Lloyd 10–2–57–1; J. Whitehouse 13–2–85–1.

County Records

First-class cricket

Highest innings totals:	For —657–6d v Hampshire (Birmingham)	1899
	Agst—887 by Yorkshire (Birmingham)	1896
Lowest innings totals:	For —16 v Kent (Tonbridge)	1913
	Agst—15 by Hampshire (Birmingham)	1922
Highest individual innings:	For —305* F. R. Foster v Worcestershire (Dudley)	1914
	Agst—316 R. H. Moore for Hants (Bournemouth)	1937
Best bowling in an innings:	For —10-41 J. D. Bannister v Combined Services (Birmingham)	1959
	Agst—10-36 H. Verity for Yorkshire (Leeds)	1931
Best bowling in a match:	For —15-76 S. Hargreave v Surrey (The Oval)	1903
	Agst—17-92 A. P. Freeman for Kent (Folkestone)	1932

Most runs in a season:	2417 (av 60.42) M. J. K. Smith	1959
runs in a career:	34172 (av 35.31) W. G. Quaife	1894–1928
100s in a season:	8 by R. E. S. Wyatt	1937
	and R. B. Kanhai	1972
100s in a career:	71 by W. G. Quaife	1894–1928
wickets in a season:	180 (av 15.13) W. E. Hollies	1946
wickets in a career:	2201 (av 20.45) W. E. Hollies	1932–1957

RECORD WICKET STANDS

1st	377* N. F. Horner & K. Ibadulla v Surrey (The Oval)	1960
2nd	465* J. A. Jameson & R. B. Kanhai v Gloucestershire (Birmingham)	1974
3rd	327 S. Kinneir & W. G. Quaife v Lancashire (Birmingham)	1901
4th	402 R. B. Kanhai & K. Ibadulla v Notts (Nottingham)	1968
5th	268 W. Quaife & W. G. Quaife v Essex (Leyton)	1900
6th	220 H. E. Dollery & J. Buckingham v Derbyshire (Derby)	1938
7th	250 H. E. Dollery & J. S. Ord v Kent (Maidstone)	1953
8th	228 A. J. Croom & R. E. S. Wyatt v Worcestershire (Dudley)	1925
9th	154 G. W. Stephens & A. J. Croom v Derbyshire (Birmingham)	1925
10th	128 F. R. Santall & W. Sanders v Yorkshire (Birmingham)	1930

One-day cricket

Highest innings totals:	Gillette Cup	307–8 v Hampshire (Birmingham)	1964
	John Player League	265–5 v Northamptonshire (Northampton)	1979
	Benson & Hedges Cup	269–9 v Worcestershire (Birmingham)	1976
Lowest innings totals:	Gillette Cup	109 v Kent (Canterbury)	1971
	John Player League	65 v Kent (Maidstone)	1979
	Benson & Hedges Cup	96 v Leicestershire (Leicester)	1972
Highest individual innings	Gillette Cup	126 R. B. Kanhai v Lincolnshire (Birmingham)	1971
	John Player League	123* J. A. Jameson v Nottinghamshire (Nottingham)	1973
	Benson & Hedges Cup	119* R. B. Kanhai v Northants (Northampton)	1975

Best bowling figures:	Gillette Cup	6–32 K. Ibadulla v Hants (Birmingham)	1965
	John Player League	5–13 D. J. Brown v Worcestershire (Birmingham)	1970
	Benson & Hedges Cup	5–21 S. J. Rouse v Worcestershire (Worcester)	1974

WORCESTERSHIRE

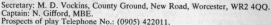

Formation of present club: 1865.
Colours: Dark Green and Black.
Badge: Shield, *Argent*, bearing *Fess* between three *Pears Sable*.
County Champions (3): 1964, 1965 and 1974.
Gillette Cup finalists (2): 1963 and 1966.
John Player League champions: 1971.
Benson & Hedges Cup finalists (2): 1973 and 1976.
Gillette Man of the Match awards: 16.
Benson & Hedges Gold awards: 20.
Secretary: M. D. Vockins, County Ground, New Road, Worcester, WR2 4QQ.
Captain: N. Gifford, MBE.
Prospects of play Telephone No.: (0905) 422011.

Hartley ALLEYNE B Barbados 28/2/1957. RHB, RFM. Debut for Barbados in one Shell Shield match in 1978–79. Has joined county for 1980.

Alan BROWN (Darwen Vale HS) B Darwen (Lancs) 23/12/1957. RHB, WK. 5ft 5ins tall. Played for 2nd XI since 1977. Debut 1979. One match v Oxford U (Oxford) and also appeared in one John Player League match.

James (Jimmy) CUMBES (Didsbury Secondary Technical School) B East Didsbury (Lancs) 4/5/1944. RHB, RFM. Debut for Lancs 1963. Not re-engaged at end of 1967 season and made debut for Surrey in 1968. Not re-engaged after 1970 season and rejoined Lancs in 1971. Made debut for Worcs in 1972 by special registration. Cap 1978. Hat-trick v Northants (Worcester) 1977. HS: 25* Surrey v West Indians (Oval) 1969. HSC: 22 v Middlesex (Lord's) 1977. HSJPL: 14* v Sussex (Eastbourne) 1978. BB: 6–24 v Yorks (Worcester) 1977. BBGC: 4–23 v Sussex (Hove) 1974. BBJPL: 3–13 v Middlesex (Worcester) 1978. BBBH: 3–34 v Somerset (Taunton) 1978. Soccer (goalkeeper) for Tranmere Rovers, West Bromwich Albion, and Aston Villa.

Timothy Stephen CURTIS (Worcester Royal GS) B Chislehurst (Kent) 15/1/1960. RHB, LB. Played for 2nd XI since 1976. Debut 1979. One match v Sri Lankans. HS: 27 v Sri Lankans (Worcester) 1979.

Norman GIFFORD B Ulverston (Lancs) 30/3/1940. LHB, SLA. Joined staff 1958 and made debut 1960. Cap 1961. Appointed county captain in 1971 after being vice-captain since 1969. Benefit (£11,047) in 1974. *Wisden* 1974. Awarded MBE in 1978 Birthday Honours list. Tests: 15 between 1964 and 1973. Played in one match for Rest of World v Australia 1971–72. Tours: Rest of World to Australia 1971–72, India, Pakistan and Sri Lanka 1972–73. 100 wkts (3)—133 wkts (av 19.66) in 1961 best. Hat-trick v Derbyshire (Chesterfield) 1965. Took 4 wkts in 6 balls v Cambridge U (Cambridge) 1972. Gillette Man of Match awards: 1. Benson & Hedges Gold awards: 2. HS: 89 v Oxford U (Oxford) 1963. HSTC: 25* v New Zealand (Nottingham) 1973. HSGC: 38 v Warwickshire (Lord's) 1966. HSJPL: 29 v Essex (Worcester) 1974. HSBH: 33 v Kent (Lord's) 1973. BB: 8–28 v Yorks (Sheffield) 1968. BBTC: 5–55 v Pakistan (Karachi) 1972–73. BBGC: 4–7 v Surrey (Worcester) 1972. BBJPL: 5–28 v Northants (Worcester) 1979. BBBH: 6–8 v Minor Counties (South) (High Wycombe) 1979.

Edward John Orton (Ted) HEMSLEY (Bridgnorth GS) B Norton, Stoke-on-Trent 1/9/1943. RHB, RM. Debut 1963. Cap 1969. Shared in 6th wkt partnership record for county, 227 with D. N. Patel v Oxford U (Oxford) 1976. Scored 1,168 runs (av 38.93) in 1978, Benson & Hedges Gold awards: 2. HS: 176* v Lancs (Worcester) 1977. HSGC: 73 v Sussex (Hove) 1972. HSJPL: 75* v Glamorgan (Cardiff) 1979. HSBH: 73 v Warwickshire (Birmingham) 1973. BB: 3–5 v Warwickshire (Worcester) 1971. BBJPL: 4–42 v Essex (Worcester) 1971. Soccer for Shrewsbury Town, Sheffield United and Doncaster Rovers.

Stephen Peter HENDERSON (Downside School) B Oxford 24/9/1958. Son of D. Henderson, former Oxford Blue. LHB, RM. Debut 1977. Did not play in 1979. HS: 52 v Northants (Worcester) 1977. HSGC: 33 v Glamorgan (Worcester) 1977. HSJPL: 19 v Hants (Worcester) 1977. Is studying at Durham University.

Vanburn Alonza (Van) HOLDER B St Michael, Barbados 8/10/1945. RHB, RFM. Debut 1966–67 for Barbados in one match in Shell Shield tournament. Debut for county 1968. Cap 1970. Benefit in 1979. Tests: 40 for West Indies between 1969 and 1978–79. Tours: West Indies to England 1969, 1973 and 1976. India, Sri Lanka and Pakistan 1974–75, Australia 1975–76, India and Sri Lanka 1978–79 (vice-captain). HS: 122 Barbados v Trinidad (Bridgetown) 1973–74. HSUK: 52 v Glos (Dudley) 1970. HSTC: 42 West Indies v New Zealand (Port of Spain) 1971–72. HSGC: 25* v Notts (Worcester) 1974. HSJPL: 35* v Middlesex (Lord's) 1970. HSBH: 17* v Minor Counties (South) (High Wycombe) 1979. BB: 7–40 v Glamorgan (Cardiff) 1974. BBTC: 6–38 West Indies v Australia (Port of Spain) 1977–78. BBGC: 3–14 v Oxfordshire (Cowley) 1970. BBJPL: 6–33 v Middlesex (Lord's) 1972. BBBH: 5–12 v Northants (Northampton) 1974.

David John HUMPHRIES B Alveley (Shropshire) 6/8/1953. LHB, WK. Played for Shropshire 1971–73. Debut for Leics 1974. Left county after 1976 season and made debut for Worcs in 1977. Cap 1978. HS: 111* v Warwickshire (Worcester) 1978. HSGC: 58 v Glamorgan (Worcester) 1977. HSJPL: 62 v Notts (Dudley) 1977. HSBH: 22* v Minor Counties (West) (Worcester) 1977.

John Darling INCHMORE (Ashington GS) B Ashington (Northumberland) 22/2/1949. RHB, RFM. Played for Northumberland in 1970. Played for both Warwickshire and Worcs 2nd XIs in 1972 and for Stourbridge in Birmingham League. Debut 1973. Cap 1976. Played for Northern Transvaal in 1976–77 Currie Cup competition. Benson & Hedges Gold awards: 1. HS: 113* v Essex (Worcester) 1974. HSGC: 19* v Leics (Leicester) 1979. HSJPL: 30* v Essex (Dudley) 1976. HSBH: 49* v Somerset (Taunton) 1976. BB: 8–58 v Yorks (Worcester) 1977. BBGC: 3–11 v Essex (Worcester) 1975. BBJPL: 4–9 v Northants (Dudley) 1975.

Barry John Richardson JONES (Wrekin College) B Shrewsbury 2/11/1955. LHB, RM. Debut 1976. HS: 65 v Warwickshire (Birmingham) 1977. HSJPL: 36* v Warwickshire (Worcester) 1978.

Philip Anthony (Phil) NEALE (Frederick Gough Comprehensive School, Bottesford and John Leggott Sixth Form College, Scunthorpe) B Scunthorpe (Lincs) 5/6/1954. RHB, RM. Played for Lincolnshire 1973–74. Debut 1975. Cap 1978. 1,000 runs (2)—1,305 runs (av 42.09) in 1979 best. HS: 163* v Notts (Worcester) 1979. HSGC: 68 v Glos (Bristol) 1976. HSJPL: 79* v Somerset (Worcester) 1976. HSBH: 52* v Combined Universities (Worcester) 1978. Soccer for Lincoln City. Studied at Leeds University and obtained degree in Russian.

Joseph Alan ORMROD (Kirkcaldy HS) B Ramsbottom (Lancs) 22/12/1942. RHB, OB. Debut 1962. Cap 1966. Benefit (£19,000) in 1977. Tour: Pakistan 1966–67. 1,000 runs (11)—1,535 runs (av 45.14) in 1978 best. Shared in 4th wkt partnership record for county, 281 with Younis Ahmed v Notts (Nottingham) 1979. Benson & Hedges Gold awards: 4. HS: 204* v Kent (Dartford) 1973. HSGC: 59 v Essex (Worcester) 1975. HSJPL: 110* v Kent ((Canterbury) 1975. HSBH: 124* v Glos (Worcester) 1976. BB: 5–27 v Glos (Bristol) 1972. BBJPL: 3–51 v Hants (Worcester) 1972.

Dipak Narshibhai PATEL (George Salter Comprehensive School, West Bromwich) B Nairobi, Kenya 25/10/1958. Has lived in UK since 1967. RHB, OB. Debut 1976. Cap 1979. Shared in 6th wkt partnership record for county, 227 with E. J. O. Hemsley v Oxford U (Oxford) 1976. HS: 118* v Sri Lankans (Worcester) 1979. HSJPL: 40 v Glos (Worcester) 1979. HSBH: 39 v Glamorgan (Cardiff) 1979. BB:5–22 v Sussex (Eastbourne) 1978. BBJPL: 3–22 v Glos (Moreton-in-Marsh) 1978.

Alan Paul PRIDGEON B Wall Heath (Staffs) 22/2/1954. RHB, RM. 6ft 3ins tall. Joined staff 1971. Debut 1972. HS: 32 v Yorks (Middlesbrough) 1978. HSJPL: 16* v Essex (Dudley) 1976. HSBH: 10 v Leics (Leicester) 1976. BB: 7–35 v Oxford U (Oxford) 1976. BBJPL: 6–26 v Surrey (Worcester) 1976. BBBH: 3–57 v Warwickshire (Birmingham) 1976. Plays amateur soccer.

Glenn Maitland TURNER (Otago Boys' HS) B Dunedin (New Zealand) 26/5/1947. RHB, OB. Debut for Otago in Plunket Shield competition 1964–65 whilst still at school. Debut for county 1967. Cap 1968. Wisden 1970. Benefit (£21,103) in 1978. Tests: 39 for New Zealand between 1968–69 and 1976–77 captaining country in 10 Tests. Tours: New Zealand to England 1969 and 1973 (vice-captain), India and Pakistan 1969–70, Australia 1969–70 and 1973–74 (vice-captain), West Indies 1971–72, Pakistan and India 1976–77 (captain). 1,000 runs (12)—2,416 runs (av 67.11) in 1973 best, including 1,018 runs (av 78.30) by 31 May—the first occasion since 1938. Scored 1,284 runs (av 85.60) in West Indies and Bermuda 1971–72. Scored 1,244 runs (av 77.75) in 1975–76—record aggregate for New Zealand season. Scored 10 centuries in 1970, a county record. Scored two centuries in a match on four occasions (122 and 128* v Warwickshire (Birmingham) 1972, (101 and 110* New Zealand v Australia (Christchurch) 1973–74, (135 and 108) Otago v Northern Districts (Gisborne) 1974–75 and (105 and 186*) Otago v Central Districts (Dunedin) 1974–75. Scored 141* out of 169—83.4% of total—v Glamorgan (Swansea) 1977—a record for first-class cricket. Benson & Hedges Gold awards: 3. HS: 259 twice in successive innings, New Zealanders v Guyana and New Zealand v West Indies (Georgetown) 1971–72. HSUK: 214* v Oxford U (Worcester) 1975. HSGC: 117* v Lancs (Worcester) 1971. HSJPL: 129* v Glamorgan (Worcester) 1973. HSBH: 143* v Warwickshire (Birmingham) 1976. BB: 3–18 v Pakistanis (Worcester) 1967. Has played hockey for Worcs and had trial for Midlands.

WORCESTERSHIRE

Martin John WESTON B Worcester 8/4/1959. RHB, RM. Played for 2nd XI since 1978. Debut 1979. One match v Sri Lankans. HS: 43 v Sri Lankans (Worcester) 1979.

Mohammad YOUNIS AHMED (Moslem HS, Lahore) B Jullundur, Pakistan 20/10/1947. LHB, LM/SLA. Younger brother of Saeed Ahmed, Pakistan Test cricketer, who has played for Surrey 2nd XI. Debut 1961–62 for Pakistan Inter Board Schools XI v South Zone at age of 14 years 4 months. Debut for Surrey 1965. Cap 1969. Played for South Australia in 1972–73 Sheffield Shield competition. Not re-engaged by county after 1978 season. Debut for Worcs and cap 1979. Tests: 2 for Pakistan v New Zealand 1969–70. 1,000 runs (8)—1,760 runs (av 47.56) in 1969 best. Shared in 4th wkt partnership record for county, 281 with J. A. Ormrod v Notts (Nottingham) 1979. Benson & Hedges Gold awards: 2 (1 for Surrey). HS: 221* v Notts (Nottingham) 1979. HSTC: 62 Pakistan v New Zealand (Karachi) 1969–70. HSGC: 87 Surrey v Middlesex (Oval) 1970. HSJPL: 113 Surrey v Warwickshire (Birmingham) 1976 and 113 v Yorks (Worcester) 1979. HSBH: 107 v Surrey (Worcester) 1979. BB: 4–10 Surrey v Cambridge (Cambridge) 1975. BBC: 3–33 v Oxford U (Oxford) 1979. BBJPL: 3–26 v Surrey (Oval) 1979.

NB, The following players whose particulars appeared in the 1979 Annual have been omitted: B. L. D'Oliveira (retired and appointed senior coach) and C. N. Boyns. G. G. Watson has returned to Australia. The career records of both players will be found elsewhere in this Annual.

COUNTY AVERAGES

Schweppes County Championship: Played 21, won 7, drawn 10, lost 4, abandoned 1
All first-class matches: Played 23, won 7, drawn 12, lost 4, abandoned 1

BATTING AND FIELDING

Cap		M	I	NO	Runs	HS	Avge	100	50	Ct	St
1979	Younis Ahmed	22	30	8	1539	221*	69.95	4	7	5	—
1968	G. M. Turner	18	31	2	1669	150*	57.55	8	5	10	—
1978	P. A. Neale	22	37	6	1305	163*	42.09	4	5	10	—
1966	J. A. Ormrod	22	38	4	1126	134	33.11	2	7	16	—
1965	B. L. D'Oliveira	7	9	1	257	112	32.12	1	2	—	—
1969	E. J. O. Hemsley	23	34	6	842	93	30.07	—	5	29	—
1979	D. N. Patel	21	29	4	698	118*	27.92	1	3	20	—
1978	D. J. Humphries	22	30	4	575	68	22.11	—	2	49	8
1976	J. D. Inchmore	21	22	9	283	37*	21.76	—	—	10	—
1970	V. A. Holder	14	12	6	119	24*	19.83	—	—	5	—
—	B. J. R. Jones	6	12	0	174	39	14.50	—	—	2	—
1978	J. Cumbes	19	15	9	58	13*	9.66	—	—	3	—
1961	N. Gifford	17	16	5	103	35	9.36	—	—	12	—
—	G. G. Watson	9	11	1	75	18*	7.50	—	—	—	—

Played in six matches: A. P. Pridgeon 0*.
Played in one match: C. N. Boyns 24*, 3*; A. Brown did not bat (2 ct); T. S. Curtis 15, 27 (1 ct); M. J. Weston 43, 16.

BOWLING	Type	O	M	R	W	Avge	Best	5 wI	10 wM
N. Gifford	SLA	798.3	237	1848	78	23.69	5–12	2	—
J. D. Inchmore	RFM	521.4	102	1572	62	25.35	6–35	3	—
B. L. D'Oliveira	RM/OB	122	37	275	10	27.50	2–15	—	—
Younis Ahmed	LM/SLA	92.5	21	229	8	28.62	3–33	—	—
V. A. Holder	RFM	405	75	1041	32	32.53	4–76	—	—
J. Cumbes	RFM	577.3	108	1591	48	33.14	6–103	3	—
G. G. Watson	RFM	272.5	49	825	22	37.50	4–29	—	—
D. N. Patel	OB	452.3	109	1461	37	39.48	5–95	1	—
A. P. Pridgeon	RM	119	20	391	6	65.16	2–84	—	—

Also bowled: C. N. Boyns 22–4–64–1; T. S. Curtis 1–0–2–0; E. J. O. Hemsley
8–3–22–1; P. A. Neale 1–0–5–0; J. A. Ormrod 1–0–14–0.

County Records

First-class cricket

Highest innings:	For —633 v Warwickshire (Worcester)	1906
totals:	Agst—701-4d by Leicestershire (Worcester)	1906
Lowest innings	For —24 v Yorkshire (Huddersfield)	1903
totals:	Agst—30 by Hampshire (Worcester)	1903
Highest indi-	For —276 F. L. Bowley v Hampshire (Dudley)	1914
vidual innings:	Agst—331* J. D. B. Robertson for Middlesex (Worcester)	1949
Best bowling	For —9–23 C. F. Root v Lancashire (Worcester)	1931
in an innings:	Agst—10–51 J. Mercer for Glamorgan (Worcester)	1936
Best bowling	For —15–87 A. J. Conway v Gloucestershire	
in a match:	(Moreton-in-Marsh)	1914
	Agst—17–212 J. C. Clay for Glamorgan (Swansea)	1937
Most runs in a season:	2654 (av 52.03) H. H. I. Gibbons	1934
runs in a career:	34490 (av 34.04) D. Kenyon	1946–1967
100s in a season:	10 by G. M. Turner	1970
100s in a career:	70 by D. Kenyon	1946–1967
wickets in a season:	207 (av 17.52) C. F. Root	1925
wickets in a career:	2143 (av 23.73) R. T. D. Perks	1930–1955

RECORD WICKET STANDS

1st	309	F. L. Bowley & H. K. Foster v Derbyshire (Derby)	1901
2nd	274	{ H. H. I. Gibbons & Nawab of Pataudi v Kent (Worcester)	1933
		{ H. H. I. Gibbons & Nawab of Pataudi v Glamorgan (Worcester)	1934
3rd	314	M. J. Horton & T. W. Graveney v Somerset (Worcester)	1962
4th	281	J. A. Ormrod & Younis Ahmed v Nottinghamshire (Nottingham)	1979
5th	393	E. G. Arnold & W. B. Burns v Warwickshire (Birmingham)	1909
6th	227	E. J. O. Hemsley & D. N. Patel v Oxford U (Oxford)	1976
7th	197	H. H. I. Gibbons & R. Howorth v Surrey (The Oval)	1938
8th	145*	F. Chester & W. H. Taylor v Essex (Worcester)	1914
9th	181	J. A. Cuffe & R. D. Burrows v Gloucestershire (Worcester)	1907
10th	119	W. B. Burns & G. A. Wilson v Somerset (Worcester)	1906

One-day cricket

Highest innings:	Gillette Cup	261–7 v Essex (Worcester)	1975
	John Player League	307–4 v Derbyshire (Worcester)	1975
	Benson & Hedges Cup	281–4 v Warwickshire (Birmingham)	1976
Lowest innings totals:	Gillette Cup	98 v Durham (Chester-le-Street)	1968
	John Player League	86 v Yorkshire (Leeds)	1969
	Benson & Hedges Cup	92 v Oxford and Cambridge Universities (Cambridge)	1975
Highest individual innings:	Gillette Cup	117* G. M. Turner v Lancashire (Worcester)	1971
	John Player League	129* G. M. Turner v Glamorgan (Worcester)	1973
	Benson & Hedges Cup	143* G. M. Turner v Warwickshire (Birmingham)	1976
Best bowling figures:	Gillette Cup	6–14 J. A. Flavell v Lancashire (Worcester)	1963
	John Player League	6–26 A. P. Pridgeon v Surrey (Worcester)	1978
	Benson & Hedges Cup	6–8 N. Gifford v Minor Counties (South) (High Wycombe)	1979

YORKSHIRE

Formation of present club: 1863, reorganised 1891.
Colours: Oxford blue, Cambridge blue, and gold.
Badge: White rose.
County Champions (31): 1867, 1870, 1893, 1896,
1898, 1900, 1901, 1902, 1905, 1908, 1912,
1919, 1922, 1923, 1924, 1925, 1931, 1932,
1933, 1935, 1937, 1938, 1939, 1946, 1959,
1960, 1962, 1963, 1966, 1967, and 1968.
Joint Champions (2): 1869 and 1949.
Gillette Cup Winners (2): 1965 and 1969.
John Player League runners-up: 1973.
Benson & Hedges Cup finalists: 1972.
Fenner Trophy Winners (2): 1972 and 1974,
Gillette Man of the Match awards: 12.
Benson & Hedges Gold awards: 20.

Secretary: J. Lister, Headingley Cricket Ground, Leeds, LS6 3 BU.
Cricket Manager: R. Illingworth, CBE.
Captain: J. H. Hampshire.

Charles William Jeffrey (Bill) ATHEY (Acklam Hall High School, Middlesbrough) B Middlesbrough 27/9/1957. RHB, RM. Toured West Indies with England Young Cricketers 1976. Debut 1976. HS: 131* v Sussex (Leeds) 1976 and 131 v Somerset (Taunton) 1978. HSGC: 35 v Middlesex (Lord's) 1979. HSJPL: 118 v Leics (Leicester) 1978. HSBH: 31 v Minor Counties (East) (Jesmond) 1977. BB: 3–38 v Surrey (Oval) 1978. BBJPL: 3–10 v Kent (Canterbury) 1978. BBBH: 3–32 v Middlesex (Lord's) 1979.

David Leslie BAIRSTOW (Hanson GS, Bradford) B Bradford 1/9/1951. RHB, WK. Can bowl RM. Debut 1970 whilst still at school. Played for MCC Schools at Lord's in 1970. Cap 1973. Played for Griqualand West in 1976–77 and 1977–78 (captain) Currie Cup and Castle Bowl competitions. Tests: 1 in 1979. Tours: Australia 1978–79 (flown out as replacement for R. W. Tolchard), Australia and India 1979–80. Dismissed 70 batsmen (64 ct 6 st) in 1971, including 9 in match and 6 in innings (all ct) v Lancs (Manchester). Benson & Hedges Gold awards: 3. HS: 106 v Glamorgan (Middlesbrough) 1976 and 106 Griqualand West v Natal B (Pietermaritzburg) 1976–77. HSTC: 59 v India (Oval) 1979. HSGC: 31* v Durham (Middlesbrough) 1978. HSJPL: 76 v Sussex (Scarborough) 1976. HSBH: 35* v Essex (Middlesbrough) 1978. BB: 3–82 Griqualand West v Transvaal B (Johannesburg) 1976–77. Soccer for Bradford City.

Geoffrey (Geoff) BOYCOTT (Hemsworth GS) B Fitzwilliam (Yorks) 21/10/1940. RHB, RM. Plays in contact lenses. Debut 1962. Cap 1963. Elected Best Young Cricketer of the Year in 1963 by the Cricket Writers' Club. *Wisden* 1964. County captain from 1971 to 1978. Played for Northern Transvaal in 1971–72. Benefit (£20,639) in 1974. Tests: 84 between 1964 and 1979 captaining England in 4 Tests in 1977–78. Played in 2 matches against Rest of World in 1970. Tours: South Africa 1964–65, Australia and New Zealand 1965–66 and 1970–71 (returned home early through broken arm injury), West Indies 1967–68 and 1973–74, Pakistan and New Zealand 1977–78 (vice-captain), Australia 1978–79, Australia and India 1979–80. 1,000 runs (17)—2,503 runs (av 100.12) in 1971 best. Only English batsman ever to have an average of 100 for a season and repeated the feat in 1979 with 1,538 runs (av 102.53). Also scored 1,000 runs in South Africa 1964–65 (1,135 runs, av 56,75), West Indies 1967–68 (1,154 runs, av 82.42), Australia 1970–71 (1,535 runs, av 95.93). Scored two centuries in match (103 and 105) v Notts (Sheffield) 1966 and (160* and 116) England v The Rest (Worcester) 1974. Completed 30,000 runs in 1977 and scored his 100th century in Leeds Test of that year – only player to have done so in a Test match. Scored 155 v India (Birmingham) 1979 to become the second batsman to have scored a century in a Test on all six grounds in this country. Gillette Man of Match awards: 2. Benson & Hedges Gold awards: 7. HS: 261* MCC v President's XI (Bridgetown) 1973–74. HSUK: 260* v Essex (Colchester) 1970. HSTC: 246 v India (Leeds) 1967. HSGC: 146 v Surrey (Lord's) 1965. HSJPL: 108* v Northants (Huddersfield) 1974. HSBH: 102 v Northants (Middlesbrough) 1977. BB: 4–14 v Lancs (Manchester) 1979. BBTC: 3–47 England v South Africa (Cape Town) 1964–65.

Philip (Phil) CARRICK B Armley, Leeds 16/7/1952. RHB, SLA. Debut 1970. Cap 1976. Played for Eastern Province in 1976–77 Currie Cup competition. HS: 128* v Glos (Cheltenham) 1979. HSGC: 18 v Durham (Harrogate) 1973 and 18 v Notts (Bradford) 1978. HSJPL: 21 v Hants (Leeds) 1979. HSBH: 19* v Notts (Bradford) 1979. BB: 8–33 v Cambridge U (Cambridge) 1973. BBJPL: 3–32 v Hants (Bournemouth) 1976 and 3–32 v Notts (Nottingham) 1979.

Howard Pennett COOPER (Buttershaw Comprehensive School, Bradford) B Bradford 17/4/1949. LHB, RM. Debut 1971. Played for Northern Transvaal in 1973–74 Currie Cup competition. HS: 56 v Notts (Worksop) 1976. HSGC: 17 v Hants (Bournemouth) 1977. HSJPL: 29* v Hants (Bournemouth) 1976. HSBH: 20* v Minor Counties (East) (Jesmond) 1977. BB: 8–62 v Glamorgan (Cardiff) 1975. BBGC: 4–18 v Leics (Leeds) 1975. BBJPL: 6–14 v Worcs (Worcester) 1975. BBBH: 4–28 v Middlesex (Lord's) 1979.

YORKSHIRE

Geoffrey Alan COPE (Temple Moor School, Leeds) B Leeds 23/2/1947. RHB, OB. Wears glasses. Debut 1966. Cap 1970. Suspended from playing in second half of 1972 season by TCCB, owing to unsatisfactory bowling action. Action cleared in 1973 by TCCB sub-committee after watching film of him bowling. Suspended again in 1978 but subsequently cleared. Joint benefit in 1980 with B. Leadbeater. Tours: India, Sri Lanka and Australia 1976–77, Pakistan and New Zealand 1977–78. Hat-trick v Essex (Colchester) 1970. HS: 78 v Essex (Middlesbrough) 1977. HSJPL: 16* v Sussex (Bradford) 1974. HSBH: 18* v Surrey (Bradford) 1976. BB: 8–73 v Glos (Bristol) 1975. BBJPL: 3–24 v Northants (Bradford) 1969.

John Harry HAMPSHIRE (Oakwood Technical HS, Rotherham) B Thurnscoe (Yorks) 10/2/1941. RHB, LB. Debut 1961. Cap 1963. Played for Tasmania in 1967–68, 1968–69, 1977–78 and 1978–79. Benefit (£28,425) in 1976. Appointed county captain in 1979. Tests: 8 between 1969 and 1975. Scored 107 in his first Test v West Indies (Lord's) and is only English player to have scored a century on debut in Test cricket when this has occurred at Lord's. Tour: Australia and New Zealand 1970–71. 1,000 runs (13)—1,596 runs (av 53.20) in 1978 best. Gillette Man of Match awards: 4. Benson & Hedges Gold awards: 1. HS: 183* v Sussex (Hove) 1971. HSTC: 107 v West Indies (Lord's) 1969. HSGC: 110 v Durham (Middlesbrough) 1978. HSJPL: 119 v Leics (Hull) 1971. HSBH: 73 v Kent (Leeds) 1979. BB: 7–52 v Glamorgan (Cardiff) 1963.

Stuart Neil HARTLEY (Beckfoot GS) B Shipley (Yorks) 18/3/1956. RHB, RM. Played for 2nd XI since 1975. Debut 1978. HS: 53* v Lancs (Manchester) 1979. HSJPL: 54* v Warwickshire (Birmingham) 1979.

Peter Geoffrey INGHAM (Ashville College, Harrogate) B Sheffield 28/9/1956. RHB, RM. Played for 2nd XI since 1974. Debut 1979 (two matches). HS: 17 v Warwickshire (Sheffield) 1979.

Colin JOHNSON (Pocklington School) B Pocklington (Yorks) 5/9/1947. RHB, OB. Played in MCC Schools matches at Lord's 1966. Debut 1969. Benson & Hedges Gold awards: 1. HS: 107 v Somerset (Sheffield) 1973. HSGC: 44 v Durham (Harrogate) 1973. HSJPL: 67* v Glamorgan (Ebbw Vale) 1978. HSBH: 73* v Middlesex (Lord's) 1977.

James Derek LOVE B Leeds 22/4/1955. RHB, RM. Debut 1975. HS: 170* v Worcs (Worcester) 1979. HSJPL: 90* v Derbyshire (Chesterfield) 1979. HSBH: 18 v Notts (Nottingham) 1978.

Richard Graham LUMB (Percy Jackson GS, Doncaster and Mexborough GS) B Doncaster 27/2/1950. RHB, RM. Played in MCC Schools matches at Lord's 1968. Debut 1970 after playing in one John Player League match in 1969. Cap 1974. 1,000 runs (4)—1,532 runs (av 41.40) in 1975 best. HS: 159 v Somerset (Harrogate) 1979. HSGC: 56 v Shropshire (Wellington) 1976. HSJPL: 101 v Notts (Scarborough) 1976. HSBH: 75 v Essex (Chelmsford) 1979.

Christopher Middleton (Chris) OLD (Acklam Hall Secondary GS, Middlesbrough) B Middlesbrough 22/12/1948. LHB, RFM. Debut 1966. Cap 1969. Elected Best Young Cricketer of the Year in 1970 by the Cricket Writers' Club. *Wisden* 1978. Benefit in 1979. Tests: 41 between 1972–73 and 1978–79. Played in 2 matches against Rest of World 1970. Tours: India, Pakistan and Sri Lanka 1972–73, West Indies 1973–74, Australia and New Zealand 1974–75, India, Sri Lanka and Australia 1976–77, Pakistan and New Zealand 1977–78, Australia 1978–79. Scored century in 37 minutes v Warwickshire (Birmingham) 1977—second fastest ever in first-class cricket. Took 4 wickets in 5 balls, England v Pakistan (Birmingham) 1978. Benson & Hedges Gold awards: 3. HS: 116 v Indians (Bradford) 1974. HSTC: 65 v

156

Pakistan (Oval) 1974. HSGC: 29 v Lancs (Leeds) 1974. HSJPL: 82 v Somerset (Bath) 1974 and 82* v Somerset (Glastonbury) 1976. HSBH: 72 v Sussex (Hove) 1976. BB: 7–20 v Glos (Middlesbrough) 1969. BBTC: 7–50 v Pakistan (Birmingham) 1978. BBGC: 4–9 v Durham (Middlesbrough) 1978. BBJPL: 5–53 v Sussex (Hove) 1971. BBBH: 4–17 v Derbyshire (Bradford) 1973.

Alan RAMAGE (Warsett School, Brotton) B Guisborough 29/11/1957. LHB, RFM. Played for 2nd XI since 1974 and in six John Player League matches and one Benson & Hedges Cup match between 1975 and 1977. Debut 1979. HS: 19 v Cambridge U (Cambridge) 1979. HSBH: 17* v Combined Universities (Barnsley) 1976. BB: 3–24 v Cambridge U (Cambridge) 1979. BBJPL: 3–51 v Kent (Canterbury) 1977. Plays soccer for Middlesbrough.

Kevin SHARP (Abbey Grange C.E. High School, Leeds) B Leeds 6/4/1959. LHB, OB. Debut 1976. Captained England under-19 v West Indies under-19 in 1978 and scored 260* in match at Worcester. HS: 91 v Middlesex (Bradford) 1978. HSGC: 25 v Middlesex (Lord's) 1979. HSJPL: 40 v Surrey (Oval) 1978. HSBH: 41 v Notts (Bradford) 1979.

Arnold SIDEBOTTOM (Broadway GS, Barnsley) B Barnsley 1/4/1954. RHB, RFM. Played for 2nd XI since 1971 and in Schools matches at Lord's in that year. Debut 1973. HS: 124 v Glamorgan (Cardiff) 1977. HSGC: 45 v Hants (Bournemouth) 1977. HSJPL: 31 v Sussex (Hove) 1975. HSBH: 15 v Notts (Bradford) 1979. BB: 4–47 v Derbyshire (Chesterfield) 1975. BBGC: 4–36 v Hants (Bournemouth) 1977. BBJPL: 4–24 v Surrey (Scarborough) 1975. BBBH: 3–21 v Minor Counties (North) (Jesmond) 1979. Soccer for Manchester United and Huddersfield Town.

Graham Barry STEVENSON (Minsthorpe GS) B Ackworth (Yorks) 16/12/1955. RHB, RM. Played for 2nd XI in 1972. Debut 1973. Cap 1978. Tour: Australia and India 1979–80 (flown out as replacement for M. Hendrick). HS: 83 v Derbyshire (Chesterfield) 1976. HSGC: 27 v Glos (Leeds) 1976. HSJPL: 33* v Derbyshire (Huddersfield) 1978. HSBH: 13 v Essex (Chelmsford) 1979. BB:8–65 v Lancs (Leeds) 1978. BBGC: 4–57 v Lancs (Leeds) 1974. BBJPL: 5–41 v Leics (Leicester) 1976. BBBH: 5–28 v Kent (Canterbury) 1978.

Stephen STUCHBURY (Ecclesfield GS) B Sheffield 22/6/1954. LHB, LFM. Played for 2nd XI since 1975. Debut 1978. One match v New Zealanders (Leeds) and also played in six John Player League matches. Did not play in 1979.

John Peter WHITELEY (Ashville College, Harrogate) B Otley (Yorks) 28/2/1955. RHB, OB. Played for 2nd XI since 1972. Debut 1978. HS: 20 v Northants (Northampton) 1979. BB: 4–14 v Notts (Scarborough) 1978. Studied at Bristol University.

NB. The following players whose particulars appeared in the 1979 Annual have been omitted: B. Leadbeater (not re-engaged) and A. L. Robinson (left staff owing to injury).

The career record of Leadbeater will be found elsewhere in this Annual.

COUNTY AVERAGES

Schweppes County Championship: Played 21, won 5, drawn 13, lost 3, abandoned 1
All first-class matches: Played 22, won 6, drawn 13, lost 3, abandoned 1

BATTING AND FIELDING

Cap		M	I	NO	Runs	HS	Avge	100	50	Ct	St
1963	G. Boycott	11	15	5	1160	175*	116.00	4	7	3	—
1974	R. G. Lumb	22	35	4	1465	159	44.39	5	4	12	—
1976	P. Carrick	22	27	8	639	128*	33.63	1	3	12	—
—	S. N. Hartley	3	5	1	126	53*	31.50	—	1	1	—
1970	G. A. Cope	9	9	6	92	39*	30.66	—	—	3	—
1963	J. H. Hampshire	21	31	2	880	96	30.34	—	6	21	—
—	J. D. Love	12	21	3	496	170*	27.55	1	1	7	—
—	K. Sharp	15	23	2	548	80	26.09	—	2	2	—
—	H. P. Cooper	6	3	0	69	40	23.00	—	—	1	—
1973	D. L. Bairstow	22	34	9	569	61	22.76	—	2	46	9
—	C. W. J. Athey	21	34	3	679	79*	21.90	—	2	14	1
1978	G. B. Stevenson	17	20	5	317	73*	21.13	—	1	8	—
—	A. Sidebottom	13	14	5	184	51	20.44	—	1	2	—
—	A. Ramage	5	5	3	33	19	16.50	—	—	—	—
1969	C. M. Old	13	15	5	110	23	11.00	—	—	8	—
—	S. Oldham	13	6	1	53	50	10.60	—	1	5	—
—	J. P. Whiteley	12	7	2	46	20	9.20	—	—	3	—

Played in two matches: P. G. Ingham 17, 4, 11; B. Leadbeater 15, 1*, 1, 49.
Played in one match: C. Johnson 1, 13.

BOWLING

	Type	O	M	R	W	Avge	Best	5 wI	10 wM
G. Boycott	RM	45.2	20	84	9	9.33	4–14	—	—
A. Ramage	RM	129	38	348	15	23.20	3–24	—	—
C. M. Old	RFM	360.5	96	904	36	25.11	5–72	1	—
A. Sidebottom	RFM	294	72	826	31	26.64	4–59	—	—
G. B. Stevenson	RM	498.3	124	1440	50	28.80	6–14	1	—
P. Carrick	SLA	668.2	218	1717	55	31.21	5–32	1	—
H. P. Cooper	RM	142	36	387	11	35.18	2–16	—	—
S. Oldham	RFM	279.2	64	803	22	36.50	4–76	—	—
G. A. Cope	OB	191.3	58	490	13	37.69	6–37	1	—
J. P. Whiteley	OB	209.2	67	546	10	54.60	3–85	—	—

Also bowled: C. W. J. Athey 101.3–21–325–2; D. L. Bairstow 5–1–16–1; J. D. Love 10–1–35–0.

County Records

First-class cricket

Highest innings totals:	For —887 v Warwickshire (Birmingham)	1896
	Agst—630 by Somerset (Leeds)	1901
Lowest innings totals:	For —23 v Hampshire (Middlesbrough)	1965
	Agst—13 by Nottinghamshire (Nottingham)	1901
Highest individual innings:	For —341 G. H. Hirst v Leicestershire (Leicester)	1905
	Agst—318* W. G. Grace for Gloucester (Cheltenham)	1876
Best bowling in an innings:	For —10–10 H. Verity v Nottinghamshire (Leeds)	1932
	Agst—10–37 C. V. Grimmett for Australians (Sheffield)	1930
Best bowling in a match:	For —17–91 H. Verity v Essex (Leyton)	1933
	Agst—17–91 H. Dean for Lancashire (Liverpool)	1913

Most runs in a season:	2883 (av 80.08) H. Sutcliffe	1932
runs in a career:	38561 (av 50.21) H. Sutcliffe	1919–1945
100s in a season:	12 by H. Sutcliffe	1932
100s in a career:	112 by H. Sutcliffe	1919–1945
wickets in a season:	240 (av 12.72) W. Rhodes	1900
wickets in a career:	3608 (av 16.00) W. Rhodes	1898–1930

RECORD WICKET STANDS

1st	555	P. Holmes & H. Sutcliffe v Essex (Leyton)	1932
2nd	346	W. Barber & M. Leyland v Middlesex (Sheffield)	1932
3rd	323*	H. Sutcliffe & M. Leyland v Glamorgan (Huddersfield)	1928
4th	312	G. H. Hirst & D. Denton v Hampshire (Southampton)	1914
5th	340	E. Wainwright & G. H. Hirst v Surrey (The Oval)	1899
6th	276	M. Leyland & E. Robinson v Glamorgan (Swansea)	1926
7th	254	D. C. F. Burton & W. Rhodes v Hampshire (Dewsbury)	1919
8th	292	Lord Hawke & R. Peel v Warwickshire (Birmingham)	1896
9th	192	G. H. Hirst & S. Haigh v Surrey (Bradford)	1898
10th	148	Lord Hawke & D. Hunter v Kent (Sheffield)	1898

One-day cricket

Highest innings totals:	Gillette Cup	317–4 v Surrey (Lord's)	1965
	John Player League	248–5 v Derbyshire (Chesterfield)	1979
	Benson & Hedges Cup	218–3 v Minor Counties (North) (Scunthorpe)	1975
		218–9 v Minor Counties (East) (Jesmond)	1977
Lowest innings totals:	Gillette Cup	76 v Surrey (Harrogate)	1970
	John Player League	74 v Warwickshire (Birmingham)	1972
	Benson & Hedges Cup	114 v Kent (Canterbury)	1978
Highest individual innings:	Gillette Cup	146 G. Boycott v Surrey (Lord's)	1965
	John Player League	119 J. H. Hampshire v Leicestershire (Hull)	1971
	Benson & Hedges Cup	102 G. Boycott v Northamptonshire (Middlesbrough)	1977
Best bowling figures:	Gillette Cup	6–15 F. S. Trueman v Somerset (Taunton)	1965
	John Player League	7–15 R. A. Hutton v Worcestershire (Leeds)	1969
	Benson & Hedges Cup	6–27 A. G. Nicholson v Minor Counties (North) (Middlesbrough)	1972

THE FIRST-CLASS UMPIRES FOR 1980

NB The abbreviations used below are identical with those given at the beginning of the section 'The Counties and their Players'.

William Edward (Bill) ALLEY B Sydney (Australia) 3/2/1919. LHB, RM. Played for New South Wales 1945–46 to 1947–48. Subsequently came to England to play League cricket and then for Somerset from 1957 to 1968, *Wisden* 1961. Testimonial (£2,700) in 1961. Tours: India and Pakistan 1949–50, Pakistan 1963–64 with Commonwealth team. Scored 3,019 runs (av 56.96) in 1961 including 2,761 runs and 10 centuries for county, both being records. Won Man of the Match award in Gillette Cup Competition on three occasions. HS: 221* v Warwickshire (Nuneaton) 1961. BB: 8–65 v Surrey (Oval) 1962. Career record: 19,612 runs (av 31.88), 31 centuries, 768 wkts (av 22.68) Appointed 1969. Umpired in 7 Tests between 1974 and 1977.

Ronald (Ron) ASPINALL B Almondbury (Yorks) 26/10/1918. RHB, RFM. Played for Yorkshire from 1946 to 1950 (retiring early through injury) and for Durham from 1951 to 1957. HS: 57* v Notts (Nottingham) 1948. BB: 8–42 v Northants (Rushden) 1949. Career record: 763 runs (av 19.07), 131 wkts (av 20.38). Appointed 1960.

Harold Denis BIRD B Barnsley 19/4/1933. RHB, RM. Played for Yorks from 1956 to 1959 and for Leics from 1960 to 1964. Was subsequently professional at Paignton CC. HS: 181* Yorks v Glamorgan (Bradford) 1959. Career record: 3,315 runs (av 20.71), 2 centuries. Appointed 1970. Umpired in 17 Tests between 1973 and 1979.

William Lloyd BUDD B Hawkley (Hants) 25/10/1913. RHB, RFM. Played for Hampshire from 1934 to 1946. HS: 77* v Surrey (Oval) 1937. BB: 4–22 v Essex (Southend) 1937. Career record: 941 runs (av 11,47). 64 wkts (av 39.15). Was on Minor Counties list for some years. Appointed 1969. Umpired in 4 Tests between 1976 and 1978.

David John CONSTANT B Bradford-on-Avon (Wilts) 9/11/1941. LHB, SLA. Played for Kent from 1961 to 1963 and for Leics from 1965 to 1968. HS: 80 v Glos (Bristol) 1966. Career record: 1,517 runs (av 19.20), 1 wkt (av 36,00). Appointed 1969. Umpired in 18 Tests between 1971 and 1979.

Cecil (Sam) COOK B Tetbury (Glos) 23/8/1921. RHB, SLA. Played for Gloucestershire from 1946 to 1964. Benefit (£3,067) in 1957. Took wicket with first ball in first-class cricket. Tests: 1 v SA 1947. HS: 35* v Sussex (Hove) 1957. BB: 9–42 v Yorks (Bristol) 1947. Career record: 1,964 runs (av 5,39), 1,782 wkts (av 20.52). Appointed 1971, after having withdrawn from appointment in 1966.

Derek James DENNIS B Swansea 1/1/1929. Has not played first-class cricket. Umpired in Minor Counties matches since 1975. Appointed 1979.

David Gwilliam Lloyd EVANS B Lambeth (London) 27/7/1933. RHB, WK. Played for Glamorgan from 1956 to 1960. Benefit (£3,500) in 1969. HS: 46* v Oxford U (Oxford) 1961. Career record: 2,875 runs (av 10.53). 558 dismissals (502 ct 56 st). Appointed 1971.

David John HALFYARD B Winchmore Hill (Middlesex) 3/4/1931. RHB, RM. Played for Kent from 1956 to 1964 retiring through leg injury. Testimonial (£3,216) in 1965. Played for Notts from 1968 to 1970. Not re-engaged and has subsequently played in Minor Counties competition for Durham in 1971 and 1972, Northumberland in 1973 and Cornwall from 1974. HS: 79 Kent v Middlesex (Lord's) 1960. BB: 9–39 Kent v Glamorgan (Neath) 1957. Career record: 3,242 runs (av 10.91), 963 wkts (av 25.77). Appointed 1977, after having been on list in 1967.

Robert Stephen (Bob) HERMAN B Southampton 30/11/1946. Son of O. W. ('Lofty') Herman (former Hants player and first-class umpire). RHB, RFM. Played for Middlesex from 1965 to 1971 and for Hants from 1972 to 1977. Played for Dorset in 1978 and 1979. Won Benson & Hedges Gold award on two occasions. HS: 56 v Worcs (Portsmouth) 1972. BB: 8–42 v Warwickshire (Portsmouth) 1972. Career record: 1,426 runs (av 10.25), 506 wkts (av 26.28). Appointed 1980.

Arthur JEPSON B Selston (Notts) 12/7/1915. RHB, RFM. Played for Notts from 1938 to 1959. Benefit (£2,000) in 1951. HS: 130 v Worcs (Nottingham) 1950. BB: 8–45 v Leics (Nottingham) 1958. Career record: 6,369 runs (av 14.31), 1 century, 1,051 wkts (av 29.08). Soccer (goalkeeper) for Port Vale, Stoke City and Lincoln City. Appointed 1960. Umpired in 4 Tests between 1966 and 1969.

Raymond (Ray) JULIAN B Cosby (Leics) 23/8/1936. RHB, WK. Played for Leicestershire from 1953 (debut at age of 16) to 1971, but lost regular place in side to R. W. Tolchard in 1966. HS: 51 v Worcs (Worcester) 1962. Career record: 2,581 runs (av 9.73), 421 dismissals (382 ct 39 st). Appointed 1972.

John George LANGRIDGE B Chailey (Sussex) 10/2/1910. Younger brother of late James Langridge. Opening RHB and outstanding slip field. Played for Sussex from 1928 to 1955. *Wisden* 1949. Shared joint benefit (£1,930) with H. W. Parks in 1948. Testimonial (£3,825) in 1953. Awarded MBE in 1979 Birthday Honours List. Scored more runs and centuries in first-class cricket than any other player who never appeared in a Test match. Only F. E. Woolley, W. G. Grace, W. R. Hammond, G. A. R. Lock and D. B. Close have held more catches than his total of 786. HS: 250* v Glamorgan (Hove) 1933. Career record: 34,380 runs (av 37.45), 76 centuries, 44 wkts (av 42,00). Appointed 1956. Umpired in 7 Tests between 1960 and 1963.

Barrie John MEYER B Bournemouth 21/8/1932. RHB, WK. Played for Gloucestershire from 1957 to 1971. Benefit 1971. HS: 63 v Indians (Cheltenham) 1959 v Oxford U (Bristol) 1962 and v Sussex (Bristol) 1964. Career record: 5,367 runs (av 14.19), 826 dismissals (707 ct 119 st). Soccer for Bristol Rovers, Plymouth Argyle, Newport County and Bristol City. Appointed 1973. Umpired in 4 Tests in 1978 and 1979.

Donald Osmund OSLEAR B Cleethorpes (Lincs) 3/3/1929. Has not played first-class cricket. Played soccer for Grimsby Town, Hull City, and Oldham Athletic. Also played ice hockey. Has umpired in county second XI matches since 1972. Appointed in 1975.

Kenneth Ernest (Ken) PALMER B Winchester 22/4/1937. RHB, RFM. Played for Somerset from 1955 to 1969. Testimonial (£4,000) in 1968. Tour: Pakistan with Commonwealth team 1963–64. Coached in Johannesburg 1964–65 and was called upon by MCC to play in final Test v South Africa owing to injuries to other bowlers. Tests (1): v SA 1964–65. HS: 125* v Northants (Northampton) 1961. BB: 9–57 v Notts (Nottingham) 1963. Career record: 7,771 runs (av 20.66), 2 centuries, 866 wkts (av 21.34). Appointed 1972. Umpired in 4 Tests in 1978 and 1979.

161

Roy PALMER B Devizes (Wilts) 12/7/1942. RHB, RFM. Younger brother of K. E. Palmer. Played for Somerset from 1965 to 1970. Won Man of the Match award in Gillette Cup competition on two occasions. HS: 84 v Leics (Taunton) 1967. BB: 6–45 v Middlesex (Lord's) 1967. Career record: 1,037 runs (av 13.29), 172 wkts (av 31.62). Appointed 1980.

Derek SHACKLETON B Todmorden (Yorks) 12/8/1924. RHB, RM. Played for Hampshire from 1948 to 1969. *Wisden* 1958. Benefit (£5,000) in 1958. Testimonial (£5,000) in 1967. Played for Dorset from 1971 to 1974. Tests: 7 between 1950 and 1963. Tours: India with Commonwealth XI 1950–51 and MCC 1952–52. Took 100 wkts in 20 consecutive seasons from 1949 to 1968, to create record. Only W. Rhodes has taken 100 wkts in more seasons (23). Took more wkts (2,669, av 18.22) than any other Hants bowler. HS: 87* v Essex (Bournemouth) 1949. BB: 9–30 v Warwickshire (Portsmouth) 1960. Career record: 9,561 runs (av 14.59), 2,857 wkts (av 18.65). The eighth highest aggregate by a bowler in first-class cricket. Appointed 1979.

Charles Terry SPENCER B Leicester 18/8/1931. RHB, RFM. Played for Leicestershire from 1952 to 1974. Benefit (£3,500) in 1964. HS: 90 v Essex (Leicester) 1964. BB: 9–63 v Yorks (Huddersfield) 1954. Career record: 5,871 runs (av 10.77), 1,367 wkts (av 26.69). Appointed 1979.

Thomas William (Tom) SPENCER B Deptford 22/3/1914. RHB, RM. Played for Kent from 1935 to 1946. HS: 96 v Sussex (Tunbridge Wells) 1946. Career record: 2,152 runs (av 20.11), 1 wkt (av 19.00). Appointed 1950 (longest serving umpire on list). Has umpired in 17 Tests between 1954 and 1978.

Peter Samuel George STEVENS B Reading 27/7/1934. Has not played first-class cricket. Umpired in Minor Counties matches since 1975. Appointed 1980.

Jack VAN GELOVEN B Leeds 4/1/1934. RHB, RM. Played for Yorkshire in 1955 and for Leicestershire from 1956 to 1965. Subsequently played for Northumberland in Minor Counties competition from 1966 to 1973. HS: 157* v Somerset (Leicester) 1961. BB: 7–56 v Hants (Leicester) 1959. Career record: 7,522 runs (av 19.43), 5 centuries, 486 wkts (av 28.62). Appointed 1977.

Alan Geoffrey Thomas WHITEHEAD B Butleigh (Somerset) 28/10/1940. LHB, SLA. Played for Somerset from 1957 to 1961. HS: 15 v Hants (Southampton) 1959 and 15 v Leics (Leicester) 1960. BB: 6–74 v Sussex (Eastbourne) 1959. Career record: 137 runs (av 5.70), 67 wkts (av 34.41). Served on Minor Counties list in 1969. Appointed 1970.

Peter Bernard WIGHT B Georgetown (British Guiana) 25/6/1930. RHB, OB. Played for British Guyana in 1950–51 and for Somerset from 1953 to 1965. Benefit (£5,000) in 1963. HS: 222* v Kent (Taunton) 1959. BB: 6–29 v Derbyshire (Chesterfield) 1957. Career record: 17.773 runs (av 33.09), 28 centuries, 68 wkts (av 32.26). Appointed 1966.

NB The Test match panel for 1980 is W. E. Alley, H. D. Bird, D. J. Constant, B. J. Meyer, D. O. Oslear and K. E. Palmer.

The Winners.

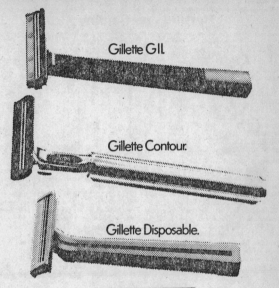

Gillette G II.

Gillette Contour.

Gillette Disposable.

Number One in Twin Blade shaving.

FIRST-CLASS AVERAGES 1979

The following averages include everyone who appeared in first-class cricket during the season.
†*Indicates left-handed batsman.*

Batting and fielding

	Cap	M	I	NO	Runs	HS	Avge	100	50	Ct	St
Aamer Hameed (OU)	—	9	13	0	217	52	16.69	—	1	2	—
Abberley, R. N. (Wa)	1966	6	9	2	79	22*	11.28	—	—	3	—
†Abrahams, J. (La)	—	15	25	1	633	79	26.37	—	6	12	—
Acfield, D. L. (Ex)	1970	19	16	9	55	12*	7.85	—	—	5	—
Agnew, J. P. (Le)	—	3	2	0	10	9	5.00	—	—	—	—
Allott, P. J. W. (La)	—	12	6	2	19	14	4.75	—	—	4	—
Amarnath, M. (Ind)	—	11	16	3	592	123	45.53	1	3	2	—
Amiss, D. L. (Wa)	1965	22	37	3	1672	232*	49.17	6	6	15	—
Anderson, I. J. (Ire)	—	2	4	1	133	110	44.33	1	—	2	—
Anderson, I. S. (D)	—	5	9	3	98	38	16.33	—	—	1	—
Arnold, G. G. (Sx)	1979	18	19	2	163	51	9.58	—	1	5	—
Arrowsmith, R. (La)	—	8	7	4	73	39	24.33	—	—	3	—
Asif Iqbal (K)	1968	10	16	1	506	152	33.73	1	—	3	—
Athey, C. W. J. (Y)	—	21	34	3	679	79*	21.90	—	2	14	1
Bailey, D. (MCo)	—	1	2	0	162	95	81.00	—	2	—	—
†Bailey, M. J. (H)	—	4	6	1	76	24	15.20	—	—	1	—
Bainbridge, P. (Gs)	—	8	14	2	149	81*	12.41	—	1	1	—
Bairstow, D.L.(E/Y/MCC)	1973	24	37	9	680	61	24.28	—	3	50	9
Balderstone, J. C. (Le)	1973	24	41	7	1393	122*	40.97	1	11	15	—
Barclay, J. R. T. (Sx)	1976	23	39	5	1093	104*	32.14	2	7	18	—
†Barlow, G. D. (M)	1976	20	33	9	1000	133	41.66	1	5	9	—
Barnett, K. J. (D)	—	23	36	6	752	96	25.06	—	4	13	—
Bedi, B. S. (Ind)	—	11	7	4	28	20	9.33	—	—	5	—
Bell, D. L. (Sc)	—	2	4	1	37	13*	12.33	—	—	1	—
†Bennett, B. W. P. (CU)	—	2	2	0	4	4	2.00	—	—	—	—
Birch, J. D. (Nt)	—	13	21	5	440	94*	27.50	—	2	12	—
†Birkenshaw, J. (Le)	1965	9	10	5	119	33*	23.80	—	—	7	—
Black, T. M. (Sc)	—	1	2	0	88	57	44.00	—	1	2	—
Booth, P. (Le)	1976	10	8	3	64	20	12.80	—	—	4	—
Bore, M. K. (Nt)	—	22	17	8	45	13*	5.00	—	—	4	—
Borrington, A. J. (D)	1977	19	28	4	563	64	23.45	—	3	9	—
Botham, I. T. (E/So)	1976	15	20	1	731	137	38.47	2	1	21	—
Boycott, G. (E/Y)	1963	15	20	5	1538	175*	102.53	6	7	4	—
Boyns, C. M. (Wo)	—	1	2	2	27	24*	—	—	—	—	—
Brain, B. M. (Gs)	1977	23	18	0	123	24	6.83	—	—	3	—
Brassington, A. J. (Gs)	1978	20	21	8	74	17	5.69	—	—	17	4
†Breakwell, D. (So)	1976	24	31	9	510	54*	23.18	—	2	9	—
Brearley, J.M.(E/M/MCC)	1964	14	20	3	564	148*	33.17	1	1	21	—
Briers, N. E. (Le)	—	19	32	2	620	119	20.66	2	1	9	—
†Broad, B. C. (Gs)	—	9	16	2	512	129	36.57	1	2	3	—
Brown, A. (Wo)	—	1	—	—	—	—	—	—	—	2	—
Brown, D. J. (Wa)	1964	9	7	1	103	33	17.16	—	—	2	—
Burgess, G. I. (So)	1968	1	2	0	20	11	10.00	—	—	—	—
Bury, T. E. O. (OU)	—	1	—	—	—	—	—	—	—	—	—

164

	Cap	M	I	NO	Runs	HS	Avge	100	50	Ct	St
Bushe, E. A. (Ire)	—	1	1	0	14	14	14.00	—	—	5	1
†Butcher, A. R. (E/Sy)	1975	24	42	5	1398	169	37.78	4	6	14	—
Butcher, R. O. (M)	1979	14	22	0	513	106	23.31	1	2	13	—
Carrick, P. (Y)	1976	22	27	8	639	128*	33.63	1	3	12	—
Carter, R. M. (No)	—	10	10	3	94	26*	13.42	—	—	4	—
Cartwright, H. (D)	1978	2	2	0	72	72	36.00	—	1	—	—
Chandrasekhar, B. S. (Ind)	—	9	5	3	2	1*	1.00	—	—	—	—
Chauhan, C. P. S. (Ind)	—	13	22	2	561	108	28.05	1	3	4	—
†Cheatle, R. G. L. (Sx)	—	8	5	1	38	15	9.50	—	—	11	—
†Childs, J. H. (Gs)	1977	21	15	9	47	9	7.83	—	—	5	—
Clark, J. (Sc)	—	2	3	0	8	6	2.66	—	—	—	—
Clarke, S. T. (Sy)	—	11	11	3	90	25	11.25	—	—	6	—
Claughton, J. A. (Wa/OU)	—	9	16	0	289	82	18.06	—	1	2	—
†Clements, S. M. (OU)	—	11	19	3	420	57*	26.25	—	1	3	—
Clifford, C. C. (Wa)	—	20	17	5	88	26	7.33	—	—	4	—
Clift, P. B. (Le)	1976	24	34	10	741	88*	30.87	—	3	7	—
†Clinton, G. S. (Sy)	—	22	38	5	1082	134	32.78	2	6	13	—
Cockbain, I. (La)	—	1	1	0	23	23	23.00	—	—	—	—
Colhoun, O. D. (Ire)	—	1	—								
Collins, B. G. (MCo)	—	1	—								
Collyer, F. E. (MCo)	—	1	1	0	46	46	46.00	—	—	2	—
Cook, G. (No)	1975	22	37	2	1241	130	35.45	3	4	17	—
Cook, N. G. B. (Le)	—	14	12	5	74	18*	10.57	—	—	3	—
†Cooper, H. P. (Y)	—	6	3	0	69	40	23.00	—	—	1	—
Cooper, K. E. (Nt)	—	12	9	4	79	18*	15.80	—	—	3	—
†Cooper, N. H. C. (CU)	—	7	8	1	264	54	37.71	—	2	3	—
Cope, G. A. (Y)	1970	9	9	6	92	39*	30.66	—	—	3	—
Cordle, A. E. (Gm)	1967	22	28	6	316	51	14.36	—	1	12	—
Corlett, S. C. (Ire)	—	2	1	0	9	9	9.00	—	—	2	—
Cottrell, P. R. (CU)	—	10	9	1	119	34	14.87	—	—	17	4
Cowdrey, C. S. (K)	1979	21	30	4	692	83	26.61	—	4	12	—
Cowley, N. G. (H)	1978	23	39	6	611	85	18.51	—	2	7	—
Crawford, N. C. (CU)	—	9	9	1	107	46	13.37	—	—	2	—
Cumbes, J. (Wo)	1978	19	15	9	58	13*	9.66	—	—	3	—
Curtis, T. S. (Wo)	—	1	2	0	42	27	21.00	—	—	1	—
Curzon, C. C. (Nt)	—	3	4	3	36	18*	36.00	—	—	3	1
Daniel, W. W. (M)	1977	17	13	6	72	18	10.28	—	—	5	—
Davies, T. (Gm)	—	1	—								3
Davison, B. F. (Le)	1971	24	39	0	1245	84	31.92	—	8	16	—
Denness, M. H. (Ex)	1977	21	35	2	1032	136	31.27	2	4	8	—
†Denning, P. W. (So)	1973	22	35	6	1222	106	42.13	2	7	18	—
De Silva, D. L. S. (SL)	—	4	3	1	11	7	5.50	—	—	2	—
De Silva, D. S. (SL)	—	6	7	1	291	76*	48.50	—	2	3	—
†De Silva, G. R. A. (SL)	—	7	5	1	23	16	5.75	—	—	2	—
Dewes, A. R. (CU)	—	9	13	1	269	84	22.41	—	2	2	—
Dexter, R. E. (Nt)	—	1	1	0	1	1	1.00	—	—	—	—
Dias, R. L. (SL)	—	8	10	2	306	84*	38.25	—	2	2	—
†Dilley, G. R. (K)	—	21	23	10	262	81	20.15	—	1	16	—
D'Oliveira, B. L. (Wo)	1965	7	9	1	257	112	32.12	1	2	—	—
Downton, P. R. (K)	1979	14	18	1	162	29	9.52	—	—	26	4
†Dredge, C. H. (So)	1978	11	11	5	215	55	35.83	—	1	5	—
Dudleston, B. (Le)	1969	21	35	0	1258	202	35.94	2	8	17	1

	Cap	M	I	NO	Runs	HS	Avge	100	50	Ct	St
Ealham, A. G. E. (K)	1970	24	33	4	760	153	26.20	1	3	13	—
East, R. E. (Ex)	1967	20	26	5	401	70	19.09	—	1	8	—
Edmonds,P.H.(E/M/MCC)	1974	15	17	6	490	141*	44.54	1	1	10	—
†Edwards, T. D. W. (CU)	—	2	3	1	27	18	13.50	—	—	1	—
Elder, J. W. G. (Ire)	—	2	1	0	7	7	7.00	—	—	1	—
Emburey, J. E. (M/MCC)	1977	20	22	6	477	91*	29.81	—	1	21	—
Featherstone, N. G. (M)	1971	10	14	3	260	59*	23.63	—	1	10	—
Ferreira, A. M. (Wa)	—	16	17	6	219	57	19.90	—	1	7	—
Finan, N. H. (Gs)	—	3	1	1	4	4*	—	—	—	—	—
Fisher, P. B. (M)	—	2	2	0	6	6	3.00	—	—	5	—
†Fletcher, C. D. B. (Sx)	—	1	—	—	—	—	—	—	—	—	—
Fletcher, K. W. R. (Ex)	1963	23	34	4	1006	140*	33.53	1	8	19	—
Foat, J. C. (Gs)	1979	10	17	2	463	126	30.86	2	1	5	—
Fowler, G. (La)	—	2	4	0	24	20	6.00	—	—	—	—
Francis, D. A. (Gm)	—	15	26	7	446	56*	23.47	—	1	3	—
French, B. N. (Nt)	—	19	20	5	223	41	14.86	—	—	38	4
Gaekwad, A. D. (Ind)	—	12	20	2	574	109	31.88	2	1	4	—
Gandon, N. J. C. (OU)	—	8	13	1	170	38	14.16	—	—	6	—
Gard, T. (So)	—	4	4	1	71	51*	71.00	—	1	6	3
Garner, J. (So)	1979	14	10	4	106	53	17.66	—	1	4	—
Garnham, M. A. (Gs)	—	3	4	2	50	21	25.00	—	—	2	2
Gatting, M. W. (M/MCC)	1977	16	24	5	580	93*	30.52	—	2	12	—
Gavaskar, S. M. (Ind)	—	13	20	1	1062	221	55.89	3	5	15	—
†Ghavri, K. D. (Ind)	—	12	12	5	143	33*	20.42	—	—	1	—
†Gifford, N. (Wo)	1961	17	16	5	103	35	9.36	—	—	12	—
Gill, P. N. (MCo)	—	1	2	0	38	20	19.00	—	—	—	—
Goddard, G. F. (Sc)	—	2	3	0	16	7	5.33	—	—	—	—
Gooch, G. A. (E/Ex/MCC)	1975	17	25	2	838	109	36.43	1	6	28	—
Goonetilleke,F.R.M.(SL)	—	6	5	1	41	24*	10.25	—	—	—	—
†Gould, I. J. (M/MCC)	1977	19	22	1	370	89	17.61	—	2	24	3
†Gower, D. I. (E/Le/MCC)	1977	17	27	4	957	200*	41.60	1	8	9	—
Graveney, D. A. (Gs)	1976	22	27	10	301	56*	17.70	—	1	5	—
†Graves, P. J. (Sx)	1969	17	24	2	501	59	22.77	—	1	5	—
Greenidge, C. G. (H)	1972	17	30	2	1404	145	50.14	3	8	27	—
Greig, I. A. (CU)	—	8	11	1	249	58	24.90	—	2	7	—
Griffiths, B. J. (No)	1978	14	14	6	36	10*	4.50	—	—	2	—
Gurr, D. R. (So)	—	4	2	2	31	20*	—	—	—	—	—
Hacker, P. J. (Nt)	—	10	11	3	40	9	5.00	—	—	2	—
†Hadlee, R. J. (Nt)	1978	12	16	4	193	41	16.08	—	—	5	—
Halliday, M. (Ire)	—	2	1	1	13	13*	—	—	—	—	—
Hampshire, J. H. (Y)	1963	21	31	2	880	96	30.34	—	6	21	—
Hardie, B. R. (Ex)	1974	23	34	5	1170	146*	40.34	3	5	30	—
Harris, M. J. (Nt)	1970	21	38	4	1368	133*	40.23	2	10	9	—
Harrison, D. W. (Ire)	—	1	1	0	0	0	0.00	—	—	2	—
Hartley, S. N. (Y)	—	3	5	1	126	53*	31.50	—	1	1	—
Hassan, B. (Nt)	1970	11	16	1	257	49	17.13	—	—	7	—
Hayes, F. C. (La)	1972	18	22	5	747	88	43.94	—	6	8	—
Hayward, R. E. (MCo)	—	1	1	0	0	0	0.00	—	—	1	—
Head, T. J. (Sx)	—	7	6	2	70	22	17.50	—	—	21	1
Hemmings, E. E. (Nt)	—	21	31	6	453	85*	18.12	—	2	9	—
Hemsley, E. J. O. (Wo)	1969	23	34	6	842	93	30.07	—	5	29	—

166

	Cap	M	I	NO	Runs	HS	Avge	100	50	Ct	St
Hendrick, M. (E/D/MCC)	1972	15	12	7	100	36	20.00	—	—	11	—
Herkes, R. (M)	—	2	4	2	0	0*	0.00	—	—	—	—
†Higgs, K. (Le)	1972	19	13	6	42	9	6.00	—	—	19	—
Hignell, A. J. (Gs)	1977	16	27	6	736	149*	35.04	2	3	19	—
Hill, A. (D)	1976	19	35	3	887	99	27.71	—	6	8	—
Hills, R. W. (K)	1977	10	11	4	73	27	10.42	—	—	4	—
Hoadley, S. P. (Sx)	—	5	7	0	97	23	13.85	—	—	1	—
Hobbs, R. N. S. (Gm)	1979	19	21	7	111	29	7.92	—	—	12	—
†Hodgson, A. (No)	1976	11	11	3	39	10	4.87	—	—	4	—
Hogg, W. (La/MCC)	—	12	9	2	33	11	4.71	—	—	5	—
Holder, V. A. (Wo)	1970	14	12	6	119	24*	19.83	—	—	5	—
Holliday, D. C. (CU)	—	10	14	3	145	55*	13.18	—	1	6	—
Holmes, G. C. (Gm)	—	10	14	3	246	100*	22.36	1	—	1	—
Hopkins, D. C. (Wa)	—	12	14	2	103	34*	8.58	—	—	3	—
Hopkins, J. A. (Gm)	1977	23	42	1	1174	94	28.63	—	8	18	—
Howarth, G. P. (Sy)	1974	19	30	4	1238	183	47.61	4	7	12	—
Howat, M. G. (CU)	—	2	—	—	—	—	—	—	—	—	—
Hughes, D. P. (La)	1970	15	14	3	188	60*	17.09	—	1	14	—
Humpage, G. W. (Wa)	1976	17	24	2	755	96	34.31	—	2	21	2
†Humphries, D. J. (Wo)	1978	22	30	4	575	68	22.11	—	2	49	8
†Ikin, M. J. (MCo)	—	1	1	0	31	31	31.00	—	—	—	—
Imran Khan (Sx)	1976	16	25	5	700	154*	35.00	1	6	6	—
Inchmore, J. D. (Wo)	1976	21	22	9	283	37*	21.76	—	—	10	—
Ingham, P. G. (Y)	—	2	3	0	32	17	10.66	—	—	—	—
Intikhab Alam (Sy)	1969	15	21	4	345	52	20.29	—	2	8	—
Jackman, R. D. (Sy)	1970	21	25	8	287	82	16.88	—	1	12	—
Jarvis, K. B. S. (K)	1977	19	15	5	38	8	3.80	—	—	3	—
Javed Miandad (Sx)	1977	3	6	2	76	30*	19.00	—	—	4	—
Jayasekera, R. S. A. (SL)	—	5	7	1	230	79*	38.33	—	2	5	2
Jayasinghe, S. A. (SL)	—	6	7	1	183	64	30.50	—	2	10	4
Jeganathan, S. (SL)	—	5	6	1	21	8	4.20	—	—	2	—
Jennings, K. F. (So)	1978	19	11	5	19	11*	3.16	—	—	9	—
Jesty, T. E. (H)	1971	19	35	3	1100	76	34.37	—	10	16	—
Johnson, C. (Y)	—	1	2	0	14	13	7.00	—	—	—	—
Johnson, G. W. (K)	1970	24	31	7	726	82	30.25	—	5	17	—
Johnson, J. S. (MCo)	—	1	2	1	170	146*	170.00	1	—	—	—
Johnson, P. D. (MCo)	—	1	2	0	24	13	12.00	—	—	1	—
Johnston, R. I. (Ire)	—	2	3	1	70	34	35.00	—	—	1	—
†Jones, A. (Gm)	1962	22	40	0	1198	115	29.95	2	8	12	—
Jones, A. A. (M)	1976	11	8	3	29	12	5.80	—	—	3	—
†Jones, A. L. (Gm)	—	15	27	3	498	83	20.75	—	4	10	—
†Jones, B. J. R. (Wo)	—	6	12	0	174	39	14.50	—	—	2	—
Jones, E. W. (Gm)	1967	21	34	6	368	108	13.14	1	—	39	3
†Kallicharran, A. I. (Wa)	1972	17	26	5	1098	170*	52.28	4	6	14	—
Kapil Dev (Ind)	—	13	15	0	287	102	19.13	1	—	4	—
Kemp, N. J. (K)	—	1	2	0	12	10	6.00	—	—	—	—
†Kennedy, A. (La)	1975	9	11	3	135	21	16.87	—	—	—	—
Ker, J. E. (Sc)	—	2	3	1	29	14*	14.50	—	—	1	—
Khanna, S. C. (Ind.)	—	6	4	1	41	20	13.66	—	—	6	4
Kirsten, P. N. (D)	1978	23	38	2	1148	135*	31.88	2	5	21	—
†Kitchen, M. J. (So)	1966	7	10	0	146	36	14.60	—	—	8	—

167

	Cap	M	I	NO	Runs	HS	Avge	100	50	Ct	St
Knight, J. M. (OU)	—	11	16	0	117	20	7.31	—	—	1	—
†Knight, R. D. V. (Sy)	1978	22	33	5	946	117*	33.78	2	4	15	—
Knott, A. P. E. (K)	1965	10	11	2	243	63	27.00	—	1	15	1
†Laing, J. R. (Sc)	—	2	4	0	50	23	12.50	—	—	1	—
Lamb, A. J. (No)	1978	21	34	8	1747	184	67.19	4	11	19	—
Lamb, T. M. (No)	1978	17	17	7	72	14	7.20	—	—	2	—
Larkins, W. (No/MCC)	1976	16	27	1	1079	136	41.50	3	7	12	—
Lawson, G. F. (La)	—	1	2	0	19	17	9.50	—	—	—	—
Leadbeater, B. (Y)	1969	2	4	1	66	49	22.00	—	—	—	—
Lee, P. G. (La)	1972	16	14	7	68	19	9.71	—	—	—	—
†L'Estrange, M. G. (OU)	—	11	19	1	278	63	15.44	—	1	12	—
Lever, J. K. (E/Ex/MCC)	1970	21	16	6	81	14	8.10	—	—	3	—
Lewis, R. V. (MCo)	—	1	2	0	89	88	44.50	—	1	—	—
Lilley, A. W. (Ex)	—	4	5	0	76	35	15.20	—	—	1	—
Lister, J. W. (D)	—	2	4	0	68	44	17.00	—	—	—	—
†Llewellyn, M. J. (Gm)	1977	10	15	1	285	106*	20.35	1	1	4	—
Lloyd, B. J. (Gm)	—	16	25	6	293	43	15.42	—	—	13	—
†Lloyd, C. H. (La)	1969	17	22	4	880	104*	48.88	3	3	11	—
†Lloyd, D. (La)	1968	22	34	3	1078	135*	34.77	4	4	14	—
†Lloyd, T. A. (Wa)	—	15	26	5	613	104	29.19	1	1	16	—
†Lloyds, J. W. (So)	—	4	7	0	117	43	16.71	—	—	2	—
†Long, A. (Sx)	1976	16	17	10	200	35*	28.57	—	—	36	5
Love, J. D. (Y)	—	12	21	3	496	170*	27.55	1	1	7	—
Lumb, R. G. (Y)	1974	22	35	2	1465	159	44.39	5	4	12	—
Lynch, M. A. (Sy)	—	7	12	2	153	45	15.30	—	—	3	—
Lyon, J. (La)	1975	21	22	8	313	123	22.35	1	—	30	2
McCurdy, R. J. (D)	—	1	—	—	—	—	—	—	—	—	—
McEvoy, M. S. A. (Ex)	—	7	12	0	108	28	9.00	—	—	11	—
McEwan, K. S. (Ex)	1974	23	35	2	1387	208*	42.03	3	6	19	—
McFarlane, L. (No)	—	8	2	0	0	0	0.00	—	—	3	—
†Mack, A. J.(Gm)	—	8	12	4	35	18	4.37	—	—	2	—
Mackintosh, K. S. (Nt)	—	1	2	0	16	8	8.00	—	—	2	—
McLellan, A. J. (D)	—	12	10	3	72	41	10.28	—	—	24	2
†McPherson, T. I. (Sc)	—	2	3	2	26	21	26.00	—	—	1	—
Madugalle, R. S. (SL)	—	7	8	0	242	88	30.25	—	2	8	—
Malone, M. F. (La)	—	3	2	0	0	0	0.00	—	—	—	—
Marie, G. V. (OU)	—	1	2	2	17	11*	—	—	—	—	—
Marks, V. J. (So)	1979	24	33	9	894	93	37.25	—	7	8	—
Marsden, R. (OU)	—	1	1	0	3	3	3.00	—	—	1	—
Marshall, M. D. (H)	—	19	25	2	197	38	8.56	—	—	12	—
Maynard, C. (Wa)	—	12	12	3	310	85	34.44	—	2	27	1
Mellor, A. J. (D)	—	7	6	4	7	3*	3.50	—	—	4	—
Mendis, G. D. (Sx)	—	22	37	4	929	118	28.15	1	6	24	—
Mendis, L. R.D. (SL)	—	7	10	1	329	82	36.55	—	3	2	—
Merry, W. G. (M)	—	8	6	4	7	4*	3.50	—	—	1	—
Miller, G. (E/D)	1976	16	19	5	512	82	36.57	—	4	9	—
Mills, J. P. C. (CU)	—	10	13	0	198	46	15.23	—	—	4	—
Monteith, J. D. (Ire)	—	2	2	1	31	27	31.00	—	—	1	—
Morrill, N. D. (OU)	—	9	14	2	158	45	13.16	—	—	2	—
Moseley, H. R. (So)	1972	8	5	2	25	15	8.33	—	—	1	—
Moulding, R. P. (OU)	—	8	13	1	146	57*	12.16	—	1	4	—
Mubarak, A. M. (CU)	—	9	13	2	201	58*	18.27	—	1	6	—

	Cap	M	I	NO	Runs	HS	Avge	100	50	Ct	St
†Nash, M. A. (Gm)	1969	9	11	0	123	41	11.18	—	—	5	—
Neale, P. A. (Wo)	1978	22	37	6	1305	163*	42.09	4	5	10	—
Needham, A. (Sy)	—	1	1	0	2	2	2.00	—	—	2	—
Nicholas, M. C. J. (H)	—	4	7	1	133	105*	22.16	1	—	1	—
Northcote-Green, S. R. (OU)	—	6	10	2	100	38*	12.50	—	—	1	—
O'Brien, B. A. (Ire)	—	2	4	1	89	45*	29.66	—	—	1	—
O'Brien, N. T. (MCo)	—	1	1	0	13	13	13.00	—	—	—	—
†Old, C. M. (Y/MCC)	1969	14	16	5	112	23	10.18	—	—	9	—
Oldham, S. (Y)	—	13	6	1	53	50	10.60	—	1	5	—
Olive, M. (So)	—	1	2	0	77	39	38.50	—	—	2	—
Oliver, P. R. (Wa)	—	16	18	3	394	83	26.26	—	2	9	—
Ontong, R. C. (Gm)	1979	23	41	7	1157	135*	34.02	3	7	8	—
Opatha, A. R. M. (SL)	—	7	8	1	101	24	14.42	—	—	5	—
Orders, J. O. D. (OU)	—	5	10	0	201	70	20.10	—	2	1	—
Ormrod, J. A. (Wo)	1966	22	38	4	1126	134	33.11	2	7	16	—
Parker, P. W. G. (Sx/MCC)	1979	23	37	7	1330	103	44.33	4	5	15	—
†Parsons, G. J. (Le)	—	3	4	1	21	17	7.00	—	—	—	—
†Partridge, M. D. (Gs)	—	23	31	10	717	90	34.14	—	6	8	—
Parvez Mir (Gm)	—	1	2	0	16	10	8.00	—	—	—	—
Pasqual, S. P. (SL)	—	7	9	2	250	101*	35.71	1	—	3	—
Patel, B. P. (Ind)	—	7	10	4	137	36*	22.83	—	—	1	—
Patel, D. N. (Wo)	1979	21	29	4	698	118*	27.92	1	3	20	—
Pauline, D. B. (Sy)	—	1	—	—	—	—	—	—	—	1	—
Pearce, J. P. (OU)	—	5	8	2	16	8*	2.66	—	—	2	—
Peck, I. G. (CU)	—	1	2	0	4	4	2.00	—	—	1	—
Perry, N. J. (Gm)	—	6	6	3	8	5*	2.66	—	—	1	—
Perryman, S. P. (Wa)	1977	19	13	4	68	12	7.55	—	—	6	—
Phillip, N. (Ex)	1978	22	30	5	425	66	17.00	—	2	6	—
Phillipson, C. P. (Sx)	—	23	31	6	460	47	18.40	—	—	19	—
Pigott, A. C. S. (Sx)	—	14	20	3	328	55	19.29	—	1	6	—
Pilling, H. (La)	1965	1	—	—	—	—	—	—	—	—	—
Pocock, N. E. J. (H)	—	12	22	2	393	143*	19.65	1	—	14	—
Pocock, P. I. (Jy)	1967	22	19	7	131	20	10.91	—	—	5	—
Pont, K. R. (Ex)	1976	13	20	3	346	77	20.35	—	2	6	—
Popplewell, N. F. M. (So/CU)	—	16	20	2	400	92	22.22	—	1	4	—
Pridgeon, A. P. (Wo)	—	6	1	1	0	0*	—	—	—	—	—
Pringle, D. R. (CU)	—	10	13	3	404	103*	40.40	1	2	7	—
Procter, M. J. (Gs)	1968	21	36	2	1241	122	38.78	3	7	11	—
Racionzer, T. B. (Sc)	—	1	2	0	13	12	6.50	—	—	2	—
Radley, C. T. (M)	1967	20	35	6	1128	118*	38.89	2	8	23	—
†Ramage, A. (Y)	—	5	5	3	33	19	16.50	—	—	—	—
Randall, D. W. (E/Nt)	1973	14	25	1	1138	209	47.41	3	5	12	—
Ratcliffe, R. M. (La)	1976	17	16	5	285	101*	25.90	1	—	3	—
Rawlinson, J. L. (OU)	—	4	6	2	27	13*	6.75	—	—	2	—
Reddy, B. (Ind)	—	10	12	2	101	23	10.10	—	—	21	2
†Reidy, B. W. (La)	—	18	26	6	547	131*	27.35	1	1	6	—
†Reith, M. S. (Ire)	—	2	4	0	77	30	19.25	—	—	2	—
Rice, C. E. B. (Nt)	1975	21	34	3	1297	129	41.83	1	10	22	—
Rice, J. M. (H)	1975	23	41	3	927	84*	24.39	—	4	16	—

	Cap	M	I	NO	Runs	HS	Avge	100	50	Ct	St
Richards, C. J. (Sy)	1978	23	20	1	183	29	9.63	—	—	50	8
Richards, G. (Gm)	1976	10	13	1	155	34	12.91	—	—	3	—
†Richards, I. M. (No)	—	11	15	1	312	47	22.28	—	—	3	—
Richards, I. V. A. (So)	1974	16	26	0	1043	156	40.11	3	4	13	—
Robertson, F. (Sc)	—	2	3	0	57	51	19.00	—	1	1	—
Robinson, P. A. (La)	—	1	1	0	15	15	15.00	—	—	—	—
Robinson, R. T. (Nt)	—	1	2	0	68	40	34.00	—	—	—	—
Rock, D. J. (H)	—	16	27	1	473	104	18.19	1	1	8	—
Roebuck, P. M. (So)	1978	23	37	10	1273	89	47.14	—	11	22	—
Rogers, J. J. (OU)	—	11	19	2	237	33*	13.94	—	—	3	—
Roope, G. R. J. (Sy)	1969	23	35	7	939	114	33.53	1	5	41	—
†Rose, B. C. (So)	1975	21	33	1	1317	133	41.15	2	8	12	—
Ross, C. J. (OU)	—	10	14	7	40	16*	5.71	—	—	3	—
†Rouse, S. J. (Wa)	1974	1	1	0	21	21	21.00	—	—	1	—
Rowe, C. J. C. (K)	1977	23	39	5	945	147*	27.79	3	3	7	—
Russell, P. E. (D)	1975	5	4	0	8	4	2.00	—	—	1	—
Russom, N. (CU)	—	3	3	1	32	12	16.00	—	—	—	—
†Sadiq Mohammad (Gs)	1973	17	30	2	1595	171	56.96	8	5	16	—
Sainsbury, G. E. (Ex)	—	1	—	—	—	—	—	—	—	1	—
Sanderson, J. F. W. (OU)	—	1	1	0	2	2	2.00	—	—	1	—
Sarfraz Nawaz (No)	1975	13	15	2	220	46	16.92	—	—	7	—
Savage, R. L. (Wa)	—	7	8	5	39	15*	13.00	—	—	3	—
Schepens, M. (Le)	—	5	7	2	132	57	26.40	—	1	6	—
†Scott, C. J. (La)	—	3	4	1	24	16	8.00	—	—	10	1
Selvey, M. W. W. (M)	1973	20	18	1	237	45	13.94	—	—	7	—
†Shantry, B. K. (Gs)	—	1	—	—	—	—	—	—	—	—	—
Sharp, G. (No)	1973	22	26	2	386	51	16.08	—	1	34	6
†Sharp, K. (Y/MCC)	—	16	24	2	566	80	25.72	—	2	2	—
Shepherd, D. R. (Gs)	1969	8	10	2	223	70	27.87	—	1	—	—
Shepherd, J. N. (K)	1967	16	20	1	370	86	19.47	—	1	9	—
Short, J. F. (Ire)	—	2	4	1	165	80†	55.00	—	2	3	—
Shuttleworth, K. (Le)	1977	19	20	9	279	44	25.36	—	—	17	—
Sidebottom, A. (Y)	—	13	14	5	184	51	20.44	—	1	2	—
Simmons, J. (La)	1971	23	25	5	469	74*	23.45	—	1	17	—
Skala, S. M. (OU)	—	2	3	0	18	11	6.00	—	—	6	1
†Slack, W. N. (M)	—	6	12	0	236	66	19.66	—	1	2	—
Slocombe, P. A. (So)	1978	23	38	3	956	103*	27.31	1	6	8	—
Smedley, M. J. (Nt)	1966	12	16	1	351	91	23.40	—	1	12	—
†Smith, A. V. (Ire)	—	1	1	1	11	11*	—	—	—	—	—
Smith, C. L. (Gm)	—	1	2	0	81	67	81.00	—	1	1	—
†Smith, D. M. (Sy)	—	19	23	7	555	79	34.68	—	4	8	—
Smith, K. D. (Wa)	1978	20	34	3	739	71	23.83	—	7	9	—
Smith, M. J. (M)	1967	19	34	4	1109	137	36.96	5	1	2	—
Smith, N. (Ex)	1975	23	29	7	417	90*	18.95	—	3	51	3
Southern, J. W. (H)	1978	16	21	9	247	61*	20.58	—	1	5	—
Spencer, J. (Sx)	1973	17	16	3	145	35	11.15	—	—	3	—
Steele, A. (Sc)	—	2	3	0	70	49	23.33	—	—	4	—
Steele, D. S. (D)	1979	23	38	8	1190	127*	39.66	2	7	22	—
Steele, J. F. (Le)	1971	23	38	5	1301	187	39.42	3	6	21	—
Stephenson, G. R. (H)	1969	23	33	3	333	43	11.10	—	—	31	4
Stevenson, G. B. (Y)	1978	17	20	5	317	73*	21.13	—	1	8	—
Stevenson, K. (H)	1979	23	28	15	96	24	7.38	—	—	6	—
Stewart, D. E. R. (Sc)	—	2	4	0	15	11	3.75	—	—	2	—

	Cap	M	I	NO	Runs	HS	Avge	100	50	Ct	St
Stovold, A. W. (Gs)	1976	22	39	1	1388	156	35.52	1	10	18	—
†Stovold, M. W. (Gs)	—	7	10	1	84	27	9.33	—	—	1	—
Surridge, D. (CU)	—	9	8	6	40	14*	20.00	—	—	3	—
†Swarbrook, F. W. (D)	1975	6	7	2	163	52	32.60	—	1	4	—
Swart, P. D. (Gm)	1979	21	36	5	918	122	29.61	1	4	15	—
Tavare, C. J. (K)	1978	24	38	6	1328	150*	41.50	3	7	21	—
Taylor, D. J. S. (So)	1971	20	20	10	318	50*	31.80	—	1	29	10
Taylor, L. B. (Le)	—	15	9	5	25	11*	6.25	—	—	3	—
Taylor, M. N. S. (H)	1973	21	30	3	495	75	18.33	—	3	9	—
Taylor, N. (K)	—	1	2	0	121	110	60.50	1	—	—	—
Taylor, R. W. (E/D)	1962	14	14	3	286	64	26.00	—	1	31	3
Tennekoon, A. P. B. (SL)	—	7	11	1	491	112	49.10	1	3	5	—
Terry, V. P. (H)	—	5	7	0	86	21	12.28	—	—	4	—
†Thomas, D. J. (Sy)	—	7	8	2	48	15*	8.00	—	—	2	—
Thomas, G. P. (Wa)	—	1	1	0	9	9	9.00	—	—	—	—
Thomas, J. G. (Gm)	—	1	1	0	34	34	34.00	—	—	—	—
Titmus, F. J. (M)	1953	2	2	0	30	25	15.00	—	—	1	—
Todd, P. A. (Nt)	1977	19	34	2	1164	176	36.37	2	4	14	—
Tolchard, R. W. (Le)	1966	20	30	7	688	109	29.91	1	2	43	3
Tomlins, K. P. (M)	—	1	1	0	4	4	4.00	—	—	1	—
Tremlett, T. M. (H)	—	6	11	2	51	18	5.66	—	—	3	—
Trim, G. E. (La)	—	8	13	0	258	91	19.84	—	1	9	—
Tunnicliffe, C.J. (D)	1977	20	22	4	403	57	22.38	—	2	8	—
Tunnicliffe, H. T. (Nt)	—	22	39	12	883	97	32.70	—	6	16	—
†Turner, D. R. (H)	1970	22	39	1	815	129	21.44	1	3	3	—
Turner, G. M. (Wo)	1968	18	31	2	1669	150*	57.55	8	5	10	—
Turner, S. (Ex)	1970	23	30	4	561	102	21.57	1	1	14	—
Underwood, D. L. (K)	1964	23	24	5	210	45	11.05	—	—	17	—
Vengsarkar, D. B. (Ind)	—	12	19	1	751	138	41.72	3	4	12	—
Venkataraghavan, S. (Ind)	—	13	10	0	101	28	10.10	—	—	3	—
Viswanath, G. R. (Ind)	—	13	17	2	757	113	50.46	3	4	4	—
Waller, C. E. (Sx)	1976	16	13	7	69	18*	11.50	—	—	12	—
†Walters, J. (D)	—	22	28	7	291	54	13.85	—	1	8	—
Warnapura, B. (SL)	—	5	7	1	232	73	38.66	—	3	1	—
†Warner, C. J. (Sc)	—	1	2	1	39	27	39.00	—	—	1	—
Watson, G. G. (Wo)	—	9	11	1	75	18*	7.50	—	—	—	—
Watson, W. K. (Nt)	—	10	10	5	89	25	17.80	—	—	7	—
†Watts, P. J. (No)	1962	18	24	7	323	42*	19.00	—	—	11	—
Wells, C. M. (Sx)	—	5	6	1	60	29	12.00	—	—	1	—
†Wessels, K. C. (Sx)	1977	21	36	2	1800	187	52.94	6	11	21	—
Weston, M. J. (Wo)	—	1	2	0	59	43	29.50	—	—	—	—
Wettimuny, S. R. D. (SL)	—	7	11	0	182	83	16.54	—	1	8	—
Whitehouse, J. (Wa)	1973	21	34	4	624	98	20.80	—	3	10	—
Whiteley, J. P. (Y)	—	12	7	2	46	20	9.20	—	—	3	—
Wijesuriya, R. G. C. E. (SL)	—	5	4	2	38	25	19.00	—	—	6	—
Wilkins, A. H. (Gm)	—	10	12	2	81	43	8.10	—	—	1	—
Willey, P. (E/No/MCC)	1971	22	34	7	1109	131	41.07	2	6	10	—
Williams, R. G. (No)	1979	22	35	3	1057	151*	33.03	4	3	7	—
Willis, R. G. D. (E/Wa)	1972	12	8	5	98	42*	32.66	—	—	1	—
Wilson, P. H. L. (Sy)	—	17	11	7	48	15	12.00	—	—	3	—

	Cap	M	I	NO	Runs	HS	Avge	100	50	Ct	St
†Wincer, R. C. (D)	—	11	11	4	88	26	12.57	—	—	3	—
Windaybank, S. J. (Gs)	—	2	3	0	101	53	33.66	—	1	—	—
Wood, B. (La)	1968	22	35	7	1144	135*	40.85	2	6	12	—
Woolmer, R. A. (K)	1970	24	39	5	1382	169	40.64	4	5	12	—
†Wright, J. G. (D)	1977	19	35	3	1249	142*	39.03	5	5	9	—
Yajurvindra Singh (Ind)	—	9	14	6	293	59	36.62	—	1	10	—
†Yardley, T. J. (No)	1978	19	29	6	623	66*	27.08	—	4	17	—
Yashpal Sharma (Ind)	—	12	21	6	884	111	58.93	3	3	6	1
†Yeabsley, D. I. (MCo)	—	1	1	1	9	9*	—	—	—	—	—
†Younis Ahmed (Wo)	1979	22	30	8	1539	221*	69.95	4	7	5	—
Zaheer Abbas (Gs)	1975	17	30	2	1304	151*	46.57	3	8	9	—
Zuill, A. M. (Sc)	—	1	2	0	30	21	15.00	—	—	—	—

WINNERS OF THE 1979 GILLETTE 'PICK A TEAM' COMPETITION

Readers were asked to pick the best Gillette Cup team from a list of 40 cricketers who have played in a winning Gillette Cup Final team assuming them all to be at the top of their form. The team picked by a panel of judges was: **Dennis Amiss (1), Farokh Engineer (2), Rohan Kanhai (3), Zaheer Abbas (4), Clive Lloyd (5), Ted Dexter (6), Mike Procter (Captain) (7), Imran Khan (8), Chris Old (9), Fred Trueman (10), Derek Underwood (11).** The batting order is in brackets.

First Prize: £200 D. Cohen, The Ranch House, Willowmere, Sandown Road, Esher, Surrey. **Second Prize: £100** P. A. Farrell, 612 Allesley Old Road, Coventry CV5 8EB; **Third Prize: £50** C. M. Spencer, 12 Coughton Place, Walford, Ross-on-Wye, Herefordshire; **Fourth Prize: £25** R. M. Barlow, 73 Enfield Road, Acton, London W3; **25 Runners-up: £5 each** A. Spalding, 25 Regent Road, Lowestoft, Suffolk; P. Billington, 44 Clewer Hill Road, Windsor, Berkshire SL4 4BW; J. Pinder, 18 Chestnut Drive, Thorney, Peterborough; M. A. Field, Napoleon Cottage, Bilting, Near Ashford, Kent; M. Chandler, 2 Scowsdown, Ewhurst Green, Robertsbridge, Sussex; M. Reischman, 129 Carr Road, Calverley, Pudsey, West Yorkshire; N. D. Redwood, 11 Clifton Road, Weston-Super-Mare, Somerset; M. Pickett, 15 Taylor Avenue, Ormskirk, Lancashire; G. Jessop, The Master's Lodge, St. John's Hospital, Bath, Avon; G. Owens, 56 Sledgwick Road, Billingham, Cleveland TS23 3HLL; S. J. C. Lockwood, 1 Meadow Way, Westergate, Chichester, Sussex PO20 6QT; R. E. Withers, 10 Allcroft Road, Reading, Berkshire RG1 5HH; R. L. Sloan, No. 5 Cottage, Lauriston Farm, Goldhanger, Maldon, Essex; Ian Ross, 34 High Street, Wick, Caithness, Scotland; G. Brock, 119 Grove Lane, Cheadle Hume, Cheadle, Cheshire SK8 7NE; D. R. Harris, 2 Verney Mews, Reading, Berkshire RG3 2NT; N. D. Davies, 27 Union Road, Abergavenny, Gwent NP7 5UW; J. O'Dea, 35 King's Avenue, Muswell Hill, London N10 1PA; D. O'Callaghan, 42 Kirkham Road, Nunthorpe, Middlesbrough, Cleveland TS7 0HF; M. Lee, 40 John Street, Meadowfield, Durham DH7 8RS; R. Langley, 4 Glenwood Drive, Romford, Essex; F. D. Morgan, Cedarwood, Old Hill Crescent, Newport, Gwent; T. J. A. Young, Beacon Down House, Ham Road, Liddington, Swindon, Wiltshire; J. Yates, 9 Hamilton Road, Oxford; G. Hill, Valley View, Kirkby-Overblow, Harrogate, North Yorkshire.

Each prize carries with it a selection of Gillette products.

BOWLING

	Type	Overs	Mds	Runs	Wkt	Avge	Best	5 wI	10 wM
Aamer Hameed (OU)	RFM	150	25	521	7	74.42	2–85	—	—
Abberley, R. N. (Wa)	OB	3	1	9	1	9.00	1–9	—	—
Abrahams, J. (La)	OB	2	1	3	0		—	—	—
Acfield, D. L. (Ex)	OB	489.2	143	1048	41	25.56	6–56	3	—
Agnew, J. P. (Le)	RF	69	16	199	7	28.42	2–33	—	—
Allott, P. J. W. (La)	RFM	223.2	41	609	13	46.84	5–39	1	—
Amarnath, M. (Ind)	RM	194.5	47	533	14	38.07	4–88	—	—
Amiss, D. L. (Wa)	—						—	—	—
Anderson, I. J. (Ire)	OB	14	10	16	0		—	—	—
Anderson, I. S. (D)	OB	4	0	13	0		—	—	—
Arnold, G. G. (Sx)	RFM	435.5	147	950	52	18.26	6–41	2	—
Arrowsmith, R. (La)	SLA	96.1	22	316	10	31.60	2–22	—	—
Asif Iqbal (K)	RM	17	3	71	1	71.00	1–29	—	—
Athey, C. W. J. (Y)	RM	101.3	21	325	2	162.50	1–2	—	—
Bailey, D. (MCo)	OB	14	3	72	0		—	—	—
Bailey, M. J. (H)	OB	50.4	9	151	3	50.33	2–65	—	—
Bainbridge, P. (Gs)	RM	72	19	240	7	34.28	2–30	—	—
Bairstow, D. L. (E/Y/MCC)	RM	5	1	16	1	16.00	1–16	—	—
Balderstone, J. C. (Le)	SLA	265.5	80	681	23	29.60	3–38	—	—
Barclay, J. R. T. (Sx)	OB	412.4	85	1250	52	24.03	6–61	2	—
Barlow, G. D. (M)	RM	2	1	1	0		—	—	—
Barnett, K. J. (D)	LB	98.5	12	387	4	96.75	1–14	—	—
Bedi, B. S. (Ind)	SLA	377.5	113	847	33	25.66	6–28	2	1
Bell, D. L. (Sc)	—						—	—	—
Bennett, B. W. P. (CU)	—						—	—	—
Birch, J. D. (Nt)	RM	25	6	76	1	76.00	1–63	—	—
Birkenshaw, J. (Le)	OB	151.3	40	381	12	31.75	3–20	—	—
Black, T. M. (Sc)	—						—	—	—
Booth, P. (Le)	RFM	111	28	379	10	37.90	3–46	—	—
Bore, M. K. (Nt)	LM	731	226	1885	61	30.90	8–89	3	—
Borrington, A. J. (D)	—						—	—	—
Botham, I. T. (E/So)	RFM	436.4	111	1318	46	28.65	6–81	4	—
Boycott, G. (E/Y)	RM	52.2	23	92	9	10.22	4–14	—	—
Boyns, C. M. (Wo)	RM	22	4	64	1	64.00	1–50	—	—
Brain, B. M. (Gs)	RFM	495.5	125	1355	49	27.65	5–33	2	—
Brassington, A. J. (Gs)	—						—	—	—
Breakwell, D. (So)	SLA	567.3	193	1311	47	27.89	6–41	1	—
Brearley, J. M. (E/M/MCC)	—						—	—	—
Briers, N. E. (Le)	—	3	2	1	0		—	—	—
Broad, B. C. (Gs)	—						—	—	—
Brown, A. (Wo)	—						—	—	—
Brown, D. J. (Wa)	RFM	243.4	60	653	21	31.09	7–73	2	—
Burgess, G. I. (So)	RM	5	3	8	0		—	—	—
Bury, T. E. O. (OU)	—						—	—	—
Bushe, E. A. (Ire)	—						—	—	—
Butcher, A. R. (E/Sy)	SLA	29	8	123	1	123.00	1–12	—	—
Butcher, R. O. (M)	RM	1	0	4	0		—	—	—

173

	Type	Overs	Mds	Runs	Wkt	Avge	Best	5 wI	10 wM
Carrick, P. (Y)	SLA	668.2	218	1717	55	31.21	5-32	3	—
Carter, R. M. (No)	RM	99	26	316	8	39.50	2-12	—	—
Cartwright, H. (D)	—								
Chandrasekhar, B. S. (Ind)	LBG	204.2	32	655	14	46.78	4-30	—	—
Chauhan, C. P. S. (Ind)	OB	38.3	5	132	4	33.00	1-7	—	—
Cheatle, R. G. L. (Sx)	SLA	185.1	49	467	21	22.23	6-32	2	—
Childs, J. H. (Gs)	SLA	658.3	195	1861	48	38.77	5-118	1	—
Clark, J. (Sc)	RM	43	14	101	5	20.20	4-53	—	—
Clarke, S. T. (Sy)	RFM	320.1	106	757	43	17.60	6-61	3	—
Claughton, J. A. (Wa/OU)	—								
Clements, S. M. (OU)	RM	38	9	160	3	53.33	1-29	—	—
Clifford, C. C. (Wa)	OB	682.4	154	2166	49	44.20	5-37	3	—
Clift, P. B. (Le)	RM	560.1	151	1412	50	28.24	5-57	1	—
Clinton, G. S. (Sy)	—								
Cockbain, I. (La)	—								
Colhoun, O. D. (Ire)	—								
Collins, B. G. (MCo)	RFM	37	6	110	3	36.66	3-83	—	—
Collyer, F. E. (MCo)	—								
Cook, G. (No)	SLA	11.3	4	31	0			—	—
Cook, N. G. B. (Le)	SLA	359.5	119	870	36	24.16	6-57	2	—
Cooper, H. P. (Y)	RM	142	36	387	11	35.18	2-16	—	—
Cooper, K. E. (Nt)	RM	177.4	45	536	15	35.73	4-42	—	—
Cooper, N. H. C. (CU)	OB	72	15	216	6	36.00	2-11	—	—
Cope, G. A. (Y)	OB	191.3	58	490	13	37.69	6-37	1	—
Cordle, A. E. (Gm)	RFM	609.3	133	1604	58	27.65	6-49	1	—
Corlett, S. C. (Ire)	RM	55	18	143	7	20.42	4-37	—	—
Cottrell, P. R. (CU)	—								
Cowdrey, C. S. (K)	RM	13.4	2	72	4	18.00	3-40	—	—
Cowley, N. G. (H)	OB	507.4	146	1306	37	35.29	5-44	1	—
Crawford, N. C. (CU)	RM	131.2	31	429	18	23.83	6-80	1	—
Cumbes, J. (Wo)	RFM	577.3	108	1591	48	33.14	6-103	3	—
Curtis, T. S. (Wo)	LB	1	0	2	0			—	—
Curzon, C. C. (Nt)	—								
Daniel, W. W. (M)	RF	429.2	100	1170	52	22.50	6-38	2	—
Davies, T. (Gm)	—								
Davison, B. F. (Le)	RM	0.5	0	7	0			—	—
Denness, M. H. (Ex)	—								
Denning, P. W. (So)	—								
De Silva, D. L. S. (SL)	RFM	79	23	199	6	33.16	2-28	—	—
De Silva, D. S. (SL)	LBG	298.1	89	781	35	22.31	8-46	3	2
De Silva, G. R. A. (SL)	SLA	291.3	85	699	30	23.30	6-30	1	—
Dewes, A. R. (CU)	—								
Dexter, R. E. (Nt)	—								
Dias, R. L. (SL)	RM	1	0	3	0			—	—
Dilley, G. R. (K)	RFM	446.4	110	1151	49	23.48	6-66	1	—
D'Oliveira, B. L. (Wo)	RM/OB	122	37	275	10	27.50	2-15	—	—
Downton, P. R. (K)	—								
Dredge, C. H. (So)	RM	251	60	759	25	30.36	4-40	—	—
Dudleston, B. (Le)	SLA	55	25	104	6	17.33	3-25	—	—
Ealham, A. G. E. (K)	OB	8.3	2	49	1	49.00	1-44	—	—
East, R. E. (Ex)	SLA	561.3	168	1290	43	30.00	5-56	1	—

174

	Type	Overs	Mds	Runs	Wkt	Avge	Best	5 wI	10 wM
Edmonds, P. H. (E/M/MCC)	SLA	564.4	181	1230	39	31.53	4-30	—	—
Edwards, T. D. W. (CU)	—								
Elder, J. W. G. (Ire)	RFM	33.2	12	85	3	28.33	2-28	—	—
Emburey, J. E. (M/MCC)	OB	746.2	225	1619	59	27.44	4-31	—	—
Featherstone, N. G. (M)	OB	191.1	40	568	23	24.69	4-28	—	—
Ferreira, A. M. (Wa)	RM	426	102	1210	31	39.03	5-66	·1	—
Finan, N. H. (Gs)	RM	16	4	61	0	—	—	—	—
Fisher, P. B. (M)	—								
Fletcher, C. D. B. (Sx)	RFM	19	4	51	1	51.00	1-35	—	—
Fletcher, K. W. R. (Ex)	LB	34.3	5	134	9	14.88	5-41	1	—
Foat, J. C. (Gs)	RM	4	0	17	0	—	—	—	—
Fowler, G. (La)	—								
Francis, D. A. (Gm)	—								
French, B. N. (Nt)	—								
Gaekwad, A. D. (Ind)	OB	13	4	55	1	55.00	1-10	—	—
Gandon, N. J. C. (OU)	—								
Gard, T. (So)	—								
Garner, J. (So)	RFM	393.1	127	761	55	13.83	6-80	4	—
Garnham, M. A. (Gs)	—								
Gatting, M. W. (M/MCC)	RM	69.4	11	222	4	55.50	2-57	—	—
Gavaskar, S. M. (Ind)	RM	8	1	23	0	—	—	—	—
Ghavri, K. D. (Ind)	LM/SLA	345.5	68	1122	27	41.55	5-23	1	—
Gifford, N. (Wo)	SLA	798.3	237	1848	78	23.69	5-12	2	—
Gill, P. N. (MCo)	—								
Goddard, G. F. (Sc)	OB	53.1	21	118	7	16.85	7-56	1	—
Gooch, G. A. (E/Ex/MCC)	RM	78	18	201	4	50.25	1-10	—	—
Goonetilleke, F. R. M.(SL)	RM	125	34	360	7	51.42	3-32	—	—
Gould, I. J. (M/MCC)	—								
†Gower, D. I. (E/Le/MCC)	—								
Graveney, D. A. (Gs)	SLA	417	98	1311	39	33.61	5-59	3	1
Graves, P. J. (Sx)	—								
Greenidge, C. G. (H)	—								
Greig, I. A. (CU)	RM	90	18	277	6	46.16	3-33	—	—
Griffiths, B. J. (No)	RFM	422.5	89	1222	50	24.44	5-76	1	—
Gurr, D. R. (So)	RFM	71	17	189	2	94.50	2-36	—	—
Hacker, P. J. (Nt)	LFM	177	42	639	15	42.60	4-46	—	—
Hadlee, R. J. (Nt)	RFM	317	103	753	47	16.02	7-23	2	—
Halliday, M. (Ire)	OB	65.2	29	110	5	22.00	5-39	1	—
Hampshire, J. H. (Y)	—								
Hardie, B. R. (Ex)	RM	5	0	39	2	19.50	2-39	—	—
Harris, M. J. (Nt)	LBG	10	2	31	0	—	—	—	—
Harrison, D. W. (Ire)	—								
Hartley, S. N. (Y)	—								
Hassan, B. (Nt)	—								
Hayes, F. C. (La)	—								
Hayward, R. E. (MCo)	—								
Head, T. J. (Sx)	—								
Hemmings, E. E. (Nt)	OB	738	226	1770	62	28.54	5-74	2	—
Hemsley, E. J. O. (Wo)	RM	8	3	22	1	22.00	1-11	—	—

	Type	Overs	Mds	Runs	Wkt	Avge	Best	5 wI	10 wM
Hendrick, M. (E/D/MCC)	RFM	456	150	885	42	21.07	4-32	—	—
Herkes, R. (M)	RM	25.4	2	84	6	14.00	6-60	1	—
Higgs, K. (Le)	RM	404.5	133	872	47	18.55	6-33	4	—
Hignell, A. J. (Gs)	LB	1	0	4	0	—	—	—	—
Hill, A. (D)	OB	11	1	61	2	30.50	1-15	—	—
Hills, R. W. (K)	RM	151	34	437	14	31.21	4-58	—	—
Hoadley, S. P. (Sx)	—	—	—	—	—	—	—	—	—
Hobbs, R. N. S. (Gm)	LBG	269.3	77	805	22	36.59	3-21	—	—
Hodgson, A. (No)	RFM	234	39	819	18	45.50	3-41	—	—
Hogg, W. (La/MCC)	RFM	240.4	48	791	27	29.29	4-26	—	—
Holder, V. A. (Wo)	RFM	405	75	1041	32	32.53	4-76	—	—
Holliday, D. C. (CU)	LB	53	12	181	4	45.25	2-23	—	—
Holmes, G. C. (Gm)	RM	41.9	9	201	7	28.71	4-78	—	—
Hopkins, D. C. (Wa)	RM	275	59	886	27	32.81	6-67	1	—
Hopkins, J. A. (Gm)	—	—	—	—	—	—	—	—	—
Howarth, G. P. (Sy)	OB	20	6	46	1	46.00	1-19	—	—
Howat, M. G. (CU)	RFM	30	3	116	1	116.00	1-47	—	—
Hughes, D. P. (La)	SLA	226.2	56	646	15	43.06	4-77	—	—
Humpage, G. W. (Wa)	RM	16	1	96	0	—	—	—	—
Humphries, D. J. (Wo)	—	—	—	—	—	—	—	—	—
Ikin, M. J. (MCo)	OB	35	8	112	0	—	—	—	—
Imran Khan (Sx)	RF	415.4	106	1091	73	14.94	6-37	7	—
Inchmore, J. D. (Wo)	RFM	521.4	102	1572	62	25.35	6-35	3	—
Ingham, P. G. (Y)	—	—	—	—	—	—	—	—	—
Intikhab Alam (Sy)	LBG	345.1	100	959	18	53.27	3-44	—	—
Jackman, R. D. (Sy)	RFM	628.1	173	1595	93	17.15	8-64	8	—
Jarvis, K. B. S. (K)	RFM	414.2	104	1275	38	33.55	4-42	—	—
Javed Miandad (Sx)	LBG	24	4	73	1	73.00	1-26	—	—
Jayasekera, R. S. A. (SL)	—	—	—	—	—	—	—	—	—
Jayasinghe, S. A. (SL)	—	—	—	—	—	—	—	—	—
Jeganathan, S. (SL)	SLA	87	25	265	7	37.85	4-92	—	—
Jennings, K. F. (So)	RM	245.3	78	620	20	31.00	4-25	—	—
Jesty, T. E. (H)	RM	44	12	140	3	46.66	2-17	—	—
Johnson, C. (Y)	—	—	—	—	—	—	—	—	—
Johnson, G. W. (K)	OB	448	143	1087	24	45.29	5-12	1	—
Johnson, J. S. (MCo)	—	—	—	—	—	—	—	—	—
Johnson, P. D. (MCo)	—	—	—	—	—	—	—	—	—
Johnston, R. I. (Ire)	RM	1	0	3	0	—	—	—	—
Jones, A. (Gm)	—	—	—	—	—	—	—	—	—
Jones, A. A. (M)	RFM	221.2	49	646	17	38.00	3-39	—	—
Jones, A. L. (Gm)	—	—	—	—	—	—	—	—	—
Jones, B. J. R. (Wo)	—	—	—	—	—	—	—	—	—
Jones, E. W. (Gm)	—	—	—	—	—	—	—	—	—
Kalicharran, A. I. (Wa)	OB	119.1	20	403	6	67.16	2-13	—	—
Kapil Dev (Ind)	RFM	422	96	1327	31	42.80	5-146	1	—
Kemp, N. J. (K)	RM	22	2	102	2	51.00	2-102	—	—
Kennedy, A. (La)	—	—	—	—	—	—	—	—	—
Ker, J. E. (Sc)	RM	17	6	45	2	22.50	1-2	—	—
Khanna, S. C. (Ind)	—	—	—	—	—	—	—	—	—
Kirsten, P. N. (D)	OB	269.3	65	752	19	39.57	4-44	—	—
Kitchen, M. J. (So)	—	—	—	—	—	—	—	—	—

176

	Type	Overs	Mids	Runs	Wkt	Avge	Best	5 wI	10 wM
Knight, J. M. (OU)	RFM	259.1	46	795	21	37.85	4-69	—	—
Knight, R. D. V. (Sy)	RM	260	66	728	29	25.10	5-44	2	—
Knott, A. P. E. (K)	—	—	—	—	—	—	—	—	—
Laing, J. R. (Sc)	—	—	—	—	—	—	—	—	—
Lamb, A. J. (No)	RM	6	1	15	1	15.00	1-13	—	—
Lamb, T. M. (No)	RM	329.5	94	997	24	41.54	4-58	—	—
Larkins, W. (No/MCC)	RM	33	8	117	3	39.00	1-14	—	—
Lawson, G. F. (La)	RFM	30	6	88	5	17.60	4-81	—	—
Leadbeater, B. (Y)	—	—	—	—	—	—	—	—	—
Lee, P. G. (La)	RFM	288.5	61	901	23	39.17	3-50	—	—
L'Estrange, M. G. (OU)	—	—	—	—	—	—	—	—	—
Lever, J. K. (E/Ex/MCC)	LFM	700	166	1834	106	17.30	8-49	8	2
Lewis, R. V. (MCo)	—	—	—	—	—	—	—	—	—
Lilley, A. W. (Ex)	—	—	—	—	—	—	—	—	—
Lister, J. W. (D)	—	—	—	—	—	—	—	—	—
Llewellyn, M. J. (Gm)	—	—	—	—	—	—	—	—	—
Lloyd, B. J. (Gm)	OB	396.1	89	1102	26	42.38	4-55	—	—
Lloyd, C. H. (La)	—	—	—	—	—	—	—	—	—
Lloyd, D. (La)	SLA	59.3	19	164	11	14.90	6-60	2	—
Lloyd, T. A. (Wa)	RM	10	2	57	1	57.00	1-26	—	—
Loyds, J. W. (So)	RM	6	3	14	0	—	—	—	—
Long, A. (Sx)	—	—	—	—	—	—	—	—	—
Love, J. D. (Y)	RM	10	1	35	0	—	—	—	—
Lumb, R. G. (Y)	—	—	—	—	—	—	—	—	—
Lynch, M.A. (Sy)	—	—	—	—	—	—	—	—	—
Lyon, J. (La)	—	—	—	—	—	—	—	—	—
McCurdy, R. J. (D)	RF	18	4	50	1	50.00	1-50	—	—
McEvoy, M. S. A. (Ex)	—	—	—	—	—	—	—	—	—
McEwan, K. S. (Ex)	—	—	—	—	—	—	—	—	—
McFarlane, L. (No)	RM	181	34	569	13	43.76	3-83	—	—
Mack, A. J. (Gm)	LM	176.3	27	572	14	40.85	4-62	—	—
Mackintosh, K. S. (M)	RM	10	3	23	0	—	—	—	—
McLellan, A. J. (D)	—	—	—	—	—	—	—	—	—
McPherson, T. I. (Sc)	SLA	18	6	46	1	46.00	1-46	—	—
Madugalle, R. S. (SL)	OB	9	0	32	0	—	—	—	—
Malone, M. F. (La)	RFM	102.3	32	230	19	12.10	7-88	3	1
Marie, G. V. (OU)	RM	21	4	46	5	9.20	5-46	1	—
Marks, V. J. (So)	OB	568.4	153	1581	57	27.73	6-33	4	—
Marsden, R. (OU)	—	—	—	—	—	—	—	—	—
Marshall, M. D. (H)	RFM	467	146	1051	47	22.36	5-56	1	—
Maynard, C. (Wa)	—	—	—	—	—	—	—	—	—
Mellor, A. J. (D)	SLA	97.1	19	311	8	38.87	3-28	—	—
Mendis, G. D. (Sx)	—	—	—	—	—	—	—	—	—
Mendis, L. R. D. (SL)	—	—	—	—	—	—	—	—	—
Merry, W. G. (M)	RM	150	36	431	10	43.10	3-46	—	—
Miller, G. (E/D)	OB	452.1	138	1047	37	28.29	6-53	2	—
Mills, J. P. C. (CU)	RM	1	0	5	0	—	—	—	—
Monteith, J. D. (Ire)	SLA	86	28	194	10	19.40	4-52	—	—
Morrill, N. D. (OU)	OB	145.4	28	490	8	61.25	3-53	—	—
Moseley, H. R. (So)	RFM	196.4	50	495	31	15.96	6-52	2	1
Moulding, R. P. (OU)	—	—	—	—	—	—	—	—	—
Mubarak, A. M. (CU)	RM/OB	1	0	6	0	—	—	—	—

177

	Type	Overs	Mds	Runs	Wkt	Avge	Best	5 wI	10 wM
Nash, M. A. (Gm)	LM	226.3	66	619	16	38.68	4-50	—	—
Neale, P. A. (Wo)	RM	1	0	5	0	—	—	—	—
Needham, A. (Sy)	—								
Nicholas, M. C. J. (H)	RFM	0.1	0	1	0	—	—	—	—
Northcote-Green, S. R. (OU)	—								
O'Brien, B. A. (Ire)	—								
O'Brien, N. T. (MCo)	RM	21	4	78	0	—	—	—	—
Old, C. M. (Y/MCC)	RFM	381.1	103	938	42	22.33	6-34	2	—
Oldham, S. (Y)	RFM	279.2	64	803	22	36.50	4-76	—	—
Olive, M. (Sc)	—								
Oliver, P. R. (Wa)	OB	141	27	482	7	68.85	2-50	—	—
Oliver, P. R. (wa)	OB	141	27	482	7	68.85	2-50	—	—
Ontong, R. C. (Gm)	RFM	302	62	927	32	28.96	5-40	2	—
Opatha, A. R. M. (SL)	RM	141	32	443	12	36.91	3-27	—	—
Orders, J. O. D. (OU)	LM	34	5	104	1	104.00	1-16	—	—
Ormrod, J. A. (Wo)	OB	1	0	14	0	—	—	—	—
Parker, P. W. G. (Sx/MCC)	RM	28	4	117	1	117.00	1-55	—	—
Parsons, G. J. (Le)	RM	54	17	179	9	19.88	4-43	—	—
Partridge, M. D. (Gs)	RM	296.4	51	1072	21	51.04	5-29	1	—
Parvez Mir (Gm)	RM	4	0	21	0	—	—	—	—
Pasqual, S. P. (SL)	RM	42.1	12	144	2	72.00	1-22	—	—
Patel, B. P. (Ind)	—								
Patel, D. N. (Wo)	OB	452.3	109	1461	37	39.48	5-95	1	—
Pauline, D. B. (Sy)	—								
Pearce, J. P. (OU)	SLA	97.2	17	344	7	49.14	4-94	—	—
Peck, I. G. (CU)	—								
Perry, N. J. (Gm)	SLA	174.4	39	563	13	43.30	3-51	—	—
Perryman, S. P. (Wa)	RM	671	224	1662	51	32.58	6-69	4	1
Phillip, N. (Ex)	RFM	548.1	128	1506	72	21.51	5-23	1	—
Phillipson, C. P. (Sx)	RM	203.5	53	477	20	23.85	4-24	—	—
Pigott, A. C. S. (Sx)	RFM	269	48	917	28	32.75	4-40	—	—
Pilling, H. (La)	—								
Pocock, N. E. J. (H)	LM	7	3	25	1	25.00	1-4	—	—
Pocock, P. I. (Sy)	OB	595.5	189	1435	70	20.50	9-57	4	1
Pont, K. R. (Ex)	RM	96	18	251	9	27.88	3-34	—	—
Popplewell, N. F. M. (So/CU)	RM	251	66	747	22	33.95	3-18	—	—
Pridgeon, A. P. (Wo)	RM	119	20	391	6	65.16	2-84	—	—
Pringle, D. R. (CU)	RM	247.3	74	559	22	25.40	4-43	—	—
Procter, M. J. (Gs)	RF/OB	574.5	140	1532	81	18.91	8-30	7	1
Racionzer, T. B. (Sc)	—								
Radley, C. T. (M)	LB	2	0	9	1	9.00	1-9	—	—
Ramage, A. (Y)	RM	129	38	348	15	23.20	3-24	—	—
Randall, D. W. (E/Nt)	—								
Ratcliffe, R. M. (La)	RM	450.5	131	1103	38	29.02	6-84	3	1
Rawlinson, J. L. (OU)	—								
Reddy, B. (Ind)	—								
Reidy, B. W. (La)	LM	148.4	2	468	16	29.25	5-61	1	—
Reith, M. S. (Ire)	RM	15	7	28	1	28.00	1-24	—	—

178

	Type	Overs	Mds	Runs	Wkt	Avge	Best	5wI	10wM
Rice, C. E. B. (Nt)	RFM	448	134	1139	58	19.63	6–49	3	—
Rice, J. M. (H)	RM	270.4	58	760	24	31.66	5–17	1	—
Richards, C. J. (Sy)	—	—	—	—	—	—	—	—	—
Richards, G. (Gm)	OB	57	15	164	9	18.22	3–4	—	—
Richards, I. M. (No)	RM	5	2	25	0		—	—	—
Richards, I. V. A. (So)	OB	77.3	11	270	5	54.00	2–47	—	—
Robertson, F. (Sc)	RM	42.3	14	91	8	11.37	5–35	1	—
Robinson, P. A. (La)	RFM	19.5	4	58	2	29.00	2–57	—	—
Robinson, R. T. (Nt)	—	—	—	—	—	—	—	—	—
Rock, D, J, (H)	—	—	—	—	—	—	—	—	—
Roebuck, P. M. (So)	OB	6	0	22	1	22.00	1–2	—	—
Rogers, J. J. (OU)	OB/LB	8	1	39	1	39.00	1–24	—	—
Roope, G. R. J. (Sy)	RM	40.4	6	167	5	33.40	2–5	—	—
Rose, B. C. (So)	LM	5	0	14	0		—	—	—
Ross, C. J. (OU)	RM	263.5	60	691	26	26.57	4–66	—	—
Rouse, S. J. (Wa)	LFM	20.3	3	80	6	13.33	4–41	—	—
Rowe, C. J. C. (K)	OB	53	17	150	6	25.00	4–4	—	—
Russell, P. E. (D)	RM/OB	121	29	335	6	55.83	3–102	—	—
Russom, N. (CU)	RM	27	5	88	2	44.00	1–28	—	—
Sadiq Mohammad (Gs)	LBG	48	7	180	4	45.00	3–97	—	—
Sainsbury, G. E. (Ex)	LM	23	2	79	1	79.00	1–38	—	—
Sanderson, J. F. W. (OU)	RM	23	8	66	2	33.00	2–52	—	—
Sarfraz Nawaz (No)	RFM	408.5	130	913	45	20.28	6–60	2	—
Savage, R. L. (Wa)	RM/OB	177.4	39	566	11	51.45	4–83	—	—
Schepens, M. (Le)	—	—	—	—	—	—	—	—	—
Scott, C. J. (La)	—	—	—	—	—	—	—	—	—
Selvey, M. W. W. (M)	RFM	576.3	177	1443	56	25.76	5–42	3	—
Shantry, B. K. (Gs)	—	—	—	—	—	—	—	—	—
Sharp, G. (No)	—	—	—	—	—	—	—	—	—
Sharp, K. (Y/MCC)	—	—	—	—	—	—	—	—	—
Shepherd, D. R. (Gs)	—	—	—	—	—	—	—	—	—
Shepherd, J. N. (K)	RM	418.3	114	1075	34	31.61	4–55	—	—
Short, J. F. (Ire)	—	—	—	—	—	—	—	—	—
Shuttleworth, K. (Le)	RFM	444	101	1273	45	28.28	4–59	—	—
Sidebottom, A. (Y)	RFM	294	72	826	31	26.64	4–59	—	—
Simmons, J. (La)	OB	454	112	1231	51	24.13	7–86	1	—
Skala, S. M. (OU)	—	—	—	—	—	—	—	—	—
Slack, W. N. (M)	RM	6	3	3	0		—	—	—
Slocombe, P. A. (So)	—	—	—	—	—	—	—	—	—
Smedley, M. J. (Nt)	—	—	—	—	—	—	—	—	—
Smith, A. V. (Ire)	—	—	—	—	—	—	—	—	—
Smith, C. L. (Gm)	—	—	—	—	—	—	—	—	—
Smith, D. M. (Sy)	RM	12	1	55	0		—	—	—
Smith, K. D. (Wa)	—	—	—	—	—	—	—	—	—
Smith, M. J. (M)	SLA	5	0	22	0		—	—	—
Smith, N. (Ex)	—	—	—	—	—	—	—	—	—
Southern, J. W. (H)	SLA	370.2	120	951	29	32.79	6–81	1	—
Spencer, J. (Sx)	RM	365.1	107	888	33	26.90	6–40	2	—
Steele, A. (Sc)	—	—	—	—	—	—	—	—	—
Steele, D. S. (D)	SLA	503.4	135	1459	48	30.39	6–91	1	—
Steele, J. F. (Le)	SLA	273.2	91	654	27	24.22	6–36	1	—
Stephenson, G. R. (H)	RM	1	1	0	0		—	—	—
Stevenson, G. B. (Y)	RM	498.3	124	1440	50	28.80	6–14	1	—

179

	Type	Overs	Mds	Runs	Wkt	Avge	Best	5 wI	10 wM
Stevenson, K. (H)	RFM	548.3	133	1567	69	22.71	7-22	4	—
Stewart, D. E. R. (Sc)	—	—	—	—	—	—	—	—	—
Stovold, A. W. (Gs)		13.4	4	39	1	39.00	1-4	—	—
Stovold, M. W. (Gs)	—	—	—	—	—	—	—	—	—
Surridge, D. (CU)	RFM	208.2	44	583	27	21.59	4-22	—	—
Swarbrook, F. W. (D)	SLA	41	5	161	0	—	—	—	—
Swart, P. D. (Gm)	RM	234.3	48	673	21	32.04	4-61	—	—
Tavare, C. J. (K)	RM	9.5	2	39	1	39.00	1-38	—	—
Taylor, D. J. S. (So)	—	—	—	—	—	—	—	—	—
Taylor, L. B. (Le)	RFM	352.3	77	958	44	21.77	6-61	2	—
Taylor, M. N. S. (H)	RM	265.5	70	746	27	27.62	5-33	1	—
Taylor, N. (K)	—	—	—	—	—	—	—	—	—
Taylor, R. W. (D)	—	—	—	—	—	—	—	—	—
Tennekoon, A. P. B. (SL)	—	—	—	—	—	—	—	—	—
Terry, V. P. (H)	—	—	—	—	—	—	—	—	—
Thomas, D. J. (Sy)	LM	169	32	556	13	42.76	6-84	1	—
Thomas, G. P. (Wa)	—	—	—	—	—	—	—	—	—
Thomas, J. G. (Gm)	RM	25	4	132	1	132.00	1-65	—	—
Titmus, F. J. (M)	OB	76	16	177	3	59.00	1-32	—	—
Todd, P. A. (Nt)	—	—	—	—	—	—	—	—	—
Tolchard, R. W. (Le)	—	—	—	—	—	—	—	—	—
Tomlins, K. P. (M)	RM	2	0	13	0	—	—	—	—
Tremlett, T. M. (H)	RM	89.2	21	248	8	31.00	2-9	—	—
Trim, G. E. (La)	LB	2	0	13	0	—	—	—	—
Tunnicliffe, C. J. (D)	LFM	454.5	107	1307	37	35.32	4-35	—	—
Tunnicliffe, H. T. (Nt)	RM	166.2	50	511	13	39.30	4-30	—	—
Turner, D. R. (H)	RM	15.2	5	66	3	22.00	1-1	—	—
Turner, G. M. (Wo)	—	—	—	—	—	—	—	—	—
Turner, S. (Ex)	RFM	576.3	164	1285	61	21.06	5-35	4	1
Underwood, D. L. (K)	LM	799.2	335	1575	106	14.85	8-28	10	4
Vengsarkar, D. B. (Ind)	—	—	—	—	—	—	—	—	—
Venkataraghavan, S. (Ind)	OB	391.5	96	1065	34	31.22	5-33	1	—
Viswanath, G. R. (Ind)	—	—	—	—	—	—	—	—	—
Waller, C. E. (Sx)	SLA	487.1	126	1262	39	32.35	4-18	—	—
Walters, J. (D)	RFM	380	80	1209	29	41.86	4-100	—	—
Warnapura, B. (SL)	RM	20.5	6	54	2	27.00	1-12	—	—
Warner, C. J. (Sc)	—	—	—	—	—	—	—	—	—
Watson, G. G. (Wo)	RFM	272.5	49	825	22	37.50	4-29	—	—
Watson, W. K. (Nt)	RFM	213.5	69	560	20	28.00	6-51	1	—
Watts, P. J. (No)	RM	107	24	304	7	43.42	2-10	—	—
Wells, C. M. (Sx)	RM	73.1	30	137	10	13.70	4-23	—	—
Wessels, K. C. (Sx)	OB	1	0	4	0	—	—	—	—
Weston, M. J. (Wo)	—	—	—	—	—	—	—	—	—
Wettimuny, S. R. D. (SL)	RM	1.3	0	10	1	10.00	1-10	—	—
Whitehouse, J. (Wa)	OB	13	2	85	1	85.00	1-17	—	—
Whiteley, J. P. (Y)	OB	209.2	67	546	10	54.60	3-85	—	—

180

	Type	Overs	Mds	Runs	Wkt	Avge	Best	5 wI	10 wM
Wijesuriya, R. G. C. E. (SL)	SLA	153	41	377	10	37.70	3–13	—	—
Wilkins, A. H. (Gm)	LM	248.5	56	717	30	23.90	6–79	3	—
Willey, P. (E/No/MCC)	OB	716.1	190	1697	52	32.63	5–46	3	—
Williams, R. G. (No)	OB	430	119	1184	36	32.88	5–57	1	—
Willis, R. G. D. (E/Wa)	RF	261	68	699	21	33.28	5–41	1	—
Wilson, P. H. L. (Sy)	RFM	284.5	63	861	30	28.79	4–39	—	—
Wincer, R. C. (D)	RFM	235.5	40	864	24	36.00	4–79	—	—
Windaybank, S. J. (Gs)	—	—	—	—	—	—	—	—	—
Wood, B. (La)	RM	161.2	30	513	18	28.50	4–58	—	—
Woolmer, R. A. (K)	RM	107	20	301	3	100.33	1–22	—	—
Wright, J. G. (D)	—	—	—	—	—	—	—	—	—
Yajurvindra Singh (Ind)	RM	138	26	437	15	29.13	5–75	1	—
Yardley, T. J. (No)	RM	0.3	0	3	0			—	—
Yashpal Sharma (Ind)	RM	31.1	3	123	3	41.00	1–13	—	—
Yeabsley, D. I. (MCo)	LM	44.3	11	120	3	40.00	2–53	—	—
Younis Ahmed (Wo)	LM/SLA	92.5	21	229	8	28.62	3–33	—	—
Zaheer Abbas (Gs)	OB	2	0	2	0			—	—
Zuill, A. M. (Sc)	—	—	—	—	—	—	—	—	—

Young Cricketer of the Year

At the end of each season the members of the Cricket Writers' Club select by ballot the player they consider the best young cricketer of the season.

P. W. G. Parker (Sussex) was elected last year.

The selections to date are:

1950 R. Tattersall (Lancashire)
1951 P. B. H. May (Surrey)
1952 F. S. Trueman (Yorkshire)
1953 M. C. Cowdrey (Kent)
1954 P. J. Loader (Surrey)
1955 K. F. Barrington (Surrey)
1956 B. Taylor (Essex)
1957 M. J. Stewart (Surrey)
1958 A. C. D. Ingleby-Mackenzie (Hampshire)
1959 G. Pullar (Lancashire)
1960 D. A. Allen (Gloucestershire)
1961 P. H. Parfitt (Middlesex)
1962 P. J. Sharpe (Yorkshire)
1963 G. Boycott (Yorkshire)
1964 J. M. Brearley (Middlesex)
1965 A. P. E. Knott (Kent)
1966 D. L. Underwood (Kent)
1967 A. W. Greig (Sussex)
1968 R. H. M. Cottam (Hampshire)
1969 A. Ward (Derbyshire)
1970 C. M. Old (Yorkshire)
1971 J. Whitehouse (Warwickshire)
1972 D. R. Owen-Thomas (Surrey)
1973 M. Hendrick (Derbyshire)
1974 P. H. Edmonds (Middlesex)
1975 A. Kennedy (Lancashire)
1976 G. Miller (Derbyshire)
1977 I. T. Botham (Somerset)
1978 D. I. Gower (Leicestershire)
1979 P. W. G. Parker (Sussex)

CAREER FIGURES FOR THE LEADING PLAYERS

The following are the abbreviated figures of the leading batsmen and bowlers based on their career averages, and fielders and wicket-keepers based on the number of their catches and dismissals. The figures are complete to the end of the 1979 season and the full career records will be found in the main tables on pages 184 to 201. The qualification for inclusion for batsmen and bowlers are 100 innings and 100 wickets respectively.

Only those players likely to play in first-class county cricket in 1980 have been included.

BATTING AND FIELDING

BATSMEN	Runs	Avge	100s	BOWLERS	Wkts	Avge
G. Boycott	35,761	56.94	115	J. Garner	185	18.20
Zaheer Abbas	22.739	50.31	68	W. W. Daniel	227	18.72
C. H. Lloyd	22,401	49.89	60	M. J. Procter	1,231	19.09
G. M. Turner	28.797	48.72	81	D. L. Underwood	1,840	19.28
I. V. A. Richards	14,108	47.34	38	M. D. Marshall	121	19.49
Javed Miandad	9.195	46.91	25	M. F. Malone	143	20.16
A. J. Lamb	4,666	46.19	10	G. S. Le Roux	133	20.73
D. L. Amiss	30,038	43.53	74	M. Hendrick	575	20.78
A. I. Kallicharran	17.150	43.30	40	G. G. Arnold	1,037	21.53
C. G. Greenidge	16,594	43.10	38	N. Gifford	1,565	21.68
P. N. Kirsten	5,957	38.93	16	C. M. Old	761	21.90
Sadiq Mohammad	17.940	38.49	41	R. J. Hadlee	420	22.24
K. W. R. Fletcher	28,521	38.38	48	S. T. Clarke	121	22.32
K. S. McEwan	11,305	38.32	27	G. Miller	399	22.91
B. F. Davison	17,304	38.03	30	I. T. Botham	471	22.93

FIELDERS	CT	WICKET-KEEPERS	Total	Ct	St
G. R. J. Roope	511	R. W. Taylor	1,316	1,174	142
K. W. R. Fletcher	487	A. P. E. Knott	1,048	943	105
D. S. Steele	429	A. Long	1,014	892	122
M. H. Denness	404	R. W. Tolchard	857	757	100
C. T. Radley	383	E. W. Jones	766	690	76
J. H. Hampshire	376	G. R. Stephenson	641	565	76
J. M. Brearley	362	D. L. Bairstow	613	528	85
J. A. Ormrod	352	D. J. S. Taylor	562	492	70
G. M. Turner	352	G. Sharp	429	361	68
K. Higgs	309	N. Smith	378	333	45
J. Birkenshaw	300	D. Nicholls	339	326	13
D. L. Amiss	299	M. J. Harris	282	268	14
D. Lloyd	292	G. W. Humpage	203	189	14
Asif Iqbal	287	A. W. Stovold	168	143	25
R. N. S. Hobbs	287	D. J. Humphries	152	130	22

Swivel head winner.

CAREER RECORDS
Compiled by Michael Fordham

The following career records are for all players appearing in first-class cricket in the 1979 season.

A few cricketers who did not re-appear for their counties in 1979, but who may do so in 1980 as well as others who appeared only in John Player League or other one-day matches.

†*Figures are incomplete for performances in Pakistan in 1977–78*

BATTING AND FIELDING

	M	I	NO	Runs	HS	Avge	100s	1000 runs S	Ct	St
†Aamer Hameed	51	68	10	846	103	14.58	2	—	15	—
Abberley, R. N.	261	439	27	10082	117*	24.47	3	3	171	—
Abrahams, J.	98	148	18	3174	126	24.41	2	—	62	—
Acfield, D. L.	267	278	136	1284	42	9.04	—	—	92	—
Agnew, J. P.	7	3	0	11	9	3.66	—	—	—	—
Allbrook, M. E.	44	55	18	320	39	8.64	—	—	14	—
Alleyne, H.	1	1	1	8	8*	—	—	—	—	—
Allott, P. J. W.	16	8	3	20	14	4.00	—	—	5	—
Amarnath, M.	137	219	39	6580	103*	36.55	10	0+2	91	—
Amiss, D. L.	459	783	93	30038	262*	43.53	74	15+1	299	—
Anderson, I. J.	16	28	7	801	147	38.14	3	—	9	—
Anderson, I. S.	11	19	4	238	75	15.86	—	—	4	—
Arnold, G. G.	323	340	77	3606	73	13.71	—	—	109	—
Arrowsmith, R.	43	40	12	286	39	10.21	—	—	13	—
Asif Iqbal	391	621	66	20715	196	37.37	40	6+2	287	—
Athey, C. W. J.	70	110	8	2337	131*	22.91	3	—	64	2
Bailey, D	31	44	1	1212	136	28.18	1	—	12	—
Bailey, M. J.	4	6	1	76	24	15.20	—	—	1	—
Bainbridge, P.	19	30	4	593	81*	22.80	—	—	8	—
Bairstow, D. L.	237	344	58	5987	106	20.93	2	—	528	85
Balderstone, J. C.	233	354	38	10193	178*	32.25	14	5	116	—
Barclay, J. R. T.	142	245	18	5462	112	24.06	5	4	103	—
Barlow, G. D.	131	209	29	5888	160*	32.71	8	3	71	—
Barnett, K. J.	23	36	6	752	96	25.06	—	—	13	—
Bedi, B. S.	353	408	106	3375	61	11.17	—	—	165	—
Bell, D. L.	5	9	1	88	20	11.00	—	—	2	—
Bennett, B. W. P.	2	2	0	4	4	2.00	—	—	—	—
Birch, J. D.	62	92	14	1465	94*	18.78	—	—	40	—
Birkenshaw, J.	466	637	119	12203	131	23.55	4	—	300	—
Black, T. M.	1	2	0	88	57	44.00	—	—	2	—
Booth, P.	79	68	19	576	58*	11.75	—	—	25	—
Bore, M. K.	96	95	29	526	37*	7.96	—	—	32	—
Borrington, A. J.	116	193	23	4137	137	24.33	3	—	57	—
Botham, I. T.	127	193	20	4812	167*	27.81	8	1	117	—
Boycott, G.	449	739	111	35761	261*	56.94	115	17+3	181	—
Boyns, C. N.	37	54	7	871	95	18.53	—	—	37	—
Brain, B. M.	228	239	61	1460	57	8.20	—	—	44	—
Brassington, A. J.	75	97	29	592	28	8.70	—	—	122	24
Breakwell, D.	205	276	58	4160	100*	19.08	1	—	77	—
Brearley, J. M.	383	654	86	20878	312*	36.75	31	8	362	12

184

	M	I	NO	Runs	HS	Avge	100s	1000 runs S	Ct	St
Briers, N. E.	51	86	7	1874	119	23.72	4	—	19	—
Broad, B. C.	9	16	2	512	129	36.57	1	—	3	—
Brown, A.	1	—	—	—	—	—	—	—	2	—
Brown, D. J.	387	445	110	4103	79	12.24	—	—	156	—
Burgess, G. I.	252	414	37	7129	129	18.90	2	—	119	—
Bury, T. E. O.	1	—	—	—	—	—	—	—	—	—
Bushe, E. A.	1	1	0	14	14	14.00	—	—	5	1
Butcher, A. R.	131	210	18	5237	188	27.27	8	1	41	—
Butcher, R. O.	55	91	3	2212	142	25.13	2	—	59	—
Carrick, P.	147	182	36	3178	128*	21.70	2	—	81	—
Carter, R. M.	12	11	4	102	26*	14.57	—	—	4	—
Cartwright, H.	82	128	16	2384	141*	21.28	1	—	31	—
Chandrasekhar, B. S.	240	240	113	597	25	4.70	—	—	106	—
Chauhan, C. P. S.	122	204	16	8189	207	43.55	20	0+2	138	—
Cheatle, R. G. L.	40	31	9	276	49	12.54	—	—	43	—
Childs, J. H.	80	69	43	145	12	5.57	—	—	30	—
Clark, J.	10	13	3	64	29	6.40	—	—	12	—
Clarke, S. T.	31	37	11	256	25	9.84	—	—	16	—
Claughton, J. A.	39	68	2	1377	130	20.86	2	—	16	—
Clements, S. M.	29	47	5	860	91	20.47	—	—	18	—
Clifford, C. C.	42	41	14	203	26	7.51	—	—	16	—
Clift, P. B.	145	212	53	3639	88*	22.88	—	—	72	—
Clinton, G. S.	54	88	8	2224	134*	27.80	2	1	23	—
Cockbain, I.	1	1	0	23	23	23.00	—	—	—	—
Colhoun, O. D.	28	35	18	74	9*	4.35	—	—	45	1
Collins, B. G.	1	—	—	—	—	—	—	—	—	—
Collyer, F. E.	5	8	1	96	46	13.71	—	—	11	1
Cook, G.	196	342	25	8956	155	28.25	10	5	206	—
Cook, N. G. B.	16	14	6	107	31	13.37	—	—	4	—
Cooper, H. P.	94	106	28	1134	56	14.53	—	—	58	—
Cooper, K. E.	56	50	12	270	19	7.10	—	—	19	—
Cooper, N. H. C.	24	39	2	825	106	22.29	1	—	10	—
Cope, G. A.	225	249	85	2298	78	14.01	—	—	68	—
Cordle, A. E.	307	429	75	5222	81	14.75	—	—	139	—
Corlett, S. C.	25	36	6	449	60	14.96	—	—	22	—
Cottrell, P. R.	10	9	1	119	34	14.87	—	—	17	4
Cowdrey, C. S.	54	67	12	1408	101*	25.60	1	—	31	—
Cowley, N. G.	90	143	24	2573	109*	21.62	1	—	40	—
Crawford, N. C.	14	15	1	178	46	12.71	—	—	3	—
Cumbes, J.	129	105	53	361	25*	6.94	—	—	28	—
Curtis, T. S.	1	2	0	42	27	21.00	—	—	1	—
Curzon, C. C.	7	8	3	62	26	12.40	—	—	5	2
Daniel, W. W.	84	73	31	414	30*	9.85	—	—	18	—
Davies, T.	1	—	—	—	—	—	—	—	3	—
Davison, B. F.	303	498	43	17304	189	38.03	30	9	230	—
Denness, M. H.	483	808	61	25081	195	33.57	33	14+1	404	—
Denning, P. W.	182	311	29	7823	122	27.74	6	4	89	—
De Silva, D. L. S.	4	3	1	11	7	5.50	—	—	2	—
De Silva, D. S.	36	55	9	851	76*	18.50	—	—	22	—
De Silva, G. R. A.	34	40	19	178	75	8.47	—	—	15	—
Dewes, A. R.	14	21	1	368	84	18.40	—	—	3	—
Dexter, R. E.	9	14	2	172	48	14.33	—	—	3	—

	M	I	No	Runs	HS	Avge	100s	1000 runs S	Ct	St
Dias, R. L.	28	49	8	1120	84*27.31		—	—	9	—
Dilley, G. R.	26	29	12	304	81	17.88	—	—	19	—
D'Oliveira, B. L.	361	564	88	18882	227	39.66	43	9	211	—
Downton, P. R.	52	48	10	405	31*10.65		—	—	114	12
Dredge, C. H.	58	69	22	758	56*16.12		—	—	24	—
Dudleston, B.	276	467	44	13920	202	32.90	31	8	223	7
Ealham, A. G. E.	281	430	65	10007	153	27.41	6	3	168	—
East, R. E.	323	413	97	5643	113	17.85	1	—	204	—
Edmonds, P. H.	203	282	48	4654	141*19.88		2	—	214	—
Edwards, T. D. W.	2	3	1	27	18	13.50	—	—	1	—
Elder, J. W. G.	7	7	2	19	7	3.80	—	—	6	—
Embnrey, J. E.	91	111	35	1323	91*17.40		—	—	96	—
Featherstone, N. G.	277	442	43	11578	147	29.01	9	2	231	—
Ferreira, A. M.	34	44	10	1016	84	29.88	—	—	22	—
Finan, N. H.	8	4	2	26	18	13.00	—	—	1	—
Fisher, P. B.	43	67	6	540	42	8.85	—	—	65	9
Fletcher, C. D. B.	1	—					—	—		—
Fletcher, K. W..R	522	868	125	28521	228*38.38		48	15	487	—
Flynn, V. A	3	2	1	21	15	21.00	—	—	4	—
Foat, J. C.	91	150	15	2512	126	18.60	5	—	39	—
Fowler, G.	2	4	0	24	20	6.00	—	—	1	—
Francis, D. A.	82	143	23	2589	110	21.57	1	—	41	—
French, B. N.	62	74	24	677	66	13.54	—	—	103	16
Gaekwad, A. D.	103	173	21	5330	155	35.06	12	0+1	52	—
Gandon, N. J. C	8	13	1	170	38	14.16	—	—	6	—
Gard, T.	9	9	5	83	51*20.75		—	—	13	4
Garner, J.	40	41	13	522	53	18.64	—	—	23	—
Garnham, M. A.	3	4	2	50	21	25.00	—	—	2	2
Gatting, M. W.	93	142	22	3555	128.	29.62	2	2	80	—
Gavaskar, S. M.	199	333	35	15508	282	52.04	51	2+6	197	—
Ghavri, K. D.	112	143	35	3175	102	29.39	1	—	43	—
Gifford, N.	510	604	185	5511	89	13.15	—	—	255	—
Gill, P. N.	2	4	0	64	20	16.00	—	—	1	—
Goddard, G. F.	21	32	4	357	39	12.75	—	—	7	—
Gooch, G. A.	135	220	19	6518	136	32.42	9	3	113	—
Goonetilleke,F.R.M.deS	11	12	4	130	60*16.25		—	—		—
Gould, I. J.	74	100	14	1653	128	19.22	1	—	131	20
Gower, D. I.	87	132	13	3887	200*32.66		6	1	35	—
Graveney, D. A.	153	214	49	2801	92	16.97	—	—	69	—
Graves, P. J.	288	495	51	11870	145*26.73		14	5	222	—
Greenidge, C. G.	235	410	25	16594	273*43.10		38	9	254	—
Greig, I. A.	27	38	3	798	96	22.80	—	—	12	—
Griffiths, B. J.	50	46	23	76	11	3.30	—	—	11	—
Gurr, D. R.	41	48	23	410	46*16.40		—	—	9	—
Hacker, P. J.	37	46	16	323	35	10.76	—	—	8	—
Hadlee, R. J.	106	147	28	2562	101*21.52		1	—	44	—
Halliday, M.	6	4	2	35	13*17.50		—	—	2	—
Hampshire, J. H.	478	765	87	22744	183*33.54		34	13	376	—
Hardie, D. R.	138	232	29	6605	162	32.53	9	4	131	—

186

	M	I	NO	Runs	HS	Avge	100s	S	Ct	St
Harris, M. J.	322	548	50	18630	201*37.40		41	11	268	14
Harrison, D. W.	2	1	0	0	0	0.00	—	—	2	—
Hartley, S. N.	4	7	1	157	53*26.16		—	—	1	—
Hassan, B.	243	402	36	10565	182*28.86		13	5	212	1
Hayes, F. C.	212	329	47	10313	187	36.57	18	5	152	—
Hayward, R. E.	1	1	0	0	0	0.00	—	—	1	—
Head, T. J.	12	14	5	175	31	19.44	—	—	35	2
Hemmings, E. E.	200	288	65	4759	85*21.34		—	—	96	—
Hemsley, E. J. O.	189	308	47	7979	176*30.57		8	1	147	—
Henderson, S. P.	12	19	3	237	52	14.81	—	—	6	—
Hendrick, M.	202	199	77	1209	46	9.90	—	—	132	—
Herbert, R.	3	5	0	33	12	6.60	—	—	2	—
Herkes, R.	3	5	3	0	0	0.00	—	—		—
Higgs, K.	505	526	204	3628	98	11.26	—	—	309	—
Hignell, A. J.	98	168	14	4142	149*26.89		7	2	104	—
Hill, A.	144	259	19	6749	160*28.12		7	2	57	—
Hills, R. W.	74	79	21	913	45	15.74	—	—	22	—
Hoadley, S. P.	12	19	0	329	112	17.31	1	—	5	—
Hobbs, R. N. S.	418	523	126	4805	100	12.10	2	—	287	—
Hodgson, A	99	118	24	909	41*	9.67	—	—	31	—
Hogg, W.	30	28	8	102	19	5.10	—	—	7	—
Holder, V. A.	305	346	80	3481	122	13.08	1	—	94	—
Holliday, D. C.	10	14	3	145	55*13.18		—	—	6	—
Holmes, G. C.	12	18	5	283	100*21.76		1	—	2	—
Hopkins, D. C.	23	25	3	159	34*	7.22	—	—	7	—
Hopkins, J. A.	115	203	13	5245	230	27.60	5	3	84	1
Howarth, G. P.	190	335	23	10187	183	32.65	19	3	124	—
Howat, M. G.	17	16	3	133	31	10.23	—	—	3	—
Hughes, D. P.	241	291	59	4263	101	18.37	1	—	151	—
Humpage, G. W.	95	145	18	4212	125*33.16		4	2	189	14
Humphries, D. J.	73	103	17	1905	111*22.15		1	—	130	22
Ikin, M. J.	2	3	0	40	31	13.33	—	—		—
Imran Khan	184	297	39	8168	170	31.65	14	3	69	—
Inchmore, J. D.	100	118	30	1337	113	15.19	1	—	37	—
Ingham, P. G.	2	3	0	32	17	10.66	—	—		—
Intikhab Alam	460	682	72	13646	182	22.37	9	—	225	—
Jackman, R. D.	325	390	126	4391	92*16.63		—	—	149	—
Jarvis, K. B. S.	97	68	34	118	12*	3.47	—	—	27	—
†Javed Miandad	140	233	37	9195	311	46.91	25	1+3	152	2
Jayasekera, R. S. A.	5	7	1	230	79*38.33		—	—	5	2
Jayasinghe, S. A.	6	7	1	183	64	30.50	—	—	10	4
Jeganathan, S.	17	22	3	181	20*	9.52	—	—	8	—
Jennings, K. F.	55	62	20	413	49	9.83	—	—	33	—
Jesty, T. E.	247	393	49	9760	159*28.37		12	4	149	1
Johnson, C.	100	152	14	2960	107	21.44	2	—	49	—
Johnson, G. W.	256	411	39	9612	168	25.56	10	3	205	—
Johnson, J. S.	1	2	1	170	146*170.00		1	—		—
Johnson, P. D.	88	147	14	3297	106*24.78		2	1	33	—
Johnston, R. I.	2	3	1	70	34	35.00	—	—	3	—
Jones, A.	554	1006	59	30914	187*32.64		48	19	269	—
Jones, A. A.	195	199	63	735	33	5.40	—	—	45	—
Jones, A. L.	47	84	6	1485	83	19.03	—	—	20	—

	M	I	NO	Runs	HS	Avge	100s	1000 runs S	Ct	St
Jones, B. J. R.	36	64	3	849	65	13.91	—	—	19	—
Jones, E. W.	330	493	105	7120	146*18.35		3	—	690	76
Kallicharran, A. I.	267	438	42	17150	197	43.30	40	7+1	185	—
Kapil Dev	50	68	5	1516	126*24.06		2	—	29	—
Kemp, N. J.	7	7	1	36	14	6.00	—	—	1	—
Kennedy, A	95	151	16	3818	176*28.28		4	1	61	—
Ker, J. E.	5	8	2	89	50	14.83	—	—	1	—
Khanna, S. C.	26	34	7	1279	136	47.37	4	—	51	15
Kirsten, P. N.	94	165	12	5957	206*38.93		16	2+1	65	—
Kitchen, M. J.	354	612	32	15230	189	26.25	17	7	157	—
Knight, J. M.	17	24	1	178	20	7.73	—	—	2	—
Knight, R. D. V.	268	474	38	13612	165*31.22		21	8	199	—
Knott, A. P. E.	389	571	104	14243	156	30.49	16	2	943	105
Laing, J. R.	8	15	1	301	127*21.50		1	—	6	—
Lamb, A. J.	74	124	23	4666	178	46.19	10	1	57	—
Lamb, T. M.	90	98	32	833	77	12.62	—	—	23	—
Larkins, W.	119	197	16	4922	170*27.19		11	2	63	—
Lawson, G. F.	15	23	4	197	39	10.36	—	—	9	—
Leadbeater, B.	147	241	29	5373	140*25.34		1	—	82	—
Lee, P. G.	179	146	63	715	26	8.61	—	—	28	—
Le Roux, G. S.	29	39	20	331	47*17.42		—	—	16	—
L'Estrange, M. G.	23	37	3	521	63	15.32	—	—	18	—
Lever, J. K.	311	323	137	1996	91	10.73	—	—	128	—
Lewis, R. V.	104	188	13	3371	136	19.26	2	—	65	—
Lilley, A. W.	5	7	1	198	100*33.00		1	—	1	—
Lister, J. W.	5	10	0	205	48	20.50	—	—	1	—
Llewellyn, M. J.	113	183	23	3762	129*23.51		3	—	74	—
Lloyd, B. J.	74	98	28	796	45*11.37		—	—	45	—
Lloyd, C. H.	342	524	75	22401	242*49.89		60	8+3	247	—
Lloyd, D.	334	536	60	15442	214*32.44		28	9	292	—
Lloyd, T. A.	36	59	11	1421	104	29.60	1	—	33	—
Lloyds, J. W.	4	7	0	117	43	16.71	—	—	2	—
Long, A.	436	522	126	6636	92	16.75	—	—	892	122
Love, J. D.	59	97	12	2388	170*28.09		4	—	35	—
Lumb, R. G.	166	277	22	8088	159	31.71	16	4	107	—
Lynch, M. A.	26	46	2	774	101	17.59	1	—	10	—
Lyon, J.	86	91	18	1016	123	13.91	1	—	159	12
McCurdy, R. J.	1	—	—	—	—	—	—	—	—	—
McEvoy, M. S. A.	16	26	1	404	67*16.16		—	—	18	—
McEwan, K. S.	189	320	25	11305	218	38.32	27	6	194	7
McFarlane, L.	8	2	0	0	0	0.00	—	—	3	—
Mack, A. J.	23	25	6	85	18	4.47	—	—	4	—
Mackintosh, K. S.	15	16	5	140	23*12.72		—	—	8	—
McLellan, A. J.	26	24	8	99	41	6.18	—	—	41	2
McPherson, T. I.	5	7	3	83	28	20.75	—	—	1	—
Madugalle, R. S.	7	8	0	242	88	30.25	—	—	8	—
Malone, M. F.	33	34	11	406	46	17.65	—	—	16	—
Malone, S. J.	2	—	—	—	—	—	—	—	—	—

	M	I	NO	runs	HS	Avge	100's	1000 runs S	Ct	St
Marie, G. V.	10	13	2	104	27	9.45	—	—	1	—
Marks, V. J.	90	146	16	3708	105	28.52	1	—	38	—
Marsden, R.	1	1	0	3	3	3.00	—	—	2	—
Marshall, M. D.	35	46	5	395	59	9.63	—	—	20	—
Maynard, C.	15	15	4	327	85	29.72	—	—	31	1
Mellor, A. J.	12	13	6	26	10*	3.71	—	—	4	—
Mendis, G. D.	61	107	12	2617	128	27.54	4	—	47	1
Mendis, L. R. D.	48	86	7	2671	194	33.81	5	—	17	1
Merry, W. G.	8	6	4	7	4*	3.50	—	—	1	—
Miller, G.	153	224	30	4961	98*25.57		—	—	87	—
Mills, J. P. C.	10	13	0	198	46	15.23	—	—	4	—
Monteith, J. D.	15	21	3	271	78	15.05	—	—	11	—
Morrill, N. D.	14	21	3	241	45	13.38	—	—	5	—
Moseley, H. R.	158	168	69	1203	67	12.15	—	—	58	—
Moulding, R. P.	17	25	4	448	77*21.33		—	—	9	—
Mubarak, A. M.	15	24	2	406	77	18.45	—	—	9	—
Nanan, N.	32	58	5	874	72	16.49	—	—	22	—
Nash, M. A.	274	392	58	6260	130	18.74	2	—	115	—
Neale, P. A.	80	140	15	4101	163*32.80		7	2	39	—
Needham, A.	13	13	1	83	21	6.91	—	—	5	—
Nicholas, M. C. J.	7	12	3	210	105*23.33		1	—	3	—
Nicholls, D.	202	342	24	7072	211	22.23	2	1	326	13
Northcote-Green, S.R.	9	16	2	138	38*	9.85	—	—	3	—
O'Brien, B. A.	9	14	1	244	45*18.76		—	—	5	—
O'Brien, N. T.	1	1	0	13	13	13.00	—	—	—	—
Old, C. M.	262	330	65	5775	116	21.79	6	—	163	—
Oldham, S.	49	31	14	119	50	7.00	—	—	15	—
Olive, M.	5	9	1	105	39	13.12	—	—	4	—
Oliver, P. R.	52	70	10	1210	83	20.16	—	—	26	—
Ontong, R. C.	101	165	16	3903	135*26.19		6	1	44	—
Opatha, A. R. M.	35	45	5	696	65	17.40	—	—	23	—
Orders, J. O. D.	13	23	1	536	79	24.36	—	—	3	—
Ormrod, J. A.	402	679	81	18230	204*30.48		24	11	352	—
Parker, P. W. G.	83	141	16	4323	215	34.58	9	3	45	—
Parsons, G. J.	5	6	1	31	17	6.20	—	—	—	—
Partridge, M. D.	35	48	15	916	90	27.75	—	—	12	—
†Parvez Mir	58	101	10	2928	155	32.17	5	—	53	—
Pasqual, S. P.	7	9	2	250	101*35.71		1	—	3	—
Patel, B. P.	141	223	33	7772	216	40.90	23	0+4	65	—
Patel, D. N.	75	107	7	2105	118*21.05		4	—	45	—
Pauline, D. B.	1	—	—	—	—	—	—	—	1	—
Payne, I. R.	12	15	1	96	29	6.85	—	—	10	—
Pearce, J. P.	7	11	5	22	8*	3.66	—	—	2	—
Peck, I. G.	6	8	0	26	11	3.25	—	—	1	—
Perry, N. J.	6	6	3	8	5*	2.66	—	—	1	—
Perryman, S. P.	103	101	39	631	43	10.17	—	—	36	—
Phillip, N.	104	157	23	3440	134	25.67	1	—	31	—

189

	M	I	NO	Runs	HS	Avge	100's	1000 runs S	Ct	St
Phillipson, C. P.	105	137	45	1563	70	16.98	—	—	58	—
Pigott, A. C. S.	20	26	3	361	55	15.69	—	—	7	—
Pilling, H.	330	536	67	15199	149*	32.40	25	8	88	—
Pocock, N. E. J.	27	48	6	838	143*	19.95	1	—	24	—
Pocock, P. I.	410	453	107	4038	75*	11.67	—	—	140	—
Pont, K. R.	114	179	24	3670	113	23.67	5	—	62	—
Popplewell, N. F. M.	32	40	7	595	92	18.03	—	—	7	—
Pridgeon, A. P.	76	70	31	277	32	7.10	—	—	20	—
Pringle, D. R.	14	18	4	464	103*	33.14	1	—	8	—
Procter, M. J.	339	568	52	19324	254	37.44	45	8	278	—
Racionzer, T. B.	42	74	9	1294	91	19.92	—	—	35	—
Radley, C. T.	378	612	82	18304	171	34.53	30	12	383	—
Ramage, A.	5	5	3	33	19	16.50	—	—	—	—
Randall, D. W.	198	342	30	10714	209	34.33	16	5	112	—
Ratcliffe, R. M.	78	81	22	984	101*	16.67	1	—	23	—
Rawlinson, J. L.	4	6	2	27	13*	6.75	—	—	2	—
Reddy, B	51	60	12	617	60	12.85	—	—	100	30
Reidy, B. W.	67	99	17	2147	131*	26.18	1	—	33	—
Reith, M. S.	8	14	0	283	82	20.21	—	—	5	—
Rice, C. E. B.	185	310	45	10075	246	38.01	11	5	134	—
Rice, J. M.	125	192	15	3504	96*	19.79	—	—	114	—
Richards, C. J.	59	64	15	630	50	12.85	—	—	99	21
Richards, G.	107	173	25	3370	102*	22.77	1	—	36	—
Richards, I. M.	23	25	4	467	50	22.23	—	—	5	—
Richards, I. V. A.	187	319	21	14108	291	47.34	38	6+2	174	—
Robertson, F.	10	15	1	151	51	10.78	—	—	3	—
Robinson, P. A.	9	8	3	105	25*	21.00	—	—	1	—
Robinson, R. T.	2	4	1	104	40	34.66	—	—	1	—
Rock, D. J.	37	65	1	1227	114	19.17	3	—	19	—
Roebuck, P. M.	92	156	29	4153	158	32.70	4	1	55	—
Rogers, J. J.	11	19	2	237	33*	13.94	—	—	3	—
Roope, G. R. J.	344	552	109	16652	171	37.58	24	8	511	1
Rose, B. C.	156	268	24	7908	205	32.40	17	5	74	—
Ross, C. J.	23	28	11	68	16*	4.00	—	—	6	—
Rouse, S. J.	109	131	26	1603	93	15.26	—	—	50	—
Rowe, C. J. C.	102	160	31	3545	147*	27.48	4	1	33	—
Russell, P. E.	167	207	44	2015	72	12.36	—	—	124	—
Russom, N.	3	3	1	32	12	16.00	—	—	—	—
Sadiq Mohammad	285	495	29	17940	184*	38.49	41	6+2	226	—
Sainsbury, G. E.	1	—	—	—	—	—	—	—	1	—
Sanderson, J. F. W.	1	1	0	2	2	2.00	—	—	1	—
Sarfraz Nawaz	220	284	58	4311	86	19.07	—	—	122	—
Savage, R. L.	44	52	25	196	22*	7.25	—	—	14	—
Saxelby, K.	2	3	1	3	3*	1.50	—	—	1	—
Schepens, M.	18	26	5	399	57	19.00	—	—	12	—
Scott, C. J.	8	9	2	49	16	7.00	—	—	16	3
Selvey, M. W. W.	187	187	69	1175	45	9.95	—	—	52	—

	M	I	NO	Runs	HS	Avge	100's	1000 runs S	Ct	St
Shantry, B. K.	3	—	—	—	—	—	—	—	—	—
Sharp, G.	192	264	52	3932	85	18.54	—	—	361	68
Sharp, K.	44	71	9	1585	91	25.56	—	—	11	—
Shepherd, D. R.	282	476	40	10672	153	24.47	12	2	95	—
Shepherd, J. N.	317	461	70	10116	170	25.87	7	1	236	—
Short, J. F.	7	11	1	393	114	39.30	1	—	4	—
Shuttleworth, K.	236	239	85	2583	71	16.77	—	—	127	—
Sidebottom, A.	48	58	11	830	124	17.65	1	—	15	—
Simmons, J.	265	314	86	4962	112	21.76	3	—	205	—
Skala, S. M.	2	3	0	18	11	6.00	—	—	6	1
Slack, W. N.	19	33	1	569	66	17.78	—	—	9	—
Slocombe, P. A.	98	169	22	4408	132	29.98	6	2	48	—
Smedley, M. J.	360	604	76	16482	149	31.21	28	9	261	—
Smith, A. V.	2	1	1	11	11*	—	—	—	1	—
Smith, C. L.	2	4	1	82	67	27.33	—	—	2	—
Smith, D. M.	75	107	27	1952	115	24.40	2	—	36	—
Smith, K. D.	83	143	12	3747	135	28.60	5	2	25	—
Smith, M. J.	417	698	78	19731	181	31.82	40	11	216	—
Smith, N.	156	202	44	2855	126	18.06	2	—	333	45
Southern, J. W.	95	107	46	695	61*	11.39	—	—	27	—
Spencer, J.	207	277	76	2721	79	13.53	—	—	72	—
Steele, A.	13	24	0	617	97	25.70	—	—	12	1
Steele, D. S.	381	637	82	18565	140*	33.45	29	10	429	—
Steele, J. F.	246	409	44	11047	195	30.26	17	6	275	—
Stephenson, G. R.	255	334	61	4477	100*	16.39	1	—	565	76
Stevenson, G. B.	80	95	14	1754	83	21.65	—	—	38	—
Stevenson, K.	91	109	38	581	33	8.18	—	—	29	—
Stewart, D. E. R.	32	51	3	854	69	17.79	—	—	17	—
Stovold, A. W.	135	242	11	6862	196	29.70	6	3	143	25
Stovold, M. W.	7	10	1	84	27	9.33	—	—	1	—
Stuchbury, S.	1	—	—	—	—	—	—	—	—	—
Surridge, D.	9	8	6	40	14*	20.00	—	—	3	—
Surridge, S. S.	1	1	1	2	2*	—	—	—	1	—
Swarbrook, F. W.	220	321	87	4859	90	20.76	—	—	137	—
Swart, P. D.	129	202	23	4457	122	24.89	6	1	73	—
Tavare, C. J.	99	164	22	5147	150*	36.24	8	3	114	—
Taylor, D. J. S.	241	340	74	5957	179	22.39	4	1	492	70
Taylor, L. B.	29	17	8	54	15	6.00	—	—	7	—
Taylor, M. N. S.	365	503	114	7752	105	19.92	3	—	211	—
Taylor, N.	1	2	0	121	110	60.50	1	—	—	—
Taylor, R. W.	503	704	129	9822	97	17.08	—	—	1174	142
Tennekoon, A. P. B.	61	107	11	3481	169*	36.26	5	—	60	—
Terry, V. P.	7	10	0	102	21	10.20	—	—	4	—
Thomas, D. J.	23	27	6	132	15*	6.28	—	—	7	—
Thomas, G. P.	2	3	0	14	9	4.66	—	—	—	—
Thomas, J. G.	1	1	0	34	34	34.00	—	—	—	—
Titmus, F. J.	786	1135	204	21564	137*	23.16	6	8	472	—
Todd, P. A.	104	183	7	4934	178	28.03	5	3	77	—
Tolchard, R. W.	390	541	157	12022	126*	31.30	10	—	757	100
Tomlins, K. P.	15	20	2	300	94	16.66	—	—	10	—

191

	M	I	NO	Runs	HS	Avge	100s	1000 runs S	Ct	St
Tremlett, T. M.	14	24	5	253	50	13.31	—	—	5	—
Trim, G. E.	10	17	0	294	91	17.29	—	—	9	—
Tunnicliffe, C. J.	76	83	20	848	82*13.46		—	—	31	—
Tunnicliffe, H. T.	55	93	24	1820	97*26.37		—	—	30	—
Turner, D. R.	263	441	36	11384	181*28.10		18	6	145	—
Turner, G. M.	391	681	90	28797	259	48.72	81	12+3	352	—
Turner, S	266	384	72	6764	121	21.67	4	—	178	—
Underwood. D. L.	470	506	130	3476	80	9.24	—	—	208	—
Vengsarkar, D. B.	74	116	12	4644	175	44.65	13	0+1	55	—
Venkataraghavan, S.	292	402	75	5936	137	18.15	1	—	273	—
Viswanath, G. R.	211	343	30	13284	247	42.44	32	0+4	160	—
Waller, C. E.	142	154	54	880	47	8.80	—	—	77	—
Walters, J.	41	54	11	836	90	19.44	—	—	10	—
Warnapura, B.	37	64	7	1624	154	28.49	2	—	20	—
Warner, C. J.	3	5	1	80	28	20.00	—	—	1	—
Watson, G. G.	44	58	15	552	38	12.83	—	—	11	—
Watson, W. K.	51	60	25	432	28*12.34		—	—	19	—
Watts, P. J.	361	592	87	14229	145	28.17	10	7	266	—
Wells, C. M.	5	6	1	60	29	12.00	—	—	1	—
Wessels, K. C.	65	113	13	4525	187	45.25	10	1	48	—
Weston, M. J.	1	2	0	59	43	29.50	—	—	—	—
Wettimony, S. R. De S	38	68	1	1681	121	25.08	2	—	17	1
White, R. A.	411	639	105	12442	116*23.29		5	1	188	—
Whitehouse, J.	170	290	30	7968	173	30.64	14	3	117	—
Whiteley, J. P.	21	12	5	60	20	8.57	—	—	9	—
Wijesuriya, R.G.C.E.	6	5	2	51	25	17.00	—	—	7	—
Wilkins, A. H.	51	58	19	317	70	8.12	—	—	16	—
Willey, P.	263	427	63	9693	227	26.62	12	2	112	—
Williams, R. G.	63	98	12	2023	151*23.52		4	1	25	—
Willis, R. G. D.	205	211	100	1626	43	14.64	—	—	92	—
Wilson, P. H. L.	26	15	11	57	15	14.25	—	—	4	—
Wincer, R. C.	21	21	8	131	26	10.07	—	—	8	—
Windaybank, S. J.	2	3	0	101	53	33.66	—	—	—	—
Wood, B.	294	484	62	14261	198	33.79	24	7	226	—
Woolmer, R. A.	268	404	64	11410	169	33.55	23	5	183	—
Wright, J. G.	92	166	12	5369	164	34.86	10	2	59	—
Yajurvindra Singh	62	94	23	3008	154*42.36		6	—	66	—
Yardley, T. J.	209	317	55	6688	135	25.52	4	1	184	2
Yashpal Sharma	48	81	17	3015	173	47.10	7	—	20	1
Yeabsley, D. I.	3	5	3	24	14*12.00		—	—	1	—
Younis Ahmed	329	555	78	17806	221*37.32		27	8	179	—
Zaheer Abbas	291	494	50	22339	274	50.31	68	8+4	212	—
Zuill, A. M.	9	17	2	231	62	15.40	—	—	1	—

BOWLING

	Runs	Wkts	Avge	BB	5 Wl	10 Wm	100 WS
†Aamer Hameed	3982	106	37.56	7–35	5	1	—
Abberley, R. N.	294	5	58.80	2–19	—	—	—
Abrahams, J.	31	0	—	—	—	—	—
Acfield, D. L.	17363	619	28.05	7–36	22	2	—
Agnew, J. P.	414	13	31.84	3–51	—	—	—
Allbrook, M. E.	3373	75	44.97	7–79	2	—	—
Alleyne, H.	41	2	20.50	1–14	—	—	—
Allott, P. J. W.	1065	27	39.44	5–39	2	—	—
Amarnath, M.	6956	218	31.90	7–27	6	1	—
Amiss, D. L.	700	18	38.88	3–21	—	—	—
Anderson, I. J.	196	16	12.25	5–21	1	—	—
Anderson, I. S.	163	2	81.50	1–24	—	—	—
Arnold, G. G.	22331	1037	21.53	8–41	44	3	1
Arrowsmith, R.	2796	99	28.24	6–29	4	—	—
Asif Iqbal	8589	288	29.82	6–45	5	—	—
Athey, C. W. J.	602	14	43.00	3–38	—	—	—
Bailey, D.	72	0	—	—	—	—	—
Bailey, M. J.	151	3	50.33	2–65	—	—	—
Bainbridge, P.	299	7	42.71	2–30	—	—	—
Bairstow, D. L.	167	5	33.40	3–82	—	—	—
Balderstone, J. C.	6686	268	24.94	6–25	5	—	—
Barclay, J. R. T.	4772	162	29.45	6–61	6	1	—
Barlow, G. D.	14	1	14.00	1–6	—	—	—
Barnett, K. J.	387	4	96.75	1–14	—	—	—
Bedi, B. S.	32725	1507	21.71	7–5	102	20	2
Bell, D. L.	—	—	—	—	—	—	—
Bennett, B. W. P.	—	—	—	—	—	—	—
Birch, J. D.	1792	36	49.77	6–64	1	—	—
Birkenshaw, J.	28258	1050	26.91	8–94	44	4	2
Black, T. M.	—	—	—	—	—	—	—
Booth, P.	4007	143	28.02	6–93	1	—	—
Bore, M. K.	6751	223	30.27	8–89	7	—	—
Borrington, A. J.	19	0	—	—	—	—	—
Botham, I. T.	10803	471	22.93	8–34	30	4	1
Boycott, G.	1114	32	34.81	4–14	—	—	—
Boyns, C. N.	1668	36	46.33	3–24	—	—	—
Brain, B. M.	17976	751	23.93	8–55	30	6	—
Brassington, A. J.	10	0	—	—	—	—	—
Breakwell, D.	11258	381	29.54	8–39	11	1	—
Brearley, J. M.	103	1	103.00	1–21	—	—	—
Briers, N. E.	41	1	41.00	1–22	—	—	—
Broad, B. C.	—	—	—	—	—	—	—
Brown, A.	—	—	—	—	—	—	—
Brown, D. J.	28757	1161	24.76	8–60	46	5	—
Burgess, G. I.	13543	474	28.57	7–43	18	2	—
Bury, T. E. O.	—	—	—	—	—	—	—
Bushe, E. A.	—	—	—	—	—	—	—
Butcher, A. R.	2976	78	38.15	6–48	1	—	—
Butcher, R. O	34	0	—	—	—	—	—

193

	Runs	Wkts	Avge	BB	5 Wl	10 Wm	100 WS
Carrick, P.	11059	410	26.97	8–33	21	2	—
Carter, R. M.	359	8	44.87	2–12	—	—	—
Cartwright, H.	11	0	—		—	—	—
Chandrasekhar, B. S.	24772	1032	24.00	9–72	73	19	—
Chauhan, C. P. S.	1398	41	34.09	6–26	1	—	—
Cheatle, R. G. L.	2409	77	31.28	6–32	4	—	—
Childs, J. H.	6290	202	31.13	8–34	9	2	—
Clark, J.	610	27	22.59	4–10	—	—	—
Clarke, S. T.	2701	121	22.32	6–39	6	1	—
Claughton, J. A.	4	0	—		—	—	—
Clements, S. M.	205	3	68.33	1–29	—	—	—
Clifford, C. C.	4052	113	35.85	6–89	6	—	—
Clift, P. B.	9787	395	24.77	8–17	13	—	—
Clinton, G. S.	9	2	4.50	2–8	—	—	—
Cockbain, I.	—	—	—		—	—	—
Colhoun, O. D.	—	—	—		—	—	—
Collins, B. G.	110	3	36.66	3–83	—	—	—
Collyer, F. E.	—	—	—		—	—	—
Cook, G.	115	0	—		—	—	—
Cook, N. G. B.	953	39	24.43	6–57	2	—	—
Cooper, H. P.	6098	222	27.46	8–62	4	1	—
Cooper, K. E.	3542	121	29.27	6–32	3	—	—
Cooper, N. H. C.	277	7	39.57	2–11	—	—	—
Cope, G. A.	15390	644	23.89	8–73	35	6	—
Cordle, A. E.	18911	693	27.28	9–49	19	2	—
Corlett, S. C.	1658	45	36.84	5–62	1	—	—
Cottrell, P. R.	—	—	—		—	—	—
Cowdrey, C. S.	183	6	30.50	3–40	—	—	—
Cowley, N. G.	4960	139	35.68	5–44	3	—	—
Crawford, N. C.	462	18	25.66	6–80	1	—	—
Cumbes, J.	9048	315	28.72	6–24	12	—	—
Curtis, T. S.	2	0	—		—	—	—
Curzon, C. C.	—	—	—		—	—	—
Daniel, W. W.	5187	277	18.72	6–21	14	3	—
Davies, T.	—	—	—		—	—	—
Davison, B. F.	2533	81	31.27	5–52	1	—	—
Denness, M. H.	62	2	31.00	1–17	—	—	—
Denning, P. W.	70	1	70.00	1–4	—	—	—
De Silva, D. L. S.	199	6	33.16	2–28	—	—	—
De Silva, D. S.	3616	151	23.94	8–46	11	5	—
De Silva, G. R. A.	3005	117	25.68	6–30	3	—	—
Dewes, A. R.	146	1	146.00	1–52	—	—	—
Dexter, R. E.	—	—	—		—	—	—
Dias, R. L.	3	0	—		—	—	—
Dilley, G. R.	1371	57	24.05	6–66	2	—	—
D'Oliveira, B. L.	15009	548	27.38	6–29	17	2	—
Downton, P. R.	—	—	—		—	—	—
Dredge, C. H.	4076	127	32.09	5–53	2	—	—
Dudleston, B.	995	35	28.42	4–6	—	—	—

	Runs	Wkts	Avge	BB	5 Wl	10 Wm	100 WS
Ealham, A. G. E.	147	3	49.00	1–1	—	—	—
East, R. E.	20639	823	25.07	8–30	38	7	—
Edmonds, P. H.	16471	661	24.91	8–132	27	4	—
Edwards, T. D. W.	—	—	—	—	—	—	—
Elder, J. W. G.	232	11	21.09	3–56	—	—	—
Emburey, J. E.	6729	291	23.12	7–36	14	3	—
Featherstone, N. C.	4434	169	26.23	5–32	3	—	—
Ferreira, A. M.	2800	100	28.00	8–38	7	1	—
Finan, N. H.	313	4	78.25	2–57	—	—	—
Fisher, P. B.	—	—	—	—	—	—	—
Fletcher, C. D. B.	51	1	51.00	1–35	—	—	—
Fletcher, K. W. R.	1644	41	40.09	5–41	1	—	—
Flynn, V. A.	—	—	—	—	—	—	—
Foat, J. C.	40	0	—	—	—	—	—
Fowler, G.	—	—	—	—	—	—	—
Francis, D. A.	6	0	—	—	—	—	—
French, B. N.	—	—	—	—	—	—	—
Gaekwad, A. D.	2406	73	32.95	6–49	2	—	—
Gandon, N. J. C.	—	—	—	—	—	—	—
Gard, T.	—	—	—	—	—	—	—
Garner, J.	3368	185	18.20	8–31	11	—	—
Garnham, M. A.	—	—	—	—	—	—	—
Gatting, M. W.	1439	56	25.69	5–59	1	—	—
Gavaskar, S. M.	909	19	47.84	3–43	—	—	—
Ghavri, K. D.	9495	359	26.44	7–34	15	2	—
Gifford, N.	33933	1565	21.68	8–28	75	11	3
Gill, P. N.	—	—	—	—	—	—	—
Goddard, G. F.	1050	41	25.60	8–34	2	1	—
Gooch, G. A.	1316	30	43.86	5–40	1	—	—
Goonetilleke,F.R.M.deS.	688	16	43.00	5–79	1	—	—
Gould, I. J.	—	—	—	—	—	—	—
Gower, D. I.	61	3	20.33	3–47	—	—	—
Graveney, D. A,	10446	356	29.34	8–85	15	3	—
Graves, P. J.	797	15	53.13	3–69	—	—	—
Greenidge, C. G.	431	16	26.93	5–49	1	—	—
Greig, I. A.	1387	35	39.62	4–76	—	—	—
Griffiths, B. J.	3831	131	29.24	5–66	3	—	—
Gurr, D. R.	3079	110	27.99	6–82	5	—	—
Hacker, P. J.	2441	51	47.86	4–46	—	—	—
Hadlee, R. J.	9341	420	22.24	7–23	20	4	—
Halliday, M.	303	14	21.64	5–39	1	—	—
Hampshire, J. H.	1585	29	54.65	7–52	2	—	—
Hardie, D. R.	60	2	30.00	2–39	—	—	—
Harris, M. J.	3384	79	42.83	4–16	—	—	—
Harrison, D. W.	—	—	—	—	—	—	—

	Runs	Wkts	Avge	BB	5 Wl	10 Wm	100 WS
Hartley, S. N.	6	0	—	—	—	—	—
Hassan, B.	407	6	67.83	3–33	—	—	—
Hayes, F. C.	15	0	—	—	—	—	—
Hayward, R. E.	—	—	—	—	—	—	—
Head, T. J.	—	—	—	—	—	—	—
Hemmings, E. E.	15967	507	31.49	7–33	21	5	—
Hemsley, E. J. O	2305	68	33.89	3–5	—	—	—
Henderson, S. P.	30	0	—	—	—	—	—
Hendrick, M.	11953	575	20.78	8–45	19	3	—
Herbert, R.	—	—	—	—	—	—	—
Herkes, R.	93	6	15.50	6–60	1	—	—
Higgs, K.	35910	1524	23.56	7–19	49	5	5
Hignell, A. J.	158	0	—	—	—	—	—
Hill, A.	128	5	25.60	3–5	—	—	—
Hills, R. W.	3970	145	27.37	6–64	2	—	—
Hoadley, S. P.	—	—	—	—	—	—	—
Hobbs, R. N. S.	28211	1056	26.71	8–63	48	8	2
Hodgson, A.	5964	206	28.95	5–30	2	—	—
Hogg, W.	1933	73	26.47	7–84	3	—	—
Holder, V. A.	22744	932	24.40	7–40	38	3	—
Holliday, D. C.	181	4	45.25	2–23	—	—	—
Holmes, G. C.	242	7	34.57	4–78	—	—	—
Hopkins, D. C.	1371	37	37.05	6–67	1	—	—
Hopkins, J. A.	27	0	—	—	—	—	—
Howarth, G. P.	2587	86	30.08	5–32	1	—	—
Howat, M. G.	881	18	48.94	3–39	—	—	—
Hughes, D. P.	15307	525	29.15	7–24	19	2	—
Humpage, G. W.	96	0	—	—	—	—	—
Humphries, D. J.	—	—	—	—	—	—	—
Ikin, M. J.	112	0	—	—	—	—	—
Imran Khan	15418	622	24.78	7–52	36	6	—
Inchmore, J. D.	7212	268	26.91	8–58	10	1	—
Ingham, P. G.	—	—	—	—	—	—	—
Intikhab Alam	41078	1469	27.96	8–54	81	13	1
Jackman, R. D.	25979	1122	23.15	8–40	53	7	—
Jarvis, K. B. S.	7134	253	28.19	8–97	6	1	—
†Javed Miandad	4859	153	31.75	6–93	5	—	—
Jayasekera, R. S. A.	—	—	—	—	—	—	—
Jayasinghe, S. A.	—	—	—	—	—	—	—
Jeganathan, S.	879	33	26.63	5–34	1	—	—
Jennings, K. F.	2714	78	34.79	5–18	1	—	—
Jesty, T. E.	10578	371	28.51	7–75	12	—	—
Johnson, C.	265	4	66.25	2–22	—	—	—
Johnson, G. W.	10693	340	31.45	6–32	9	1	—
Johnson, J. S.	—	—	—	—	—	—	—
Johnson, P. D.	972	11	38.36	3–34	—	—	—
Johnston, R. I.	3	0	—	—	—	—	—
Jones, A.	329	3	109.66	1–24	—	—	—
Jones, A. A.	13573	500	27.14	9–51	22	3	—
Jones, A. L.	17	0	—	—	—	—	—

	Runs	Wkts	Avge	BB	5 Wl	10 Wm	100 WS
Jones, B. J. R.	—	—	—	—	—	—	—
Jones, E. W.	5	0	—	—	—	—	—
Kallicharran, A. I.	1476	28	52.71	4–48	—	—	—
Kapil Dev	4254	154	27.62	8–38	7	1	—
Kemp, N. J.	241	5	48.20	3–83	—	—	—
Kennedy, A	59	2	29.50	2–29	—	—	—
Ker, J. E.	145	4	36.25	1–2	—	—	—
Khanna, S. C.	21	0	—	—	—	—	—
Kirsten, P. N.	1570	42	37.38	4–44	—	—	—
Kitchen, M. J.	109	2	54.50	1–4	—	—	—
Knight, J. M.	1032	27	38.22	4–69	—	—	—
Knight, R. D. V.	9242	260	35.54	6–44	4	—	—
Knott, A. P. E.	77	1	77.00	1–40	—	—	—
Laing, J. R.	—	—	—	—	—	—	—
Lamb, A. J.	28	3	9.33	1–1	—	—	—
Lamb, T. M.	5767	195	29.57	6–49	7	—	—
Larkins, W.	671	19	35.31	3–34	—	—	—
Lawson, G. F.	1272	39	32.61	4–71	—	—	—
Leadbeater, B.	5	1	5.00	1–1	—	—	—
Lee, P. G.	13910	554	25.10	8–53	26	6	2
Le Roux, G. S.	2758	133	20.73	7–40	7	1	—
L'Estrange, M. G.	—	—	—	—	—	—	—
Lever, J. K.	22015	950	23.17	8–49	42	4	2
Lewis, R. V.	104	1	104.00	1–59	—	—	—
Lilley, A. W.	—	—	—	—	—	—	—
Lister, J. W.	—	—	—	—	—	—	—
Llewellyn, M. J.	615	23	26.73	4–35	—	—	—
Lloyd, B. J.	4660	107	43.55	4–49	—	—	—
Lloyd, C. H.	4103	114	35.99	4–48	—	—	—
Lloyd, D.	4870	171	28.47	7–38	4	1	—
Lloyd, T. A.	92	2	46.00	1–14	—	—	—
Lloyds, J. W.	14	0	—	—	—	—	—
Long, A.	2	0	—	—	—	—	—
Love, J. D.	51	0	—	—	—	—	—
Lumb, R. G.	—	—	—	—	—	—	—
Lynch, M. A.	59	2	29.50	1–14	—	—	—
Lyon, J.	—	—	—	—	—	—	—
McCurdy, R. J.	50	1	50.00	1–50	—	—	—
McEvoy, M. S. A.	4	0	—	—	—	—	—
McEwan, K. S.	87	2	43.50	1–0	—	—	—
McFarlane, L.	569	13	43.76	3–83	—	—	—
Mack, A. J.	1527	37	41.27	4–28	—	—	—
Mackintosh, K. S.	716	16	44.75	4–49	—	—	—
McLellan, A. J.	—	—	—	—	—	—	—
McPherson, T. I.	230	10	23.00	4–74	—	—	—
Madugalle, R. S.	32	0	—	—	—	—	—
Malone, M. F.	2884	143	20.16	7–88	10	1	—
Malone, S. J.	101	2	50.50	1–28	—	—	—

197

	Runs	Wkts	Avge	BB	5 Wl	10 Wm	100 WS
Marie, G. V.	666	20	33.30	5–46	1	—	—
Marks, V. J.	5653	176	32.11	6–33	6	—	—
Marsden, R.	—	—	—	—	—	—	—
Marshall, M. D.	2359	121	19.49	6–42	7	1	—
Maynard, C.	—	—	—	—	—	—	—
Mellor, A. J.	616	17	36.23	5–52	1	—	—
Mendis, G. D.	9	0	—	—	—	—	—
Mendis, L. R. D.	30	1	30.00	1–4	—	—	—
Merry, W. G.	431	10	43.10	3–46	—	—	—
Miller, G.	9145	399	22.91	7–54	21	5	—
Mills, J. P. C.	5	0	—	—	—	—	—
Monteith, J. D.	967	60	16.11	7–38	4	1	—
Morrill, N. D.	741	12	61.75	3–53	—	—	—
Moseley, H. R.	10199	433	23.55	6–34	12	1	—
Moulding, R. P.	—	—	—	—	—	—	—
Mubarak, A. M.	6	0	—	—	—	—	—
Nanan, N.	322	9	35.77	3–12	—	—	—
Nash, M. A.	20721	806	25.70	9–56	38	3	—
Neale, P. A.	66	1	66.00	1–15	—	—	—
Needham, A.	441	9	49.00	3–25	—	—	—
Nicholas, M. C. J.	1	0	—	—	—	—	—
Nicholls, D.	23	2	11.50	1–0	—	—	—
Northcote-Green, S. R.	—	—	—	—	—	—	—
O'Brien, B. A.	—	—	—	—	—	—	—
O'Brien, N. T.	78	0	—	—	—	—	—
Old, C. M.	16671	761	21.90	7–20	29	1	—
Oldham, S.	3044	108	28.18	5–40	2	—	—
Olive, M.	—	—	—	—	—	—	—
Oliver, P. R.	1607	18	89.27	2–28	—	—	—
Ontong, R. C.	5892	198	29.75	7–60	8	—	—
Opatha, A. R. M.	2895	97	29.84	6–91	2	—	—
Orders, J. O. D.	348	6	58.00	2–16	—	—	—
Ormrod, J. A.	1089	25	43.56	5–27	1	—	—
Parker, P. W. G.	420	8	52.50	2–23	—	—	—
Parsons, G. J.	257	9	28.55	4–43	—	—	—
Partridge, M. D.	1504	30	50.13	5–29	1	—	—
Parvez Mir	3265	132	24.73	6–39	8	—	—
Pasquil, B. P.	144	2	72.00	1–22	—	—	—
Patel, S. P.	191	6	31.83	1–0	—	—	—
Patel, D. N.	2929	80	36.61	5–22	2	—	—
Pauline, D. B.	—	—	—	—	—	—	—
Payne, I. R.	325	3	108.33	2–41	—	—	—
Pearce, J. P.	501	11	45.54	4–94	—	—	—
Peck, I. G.	—	—	—	—	—	—	—
Perry, N. J.	563	13	43.30	3–51	—	—	—
Perryman, S. P.	7489	264	28.36	7–49	15	3	—
Phillip, N.	7546	325	23.21	6–33	11	1	—

	Runs	Wkts	Avge	BB	5 Wl	10 Wm	100 WS
Phillipson, C. P.	4999	151	33.10	6–56	4	—	—
Pigott, A. C. S.	1223	37	33.05	4–40	—	—	—
Pilling, H.	195	1	195.00	1–42	—	—	—
Pocock, N. E. J.	98	2	49.00	1–4	—	—	—
Pocock, P. I.	32021	1257	25.47	9–57	48	6	1
Pont, K. R.	1877	56	33.51	4–100	—	—	—
Popplewell, N. F. M.	1623	31	52.35	3–18	—	—	—
Pridgeon, A. P.	5523	140	39.45	7–35	2	1	—
Pringle, D. R.	660	23	28.69	4–43	—	—	—
Procter, M. J.	23501	1231	19.09	9–71	62	12	2
Racionzer, T. B.	5	0	—	—	—	—	—
Radley, C. T.	37	3	12.33	1–7	—	—	—
Ramage, A.	348	15	23.20	3–24	—	—	—
Randall, D. W.	100	0	—	—	—	—	—
Ratcliffe, R. M.	5173	203	25.48	7–58	15	2	—
Rawlinson, J. L.	—	—	—	—	—	—	—
Reddy, B.	—	—	—	—	—	—	—
Reidy, B. W.	1072	23	46.60	5–61	1	—	—
Reith, M. S.	48	1	48.00	1–24	—	—	—
Rice, C. E. B.	10669	461	23.14	7–62	13	1	—
Rice, J. M.	6940	219	31.68	7–48	3	—	—
Richards, C. J.	—	—	—	—	—	—	—
Richards, G.	2257	48	47.02	5–55	1	—	—
Richards, I. M.	201	7	28.71	4–57	—	—	—
Richards, I. V. A.	2627	64	41.04	3–15	—	—	—
Robertson, F.	582	32	18.18	6–58	2	—	—
Robinson, P. A.	625	21	29.76	3–33	—	—	—
Robinson, R. T.	—	—	—	—	—	—	—
Rock, D. J.	0	0	—	—	—	—	—
Roebuck, P. M.	1757	39	45.05	6–50	1	—	—
Rogers, J. J.	39	1	39.00	1–24	—	—	—
Roope, G. R. J.	8146	217	37.53	5–14	4	—	—
Rose, B. C.	179	6	29.83	3–9	—	—	—
Ross, C. J.	1349	43	31.37	4–34	—	—	—
Rouse, S. J.	7253	252	28.78	6–34	5	—	—
Rowe, C. J. C.	2080	55	37.81	6–46	3	1	—
Russell, P. E.	10108	335	30.17	7–46	5	—	—
Russom, N.	88	2	44.00	1–28	—	—	—
Sadiq Mohammad	6016	200	30.08	7–34	7	—	—
Sainsbury, G. E.	79	1	79.00	1–38	—	—	—
Sanderson, J. F. W.	66	2	33.00	2–52	—	—	—
Sarfraz Nawaz	18637	802	23.23	9–86	40	4	1
Savage, R. L.	3787	127	29.81	7–50	6	1	—
Saxelby, K.	123	1	123.00	1–32	—	—	—
Schepens, M.	13	0	—	—	—	—	—
Scott, C. J.	—	—	—	—	—	—	—
Selvey, M. W. W.	14466	582	24.85	7–20	29	4	1

	Runs	Wkts	Avge	BB	5 Wl	10 Wm	100 WS
Shantry, B. K.	167	3	55.66	2–63	—	—	—
Sharp, G.	2	0	—	—	—	—	—
Sharp, K.	22	0	—	—	—	—	—
Shepherd, D. R.	106	2	53.00	1–1	—	—	—
Shepherd, J. N.	23281	881	26.42	8–40	45	2	—
Short, J. F.							
Shuttleworth, K.	15130	622	24.32	7–41	21	1	—
Sidebottom, A.	2270	76	29.86	4–47	—	—	—
Simmons, J.	15895	587	27.07	7–59	18	2	—
Skala, S. M.							
Slack, W. N.	3	0	—	—	—	—	—
Slocombe, P. A.	25	0	—	—	—	—	—
Smedley, M. J.	4	0	—	—	—	—	—
Smith, A. V.	—	—	—	—	—	—	—
Smith, C. L.							
Smith, D. M.	1160	21	55.23	3–40	—	—	—
Smith, K. D.	3	0	—	—	—	—	—
Smith, M. J.	1866	57	32.73	4–13	—	—	—
Smith, N.							
Southern, J. N.	7521	259	29.03	6–46	10	—	—
Spencer, J.	14085	540	26.08	6–19	20	1	—
Steele, A.							
Steele, D. S.	7786	320	24.33	8–29	8	1	—
Steele, J. F.	8916	337	26.45	7–29	8	—	—
Stephenson, G. R.	39	0	—	—	—	—	—
Stevenson, G. B.	5745	205	28.02	8–65	6	1	—
Stevenson, K.	6270	223	28.11	7–22	10	—	—
Stewart, D. E. R.	72	0	—	—	—	—	—
Stovold, A. W.	62	2	31.00	1–0	—	—	—
Stovold, M. W.							
Stuchbury, S.	60	2	30.00	2–39	—	—	—
Surridge, D.	583	27	21.59	4–22	—	—	—
Surridge, S. S.	—	—	—	—	—	—	—
Swarbrook, F. W.	13998	467	29.97	9–20	15	2	—
Swart, P. D.	7360	280	26.28	6–85	5	1	—
Tavare, C. J.	87	2	43.50	1–20	—	—	—
Taylor, D. J. S.	14	0	—	—	—	—	—
Taylor, L. B.	2138	87	24.57	6–61	2	—	—
Taylor, M. N. S.	21755	821	26.49	7–23	24	—	—
Taylor, N.							
Taylor, R. W.	46	0	—	—	—	—	—
Tennekoon, A. P. B.	60	2	30.00	2–23	—	—	—
Terry, V. P.							
Thomas, D. J.	1580	34	46.47	6–84	1	—	—
Thomas, G. P.							
Thomas, J. G.	132	1	132.00	1–65	—	—	—
Titmus, F. J.	62908	2815	22.34	9–52	168	26	16
Todd, P. A.	3	0	—	—	—	—	—
Tolchard, R. W.	20	1	20.00	1–4	—	—	—
Tomlins, K. P.	29	0	—	—	—	—	—
Tremlett, T. M.	513	17	30.17	2–9	—	—	—
Trim, G. E.	13	0	—	—	—	—	—

200

	Runs	Wkts	Avge	BB	5 Wl	10 Wm	100 WS
Tunnicliffe, C. J.	4873	154	31.64	4–22	—	—	—
Tunicliffe, H. T.	1414	33	42.84	4–30	—	—	—
Turner, D. R.	201	5	40.20	1–1	—	—	—
Turner, G. M.	189	5	37.80	3–18	—	—	—
Turner, S.	16025	641	25.00	6–26	23	1	—
Underwood, D. L.	35492	1840	19.28	9–28	121	36	9
Vengsarkar, D. B.	20	0	—	—	—	—	—
Venkataraghavan, S.	28870	1196	24.13	9–93	70	17	—
Viswanath, G. R.	548	11	49.81	2–37	—	—	—
Waller, C. E.	10025	362	27.69	7–64	15	1	—
Walters, J.	1805	46	39.23	4–100	—	—	—
Warnapura, B.	257	6	42.83	1–2	—	—	—
Warner, C. J.	—	—	—	—	—	—	—
Watson, G. G.	3697	100	36.97	6–45	1	—	—
Watson, W. K.	4139	164	25.23	6–51	5	—	—
Watts, P. J.	8656	333	25.99	6–18	7	—	—
Wells, C. M.	137	10	13.70	4–23	—	—	—
Wessels, K. C.	83	3	27.66	1–4	—	—	—
Weston, M. J.	—	—	—	—	—	—	—
Wettimony, S. R. De S.	49	1	49.00	1–10	—	—	—
White, R. A.	21053	682	30.86	7–41	27	3	—
Whitehouse, J.	459	6	76.50	2–55	—	—	—
Whiteley, J. P.	1021	32	31.90	4–14	—	—	—
Wijesuriya, R. G. C. E.	493	14	35.21	4–62	—	—	—
Wilkins, A. H.	3384	123	27.51	6–79	6	—	—
Willey, P.	10600	375	28.26	7–37	16	2	—
Williams, R. G.	1771	50	35.42	5–57	1	—	—
Willis, R. G. D.	14726	627	23.48	8–32	27	2	—
Wilson, P. H. L.	1216	41	29.65	4–39	—	—	—
Wincer, R. C.	1544	43	35.90	4–42	—	—	—
Windaybank, S. J.	—	—	—	—	—	—	—
Wood, B.	7217	261	27.65	7–52	8	—	—
Woolmer, R. A.	10135	388	26.12	7–47	12	1	—
Wright, J. G.	—	—	—	—	—	—	—
Yajurvindra Singh	1009	34	29.67	7–20	2	—	—
Yardley, T. J.	21	0	—	—	—	—	—
Yashpal Sharma	233	4	58.25	1–13	—	—	—
Yeabsley, D. I.	326	12	27.16	3–45	—	—	—
Younis Ahmed	1313	35	37.51	4–10	—	—	—
Zaheer Abbas	682	20	34.10	5–15	1	—	—
Zuill, A. M.	—	—	—	—	—	—	—

FIRST-CLASS CRICKET RECORDS

COMPLETE TO END OF 1979 SEASON

Highest Innings Totals

1107	Victoria v New South Wales (Melbourne)	1926–27
1059	Victoria v Tasmania (Melbourne)	1922–23
951–7d	Sind v Baluchistan (Karachi)	1973–74
918	New South Wales v South Australia (Sydney)	1900–01
912–8d	Holkar v Mysore (Indore)	1945–46
910–6d	Railways v Dera Ismail Khan (Lahore)	1964–65
903–7d	England v Australia (Oval)	1938
887	Yorkshire v Warwickshire (Birmingham)	1896
849	England v West Indies (Kingston)	1929–30

NB. There are 22 instances of a side making 800 or more in an innings, the last occasion being 951–7 declared by Sind as above.

Lowest Innings Totals

12†	Oxford University v MCC and Ground (Oxford)	1877
12	Northamptonshire v Gloucestershire (Gloucester)	1907
13	Wellington v Nelson (Nelson)	1862–63
13	Auckland v Canterbury (Auckland)	1877–78
13	Nottinghamshire v Yorkshire (Nottingham)	1901
15	MCC v Surrey (Lord's)	1839
15†	Victoria v MCC (Melbourne)	1903–04
15†	Northamptonshire v Yorkshire (Northampton)	1908
15	Hampshire v Warwickshire (Birmingham)	1922
16	MCC and Ground v Surrey (Lord's)	1872
16	Derbyshire v Nottinghamshire (Nottingham)	1879
16	Surrey v Nottinghamshire (Oval)	1880
16	Warwickshire v Kent (Tonbridge)	1913
16	Trinidad v Barbados (Bridgetown)	1941–42
16	Border v Natal (East London)	1959–60

† Batted one man short

NB. There are 26 instances of a side making less than 20 in an innings, the last occasion being 16 and 18 by Border v Natal at East London in 1959–60. The total of 34 is the lowest by one side in a match.

Highest Aggregates in a Match

2376	(38)	Bombay v Maharashtra (Poona)	1948–49
2078	(40)	Bombay v Holkar (Bombay)	1944–45
1981	(35)	England v South Africa (Durban)	1938–39
1929	(39)	New South Wales v South Australia (Sydney)	1925–26
1911	(34)	New South Wales v Victoria (Sydney)	1908–09
1905	(40)	Otago v Wellington (Dunedin)	1923–24

In England the highest are:

1723	(34)	England v Australia (Leeds) 5 day match	1948
1601	(29)	England v Australia (Lord's) 4 day match	1930
1507	(28)	England v West Indies (Oval) 5 day match	1976
1502	(28)	MCC v New Zealanders (Lord's)	1927
1499	(31)	T. N. Pearce's XI v Australians (Scarborough)	1961
1496	(24)	England v Australia (Nottingham) 4 day match	1938
1494	(37)	England v Australia (Oval) 4 day match	1934
1492	(33)	Worcestershire v Oxford U (Worcester)	1904
1477	(32)	Hampshire v Oxford U (Southampton)	1913
1477	(33)	England v South Africa (Oval) 4 day match	1947
1475	(27)	Northamptonshire v Surrey (Northampton)	1920

Lowest Aggregates in a Match

105	(31)	MCC v Australia (Lord's)	1878
134	(30)	England v The B's (Lord's)	1831
147	(40)	Kent v Sussex (Sevenoaks)	1828
149	(30)	England v Kent (Lord's)	1858
151	(30)	Canterbury v Otago (Christchurch)	1866–67
153	(37)	MCC v Sussex (Lord's)	1843
153	(31)	Otago v Canterbury (Dunedin)	1896–97
156	(30)	Nelson v Wellington (Nelson)	1885–86
158	(22)	Surrey v Worcestershire (Oval)	1954

Wickets that fell are given in parentheses.

Tie Matches

Due to the change of law made in 1948 for tie matches, a tie is now a rarity. The law states that only if the match is played out and the scores are equal is the result a tie. The most recent tied matches are as follows:

Yorkshire (351–4d & 113) v Leicestershire (328 & 136) at Huddersfield	1954
Sussex (172 & 120) v Hampshire (153 & 139) at Eastbourne	1955
Victoria (244 & 197) v New South Wales (281 & 160) at Melbourne (St Kilda)	1956–57
(The first tie in Sheffield Shield cricket)	
T. N. Pearce's XI (313–7d & 258) v New Zealanders (268 & 303–8d) at Scarborough	1958
Essex (364–6d & 176–8d) v Gloucestershire (329 & 211) at Leyton	1959
Australia (505 & 232) v West Indies (453 & 284) at Brisbane	1960–61
(The first tie in Test cricket)	
Bahawalpur (123 & 282) v Lahore B (127 & 278) at Bahawalpur	1961–62
Middlesex (327–5d & 123–9d) v Hampshire (277 & 173) at Portsmouth	1967
England XI (312–8d & 190–3d) v England Under-25 XI (320–9d & 182) at Scarborough	1968
Yorkshire (106–9d & 207) v Middlesex (102 & 211) at Bradford	1973
Sussex (245 & 173–5d) v Essex (200–8d & 218) at Hove	1974
South Australia (431 & 171–7d) v Queensland (340–8d & 262) at Adelaide	1976–77
England XI (296–6d & 104) v Central Districts (198 & 202) at New Plymouth	1977–78

Highest Individual Scores

499	Hanif Mohammad, Karachi v Bahawalpur (Karachi)	1958–59
452*	D. G. Bradman, New South Wales v Queensland (Sydney)	1929–30
443*	B. B. Nimbalkar, Maharashtra v Kathiawar (Poona)	1948–49
437	W. H. Ponsford, Victoria v Queensland (Melbourne)	1927–28
429	W. H. Ponsford, Victoria v Tasmania (Melbourne)	1922–23
428	Aftab Baloch, Sind v Baluchistan (Karachi)	1973–74
424	A. C. MacLaren, Lancashire v Somerset (Taunton)	1895
385	B. Sutcliffe, Otago v Canterbury (Christchurch)	1952–53
383	C. W. Gregory, New South Wales v Queensland (Brisbane)	1906–07
369	D. G. Bradman, South Australia v Tasmania (Adelaide)	1935–36
365*	C. Hill, South Australia v New South Wales (Adelaide)	1900–01
365*	G. S. Sobers, West Indies v Pakistan (Kingston)	1957–58
364	L. Hutton, England v Australia (Oval)	1938
359*	V. M. Merchant, Bombay v Maharashtra (Bombay)	1943–44
359	R. B. Simpson, New South Wales v Queensland (Brisbane)	1963–64
357*	R. Abel, Surrey v Somerset (Oval)	1899
357	D. G. Bradman, South Australia v Victoria (Melbourne)	1935–36
356	B. A. Richards, South Australia v Western Australia (Perth)	1970–71
355	B. Sutcliffe, Otago v Auckland (Dunedin)	1949–50
352	W. H. Ponsford, Victoria v New South Wales (Melbourne)	1926–27
350	Rashid Israr, National Bank v Habib Bank (Lahore)	1976–77

NB. There are 91 instances of a batsman scoring 300 or more in an innings, the last occasion being 350 by Rashid Israr as above.

Most Centuries in a Season

18	D. C. S. Compton	1947
16	J. B. Hobbs	1925
15	W. R. Hammond	1938
14	H. Sutcliffe	1932

Most Centuries in an Innings

6	for Holkar v Mysore (Indore)	1945–46
5	for New South Wales v South Australia (Sydney)	1900–01
5	for Australia v West Indies (Kingston)	1954–55

Most Centuries in Successive Innings

6	C. B. Fry	1901
6	D. G. Bradman	1938–39
6	M. J. Procter	1970–71
5	E. D. Weekes	1955–56

NB. The feat of scoring 4 centuries in successive innings has been achieved on 31 occasions.

Most Centuries in Succession in Test Matches

5	E. D. Weekes, West Indies	1947–48 and 1948–49
4	J. H. W. Fingleton, Australia	1935–36 and 1936–37
4	A. Melville, South Africa	1938–39 and 1947

Two Double Centuries in a Match

A. E. Fagg, 244 and 202* for Kent v Essex (Colchester)	1938

A Double Century and a Century in a Match

C. B. Fry, 125 and 229, Sussex v Surrey (Hove)   1900
W. W. Armstrong, 157* and 245, Victoria v South Australia (Melbourne) 1920–21
H. T. W. Hardinge, 207 and 102* for Kent v Surrey (Blackheath)   1921
C. P. Mead, 113 and 224, Hampshire v Sussex (Horsham)   1921
K. S. Duleepsinhji, 115 and 246, Sussex v Kent (Hastings)   1929
D. G. Bradman, 124 and 225, Woodfull's XI v Ryder's XI (Sydney)   1929–30
B. Sutcliffe, 243 and 100* New Zealanders v Essex (Southend)   1949
M. R. Hallam, 210* and 157, Leicestershire v Glamorgan (Leicester)   1959
M. R. Hallam, 203* and 143* Leicestershire v Sussex (Worthing)   1961
Hanumant Singh, 109 and 213*, Rajasthan v Bombay (Bombay)   1966–67
Salahuddin, 256 and 102*, Karachi v East Pakistan (Karachi)   1968–69
K. D. Walters, 242 and 103, Australia v West Indies (Sydney)   1968–69
S. M. Gavaskar, 124 and 220, India v West Indies (P. of Spain)   1970–71
L. G. Rowe, 214 and 100* West Indies v New Zealand (Kingston)   1971–72
G. S. Chappell, 247* and 133, Australia v New Zealand (Wellington)   1973–74
L. Baichan, 216* and 102, Berbice v Demerara (Georgetown)   1973–74
Zaheer Abbas, 216* and 156*, Gloucestershire v Surrey (Oval)   1976
Zaheer Abbas, 230* and 104*, Gloucestershire v Kent (Canterbury)   1976
Zaheer Abbas, 205* and 108*, Gloucestershire v Sussex (Cheltenham)   1977
Saadat Ali, 141 and 222, Income Tax v Multan (Multan)   1977–78
Talat Ali, 214* and 104, Pakistan International Airways v Punjab (Lahore) 1978–79
Shafiq Ahmed, 129 and 217* National Bank v Muslim Commercial Bank
  (Karachi)   1978–79
D. W. Randall, 209 and 146 Nottinghamshire v Middlesex (Nottingham)   1979

Two Centuries in a Match on Most Occasions

7 W. R. Hammond   6 J. B. Hobbs   5 C. B. Fry

NB. 12 Batsmen have achieved the feat on four occasions, 23 batsmen on three occasions and 39 batsmen on two occasions.

Most Centuries

J. B. Hobbs, 197 (175 in England); E. H. Hendren 170 (151); W. R. Hammond, 167 (134); C. P. Mead 153 (145); H. Sutcliffe, 149 (135); F. E. Woolley, 145 (135); L. Hutton, 129 (105); W. G. Grace, 124 (123); D. C. S. Compton, 123 (92); T. W. Graveney, 122 (91); D. G. Bradman, 117 (41); G. Boycott 115 (93); M. C. Cowdrey, 107 (80); A. Sandham, 107 (87); T. W. Hayward, 104 (100); J. H. Edrich, 103 (90); L. E. G. Ames, 102 (89); G. E. Tyldesley, 102 (94).

Highest Individual Batting Aggregate in a Season

Runs		Season	M	Innings	NO	HS	Avge	100s
3,816	D. C. S. Compton	1947	30	50	8	246	90.85	18
3,539	W. J. Edrich	1947	30	52	8	267*	80.43	12

NB. The feat of scoring 3,000 runs in a season has been achieved on 28 occasions, the last instance being by W. E. Alley (3,019 runs, av. 59.96) in 1961.

Partnerships for First Wicket

561	Waheed Mirza and Mansoor Akhtar, Karachi Whites v Quetta (Karachi)	1976–77
555	H. Sutcliffe and P. Holmes, Yorkshire v Essex (Leyton)	1932
554	J. T. Brown and J. Tunnicliffe, Yorkshire v Derbyshire (Chesterfield)	1898
490	E. H. Bowley and J. G. Langridge, Sussex v Middlesex (Hove)	1933
456	W. H. Ponsford and E. R. Mayne, Victoria v Queensland (Melbourne)	1923–24
451*	S. Desai and R. Binny, Karnataka v Kerala (Chikmalagalor)	1977–78
428	J. B. Hobbs and A. Sandham, Surrey v Oxford U (Oval)	1926
424	J. F. W. Nicholson and I. J. Siedle, Natal v Orange Free State (Bloemfontein)	1926–27
413	V. M. H. Mankad and P. Roy, India v New Zealand (Madras)	1955–56
405	C. P. S. Chauhan and M. Gupte, Maharashtra v Vidarbha (Poona)	1972–73

Partnerships for Second Wicket

465*	J. A. Jameson and R. B. Kanhai, Warwickshire v Gloucestershire (Birmingham)	1974
455	K. V. Bhandarkar and B. B. Nimbalkar, Maharashtra v Kathiawar (Poona)	1948–49
451	D. G. Bradman and W. H. Ponsford, Australia v England (Oval)	1934
446	C. C. Hunte and G. S. Sobers, West Indies v Pakistan (Kingston)	1957–58
429*	J. G. Dewes and G. H. G. Doggart, Cambridge U v Essex (Cambridge)	1949
426	Arshad Pervez and Mohsin Khan, Habib Bank v Income Tax Department (Lahore)	1977–78
398	W. Gunn and A. Shrewsbury, Nottinghamshire v Sussex (Nottingham)	1890

Partnerships for Third Wicket

456	Aslam Ali and Khalid Irtiza, United Bank v Multan (Karachi)	1975–76
445	P. E. Whitelaw and W. N. Carson, Auckland v Otago (Dunedin)	1936–37
434	J. B. Stollmeyer and G. E. Gomez, Trinidad v British Guiana (Port of Spain)	1946–47
424*	W. J. Edrich and D. C. S. Compton, Middlesex v Somerset (Lord's)	1948
410	R. S. Modi and L. Amarnath, India v Rest (Calcutta)	1946–47
399	R. T. Simpson and D. C. S. Compton, MCC v NE Transvaal (Benoni)	1948–49

Partnerships for Fourth Wicket

577	Gul Mahomed and V. S. Hazare, Baroda v Holkar (Baroda)	1946–47
574*	C. L. Walcott and F. M. M. Worrell, Barbados v Trinidad (Port of Spain)	1945–46
502*	F. M. M. Worrell and J. D. C. Goddard, Barbados v Trinidad (Bridgetown)	1943–44
448	R. Abel and T. W. Hayward, Surrey v Yorkshire (Oval)	1899
424	I. S. Lee and S. O. Quin, Victoria v Tasmania (Melbourne)	1933–34
411	P. B. H. May and M. C. Cowdrey, England v West Indies (Birmingham)	1957
410	G. Abraham and B. Pandit, Kerala v Andhra (Pulghat)	1959–60
402	W. Watson and T. W. Graveney, MCC v British Guiana (Georgetown)	1953–54
402	R. B. Kanhai and K. Ibadulla, Warwickshire v Nottinghamshire (Nottingham)	1968

Partnerships for Fifth Wicket

405	D. G. Bradman and S. G. Barnes, Australia v England (Sydney)	1946–47
397	W. Bardsley and C. Kellaway, New South Wales v South Australia (Sydney)	1920–21
393	E. G. Arnold and W. B. Burns, Worcestershire v Warwickshire (Birmingham)	1909
360	V. M. Merchant and M. N. Raiji, Bombay v Hyderabad (Bombay)	1947–48
347	D. Brookes and D. Barrick, Northamptonshire v Essex (Northampton)	1952

Partnerships for Sixth Wicket

487*	G. A. Headley and C. C. Passailaigue, Jamaica v Lord Tennyson's XI (Kingston)	1931–32
428	W. W. Armstrong and M. A. Noble, Australians v Sussex (Hove)	1902
411	R. M. Poore and E. G. Wynyard, Hampshire v Somerset (Taunton)	1899
376	R. Subba Row and A. Lightfoot, Northamptonshire v Surrey (Oval)	1958
371	V. M. Merchant and R. S. Modi, Bombay v Maharashtra (Bombay)	1943–44

Partnerships for Seventh Wicket

347	D. S. Atkinson and C. C. Depeiza, West Indies v Australia (Bridgetown)	1954–55
344	K. S. Ranjitsinjhi and W. Newham, Sussex v Essex (Leyton)	1902
340	K. J. Key and H. Philipson, Oxford U v Middlesex (Chiswick Park)	1887
336	F. C. W. Newman and C. R. Maxwell, Cahn's XI v Leicestershire (Nottingham)	1935
335	C. W. Andrews and E. C. Bensted, Queensland v New South Wales (Sydney)	1934–35

Partnerships for Eighth Wicket

433	V. T. Trumper and A. Sims, Australians v Canterbury (Christchurch)	1913–14
292	R. Peel and Lord Hawke, Yorkshire v Warwickshire (Birmingham)	1896
270	V. T. Trumper and E. P. Barbour, New South Wales v Victoria (Sydney)	1912–13
263	D. R. Wilcox and R. M. Taylor, Essex v Warwickshire (Southend)	1946
255	E. A. V. Williams and E. A. Martindale, Barbados v Trinidad (Bridgetown)	1935–36

Partnerships for Ninth Wicket

283	A. R. Warren and J. Chapman, Derbyshire v Warwickshire (Blackwell)	1910
251	J. W. H. T. Douglas and S. N. Hare, Essex v Derbyshire (Leyton)	1921
245	V. S. Hazare and N. D. Nagarwalla, Maharashtra v Baroda (Poona)	1939–40
239	H. B. Cave and I. B. Leggat, Central Districts v Otago (Dunedin)	1952–53
232	C. Hill and E. Walkley, South Australia v New South Wales (Adelaide)	1900–01

Partnerships for Tenth Wicket

307	A. F. Kippax and J. E. H. Hooker, New South Wales v Victoria (Melbourne)	1928–29
249	C. T. Sarwate and S. N. Bannerjee, Indians v Surrey (Oval)	1946
235	F. E. Woolley and A. Fielder, Kent v Worcestershire (Stourbridge)	1909
230	R. W. Nicholls and W. Roche, Middlesex v Kent (Lord's)	1899
228	R. Illingworth and K. Higgs, Leicestershire v Northamptonshire (Leicester)	1977
218	F. H. Vigar and T. P. B. Smith, Essex v Derbyshire (Chesterfield)	1947

Most Wickets in a Season

W		Season	M	O	M	R	Avge
304	A. P. Freeman	1928	37	1,976.1	432	5,489	18.05
298	A. P. Freeman	1933	33	2,039	651	4,549	15.26

NB. The feat of taking 250 wickets in a season has been achieved on 12 occasions, the last instance being by A. P. Freeman in 1933 as above. 200 or more wickets in a season have been taken on 59 occasions, the last instance being by G. A. R. Lock (212 wkts, av 12.02) in 1957.

The most wickets taken in a season since the reduction of County Championship matches in 1969 are as follows:

W		Season	M	O	M	R	Avge
131	L. R. Gibbs	1971	23	1024.1	295	2475	18.89
119	A. M. E. Roberts	1974	21	727.4	198	1621	13.62
112	P. G. Lee	1975	21	799.5	199	2067	18.45

NB. 100 wickets in a season have been taken on 27 occasions since 1969.

All Ten Wickets in an Innings

The feat has been achieved on 69 occasions.
On three occasions: A. P. Freeman, 1929, 1930 and 1931.
On two occasions: J. C. Laker, 1956, H. Verity, 1931 and 1932, V. E. Walker 1859 and 1865.
Instances since the war:
W. E. Hollies, Warwickshire v Nottinghamshire (Birmingham) 1946; J. M. Sims of Middlesex playing for East v West (Kingston) 1948; J. K. R. Graveney, Gloucestershire v Derbyshire (Chesterfield) 1949; T. E. Bailey, Essex v Lancashire (Clacton) 1949; R. Berry, Lancashire v Worcestershire (Blackpool) 1953; S. P. Gupte, Bombay v Pakistan Services (Bombay), 1954–55; J. C. Laker, Surrey v Australians (Oval) 1956; J. C. Laker, England v Australia (Manchester) 1956; G. A. R. Lock, Surrey v Kent (Blackheath) 1956; K. Smales, Nottinghamshire v Gloucestershire (Stroud) 1956; P. Chatterjee, Bengal v Assam (Jorhat) 1956–57; J. D. Bannister, Warwickshire v Combined Services (Birmingham) 1959; A. J. G. Pearson, Cambridge U v Leicestershire (Loughborough) 1961; N. I. Thomson, Sussex v Warwickshire (Worthing) 1964; P. Allan, Queensland v Victoria (Melbourne) 1965–66; I. Brayshaw, Western Australia v Victoria (Perth) 1967–68; Shahid Mahmood, Karachi Whites v Khairpur (Karachi) 1969–70.

Nineteen Wickets in a Match

J. C. Laker 19–90 (9–37 and 10–53), England v Australia (Manchester) 1956.

Eighteen Wickets in a Match

H. A. Arkwright 18–96 (9–43 and 9–53), MCC v Gentlemen of Kent (Canterbury) 1861, (twelve-a-side match).

Seventeen Wickets in a Match

The feat has been achieved on 18 occasions.

Instances between the two wars were: A. P. Freeman (for 67 runs), Kent v Sussex (Hove) 1922; F. C. L. Matthews (89 runs), Nottinghamshire v Northamptonshire (Nottingham) 1923; C. W. L. Parker (56 runs), Gloucestershire v Essex (Glouce-ster) 1925; G. R. Cox (106 runs), Sussex v Warwickshire (Horsham) 1926; A. P. Freeman (92 runs), Kent v Warwickshire (Folkestone) 1932; H. Verity (91 runs), Yorkshire v Essex (Leyton) 1933; J. C. Clay (212 runs), Glamorgan v Worcester-shire (Swansea) 1937; T. W. J. Goddard (106 runs), Gloucestershire v Kent (Bristol) 1939. There has been no instance since the last war.

Most Hat-tricks in a Career

7 D. V. P. Wright.
6 T. W. J. Goddard, C. W. L. Parker.
5 S. Haigh, V. W. C. Jupp, A. E. G. Rhodes, F. A. Tarrant.

NB. Nine bowlers have achieved the feat on four occasions and 24 bowlers on three occasions.

The 'Double' Event

3,000 and 100 wickets: J. H. Parks, 1937.
2,000 runs and 200 wickets: H. G. Hirst, 1906.
2,000 runs and 100 wickets: F. E. Woolley (4), J. W. Hearne (3), G. H. Hirst (2). W. Rhodes (2), T. E. Bailey, D. E. Davies, W. G. Grace, G. L. Jessop, V. W. C. Jupp, James Langridge, F. A. Tarrant, C. L. Townsend, L. F. Townsend.
1,000 runs and 200 wickets: M. W. Tate (3), A. E. Trott (2), A. S. Kennedy.
Most 'Doubles': W. Rhodes (16), G .H. Hirst (14), V. W. C. Jupp (10).
'Double' in first season: D. B. Close, 1949. At the age of 18, Close is the youngest player ever to perform this feat.

The feat of scoring 1,000 runs and taking 100 wickets has been achieved on 302 occasions, the last instance being F. J. Titmus in 1967.

FIELDING

Most catches in a season:	78 W. R. Hammond	1928
	77 M. J. Stewart	1957
Most catches in a match:	10 W. R. Hammond, Gloucestershire v Surrey (Cheltenham)	1928
Most catches in an innings:	7 M. J. Stewart, Surrey v Northamptonshire (Northampton)	1957
	7 A. S. Brown, Gloucestershire v Nottinghamshire (Nottingham)	1966

WICKET-KEEPING
Most Dismissals in a Season

127 (79 ct, 48 st), L. E. G. Ames   1929

NB. The feat of making 100 dismissals in a season has been achieved on 12 occasions, the last instance being by R. Booth (100 dismissals—91 ct 9 st) in 1964.

Most dismissals in a match:	12 E. Pooley (8 ct 4 st) Surrey v Sussex (Oval)	1868
	12 D. Tallon (9 ct 3 st), Queensland v New South Wales (Sydney)	1938–39
	12 H. B. Taber (9 ct 3 st), New South Wales v South Australia (Adelaide)	1968–69
Most catches in a match:	11 A. Long, Surrey v Sussex (Hove)	1964
	11 R. W. Marsh, Western Australia v Victoria (Perth)	1975–76
Most dismissals in an innings:	8 A. T. W. Grout (8 ct) Queensland v W. Australia (Brisbane)	1959–60

TEST CRICKET RECORDS

COMPLETE TO END OF VARIOUS SERIES
IN AUSTRALIA AND INDIA

Matches between England and Rest of the World 1970 and between Australia and Rest of the World 1971–72 are excluded

HIGHEST INNINGS TOTALS

903—7d	England v Australia (Oval)	1938
849	England v West Indies (Kingston)	1929–30
790—3d	West Indies v Pakistan (Kingston)	1957–58
758—8d	Australia v West Indies (Kingston)	1954–55
729—6d	Australia v England (Lord's)	1930
701	Australia v England (Oval)	1934
695	Australia v England (Oval)	1930
687—8d	West Indies v England (Oval)	1976
681—8d	West Indies v England (Port of Spain)	1953–54
674	Australia v India (Adelaide)	1947–48
668	Australia v West Indies (Bridgetown)	1954–55
659—8d	Australia v England (Sydney)	1946–47
658—8d	England v Australia (Nottingham)	1938
657—8d	Pakistan v West Indies (Bridgetown)	1957–58
656—8d	Australia v England (Manchester)	1964
654—5d	England v South Africa (Durban)	1938–39
652—8d	West Indies v England (Lord's)	1973
650—6d	Australia v West Indies (Bridgetown)	1964–65

The highest innings for the countries not mentioned above are:

644—7d	India v West Indies (Kanpur)	1978–79
622—9d	South Africa v Australia (Durban)	1969–70
551—9d	New Zealand v England (Lord's)	1973

NB. There are 43 instances of a side making 600 or more in an innings in a Test Match.

LOWEST INNINGS TOTALS

26	New Zealand v England (Auckland)	1954–55
30	South Africa v England (Port Elizabeth)	1895–96
30	South Africa v England (Birmingham)	1924
35	South Africa v England (Cape Town)	1898–99
36	Australia v England (Birmingham)	1902
36	South Africa v Australia (Melbourne)	1931–32
42	Australia v England (Sydney)	1887–88
42	New Zealand v Australia (Wellington)	1945–46
42†	India v England (Lord's)	1974
43	South Africa v England (Cape Town)	1888–89
44	Australia v England (Oval)	1896
45	England v Australia (Sydney)	1886–87
45	South Africa v Australia (Melbourne)	1931–32
47	South Africa v England (Cape Town)	1888–89
47	New Zealand v England (Lord's)	1958

†Batted one man short.

The lowest innings for the countries not mentioned above are:

76	West Indies v Pakistan (Dacca)	1958–59
87	Pakistan v England (Lord's)	1954

HIGHEST INDIVIDUAL INNINGS

365*	G. S. Sobers: West Indies v Pakistan (Kingston)	1957–58
364	L. Hutton: England v Australia (Oval)	1938
337	Hanif Mohammad: Pakistan v West Indies (Bridgetown)	1957–58
336*	W. R. Hammond: England v New Zealand (Auckland)	1932–33
334	D. G. Bradman: Australia v England (Leeds)	1930
325	A. Sandham: England v West Indies (Kingston)	1929–30
311	R. B. Simpson: Australia v England (Manchester)	1964
310*	J. H. Edrich: England v New Zealand (Leeds)	1965
307	R. M. Cowper: Australia v England (Melbourne)	1965–66
304	D. G. Bradman: Australia v England (Leeds)	1934
302	L. G. Rowe: West Indies v England (Bridgetown)	1973–74
299*	D. G. Bradman: Australia v South Africa (Adelaide)	1931–32
291	I. V. A. Richards: West Indies v England (Oval)	1976
287	R. E. Foster: England v Australia (Sydney)	1903–04
285*	P. B. H. May: England v West Indies (Birmingham)	1957
278	D. C. S. Compton: England v Pakistan (Nottingham)	1954
274	R. G. Pollock: South Africa v Australia (Durban)	1969–70
274	Zaheer Abbas: Pakistan v England (Birmingham)	1971
270*	G. A. Headley: West Indies v England (Kingston)	1934–35
270	D. G. Bradman: Australia v England (Melbourne)	1936–37
266	W. H. Ponsford: Australia v England (Oval)	1934
262*	D. L. Amiss: England v West Indies (Kingston)	1973–74
261	F. M. M. Worrell: West Indies v England (Nottingham)	1950
260	C. C. Hunte: West Indies v Pakistan (Kingston)	1957–58
259	G. M. Turner: New Zealand v West Indies (Georgetown)	1971–72
258	T. W. Graveney: England v West Indies (Nottingham)	1957
258	S. M. Nurse: West Indies v New Zealand (Christchurch)	1968–69
256	R. B. Kanhai: West Indies v India (Calcutta)	1958–59
256	K. F. Barrington: England v Australia (Manchester)	1964
255*	D. J. McGlew: South Africa v New Zealand (Wellington)	1952–53
254	D. G. Bradman: Australia v England (Leeds)	1930
251	W. R. Hammond: England v Australia (Sydney)	1928–29
250	K. D. Walters: Australia v New Zealand (Christchurch)	1976–77
250	S. F. A. Bacchus: West Indies v India (Kanpur)	1978–79

The highest individual innings for India is:

231	V. M. H. Mankad: India v New Zealand (Madras)	1955–56

NB. There are 118 instances of a double-century being scored in a Test Match.

HIGHEST RUN AGGREGATES IN A TEST RUBBER

R		Season	T	I	NO	HS	Avge	100s	50s
974	D. G. Bradman (A v E)	1930	5	7	0	334	139.14	4	—
905	W. R. Hammond (E v A)	1928–29	5	9	1	251	113.12	4	—
834	R. N. Harvey (A v SA)	1952–53	5	9	0	205	92.66	4	3
829	I. V. A. Richards (WI v E)	1976	4	7	0	291	118.42	3	2
827	C. L. Walcott (WI v A)	1954–55	5	10	0	155	82.70	5	2
824	G. S. Sobers (WI v P)	1957–58	5	8	2	365*	137.33	3	3
810	D. G. Bradman (A v E)	1936–37	5	9	0	270	90.00	3	1
806	D. G. Bradman (A v SA)	1931–32	5	5	1	299*	201.50	4	—
779	E. D. Weekes (WI v I)	1948–49	5	7	0	194	111.28	4	2
774	S. M. Gavaskar (I v WI)	1970–71	4	8	3	220	154.80	4	3
758	D. G. Bradman (A v E)	1934	5	8	0	304	94.75	2	1
753	D. C. S. Compton (E v SA)	1947	5	8	0	208	94.12	4	2

RECORD WICKET PARTNERSHIPS—ALL TEST CRICKET

1st	413	V. M. H. Mankad & P. Roy: I v NZ (Madras)	1955–56
2nd	451	W. H. Ponsford & D. G. Bradman: A v E (Oval)	1934
3rd	370	W. J. Edrich & D. C. S. Compton: E v SA (Lord's)	1947
4th	411	P. B. H. May & M. C. Cowdrey: E v WI (Birmingham)	1957
5th	405	S. G. Barnes & D. G. Bradman: A v E (Sydney)	1946–47
6th	346	J. H. W. Fingleton & D. G. Bradman: A v E (Melbourne)	1936–37
7th	347	D. S. Atkinson & C. C. Depeiza: WI v A (Bridgetown)	1954–55
8th	246	L. E. G. Ames & G. O. Allen: E v NZ (Lord's)	1931
9th	190	Asif Iqbal & Intikhab Alam: P v E (Oval)	1967
10th	151	B. F. Hastings & R. O. Collinge: NZ v P (Auckland)	1972–73

WICKET PARTNERSHIPS OF OVER 300

451	2nd	W. H. Ponsford & D. G. Bradman: A v E (Oval)	1934
446	2nd	C. C. Hunte & G. S. Sobers: WI v P (Kingston)	1957–58
413	1st	V. M. H. Mankad & P. Roy: I v NZ (Madras)	1955–56
411	4th	P. B. H. May & M. C. Cowdrey: E v WI (Birmingham)	1957
405	5th	S. G. Barnes & D. G. Bradman: A v E (Sydney)	1946–47
399	4th	G. S. Sobers & F. M. M. Worrell: WI v E (Bridgetown)	1959–60
388	4th	W. H. Ponsford & D. G. Bradman: A v E (Leeds)	1934
387	1st	G. M. Turner & T. W. Jarvis: NZ v WI (Georgetown)	1971–72
382	2nd	L. Hutton & M. Leyland: E v A (Oval)	1938
382	1st	W. M. Lawry & R. B. Simpson: A v WI (Bridgetown)	1964–65
370	3rd	W. J. Edrich & D. C. S. Compton: E v SA (Lord's)	1947
369	2nd	J. H. Edrich and K. F. Barrington: E v NZ (Leeds)	1965
359	1st	L. Hutton & C. Washbrook: E v SA (Johannesburg)	1948–49
350	4th	Mushtaq Mohammad & Asif Iqbal: P v NZ (Dunedin)	1972–73
347	7th	D. S. Atkinson & C. C. Depeiza: WI v A (Bridgetown)	1954–55
346	6th	J. H. W. Fingleton & D. G. Bradman: A v E (Melbourne)	1936–37
344*	2nd	S. M. Gavaskar & D. B. Vengsarkar: I v WI (Calcutta)	1978–79
341	3rd	E. J. Barlow & R. G. Pollock: SA v A (Adelaide)	1963–64
338	3rd	E. D. Weekes & F. M. M. Worrell: WI v E. (P. of Spain)	1953–54
336	4th	W. M. Lawry & K. D. Walters: A v WI (Sydney)	1968–69
323	1st	J. B. Hobbs & W. Rhodes: E v A (Melbourne)	1911–12
319	3rd	A. Melville & A. D. Nourse: SA v E (Nottingham)	1947
308	7th	Waqar Hasan & Imtiaz Ahmed: P v NZ (Lahore)	1955–56
303	3rd	I. V. A. Richards & A. I. Kallicharran: WI v E (Nottingham)	1976
301	2nd	A. R. Morris & D. G. Bradman: A v E (Leeds)	1948

HAT-TRICKS

F. R. Spofforth	Australia v England (Melbourne)	1878–79
W. Bates	England v Australia (Melbourne)	1882–83
J. Briggs	England v Australia (Sydney)	1891–92
G. A. Lohmann	England v South Africa (Port Elizabeth)	1895–96
J. T. Hearne	England v Australia (Leeds)	1899
H. Trumble	Australia v England (Melbourne)	1901–02
H. Trumble	Australia v England (Melbourne)	1903–04
T. J. Matthews (2)†	Australia v South Africa (Manchester)	1912
M. J. C. Allom‡	England v New Zealand (Christchurch)	1929–30
T. W. J. Goddard	England v South Africa (Johannesburg)	1938–39
P. J. Loader	England v West Indies (Leeds)	1957
L. F. Kline	Australia v South Africa (Cape Town)	1957–58
W. W. Hall	West Indies v Pakistan (Lahore)	1958–59

G. M. Griffin	South Africa v England (Lord's)	1960
L. R. Gibbs	West Indies v Australia (Adelaide)	1960–61
P. J. Petherick	New Zealand v Pakistan (Lahore)	1976–77

† *Matthews achieved the hat-trick in each innings.*
‡ *Allom took four wickets with five consecutive balls.*

NINE OR TEN WICKETS IN AN INNINGS

10—53	J. C. Laker: England v Australia (Manchester)	1956
9—28	G. A. Lohmann: England v South Africa (Johannesburg)	1895–96
9—37	J. C. Laker: England v Australia (Manchester)	1956
9—69	J. M. Patel: India v Australia (Kanpur)	1959–60
9—86	Sarfraz Nawaz: Pakistan v Australia (Melbourne)	1978–79
9—95	J. M. Noreiga: West Indies v India (Port of Spain)	1970–71
9—102	S. P. Gupte: India v West Indies (Kanpur)	1958–59
9—103	S. F. Barnes: England v South Africa (Johannesburg)	1913–14
9—113	H. J. Tayfield: South Africa v England (Johannesburg)	1956–57
9—121	A. A. Mailey: Australia v England (Melbourne)	1920–21

NB. There are 39 instances of a bowler taking 8 wickets in an innings in a Test Match.

FIFTEEN OR MORE WICKETS IN A MATCH

19—90	J. C. Laker: England v Australia (Manchester)	1956
17—159	S. F. Barnes: England v South Africa (Johannesburg)	1913–14
16—137	R. A. L. Massie: Australia v England (Lord's)	1972
15—28	J. Briggs: England v South Africa (Cape Town)	1888–89
15—45	G. A. Lohmann: England v South Africa (Pt. Elizabeth)	1895–96
15—99	C. Blythe: England v South Africa (Leeds)	1907
15—104	H. Verity: England v Australia (Lord's)	1934
15—124	W. Rhodes: England v Australia (Melbourne)	1903–04

NB. There are 7 instances of a bowler taking 14 wickets in a Test Match.

HIGHEST WICKET AGGREGATES IN A TEST RUBBER

W		Season	Tests	Balls	Mdns	Runs	Avge	5 wI	10 M
49	S. F. Barnes (E v SA)	1913–14	4	1356	56	536	10.93	7	3
46	J. C. Laker (E v A)	1956	5	1703	127	442	9.60	4	2
44	C. V. Grimmett (A v SA)	1935–36	5	2077	140	642	14.59	5	3
41	R. M. Hogg (A v E)	1978–79	6	1740	60	527	12.85	5	—
39	A. V. Bedser (E v A)	1953	5	1591	48	682	17.48	5	1
38	M. W. Tate (E v A)	1924–25	5	2528	62	881	23.18	5	1
37	W. J. Whitty (A v SA)	1910–11	5	1395	55	632	17.08	2	—
37	H. J. Tayfield (SA v E)	1956–57	5	2280	105	636	17.18	4	1
36	A. E. E. Vogler (SA v E)	1909–10	5	1349	33	783	21.75	4	1
36	A. A. Mailey (A v E)	1920–21	5	1463	27	946	26.27	4	2
35	G. A. Lohmann (E v SA)	1895–96	3	520	38	203	5.80	4	2
35	B. S. Chandrasekhar (I v E)	1972–73	5	1747	83	662	18.91	4	—

MOST WICKET-KEEPING DISMISSALS IN AN INNINGS

7 (7 ct)	Wasim Bari, Pakistan v New Zealand (Auckland)	1978–79
7	R. W. Taylor, England v India (Bombay)	1979–80
6 (6 ct)	A. T. W. Grout, Australia v South Africa (Johannesburg)	1957–58
6 (6 ct)	D. T. Lindsay, South Africa v Australia (Johannesburg)	1966–67
6 (6 ct)	J. T. Murray, England v India (Lord's)	1967
6 (5 ct 1 st)	S. M. H. Kirmani, India v New Zealand (Christchurch)	1975–76

MOST WICKET KEEPING DISMISSALS IN A MATCH

10 (10 ct) R. W. Taylor, England v India (Bombay)   1979–80

MOST WICKET-KEEPING DISMISSALS IN A SERIES

26 (23 ct, 3 st) J. H. B. Waite, South Africa v New Zealand   1961–62
26 (26 ct) R. W. Marsh, Australia v West Indies   1975–76
24 (22 ct, 2 st) D. L. Murray, West Indies v England   1963
24 (24 ct) D. T. Lindsay, South Africa v Australia   1966–67
24 (21 ct, 3 st) A. P. E. Knott, England v Australia   1970–71

HIGHEST WICKET-KEEPING DISMISSAL AGGREGATES

Total		Tests	Ct	St
252	A. P. E. Knott (E)	89	233	19
221	R. W. Marsh (A)	58	212	9
219	T. G. Evans (E)	91	173	46
187	A. T. W. Grout (A)	51	163	24
168	D. L. Murray (WI)	54	160	8
153	Wasim Bari (P)	56	135	18
141	J. H. B. Waite (SA)	50	124	17
130	W. A. S. Oldfield (A)	54	78	52
114	J. M. Parks (E)	46	103	11

NB. Parks' figures include 2 catches as a fielder.

HIGHEST RUN AGGREGATES

Runs			Tests	Inns	NO	HS	Avge	100s	50s
8032	G. S. Sobers	(WI)	93	160	21	365*	57.78	26	30
7624	M. C. Cowdrey	(E)	114	188	15	182	44.06	22	38
7249	W. R. Hammond	(E)	85	140	16	336*	58.45	22	24
6996	D. G. Bradman	(A)	52	80	10	334	99.94	29	13
6971	L. Hutton	(E)	79	138	15	364	56.67	19	33
6806	K. F. Barrington	(E)	82	131	15	256	58.67	20	35
6557	G. Boycott	(E)	88	153	19	246*	48.93	18	34
6227	R. B. Kanhai	(WI)	79	137	6	256	47.53	15	28
6149	R. N. Harvey	(A)	79	137	10	205	48.41	21	24
5974	S. M. Gavaskar	(I)	63	114	8	221	56.35	23	25
5807	D. C. S. Compton	(E)	78	131	15	278	50.06	17	28
5410	J. B. Hobbs	(E)	61	102	7	211	56.94	15	28
5345	I. M. Chappell	(A)	75	136	10	196	42.42	14	26
5234	W. M. Lawry	(A)	67	123	12	210	47.15	13	27
5138	J. H. Edrich	(E)	77	127	9	310*	43.54	12	24
5003	G. R. Viswanath	(I)	69	121	9	179	44.66	11	30
4960	K. D. Walters	(A)	68	116	12	250	47.69	14	30
4882	T. W. Graveney	(E)	79	123	13	258	44.38	11	20
4869	R. B. Simpson	(A)	62	111	7	311	46.81	10	27
4795	C. H. Lloyd	(WI)	67	116	8	242*	44.39	12	22
4737	I. R. Redpath	(A)	66	120	11	171	43.45	8	31
4648	G. S. Chappell	(A)	57	102	15	247*	53.83	16	22
4555	H. Sutcliffe	(E)	54	84	9	194	60.73	16	23
4537	P. B. H. May	(E)	66	106	9	285*	46.77	13	22
4502	E. R. Dexter	(E)	62	102	8	205	47.89	9	27
4455	E. D. Weekes	(WI)	48	81	5	207	58.61	15	19
4334	R. C. Fredericks	(WI)	59	109	7	169	42.49	8	26
4175	A. P. E. Knott	(E)	89	138	14	135	33.66	5	28
4071	A. I. Kallicharran	(WI)	54	91	9	187	49.64	12	20

3915	Hanif Mohammad	(P)	55	97	8	337	43.98	12	15
3860	F. M. M. Worrell	(WI)	51	87	9	261	49.48	9	22
3798	C. L. Walcott	(WI)	44	74	7	220	56.68	15	14
3643	Mushtaq Mohammad	(P)	57	100	7	201	39.17	10	19
3631	P. R. Umrigar	(I)	59	94	8	223	42.22	12	14
3612	D. L. Amiss	(E)	50	88	10	262*	46.30	11	11
3599	A. W. Greig	(E)	58	93	4	148	40.43	8	20
3575	Asif Iqbal	(P)	58	99	7	175	38.85	11	12
3533	A. R. Morris	(A)	46	79	3	206	46.48	12	12
3525	E. H. Hendren	(E)	51	83	9	205*	47.63	7	21
3471	B. Mitchell	(SA)	42	80	9	189*	48.88	8	21
3448	B. E. Congdon	(NZ)	61	114	7	176	32.22	7	19
3428	J. R. Reid	(NZ)	58	108	5	142	33.28	6	22
3412	C. Hill	(A)	49	89	2	191	39.21	7	19
3363	Majid Khan	(P)	50	88	3	167	39.56	7	15
3283	F. E. Woolley	(E)	64	98	7	154	36.07	5	23
3245	C. C. Hunte	(WI)	44	78	6	260	45.06	8	13
3208	V. L. Manjrekar	(I)	55	92	10	189*	39.12	7	15
3163	V. T. Trumper	(A)	48	89	8	214*	39.04	8	13
3106	C. C. McDonald	(A)	47	83	4	170	39.31	5	17
3104	B. F. Butcher	(WI)	44	78	6	209*	43.11	7	16
3073	A. L. Hassett	(A)	43	69	3	198*	46.56	10	11
3061	C. G. Borde	(I)	55	97	11	177*	35.59	5	18

HIGHEST WICKET AGGREGATES

Wkts			Tests	Balls	Mdns	Runs	Avge	5 wI	10 wM
309	L. R. Gibbs	(WI)	79	27115	1313	8989	29.09	18	2
307	F. S. Trueman	(E)	67	15178	522	6625	21.57	17	3
278	D. L. Underwood	(E)	78	19983	1112	7033	25.29	16	6
266	B. S. Bedi	(I)	67	21364	1096	7637	28.71	14	1
252	J. B. Statham	(E)	70	16056	595	6261	24.84	9	1
248	R. Benaud	(A)	63	19090	805	6704	27.03	16	1
246	G. D. McKenzie	(A)	60	17681	547	7238	29.78	16	3
242	B. S. Chandrasekhar	(I)	58	15963	584	7199	29.74	16	2
236	A. V. Bedser	(E)	51	15923	572	5876	24.89	15	5
235	G. S. Sobers	(WI)	93	21599	995	7999	34.03	6	—
228	R. R. Lindwall	(A)	61	13666	418	5257	23.05	12	—
216	C. V. Grimmett	(A)	37	14513	735	5231	24.21	21	7
206	D. K. Lillee	(A)	38	10443	331	4770	23.15	15	5
202	J. A. Snow	(E)	49	12021	415	5387	26.66	8	1
193	J. C. Laker	(E)	46	12009	673	4099	21.23	9	3
192	W. W. Hall	(WI)	48	10415	312	5066	26.38	9	1
189	S. F. Barnes	(E)	27	7873	356	3106	16.43	24	7
189	E. A. S. Prasanna	(I)	49	14353	602	5742	30.38	10	2
186	A. K. Davidson	(A)	44	11665	432	3838	20.58	14	2
184	R. G. D. Willis	(E)	53	10210	292	4636	25.19	11	—
174	G. A. R. Lock	(E)	49	13147	819	4451	25.58	9	3
170	K. R. Miller	(A)	55	10474	338	3905	22.97	7	1
170	H. J. Tayfield	(SA)	37	13568	602	4405	25.91	14	2
162	V. M. H. Mankad	(I)	44	14686	777	5235	32.31	8	2
160	W. A. Johnston	(A)	40	11048	370	3825	23.90	7	—
158	S. Ramadhin	(WI)	43	13939	813	4579	28.98	10	1
155	M. W. Tate	(E)	39	12523	581	4055	26.16	7	1
153	F. J. Titmus	(E)	53	15118	777	4931	32.22	7	—
152	J. R. Thomson	(A)	34	7512	210	3892	25.60	6	—

215

MOST TEST APPEARANCES FOR EACH COUNTRY

NB. The abandoned match at Melbourne in 1970–71 is excluded from these figures.

England		Australia	
M. C. Cowdrey	114	R. N. Harvey	79
T. G. Evans	91	I. M. Chappell	75
A. P. E. Knott	89	K. D. Walters	68
G. Boycott	88	W. M. Lawry	67
W. R. Hammond	85	I. R. Redpath	66
K. F. Barrington	82	R. Benaud	63
T. W. Graveney	79	R. B. Simpson	62
L. Hutton	79	R. R. Lindwall	61
D. C. S. Compton	78	G. D. McKenzie	60
D. L. Underwood	78	S. E. Gregory	58
J. H. Edrich	77	R. W. Marsh	58
J. B. Statham	70	G. S. Chappell	57
F. S. Trueman	67	K. R. Miller	55
P. B. H. May	66	W. A. S. Oldfield	54
F. E. Woolley	64	D. G. Bradman	52
E. R. Dexter	62	A. T. W. Grout	51

South Africa		West Indies	
J. H. B. Waite	50	G. S. Sobers	93
A. W. Nourse	45	L. R. Gibbs	79
B. Mitchell	42	R. B. Kanhai	79
H. W. Taylor	42	C. H. Lloyd	67
T. L. Goddard	41	R. C. Fredericks	59
R. A. McLean	40	A. I. Kallicharran	54
H. J. Tayfield	37	D. L. Murray	54
D. J. McGlew	34	F. M. M. Worrell	51
A. D. Nourse	34	W. W. Hall	48
E. J. Barlow	30	E. D. Weekes	48
W. R. Endean	28	B. F. Butcher	44
P. M. Pollock	28	C. C. Hunte	44
K. G. Viljoen	27	C. L. Walcott	44
		S. Ramadhin	43

New Zealand		India	
B. E. Congdon	61	G. R. Viswanath	69
J. R. Reid	58	B. S. Bedi	67
M. G. Burgess	47	S. M. Gavaskar	63
B. Sutcliffe	42	P. R. Umrigar	59
G. T. Dowling	39	B. S. Chandrasekhar	58
G. M. Turner	39	C. G. Borde	55
R. O. Collinge	35	V. L. Manjrekar	55
K. J. Wadsworth	33	S. Venkataraghavan	50
R. C. Motz	32	E. A. S. Prasanna	49
V. Pollard	32	F. M. Engineer	46
B. F. Hastings	31	M. A. K. Pataudi	46
H. J. Howarth	30	V. M. H. Mankad	44
J. M. Parker	30	P. Roy	43
B. R. Taylor	30	S. M. H. Kirmani	42

Pakistan	
Asif Iqbal	58
Mushtaq Mohammad	57
Wasim Bari	56
Hanif Mohammad	55
Majid Khan	50
Intikhab Alam	47
Imtiaz Ahmed	41
Saeed Ahmed	41
Sadiq Mohammad	38
Zaheer Abbas	38
Fazal Mahmood	34
Sarfraz Nawaz	34
Wasim Raja	30

WISDEN CRICKETERS' ALMANACK 1980

117th Edition
Edited by Norman Preston

The 'bible' of cricket makes its appearance once more. Its pages contain complete details of the 1979 season in England and as usual there are the five cricketers of the year and full coverage of overseas cricket, including winter tours.

1110pp   illustrated   £6.75 (cloth)   £5.75 (limp)

RAY ILLINGWORTH

An Autobiography

Ray Illingworth, the distinguished Yorkshire, Leicestershire and England cricketer, tells his *own* story for the first time.

192pp   illustrated   May 1980   £5.95

Available from booksellers or in case of difficulty write to QAP Direct Sales, 9 Partridge Drive, Orpington, Kent, England, enclosing cheque/PO payable to Macdonald & Jane's Publishing Group + 10% for postage & packing (UK only). Allow up to 28 days for delivery, subject to availability.

M&J Queen Anne Press

TEST CAREER RECORDS
Compiled by Barry McCaully
(Including 1979–80 Tests in Australia and India)

ENGLAND

BATTING AND FIELDING

	M	I	NO	Runs	HS	Avge	100	50	Ct	St
D. L. Amiss	50	88	10	3612	262*	46.30	11	11	24	—
G. G. Arnold	34	46	11	421	59	12.02	—	1	9	—
D. L. Bairstow	1	2	0	68	59	34.00	—	1	3	—
J. C. Balderstone	2	4	0	39	35	9.75	—	—	1	—
G. D. Barlow	3	5	1	17	7*	4.25	—	—	—	—
J. Birkenshaw	5	7	0	148	64	21.14	—	1	3	—
I. T. Botham	25	35	2	1336	137	40.48	6	3	36	—
G. Boycott	88	153	19	6557	246*	48.93	18	34	27	—
J. M. Brearley	35	58	3	1301	91	23.65	—	8	48	—
D. J. Brown	26	34	5	342	44*	11.79	—	—	7	—
A. R. Butcher	1	2	0	34	20	17.00	—	—	—	—
G. A. Cope	3	3	0	40	22	13.33	—	—	1	—
M. H. Denness	128	45	3	1667	188	36.69	4	7	28	—
G. R. Dilley	2	4	2	80	38*	40.00	—	—	1	—
P. H. Edmonds	18	21	5	277	50	17.31	—	1	21	—
J. E. Emburey	6	9	1	77	42	9.62	—	—	8	—
K. W. R. Fletcher	52	85	11	2975	216	40.20	7	16	46	—
M. W. Gatting	2	3	0	11	6	3.66	—	—	3	—
N. Gifford	15	20	9	179	25*	16.27	—	—	8	—
G. A. Gooch	20	33	3	983	99	32.76	—	8	22	—
D. I. Gower	20	31	3	1315	200*	46.96	3	6	9	—
J. H. Hampshire	8	16	1	403	107	26.86	1	2	9	—
F. C. Hayes	9	17	1	244	106*	15.25	1	—	7	—
M. Hendrick	25	28	9	98	15	5.15	—	—	24	—
K. Higgs	15	19	3	185	63	11.56	—	1	4	—
W. Larkins	2	3	0	28	25	9.33	—	—	1	—
J. K. Lever	17	25	4	284	53	13.52	—	1	10	—
D. Lloyd	9	15	2	552	214*	42.46	1	—	11	—
G. Miller	24	32	3	817	98*	28.17	—	5	10	—
C. M. Old	41	58	7	751	65	14.72	—	2	22	—
P. I. Pocock	17	27	2	165	33	6.60	—	—	13	—
C. T. Radley	8	10	0	481	158	48.10	2	2	4	—
D. W. Randall	27	45	4	1125	174	27.43	2	6	18	—
G. R. J. Roope	21	32	4	860	77	30.71	—	7	35	—
B. C. Rose	5	8	1	100	27	14.28	—	—	2	—
M. W. W. Selvey	3	5	3	15	5*	7.50	—	—	1	—
K. Shuttleworth	5	6	0	46	21	7.66	—	—	1	—
D. S. Steele	8	16	0	673	106	42.06	1	5	7	—
G. B. Stevenson	1	1	1	27	27*	—	—	—	—	—
R. W. Taylor	26	33	3	620	97	20.66	—	2	79	6
R. W. Tolchard	4	7	2	129	47	25.80	—	1	5	—
D. L. Underwood	78	107	31	896	45*	11.78	—	—	43	—
P. Willey	6	12	0	233	52	19.41	—	1	2	—
R. G. D. Willis	53	74	35	451	24*	11.56	—	—	22	—
B. Wood	12	21	0	454	90	21.61	—	2	6	—
R. A. Woolmer	15	26	1	920	149	36.80	3	2	8	—

BOWLING

	Balls	Runs	Wkts	Avge	Best	5 wI	10 wM
G. G. Arnold	7650	3254	115	28.29	6–45	6	—
J. C. Balderstone	96	80	1	80.00	1–80	—	—
J. Birkenshaw	1017	469	13	36.07	5–57	1	—
I. T. Botham	6228	2575	139	18.52	8–34	14	3
G. Boycott	866	364	7	52.00	3–47	—	—
D. J. Brown	5098	2237	79	28.31	5–42	2	—
A. R. Butcher	12	9	0	—	—	—	—
G. A. Cope	864	277	8	34.62	3–102	—	—
G. R. Dilley	318	143	3	47.66	2–47	—	—
P. H. Edmonds	4083	1251	49	25.53	7–66	2	—
J. E. Emburey	1331	346	18	19.22	4–46	—	—
K. W. R. Fletcher	249	173	1	173.00	1–48	—	—
M. W. Gatting	8	1	0	—	—	—	—
N. Gifford	3084	1026	33	31.09	5–55	1	—
G. A. Gooch	396	132	3	44.00	2–16	—	—
M. Hendrick	5072	1766	78	22.64	4–28	—	—
K. Higgs	4112	1473	71	20.74	6–91	2	—
J. K. Lever	3510	1480	59	25.08	7–46	2	1
D. Lloyd	24	17	0	—	—	—	—
G. Miller	3693	1200	42	28.57	5–44	1	—
C. M. Old	7755	3594	129	27.86	7–50	4	—
P. I. Pocock	4482	2023	47	43.04	6–79	3	—
D. W. Randall	16	3	0	—	—	—	—
G. R. J. Roope	172	76	0	—	—	—	—
M. W. W. Selvey	492	343	6	57.16	4–41	—	—
K. Shuttleworth	1071	427	12	35.58	5–47	1	—
D. S. Steele	88	39	2	19.50	1–1	—	—
G. B. Stevenson	114	72	2	36.00	2–59	—	—
D. L. Underwood	19983	7033	278	25.29	8–51	16	6
P. Willey	425	177	2	88.50	2–96	—	—
R. G. D. Willis	10210	4636	184	25.19	7–78	11	—
B. Wood	98	50	0	—	—	—	—
R. A. Woolmer	546	299	4	74.75	1–8	—	—

AUSTRALIA

BATTING AND FIELDING

	M	I	NO	Runs	HS	Avge	100	50	Ct	St
A. R. Border	17	33	4	1260	162	43.44	3	8	13	—
R. J. Bright	5	9	2	86	17	12.28	—	—	2	—
I. W. Callen	1	2	2	26	22*	—	—	—	1	—
P. H. Carlson	2	4	0	23	21	5.75	—	—	2	—
G. S. Chappell	57	102	15	4684	247*	53.83	16	22	84	—
I. M. Chappell	75	136	10	5345	196	42.42	14	26	105	—
W. M. Clark	10	19	2	98	33	5.76	—	—	6	—
G. J. Cosier	18	32	1	897	168	28.93	2	3	14	—
W. M. Darling	14	27	1	697	91	26.80	—	6	5	—

I. C. Davis	15	27	1	692	105	26.61	1	4	9	—
G. Dymock	18	29	6	233	31*	10.13	—	—	1	—
J. Dyson	3	6	0	101	53	16.83	—	1	—	—
J. B. Gannon	3	5	4	3	3*	3.00	—	—	3	—
G. J. Gilmour	15	22	1	483	101	23.00	1	3	8	—
P. A. Hibbert	1	2	0	15	13	7.50	—	—	1	—
J. D. Higgs	17	29	14	93	16	6.20	—	—	2	—
A. M. J. Hilditch	9	18	0	452	85	25.11	—	4	9	—
R. M. Hogg	16	28	1	195	36	7.22	—	—	3	—
D. W. Hookes	7	13	0	436	85	33.53	—	3	2	—
K. J. Hughes	23	43	3	1551	130*	38.77	3	8	16	—
A. G. Hurst	12	20	3	102	26	6.00	—	—	3	—
B. M. Laird	5	10	0	472	92	47.92	—	5	2	—
T. J. Laughlin	3	5	0	87	35	17.40	—	—	3	—
D. K. Lillee	38	49	14	516	73*	14.74	—	1	11	—
R. B. McCosker	25	46	5	1622	127	39.56	4	9	21	—
J. A. Maclean	4	8	1	79	33*	11.28	—	—	18	—
A. A. Mallett	37	50	13	430	43*	11.62	—	—	30	—
M. F. Malone	1	1	0	46	46	46.00	—	—	—	—
A. L. Mann	4	8	0	189	105	23.62	1	—	2	—
R. W. Marsh	58	92	10	2523	132	30.76	3	12	212	9
J. K. Moss	1	2	1	60	38*	60.00	—	—	—	—
A. D. Ogilvie	5	10	0	178	47	17.80	—	—	5	—
L. S. Pascoe	4	7	3	33	20	8.25	—	—	1	—
S. J. Rixon	10	19	3	341	54	21.31	—	2	31	4
R. D. Robinson	3	6	0	100	34	16.66	—	—	4	—
C. S. Serjeant	12	23	1	522	124	23.72	1	2	13	—
P. R. Sleep	3	6	0	95	64	15.83	—	1	—	—
J. R. Thomson	34	46	9	433	49	11.70	—	—	14	—
P. M. Toohey	15	29	1	893	122	31.89	1	7	9	—
M. H. N. Walker	34	43	13	586	78*	19.53	—	1	12	—
K. D. Walters	68	116	12	4960	250	47.69	14	30	38	—
D. F. Whatmore	7	13	0	293	77	22.53	—	2	13	—
J. M. Wiener	4	8	0	179	58	22.37	—	1	4	—
G. M. Wood	15	30	1	953	126	32.86	2	5	14	—
K. J. Wright	10	18	5	219	55*	16.84	—	1	31	4
G. N. Yallop	21	41	3	1488	167	39.15	4	6	8	—
B. Yardley	14	26	4	576	74	26.18	—	3	12	—

BOWLING

	Balls	Runs	Wkts	Avge	Best	5 wI	10 wM
A. R. Border	794	256	7	36.57	2-35	—	—
R. J. Bright	739	288	7	41.14	3-69	—	—
I. W. Callen	440	191	6	31.83	3-83	—	—
P. H. Carlson	368	99	2	49.50	2-41	—	—
G. S. Chappell	4106	1493	37	40.35	5-61	1	—
I. M. Chappell	2873	1316	20	65.80	2-21	—	—
W. M. Clark	2793	1265	44	28.75	4-46	—	—
G. J. Cosier	899	341	5	68.20	2-26	—	—
G. Dymock	5239	1987	77	25.80	7-67	5	1
J. B. Gannon	726	361	11	32.81	4-77	—	—

G. J. Gilmour	2661	1406	54	26.03	6-85	3	—
J. D. Higgs	3989	1679	51	32.92	7-143	1	—
R. M. Hogg	3722	1500	64	23.43	6-74	5	2
D. W. Hookes	30	15	0	—	—	—	—
K. J. Hughes	6	0	0	—	—	—	—
A. G. Hurst	3114	1200	43	27.90	5-28	2	—
T. J. Laughlin	516	262	6	43.66	5-101	1	—
D. K. Lillee	10443	4770	206	23.15	6-26	15	5
A. A. Mallett	9820	3854	130	29.64	8-59	6	1
M. F. Malone	342	77	6	12.83	5-63	1	—
A. L. Mann	552	316	4	79.00	3-12	—	—
L. S. Pascoe	1069	346	16	34.12	4-80	—	—
P. R. Sleep	373	223	2	111.50	1-16	—	—
J. R. Thomson	7512	3892	152	25.60	6-48	6	—
P. M. Toohey	2	4	0	—	—	—	—
M. H. N. Walker	10094	3792	138	29.47	8-143	6	—
K. D. Walters	3211	1378	49	28.12	5-66	1	—
D. F. Whatmore	30	11	0	—	—	—	—
J. M. Wiener	48	22	0	—	—	—	—
G. N. Yallop	114	70	1	70.00	1-21	—	—
B. Yardley	3567	1437	37	38.83	4-35	—	—

WEST INDIES

BATTING AND FIELDING

	M	I	NO	Runs	HS	Avge	100	50	Ct	St
Imtiaz Ali	1	1	1	1*	—	—	—	—	—	—
Inshan Ali	12	18	2	172	25	10.75	—	—	7	—
R. A. Austin	2	2	0	22	20	11.00	—	—	2	—
S. F. A. Bacchus	8	14	0	514	250	36.71	1	2	10	—
L. Baichan	3	6	2	184	105*	46.00	1	—	2	—
G. S. Camacho	11	22	0	640	87	29.09	—	4	4	—
H. S. Chang	1	2	0	8	6	4.00	—	—	—	—
S. T. Clarke	6	9	3	50	15	8.33	—	—	1	—
C. E. H. Croft	10	14	10	75	23*	18.75	—	—	7	—
W. W. Daniel	5	5	2	29	11	9.66	—	—	2	—
J. Garner	10	14	2	203	60	16.91	—	1	9	—
H. A. Gomes	11	19	0	681	115	35.84	2	4	2	—
A. T. Greenidge	6	10	0	222	69	22.20	—	2	5	—
C. G. Greenidge	22	42	3	1814	134	46.51	5	10	25	—
D. L. Haynes	5	9	1	321	66	40.12	—	3	3	—
V. A. Holder	40	59	11	682	42	14.20	—	—	16	—
M. A. Holding	16	24	2	235	55	20.68	—	1	6	—
R. R. Jumadeen	12	14	10	84	56	21.00	—	1	4	—
A. I. Kallicharran	54	91	9	4071	187	49.64	12	20	43	—
C. L. King	5	9	2	219	63	31.28	—	2	4	—
C. H. Lloyd	67	116	8	4795	242*	44.39	12	22	47	—
M. D. Marshall	3	5	1	8	5	2.00	—	—	1	—
D. A. Murray	9	16	1	328	84	21.86	—	2	23	4
D. L. Murray	54	84	8	1782	91	23.44	—	11	160	8
A. L. Padmore	2	2	1	8	8*	8.00	—	—	—	—
D. R. Parry	11	18	3	363	65	2.20	—	3	4	—
N. Phillip	9	15	5	297	47	29.70	—	—	5	—

222

	M	I	NO	Runs	HS	Avge	9	11	29	—
I. V. A. Richards	31	51	2	2886	291	58.89	9	11	29	—
A. M. E. Roberts	30	40	5	307	54	8.77	—	1	7	—
L. G. Rowe	27	43	2	1868	302	45.56	6	6	16	—
I. T. Shillingford	4	7	0	218	120	31.14	1	—	1	—
S. Shivnarine	8	14	1	379	63	29.15	—	4	6	—
E. T. Willett	5	8	3	74	26	14.80	—	—	—	—
A. B. Williams	7	12	0	469	111	39.08	2	1	5	—

BOWLING

	Balls	Runs	Wkts	Avge	Best	5 wI	10 wM
Imtiaz Ali	204	89	2	44.50	2–37	—	—
Inshan Ali	3718	1621	34	47.67	5–59	1	—
R. A. Austin	6	5	0	—	—	—	—
G. S. Camacho	18	12	0	—	—	—	—
S. T. Clarke	1697	852	27	31.55	5–126	1	—
C. E. H. Croft	2367	1224	58	21.10	8–29	1	—
W. W. Daniel	788	381	15	25.40	4–53	—	—
J. Garner	2456	1184	52	22.76	4–48	—	—
H. A. Gomes	192	99	1	99.00	1–54	—	—
C. G. Greenidge	8	0	0	—	—	—	—
V. A. Holder	9095	3627	109	33.27	6–28	3	—
M. A. Holding	3576	1667	71	23.47	8–92	4	1
R. R. Jumadeen	3140	1141	29	39.34	4–72	—	—
A. I. Kallicharran	294	114	1	114.00	1–7	—	—
C. L. King	438	176	3	58.66	1–30	—	—
C. H. Lloyd	1710	621	10	62.10	2–13	—	—
M. D. Marshall	468	265	3	88.33	1–44	—	—
A. L. Padmore	474	135	1	135.00	1–36	—	—
D. R. Parry	1777	873	21	41.57	5–15	1	—
N. Phillip	1820	1041	28	37.17	4–48	—	—
I. V. A. Richards	656	242	4	60.50	2–34	—	—
A. M. E. Roberts	7530	3594	145	24.78	7–54	9	2
L. G. Rowe	56	40	0	—	—	—	—
S. Shivnarine	336	167	1	167.00	1–13	—	—
E. T. Willett	1326	482	11	43.81	3–33	—	—

NEW ZEALAND

BATTING AND FIELDING

	M	I	NO	Runs	HS	Avge	100	50	CtSt
R. W. Anderson	9	18	0	423	92	23.50	—	3	1 —
S. L. Boock	9	15	4	29	8	2.63	—	—	5 —
B. P. Bracewell	4	8	2	9	5	1.50	—	—	1 —
M. G. Burgess	47	86	5	2562	119*	31.62	5	14	34 —
B. L. Cairns	14	25	5	347	52*	17.35	—	1	6 —

E. J. Chatfield	4	7	3	31	13*	7.75	—	—	—	—
R. O. Collinge	35	50	13	533	68*	14.40	—	2	10	—
J. V. Coney	7	12	0	365	82	30.41	—	2	9	—
B. E. Congdon	61	114	7	3448	176	32.22	7	19	44	—
B. A. Edgar	6	11	0	296	129	26.90	1	1	6	—
G. N. Edwards	5	10	0	244	55	24.40	—	3	7	—
D. R. Hadlee	26	42	5	530	56	14.32	—	1	8	—
R. J. Hadlee	26	47	5	844	87	20.09	—	3	14	—
G. P. Howarth	17	32	3	1040	123	35.86	4	3	8	—
H. J. Howarth	30	42	18	291	61	12.12	—	1	33	-
W. K. Lees	12	23	2	557	152	26.52	1	—	22	7
J. F. M. Morrison	14	24	0	610	117	25.41	1	3	9	—
D. R. O'Sullivan	11	21	4	158	23*	9.29	—	—	2	—
J. M. Parker	30	52	2	1316	121	26.32	3	3	25	—
N. M. Parker	3	6	0	89	40	14.83	—	—	2	—
P. J. Petherick	6	11	4	34	13	4.85	—	—	4	—
J. F. Reid	1	2	0	19	19	9.50	—	—	—	—
A. D. G. Roberts	7	12	1	254	84*	23.09	—	1	4	—
M. J. F. Shrimpton	10	19	0	265	46	13.94	—	—	2	—
G. B. Troup	3	3	1	10	7	5.00	—	—	1	—
G. M. Turner	39	70	6	2920	259	45.62	7	14	40	—
G. E. Vivian	5	6	0	110	43	18.33	—	—	3	—
J. G. Wright	8	15	0	401	88	26.73	—	3	3	—

BOWLING

	Balls	Runs	Wkts	Avge	Best	5 wI	10 wM
S. L. Boock	1807	556	17	32.70	5–67	1	—
B. P. Bracewell	688	385	10	38.50	3–110	—	—
M. G. Burgess	498	212	6	35.33	3–23	—	—
B. L. Cairns	3296	1253	29	43.20	5–55	1	—
E. J. Chatfield	1054	485	8	60.62	4–100	—	—
R. O. Collinge	7689	3393	116	29.25	6–63	3	—
J. V. Coney	600	166	3	55.33	2–33	—	—
B. E. Congdon	5620	2154	59	36.50	5–65	1	—
D. R. Hadlee	4883	2389	71	33.64	4–30	—	—
R. J. Hadlee	6376	3225	107	30.14	7–23	6	2
G. P. Howarth	368	167	2	83.50	1–13	—	—
H. J. Howarth	8833	3178	86	36.95	5–34	2	—
W. K. Lees	5	4	0			—	—
J. F. M. Morrison	24	9	0			—	—
D. R. O'Sullivan	2739	1219	18	67.72	5–148	1	—
J. M. Parker	40	24	1	24.00	1–24	—	—
P. J. Petherick	1305	687	16	42.93	3–90	—	—
A. D. G. Roberts	440	182	4	45.50	1–12	—	—
M. J. F. Shrimpton	257	158	5	31.60	3–35	—	—
G. B. Troup	665	298	4	74.50	2–70	—	—
G. M. Turner	12	5	0			—	—
G. E. Vivian	198	107	1	107.00	1–14	—	—

INDIA

BATTING AND FIELDING

	M	I	NO	Runs	HS	Avge	100	500	Ct	St
S. Abid Ali	29	53	3	1018	81	20.36	—	6	33	—
M. Amarnath	26	45	3	1466	101*	34.90	2	9	23	—
S. Amarnath	10	18	0	550	124	30.55	1	3	4	—
B. S. Bedi	67	101	28	656	50*	8.98	—	1	26	—
R. Binny	7	11	1	158	46	15.80	—	—	5	—
B. S. Chandrasekhar	58	80	39	167	22	4.07	—	—	25	—
C. P. S. Chauhan	34	57	2	1696	93	30.83	—	13	33	—
D. R. Doshi	13	14	2	67	20	5.58	—	—	4	—
A. D. Gaekwad	21	37	3	1089	102	32.02	1	5	5	—
S. M. Gavaskar	63	114	8	5974	221	56.35	23	25	52	—
K. D. Ghavri	35	50	12	847	86	22.28	—	2	15	—
Kapil Dev	26	36	4	1068	126*	33.37	1	6	10	—
S. M. H. Kirmani	42	62	10	1439	101*	27.67	1	6	77	23
S. Madan Lal	16	30	6	428	55*	17.83	—	1	8	—
A. V. Mankad	22	42	3	991	97	25.41	—	6	12	—
M. V. Narasimha Rao	4	6	1	46	20*	9.20	—	—	7	—
D. D. Parsana	2	2	0	1	1	0.50	—	—	—	—
S. Patil	3	5	0	138	62	27.60	—	1	1	—
E. A. S. Prasanna	49	84	20	735	37	11.48	—	—	18	—
B. Reddy	4	5	1	38	21	9.50	—	—	9	2
P. Sharma	5	10	0	187	54	18.70	—	1	1	—
E. D. Solkar	27	48	6	1068	102	25.42	1	6	53	—
D. B. Vengsarkar	36	59	6	2058	157*	38.83	5	10	33	—
S. Venkataraghavan	50	68	11	731	64	12.82	—	2	39	—
G. R. Viswanath	69	121	9	5003	179	44.66	11	30	48	—
S. Yadav	11	13	4	122	29*	13.55	—	—	2	—
Yajurvindra Singh	4	7	1	109	43*	18.16	—	—	11	—
Yashpal Sharma	16	24	4	768	100*	38.40	1	5	2	—

BOWLING

	Balls	Runs	Wkts	Avge	Best	5 wI	10 wM
S. Abid Ali	4164	1980	47	42.12	6–55	1	—
M. Amarnath	2632	1161	23	50.47	4–63	—	—
S. Amarnath	13	5	1	5.00	1–5	—	—
B. S. Bedi	21640	7637	266	28.71	7–98	14	1
R. Binny	839	469	12	39.08	3–53	—	—
B. S. Chandrasekhar	16151	7199	242	29.74	8–79	16	2
C. P. S. Chauhan	126	72	1	72.00	1–11	—	—
D. R. Doshi	3515	1203	46	26.15	6–103	2	—
A. D. Gaekwad	106	80	0	—	—	—	—
S. M. Gavaskar	280	138	1	138.00	1–34	—	—
K. D. Ghavri	6352	3253	98	33.19	5–33	3	—
Kapil Dev	5745	2758	103	26.77	7–56	6	1

S. Madan Lal	2457	977	29	33.68	5–72	2	—
A. V. Mankad	41	43	0	—	—	—	—
M. V. Narasimha Rao	463	227	3	75.66	2–46	—	—
D. D. Parsana	120	50	1	50.00	1–32	—	—
S. Patil	18	8	0	—	—	—	—
E. A. S. Prasanna	14515	5742	189	30.38	8–76	10	2
P. Sharma	24	8	0	—	—	—	—
E. D. Solkar	2265	1070	18	59.44	3–28	—	—
D. B. Vengsarkar	11	10	0	—	—	—	—
S. Venkataraghavan	13442	4944	145	34.09	8–72	3	1
G. R. Viswanath	70	46	1	46.00	1–11	—	—
S. Yadav	2131	972	32	30.37	4–35	—	—
Yajurvindra Singh	120	50	0	—	—	—	—

PAKISTAN

BATTING AND FIELDING

	M	I	NO	Runs	HS	Avge	100	50	Ct	St
Abdul Qadir	6	8	1	108	29*	15.42	—	—	5	—
Anwar Khan	1	2	1	15	12	15.00	—	—	—	—
Asif Iqbal	58	99	7	3575	175	38.85	11	12	36	—
Ehtesham-Ud-Din	3	1	0	2	2	2.00	—	—	1	—
Haroon Rashid	14	25	1	853	122	35.54	2	3	6	—
Imran Khan	27	45	6	914	59	23.43	—	1	9	—
Iqbal Qasim	20	25	9	150	32	9.37	—	—	14	—
Javed Miandad	27	47	11	2252	206	62.55	6	12	25	—
Liaquat Ali	5	7	3	28	12	7.00	—	—	1	—
Majid Khan	50	88	3	3363	167	39.56	7	15	58	—
Mohsin Khan	6	10	0	282	46	28.20	—	—	6	—
Mudassar Nazar	16	28	1	800	126	29.62	2	3	10	26
Mushtaq Mohammad	57	100	7	3643	201	39.17	10	19	42	—
Sadiq Mohammad	38	69	2	2493	166	37.20	5	10	26	—
Salim Altaf	21	31	12	276	53*	14.52	—	1	3	—
Sarfraz Nawaz	34	47	8	626	53	16.05	—	2	21	—
Shafiq Ahmed	4	7	1	82	27*	13.66	—	—	2	—
Shahid Israr	1	1	1	7	7*	—	—	—	—	—
Sikander Bakht	19	24	8	108	22*	6.75	—	—	5	—
Talat Ali	10	18	2	370	61	23.12	—	2	4	—
Taslim Arif	1	2	0	136	90	68.00	—	1	—	—
Wasim Bari	56	83	21	1035	85	16.69	—	5	135	18
Wasim Raja	30	51	7	1709	117*	38.84	2	12	8	—
Zaheer Abbas	38	68	4	2617	274	40.89	6	9	22	—

226

BOWLING

	Balls	Runs	Wkts	Avge	Best	5 wI	10 wM
Abdul Qadir	1416	478	14	34.14	6–44	1	—
Anwar Khan	32	12	0	—	—	—	—
Asif Iqbal	3864	1502	53	28.33	5–48	2	—
Ehtesham-Ud-Din	748	270	14	19.28	5–47	1	—
Haroon Rashid	8	3	0	—	—	—	—
Imran Khan	7751	3391	112	30.27	6–63	7	—
Iqbal Qasim	4857	1729	46	37.58	6–40	1	1
Javed Miandad	1274	556	17	32.70	3–74	—	—
Liaquat Ali	808	359	6	59.83	3–80	—	—
Majid Khan	3222	1299	27	48.11	4–45	—	—
Mohsin Khan	8	3	0	—	—	—	—
Mudassar Nazar	1039	419	11	38.09	3–48	—	—
Mushtaq Mohammad	5410	2310	79	29.24	5–28	3	—
Sadiq Mohammad	208	98	0	—	—	—	—
Salim Altaf	4059	1710	46	37.17	4–11	—	—
Sarfraz Nawaz	9081	3668	120	30.56	9–86	4	1
Shafiq Ahmed	8	1	0	—	—	—	—
Sikander Bakht	3911	1878	58	32.37	8–69	3	1
Talat Ali	20	7	0	—	—	—	—
Wasim Bari	8	2	0	—	—	—	—
Wasim Raja	1786	816	26	31.38	4–68	—	—
Zaheer Abbas	20	2	0	—	—	—	—

Proposed Future Cricket Tours

TO ENGLAND	ENGLAND TOURS OVERSEAS
1981 Australia	1980–81 West Indies
1982 India and Pakistan	1981–82 India
1983 World Cup and New Zealand	1982–83 Australia
	1983–84 Pakistan and New Zealand

Other Tours

1980–81	India to Australia and New Zealand
	New Zealand to Australia
1981–82	Pakistan to Australia
	West Indies to Australia
	Australia to New Zealand
	New Zealand to West Indies
1982–83	India to Pakistan
	Pakistan to New Zealand and West Indies
1983–84	Australia to West Indies

SCORING OF POINTS IN THE SCHWEPPES CHAMPIONSHIP

The scheme is as follows:

(a) For a win, 12 points, plus any points scored in the first innings,

(b) In a tie, each side to score 6 points, plus any points scored in the first innings.

(c) If the scores are equal in a drawn match, the side batting in the fourth innings to score 6 points, plus any points scored in the first innings.

(d) First innings points (awarded only for performances in the first 100 overs of each innings and retained whatever the result of the match).

    (i) A maximum of 4 batting points to be available as follows: 150 to 199 runs—1 Point; 200 to 249 runs—2 points; 250 to 299 runs—3 points; 300 runs or over—4 points.

    (ii) A maximum of 4 bowling points to be available as follows: 3–4 wickets taken—1 point; 5–6 wickets taken—2 points; 7–8 wickets taken—3 points; 9–10 wickets taken—4 points.

(e) If play starts when less than eight hours playing time remains and a one innings match is played, no first innings points shall be scored. The side winning on the one innings to score 12 points.

(f) The side which has the highest aggregate of points gained at the end of the season shall be the Champion County. Should any sides in the Schweppes Championship Table be equal on points, the side with most wins will have priority.

PRINCIPAL FIXTURES 1980

Including play on Sunday

Wednesday 23 April
Lord's: MCC v Essex
Oxford: Oxford U v Gloucs
Cambridge: Cambridge U v Leics

Saturday 26 April
Cambridge: Cambridge U v Essex
Oxford: Oxford U v Somerset

Wednesday 30 April
Swansea: Glam v Essex
Canterbury: Kent v Northants
Old Trafford: Lancs v Derbys
Leicester: Leics v Yorks
Trent Bridge: Notts v Middx
Taunton: Somerset v Sussex
The Oval: Surrey v Hants
Worcester: Worcs v Gloucs
Oxford: Oxford U v Warwicks

Saturday 3 May
Ilford: Essex v Somerset
Bristol: Gloucs v Northants
Southampton: Hants v Warwicks
Lord's: Middx v Lancs
Hove: Sussex v Leics
Cambridge: Cambridge U v Surrey
Oxford: Oxford U v Yorks

Sunday 4 May
John Player League
Derby: Derbys v Surrey
Ilford: Essex v Somerset
Bristol: Gloucs v Northants
Southampton: Hants v Warwicks
Lord's: Middx v Lancs
Trent Bridge: Notts v Kent
Hove: Sussex v Leics
Bradford: Yorks v Worcs

Wednesday 7 May
Derby: Derbys v Northants
Ilford: Essex v Kent
Bristol: Gloucs v Glam

Old Trafford: Lancs v Worcs
Trent Bridge: Notts v Yorks
The Oval: Surrey v Sussex
Edgbaston: Warwicks v Somerset
Cambridge: Cambridge U v Middx
Oxford: Oxford U v Hants

Thursday 8 May
Arundel: Lavinia, Duchess of Norfolk's
  XI v West Indies (one day)

Saturday 10 May
Benson & Hedges Cup
Chelmsford: Essex v Sussex
Bristol: Gloucs v Glam
Canterbury: Kent v Somerset
Lord's: Middx v Surrey
Northampton: Northants v Oxford &
  Cambridge U
Trent Bridge: Notts v Derbys
Headingley: Yorks v Warwicks
Glasgow (Titwood): Scotland v Leics

Saturday 10 May
*Worcester: Worcs v West Indies

Sunday 11 May
John Player League
Canterbury: Kent v Somerset
Old Trafford: Lancs v Glam
Northampton: Northants v Sussex
Huddersfield: Yorks v Warwicks

Wednesday 14 May
Benson & Hedges Cup
Southampton: Hants v Middx
Old Trafford: Lancs v Notts
The Oval: Surrey v Kent
Hove: Sussex v Gloucs
Edgbaston: Warwicks v Northants
Watford (Town Gd): Minor Counties v
  Essex
Cambridge: Oxford & Camb U v Worcs
Glasgow (Titwood): Scotland v Derbys

Wednesday 14 May
*Leicester: Leics v West Indies

Saturday 17 May

Benson and Hedges Cup
Chesterfield: Derbys v Lancs
Swansea: Glam v Minor Counties
Bristol: Gloucs v Essex
Leicester: Leics v Notts
Taunton: Somerset v Middx
The Oval: Surrey v Hants
Edgbaston: Warwicks v Oxford &
   Cambridge U
Worcester: Worcs v Yorks

Saturday 17 May

*Milton Keynes: Northants v West Indies

Sunday 18 May

John Player League
Swansea: Glam v Essex
Leicester: Leics v Gloucs
Trent Bridge: Notts v Derbys
Taunton: Somerset v Yorks
The Oval: Surrey v Hants
Edgbaston: Warwicks v Sussex
Worcester: Worcs v Middx

Tuesday 20 May

Benson and Hedges Cup
Chelmsford: Essex v Glam
Canterbury: Kent v Hants
Leicester: Leics v Lancs
Northampton: Northants v Worcs
Trent Bridge: Notts v Scotland
Taunton: Somerset v Surrey
Hove: Sussex v Minor Counties
Oxford: Oxford & Camb U v Yorks

Tuesday 20 May

Lord's: Middx v West Indies (one day)

Wednesday 21 May

Lord's: Middx v West Indies (one day)

Thursday 22 May

Benson & Hedges Cup
Derby: Derbys v Leics
Cardiff: Glam v Sussex
Bournemouth: Hants v Somerset
Old Trafford: Lancs v Scotland
Lord's: Middx v Kent
Worcester: Worcs v Warwicks
Bradford: Yorks v Northants
Chippenham: Minor Counties v Gloucs

Thursday 22 May

Chelmsford: Essex v West Indies (one day)

Friday 23 May

Chelmsford: Essex v West Indies (one day)

Saturday 24 May

*Chesterfield: Derbys v West Indies
Chelmsford: Essex v Surrey
Swansea: Glam v Notts
Bournemouth: Hants v Kent
Lord's: Middx v Sussex
Northampton: Northants v Leics
Taunton: Somerset v Gloucs
Worcester: Worcs v Warwicks
Headingley: Yorks v Lancs
Oxford: Oxford U v Free Foresters

Sunday 25 May

John Player League
Chelmsford: Essex v Surrey
Swansea: Glam v Notts
Bournemouth: Hants v Kent
Old Trafford: Lancs v Gloucs
Lord's: Middx v Northants

Wednesday 28 May

Chesterfield: Derbys v Hants
Old Trafford: Lancs v Glam
Leicester: Leics v Gloucs
Northampton: Northants v Yorks
Trent Bridge: Notts v Warwicks
The Oval: Surrey v Somerset
Hove: Sussex v Kent
Worcester: Worcs v Middx
Oxford: Oxford U v MCC
HEADINGLEY:
PRUDENTIAL TROPHY
ENGLAND v WEST INDIES
(first one-day international match)

Friday 30 May

LORD'S: PRUDENTIAL TROPHY
ENGLAND v WEST INDIES
(second one-day international match)

Saturday 31 May

Cardiff: Glam v Northants
Gloucester: Gloucs v Essex
*Canterbury: Kent v West Indies
Liverpool: Lancs v Warwicks

Leicester: Leices v Derbys
Taunton: Somerset v Middx
The Oval: Surrey v Notts
Middlesbrough: Yorks v Sussex
Oxford: Oxford U v Worcs

Sunday 1 June

John Player League
Cardiff: Glam v Northants
Gloucester: Gloucs v Essex
Portsmouth: Hants v Worcs
Liverpool: Lancs v Warwicks
Leicester: Leices v Derbys
Taunton: Somerset v Middx
The Oval: Surrey v Notts
Middlesbrough: Yorks v Sussex

Wednesday 4 June

Southampton: Hants v Sussex
Leicester: Leics v Notts
Lord's: Middx v Surrey
Edgbaston: Warwicks v Derbys
Worcester: Worcs v Somerset
Sheffield: Yorks v Kent
Cambridge: Cambirdge U v Northants
Oxford: Oxford U v Lancs

Thursday 5 June

Trent Bridge: Cornhill Insurance Test
  Series
ENGLAND v WEST INDIES
(first Test match)

Saturday 7 June

Derby: Derbys v Glam
Old Trafford: Lancs v Notts
Lord's: Middx v Yorks
Northampton: Northants v Gloucs
The Oval: Surrey v Essex
Hove: Sussex v Worcs
Cambridge: Cambridge U v Warwicks
*Belfast (Ormeau): Ireland v MCC

Sunday 8 June

John Player League
Derby: Derbys v Glam
Canterbury: Kent v Gloucs
Leicester: Leics v Hants
Lord's: Middx v Yorks
Tring: Northants v Lancs
Horsham: Sussex v Worcs
Edgbaston: Warwicks v Surrey

Wednesday 11 June

BENSON & HEDGES CUP QUARTER-FINALS

Thursday 12 June

Cambridge: Oxford & Cam U v West
  Indies (two days)

Saturday 14 June

Southend: Essex v Warwicks
Swansea: Glam v Worcs
Bristol: Gloucs v Derbys
T Wells: Kent v Hants
Northampton: Northants v Notts
Bath: Somerset v Lancs
The Oval: Surrey v Middx
*Hove: Sussex v West Indies
Oxford: Oxford U v Leics

Sunday 15 June

John Player League
Southend: Essex v Warwicks
Swansea: Glam v Yorks
Bristol: Gloucs v Worcs
Lord's: Middx v Surrey
Trent Bridge: Notts v Northants
Bath: Somerset v Lancs

Wednesday 18 June

Southend: Essex v Middx
Cardiff: Glam v Warwicks
Bristol: Gloucs v Lancs
T Wells: Kent v Sussex
Leicester: Leics v Surrey
Northampton: Northants v Derbys
Bath: Somerset v Hants
Bradford: Yorks v Worcs
Cambridge: Cambridge U v Notts

Thursday 19 June

LORD'S: ENGLAND v WEST INDIES
  (second Cornhill Test match)

Saturday 21 June

Chesterfield: Derbys v Essex
Bournemouth: Hants v Gloucs
Old Trafford: Lancs v Kent
Cardiff: Glam v Somerset
Hastings: Sussex v Cambridge U
Nuneaton (Griff & Coton): Warwicks v
  Northants
Worcester: Worcs v Leices
Harrogate: Yorks v Notts

231

Sunday 22 June

John Player League
Chesterfield: Derbys v Essex
Old Trafford: Lancs v Kent
Bath: Somerset v Glam
The Oval: Surrey v Sussex
Nuneaton (Griff Coton): Warwicks v Northants
Worcester: Worcs v Leics
Scarborough: Yorks v Notts

Wednesday 25 June

Benson & Hedges Cup Semi-Finals
Old Trafford: Lancs v Surrey
   (Will be played on 27 Aug if either
   County in B & H Semi-finals)
Guildford: Derrick Robins' XI v
   Cambridge U
Dublin (Castle Ave): Ireland v West
   Indies (one day – 60 overs)
Harrogate: Tilcon Trophy (three days)

Thursday 26 June

Dublin (Castle Ave): Ireland v West
   Indies (one day – 60 overs)

Saturday 28 June

*Swansea: Glam v West Indies
Southampton: Hants v Yorks
Dartford: Kent v Derbys
Leicester: Leics v Lancs
Northampton: Northants v Worcs
Trent Bridge: Notts v Essex
Guildford: Surrey v Gloucs
Hove: Sussex v Somerset
Edgbaston: Warwicks v Middx
Lord's: Oxford U v Cambridge U

Sunday 29 June

John Player League
Chelmsford: Essex v Notts
Basingstoke: Hants v Yorks
Canterbury: Kent v Derbys
Leicester: Leics v Lancs
Northampton: Northants v Worcs
Guildford: Surrey v Gloucs
Hove: Sussex v Somerset
Edgbaston: Warwicks v Middx

Sunday 29 June

Swansea: Glam v West Indies (one day)

Wednesday 2 July

Burton-on-Trent (Allied): Derbys v Leics
*Bristol: Gloucs v West Indies
Basingstoke: Hants v Glam

Wednesday 2 July

Gillette Cup First Round
Exeter (City Ground): Devon v Cornwall
Lord's: Middx v Ireland
Trent Bridge: Notts v Durham
Taunton: Somerset v Worcs
The Oval: Surrey v Northants
Hove: Sussex v Suffolk
Edgbaston: Warwicks v Oxfordshire

Saturday 5 July

Bristol: Gloucs v Notts
Maidstone: Kent v Leics
Lord's: Middx v Northants
*Taunton: Somerset v West Indies
Hove: Sussex v Hants
Edgbaston: Warwicks v Lancs
Worcester: Worcs v Surrey
Bradford: Yorks v Glam

Sunday 6 July

John Player League
Bristol: Gloucs v Notts
Maidstone: Kent v Leics
Old Trafford: Lancs v Surrey
Lord's: Middx v Derbys
Hove: Sussex v Hants
Worcester: Worcs v Warwicks
Headingley: Yorks v Essex

Wednesday 9 July

Chelmsford: Essex v Yorks
Swansea: Glam v Sussex
Maidstone: Kent v Surrey
Lords: Middx v Hants
Northampton: Northants v Warwicks
Trent Bridge: Notts v Somerset

Thursday 10 July

OLD TRAFFORD:
ENGLAND v WEST INDIES
   (third Cornhill test match)

Saturday 12 July

Chesterfield: Derbys v Somerset
Chelmsford: Essex v Leics
Cardiff: Glam v Hants
Bristol: Gloucs v Sussex
Trent Bridge: Notts v Kent
The Oval: Surrey v Yorks
Stourport-on-Severn (Chain Wire):
   Worcs v Lancs

Sunday 13 July

John Player League
Chesterfield: Derbys v Somerset
Chelmsford: Essex v Leics
Cardiff: Glam v Hants
Moreton-in-Marsh: Gloucs v Sussex
Luton: Northants v Kent
Trent Bridge: Notts v Warwicks
The Oval: Surrey v Yorks
Worcester: Worcs v Lancs

Wednesday 16 July

Gillette Cup Second Round
Derby: Derbys v Hants
Leicester: Leics v Essex
Trent Bridge or Chester-le-Street: Notts
   or Durham v Middx or Ireland
Taunton or Worcester: Somerset or
   Worcs v Lancs
The Oval or Northampton: Surrey or
   Northants v Gloucs
Hove or Mildenhall: Sussex or Suffolk v
   Glam
Edgbaston or Oxford: Warwicks or
   Oxfordshire v Devon or Cornwall
Headingley: Yorks v Kent

Thursday 17 July

Broughty Ferry: Scotland v West Indies
   (two days)

Saturday 19 July

**LORD'S: BENSON & HEDGES CUP
FINAL**

Saturday 19 July

Leicester: Leics v Glam (will be played
   on 20 Aug if either county in B & H
   final)
*Headingley or Old Trafford: Yorks v
   West Indies (or Lancs if Yorks in B & H
   final)

Sunday 20 July

John Player League
Portsmouth: Hants v Somerset
Maidstone: Kent v Sussex
Leicester: Leics v Middx
Northampton: Northants v Derbys
Trent Bridge: Notts v Worcs
The Oval: Surrey v Glam
Edgbaston: Warwicks v Gloucs

Wednesday 23 July

Portsmouth: Hants v Surrey
Southport: Lancs v Northants
Leicester: Leics v Essex
Worksop: Notts v Derbys
Taunton: Somerset v Kent
Edgbaston: Warwicks v Worcs
Scarborough: Yorks v Middx

Thursday 24 July

**THE OVAL: ENGLAND v
   WEST INDIES
   (fourth Cornhill Test match)**

Saturday 26 July

Cardiff: Glam v Leics
Portsmouth: Hants v Lancs
Lord's: Middx v Kent
Hove: Sussex v Essex
Edgbaston: Warwicks v Surrey
Worcester: Worcs v Derbys
Sheffield: Yorks v Gloucs

Sunday 27 July

John Player League
Derby: Derbys v Warwicks
Ebbw Vale: Glam v Leics
Southampton: Hants v Lancs
Lord's: Middx v Kent
Taunton: Somerset v Notts
Hastings: Sussex v Essex
Worcester: Worcs v Surrey
Hull: Yorks v Gloucs

Sunday 27 July

Dublin (Rathmines): Ireland v Wales

Wednesday 30 July

GILLETTE CUP QUARTER FINALS

Thursday 31 July

Newcastle-on-Tyne (Jesmond): Minor
   Counties v West Indies (two days)

Saturday 2 August

Chesterfield: Derbys v Yorks
Cheltenham: Gloucs v Hants
Canterbury: Kent v Glam
Old Trafford: Lancs v Sussex
Lord's: Middx v Essex
Northampton: Northants v Surrey
Trent Bridge: Notts v Leics
Weston-super-Mare: Somerset v Worcs
*Edgbaston: Warwicks v West Indies

Sunday 3 August

John Player League
Cheltenham: Gloucs v Hants
Canterbury: Kent v Glam
Old Trafford: Lancs v Sussex
Lord's: Middx v Essex
Northampton: Northants v Surrey
Trent Bridge: Notts v Leics
Weston-super-Mare: Somerset v Worcs
Headingley: Yorks v Derbys

Wednesday 6 August

Cheltenham: Gloucs v Worcs
Canterbury: Kent v Warwicks
Lord's: Middx v Leics
Trent Bridge: Notts v Lancs
Weston-super-Mare: Somerset v Yorks
The Oval: Surrey v Glam
Eastbourne: Sussex v Northants

Wednesday 6 August

Southampton: Hants v Australia
   (one day)

Thursday 7 August

**HEADINGLEY: ENGLAND v WEST
INDIES
(fifth Cornhill test match)**

Thursday 7 August

Southampton: Hants v Australia (one
day)

Saturday 9 August

Buxton: Derbys v Lancs
Chelmsford: Essex v Hants
Cheltenham: Gloucs v Middx
Leicester: Leics v Kent
Northampton: Northants v Somerset
*The Oval: Surrey v Australia
Eastbourne: Sussex v Notts
Edgbaston: Warwicks v Yorks
Worcester: Worcs v Glam

Sunday 10 August

John Player League
Buxton: Derbys v Lancs
Chelmsford: Essex v Hants
Cheltenham: Gloucs v Middx
Leicester: Leics v Yorks
Northampton: Northants v Somerset
Eastbourne: Sussex v Notts
Edgbaston: Warwicks v Kent
Worcester: Worcs v Glam

Monday 11 August

Lord's: MCC v Scotland (two days)

Wednesday 13 August

GILLETTE CUP SEMI-FINALS

Wednesday 13 August

Young England v Australia

Saturday 16 August

Derby: Derbys v Surrey
Swansea: Glam v Gloucs
Folkestone: Kent v Essex
*Old Trafford or Headingley: Lancs v
   Australia (or Yorks if Lancs played
   West Indies on 19 July)
Lord's: Middx v Notts
Wellingborough: Northants v Hants
Taunton: Somerset v Leics
Edgbaston: Warwicks v Sussex

Saturday 16 August
*Perth: Scotland v Ireland

Sunday 17 August
John Player League
Swansea: Glam v Gloucs
Folkestone: Kent v Essex
Lord's: Middx v Notts
Wellingborough: Northants v Hants
Taunton: Somerset v Leices
Worcester: Worcs v Derbys

Sunday 17 (or 24) August
Warwick Under-25 Competition
semi-finals

Wednesday 20 August
**THE OVAL: PRUDENTIAL TROPHY
ENGLAND v AUSTRALIA
(first one-day international match)**

Bournemouth: Hants v Somerset
Folkestone: Kent v Gloucs
Leicester: Leics v Glam (if not played on
19 July)
Uxbridge: Middx v Derbys
Northampton: Northants v Essex
Cleethorpes: Notts v Worcs
Hove: Sussex v Surrey
Bradford: Yorks v Warwicks

Friday 22 August
**EDGBASTON: PRUDENTIAL TROPHY
ENGLAND v AUSTRALIA
(second one-day international match)**

Saturday 23 August
Colchester: Essex v Derbys
Bristol: Gloucs v Somerset
Bournemouth: Hants v Worcs
Old Trafford: Lancs v Yorks
Leicester: Leics v Northants
*Trent Bridge: Notts v Australia
The Oval: Surrey v Kent
Hove: Sussex v Middx
Edgbaston: Warwicks v Glam

Sunday 24 August
John Player League
Colchester: Essex v Worcs
Bristol: Gloucs v Somerset
Southampton: Hants v Derbys
Old Trafford: Lancs v Yorks
Leicester: Leics v Northants
The Oval: Surrey v Kent
Hove: Sussex v Middx
Edgbaston: Warwicks v Glam

Sunday 24 (or 17) August
Warwick Under-25 Competition
semi-finals

Wednesday 27 August
Ilkeston: Derbys v Notts
Colchester: Essex v Worcs
Old Trafford: Lancs v Surrey (if not
played on 25 June)
Taunton: Somerset v Glam
Edgbaston: Warwicks v Gloucs
Scarborough: Fenner Trophy KO
Competition (three days)

Thursday 28 August
**LORD'S: ENGLAND v AUSTRALIA
(Cornhill Insurance Centenary Test
match)**

Saturday 30 August
Derby: Derbys v Sussex
Cardiff: Glam v Middx
Blackpool: Lancs v Essex
Leicester: Leics v Warwicks
Trent Bridge: Notts v Hants
Worcester: Worcs v Kent
Headingley: Yorks v Northants
Scarborough: T. N. Pearce's XI v
                Selected Opponents

Sunday 31 August
John Player League
Derby: Derbys v Sussex
Cardiff: Glam v Middx
Old Trafford: Lancs v Essex
Leicester: Leics v Warwicks
Trent Bridge: Notts v Hants
Taunton: Somerset v Surrey
Worcester: Worcs v Kent
Scarborough: Yorks v Northants

Sunday 31 August

Edgbaston: Warwick Under-25
  Competition final

Wednesday 3 September

Chelmsford: Essex v Northants
Southampton: Hants v Leics
Canterbury: Kent v Middx
Taunton: Somerset v Warwicks
The Oval: Surrey v Lancs
Hove: Sussex v Gloucs
Worcester: Worcs v Notts
Scarborough: Yorks v Derbys

Saturday 6 September

LORD'S: GILLETTE CUP FINAL

Sunday 7 September

John Player League
Chesterfield: Derbys v Gloucs
Chelmsford: Essex v Northants
Bournemouth: Hants v Middx
Canterbury: Kent v Yorks
Trent Bridge: Notts v Lancs
The Oval: Surrey v Leics
Hove: Sussex v Glam
Edgbaston: Warwicks v Somerset

Saturday 13 September

The Oval: Courage Challenge Cup
  International Batsman of the Year
  (two days)

MINOR COUNTIES FIXTURES

MAY

Sun	18	Cheshire v Durham: Chester (Boughton Hall)
Sun	25	Lincolnshire v Norfolk: Sleaford
		Northumberland v Durham: Jesmond
Wed	28	Cambridgeshire v Bedfordshire: Wisbech
Thurs	29	Lancashire II v Cumberland: Pilkingtons, St. Helens

JUNE

Sun	1	Northumberland v Lincolnshire: Jesmond
Mon	2	Cheshire v Lancashire II: Neston
Wed	4	Staffordshire v Shropshire: Burton-on-Trent (Bass)
Mon	9	Northumberland v Lancashire II: Jesmond
Tues	10	Hertfordshire v Norfolk: Watford
Wed	11	Cambridgeshire v Lincolnshire: March
Sun	15	Cumberland v Lancashire II: Millom
		Staffordshire v Cheshire: Knypersley
Mon	16	Durham v Shropshire: Stockton
Wed	18	Cambridgeshire v Norfolk: Papworth
		Lincolnshire v Northumberland: Bourne
Sun	22	Durham v Cumberland: Chester-le-Street
Mon	23	Shropshire v Staffordshire: Wellington
Wed	25	Hertfordshire v Cambridgeshire: Stevenage
Sat	28	Oxfordshire v Buckinghamshire: Oxford (Christ Church)
Sun	29	Lincolnshire v Cambridgeshire: Grimsby (Ross)
		Northumberland v Cumberland: Jesmond

JULY

Wed	2	Lancashire II v Cheshire: Blackburn (East Lancs C.C.)
		Staffordshire v Lincolnshire: Stone
Sat	5	Hertfordshire v Bedfordshire: St. Albans (Clarence Park)
Sun	6	Buckinghamshire v Berkshire: Buckingham
		Shropshire v Cheshire: Newport
Sat	12	Bedfordshire v Hertfordshire: Henlow
		Berkshire v Buckinghamshire: Reading (Ibis C.C.)
Sun	13	Cheshire v Staffordshire: Macclesfield
		Cornwall v Somerset II: Troon
		Cumberland v Northumberland: Penrith
		Shropshire v Lancashire II: St. George's (Telford)
Sat	19	Bedfordshire v Buckinghamshire: Bedford School
Sun	20	Cornwall v Wiltshire: Truro
Mon	21	Cambridgeshire v Suffolk: Fenners
		Lancashire II v Northumberland: Lancaster
		Shropshire v Durham: Shrewsbury (London Rd.)
Tues	22	Dorset v Berkshire: Wimborne
Wed	23	Staffordshire v Durham: Brewood
Thurs	24	Devon v Berkshire: Sidmouth
Sat	26	Bedfordshire v Cambridgeshire: Bedford (Goldington Bury)
		Oxfordshire v Wiltshire: Oxford (St. Edward's)
Sun	27	Cheshire v Shropshire: Northwich
		Cornwall v Dorset: Helston
		Durham v Northumberland: Durham City
		Hertfordshire v Buckinghamshire: Hertford (Balls Park)
		Lincolnshire v Cumberland: Lincoln
Mon	28	Norfolk v Cambridgeshire: Lakenham
Tues	29	Devon v Dorset: Torquay
		Oxfordshire v Berkshire: Morris Motors
Wed	30	Norfolk v Buckinghamshire: Lakenham
Thurs	31	Wiltshire v Berkshire: Devizes
		MINOR COUNTIES v WEST INDIES: Jesmond

AUGUST

Fri	1	Suffolk v Buckinghamshire: G.R.E. Ipswich
Sat	2	Oxfordshire v Dorset: Abingdon School
Sun	3	Shropshire v Bedfordshire: Oswestry
Mon	4	Berkshire v Dorset: Reading C.C.
		Norfolk v Lincolnshire: Lakenham
		Somerset II v Devon: Taunton
		Staffordshire v Northumberland: West Bromwich
		Suffolk v Hertfordshire: Ransomes, Ipswich
		Wiltshire v Cornwall: Bemerton, Salisbury
Wed	6	Cheshire v Northumberland: Bowdon
		Norfolk v Hertfordshire: Lakenham
		Somerset II v Cornwall: Taunton
		Wiltshire v Oxfordshire: Swindon
Fri	8	Berkshire v Wiltshire: Reading (Courage)
		Buckinghamshire v Oxfordshire: Marlow
		Cambridgeshire v Hertfordshire: Fenners
		Dorset v Cornwall: Canford School
		Norfolk v Suffolk: Lakenham
Sun	10	Buckinghamshire v Suffolk: Chesham
		Cumberland v Lincolnshire: Kendal
		Durham v Cheshire: Hartlepool

237

Mon	11	Berkshire v Devon: Bray
		Dorset v Somerset II: Weymouth
Tues	12	Bedfordshire v Suffolk: Dunstable
		Northumberland v Cheshire: Jesmond
Wed	13	Oxfordshire v Devon: Banbury (XV Club)
Fri	15	Berkshire v Oxfordshire: Reading (Kensington Rd.)
		Dorset v Devon: Canford School
Sun	17	Buckinghamshire v Bedfordshire: Slough
		Cumberland v Durham: Whitehaven
		Hertfordshire v Suffolk: Old Merchant Taylors
Mon	18	Cornwall v Devon: Penzance
		Dorset v Oxfordshire: Weymouth
		Northumberland v Staffordshire: Jesmond
		Wiltshire v Somerset II: Trowbridge
Tues	19	Bedfordshire v Shropshire: Luton (Wardown Park)
		Suffolk v Norfolk: Mildenhall
Wed	20	Devon v Oxfordshire: Exmouth
		Durham v Staffordshire: South Shields
		Somerset II v Dorset: Taunton
Thurs	21	Suffolk v Cambridgeshire: Bury St. Edmunds
Sun	24	Buckinghamshire v Norfolk: Amersham
		Suffolk v Bedfordshire: Ransomes, Ipswich
Tues	26	Devon v Cornwall: Bovey Tracey
		Somerset II v Wiltshire: Weston-super-Mare (Westlands)
Thurs	28	Devon v Somerset II: Exeter
Sun	31	Buckinghamshire v Hertfordshire: High Wycombe
		Lincolnshire v Staffordshire: Scunthorpe

SEPTEMBER

Mon	1	Lancashire II v Shropshire: Old Trafford

BENSON & HEDGES CUP 1980

MAY

Wed	14	Minor Counties v Essex: Watford
Sat	17	Glamorgan v Minor Counties: Swansea
Tues	20	Sussex v Minor Counties: Hove
Thurs	22	Minor Counties v Gloucestershire: Chippenham

Twin blade winner.

Continued from p. 46

England v West Indies

Played in Brisbane, 23 December.
England 217–8 in 50 overs (Boycott 68, Gower 59).
West Indies 218–1 (Greenidge 85*, Richards 85*).
West Indies won by 9 wickets.

England v Australia

Played at Sydney, 26 December
Australia 194–6 in 47 overs (I. M. Chappell 60*, G. Chappell 52).
England 195–6 (Boycott 86*, Willey 51).
England won by 4 wickets.

Norman George FEATHERSTONE (Transvaal and Glamorgan) B Que Que Rhodesia 20/8/1949. RHB, OB. Debut for Transvaal B 1967–68 and for Middlesex 1968. Cap 1971. Benefit in 1979. Has joined Glamorgan for 1980. 1,000 runs in season – 2. Two centuries in Match – 1. HS: 147 Middlesex v Yorks (Scarborough) 1975. BB: 5–32 Middlesex v Notts (Nottingham) 1978. Gillette Awards: 1 (for Middlesex). Benson & Hedges Awards 1 (for Middlesex).

Allan Arthur JONES (St. John's College, Horsham) b Horley (Surrey) 9/12/1947. RHB, RFM. 6ft. 4ins. tall. Debut for Sussex 1966. Left staff in 1969 and made debut for Somerset in 1970. Cap 1972. Played for Northern Transvaal in 1972–73 Currie Cup Competition and for Orange Free State in 1976–77. Left Somerset after 1975 season and made debut for Middlesex in 1976. Cap 1976. Not re-engaged after 1979 season and has joined Glamorgan for 1980. Took 3 wkts in 4 balls, Somerset v Notts (Nottingham) 1972. Hat trick in Benson & Hedges Cup, Middlesex v Essex (Lord's) 1977. Benson & Hedges Gold Awards: 3 (2 for Middlesex, 1 for Somerset). HS: 33 Middlesex v Kent (Canterbury) 1978. HSJPL: 18* Somerset v Sussex (Hove) 1973. HSBH: 13 Somerset v Glos (Bristol) 1973. BB: 9–51 Somerset v Sussex (Hove) 1972. BBGC: 5–23 Middlesex v Kent (Canterbury) 1977. BBJPL: 6–34 Somerset v Essex (Westcliff) 1971. BBBH: 5–16 Middlesex v Minor Counties (East) (Lakenham) 1977.

ISBN 0263 02004 3
© 1980 Queen Anne Press
Macdonald and Janes'
Publishing Group, Paulton House,
8 Shepherdess Walk, London N1.
Printed by C. Nicholls & Company Ltd
The Philips Park Press, Manchester